Introduction to Professional School Counseling

Introduction to Professional School Counseling: Advocacy, Leadership, and Intervention is a comprehensive introduction to the field for school counselors in training, one that provides special focus on the topics most relevant to the school counselor's role and offers specific strategies for practical application and implementation. In addition to thorough coverage of *the ASCA National Model®* (2012), readers will find thoughtful discussions of the effects of trends and legislation, including the Every Student Succeeds Act (ESSA), Response to Intervention (RtI), and School-wide Positive Behavioral Intervention and Support (SWPBIS). The text also provides readers with an understanding of how school counselors assume counseling orientations within the specific context of an educational setting. Each chapter is intensely application oriented, with an equal emphasis both on research and on using data to design and improve school counselors' functioning in school systems.

Available for free download for each chapter: PowerPoint slides, a testbank of 20 multiple-choice questions, and short-answer, essay, and discussion questions. Visit www.routledge.com/cw/kolbert.

Jered B. Kolbert, PhD, is a professor and coordinator of the school counseling program in the Department of Counseling, Psychology, and Special Education at Duquesne University.

Rhonda L. Williams, EdD, is an associate professor in the Department of Counseling and Human Services at the University of Colorado at Colorado Springs.

Leann M. Morgan, PhD, is an assistant professor in the Department of Counseling and Human Services at the University of Colorado at Colorado Springs.

Laura M. Crothers, DEd, is a professor in the Department of Counseling, Psychology, and Special Education at Duquesne University.

Tammy L. Hughes, PhD, is the Martin A. Hehir Endowed Chair for Scholarly Excellence and professor and chair of the Department of Counseling, Psychology, and Special Education at Duquesne University.

"In *Introduction to Professional School Counseling*, modern concepts in school counseling are clearly explained in an engaging format. Descriptive examples bring research to life and allow for the transfer of concepts into actual practice. The information about the ASCA model goes above and beyond by infusing the model into the entire book and giving actual samples of RAMP-certified comprehensive programs. A highlight for me was the chapter about social justice, which focuses on fostering self-awareness to deliver culturally competent programming."

Jane V. Hale, PhD, LPC, assistant professor,
Department of Counseling and Development, Slippery Rock University

"This straightforward and concise approach to professional school counseling is unique in being not only theoretically sound but, unlike many other textbooks, refreshingly rich in its practicality. This well-sequenced and all-inclusive resource will greatly benefit future school counselors as well as the future of comprehensive school counseling programs."

Richard Joseph Behun, PhD, LPC, NCC, ACS, assistant professor,
Department of Psychology and Counseling, Marywood University

"This text provides a valuable introduction to the contemporary role and responsibilities of the professional school counselor. The chapters are organized effectively around *the ASCA National Model®*. For each component and theme of *the ASCA National Model®*, a brief background of the topic is balanced with a comprehensive discussion of appropriate intervention strategies in K-12 schools. A thorough literature review for each chapter includes multiple practical strategies and techniques for implementation and evaluation."

LeeAnn M. Eschbach, PhD, LPC, associate professor,
Counseling and Human Services Department, University of Scranton

"A practical, up-to-date, and comprehensive resource, one that can be used across the span of any school counselor training program."

Krista M. Malott, PhD, LPC, associate professor and school counselor educator,
Department of Education & Counseling, Villanova University

Introduction to Professional School Counseling

Advocacy, Leadership, and Intervention

JERED B. KOLBERT

RHONDA L. WILLIAMS

LEANN M. MORGAN

LAURA M. CROTHERS

TAMMY L. HUGHES

Routledge
Taylor & Francis Group

NEW YORK AND LONDON

First published 2016
by Routledge
711 Third Avenue, New York, NY 10017

and by Routledge
2 Park Square, Milton Park, Abingdon, Oxon, OX14 4RN

Routledge is an imprint of the Taylor & Francis Group, an informa business

Library of Congress Cataloging in Publication Data
Names: Kolbert, Jered B., author.
Title: Introduction to professional school counseling : advocacy, leadership, and
intervention / Jered B. Kolbert, Rhonda L. Williams, Leann M. Morgan,
Laura M. Crothers, Tammy L. Hughes.
Description: 1 Edition. | New York : Routledge, [2016] |
Includes bibliographical references and index. Identifiers: LCCN 2015047609 |
ISBN 9780415746755 (hardback : alk. paper) |
ISBN 9780415746748 (pbk. : alk. paper) | ISBN 9781315797441 (ebook)
Subjects: LCSH: Educational counseling–United States. |
Student counselors–In-service training–United States.
Classification: LCC LB1027.5.K5968 2016 | DDC 371.4–dc23
LC record available at https://lccn.loc.gov/2015047609

ISBN: 978-0-415-74675-5 (hbk)
ISBN: 978-0-415-74674-8 (pbk)
ISBN: 978-1-315-79744-1 (ebk)

Typeset in Minion
by Out of House Publishing

Dedicated to

Jered B. Kolbert – To my children, Kennedy Isabel and Karlena Swanhild.

Rhonda L. Williams – To my grandchildren: I pray you have excellent school counselors throughout your education to support and guide you. And to my husband and children who support my dedication to the profession of school counseling.

Leann M. Morgan – To my children, Courtney and Cash, that you may know the unwavering support of amazing school counselors throughout your journey.

Laura M. Crothers – To my children, Meredith Julia Lipinski and Samuel Conrad Lipinski.

Contents

Chapter One
History and Trends in the School Counseling Profession

Box 1.1

2016 CACREP School Counseling Specialty Area Standards

1.a History and development of school counseling
2.a School counselor roles as leaders, advocates, and systems change agents in P-12 schools
2.m Legislation and government policy relevant to school counseling

---

School counseling, in comparison to other professions and fields of study, is a relatively recent area of inquiry and practice. That said, understanding the historical struggles and successes of the school counseling profession enables its members to define its future. Since the inception of the profession of school counseling 110 years ago, there have been name changes, issues of role confusion, and shifts in professional focus as a result of political influences. This chapter will elucidate some of the dynamics and the reasons for the slow progress in other areas of the school counseling profession. Topics that have influenced the profession of school counseling will be grouped so that readers may understand the progression of each issue throughout the history of school counseling. A timeline is provided to readers to clarify and isolate significant benchmarks in the evolution of the profession (see Figure 1.1).

Establishing the Conditions for the Zeitgeist for Change

In their incisive chapter on the Historical Roots and Future Issues in Counseling in their text, *Transforming the School Counseling Profession* (2nd ed.), Herr and Erford (2007) explain that various authors during the 20th century proposed the conditions that promoted the rise of guidance and counseling activities in US schools. In particular, Brewer (1942) identified four conditions that facilitated the growth of the profession of school counseling: (1) Division of labor, as population growth and efficiency as a result of task analysis resulted in greater specialization of task completion; (2) Growth of technology, as the

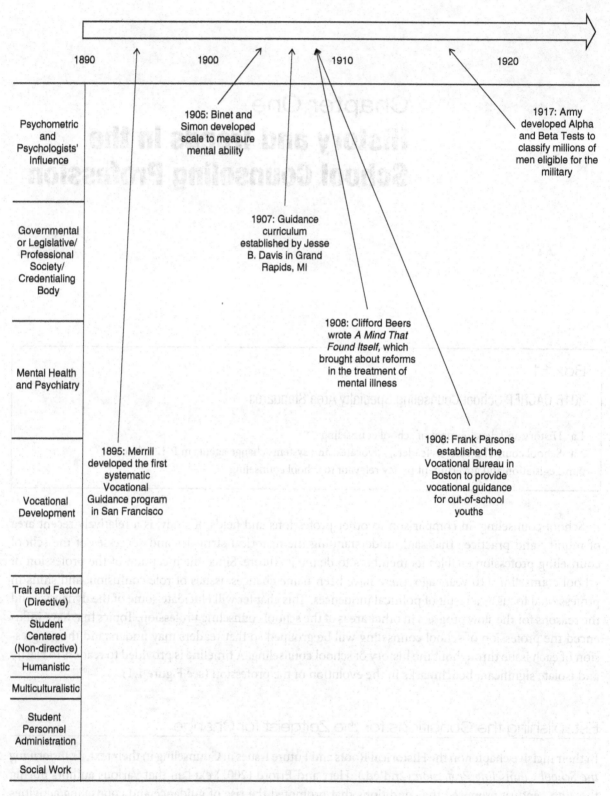

Figure 1.1 Timeline of the School Counseling Profession. Information Taken from Baker, S. B. (1999). *School counseling for the twenty-first century* (3rd ed.; pp. 10–11). Upper Saddle River, NJ: Merrill, and Herr, E. L., & Erford, B. T. (2007). Historical Roots and Future Issues. In B. T. Erford (Ed.), *Transforming the school counseling profession* (2nd ed.; pp. 13–37). Upper Saddle River, NJ: Pearson.

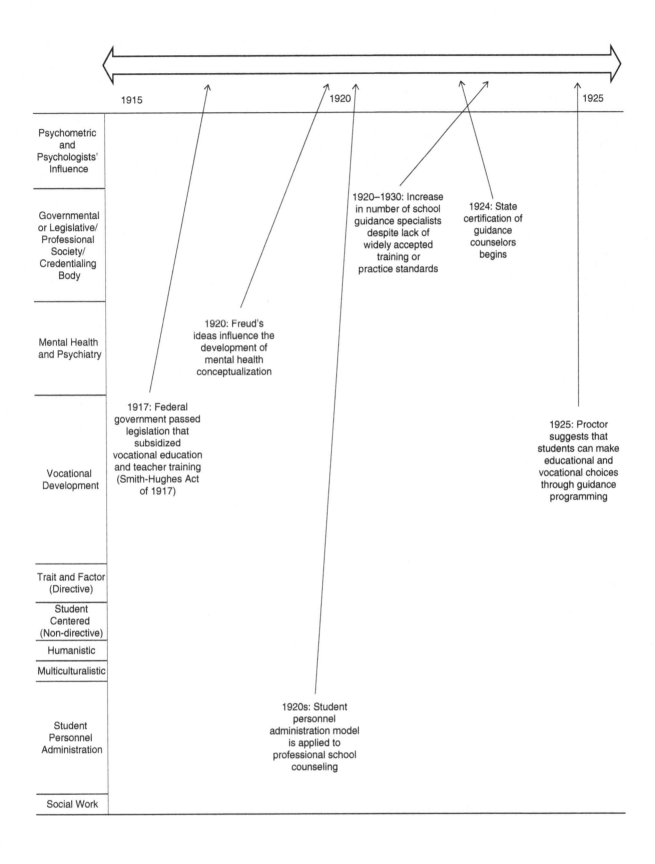

| | 1915 | | 1920 | | | 1925 |

Psychometric and Psychologists' Influence

Governmental or Legislative/ Professional Society/ Credentialing Body

1920–1930: Increase in number of school guidance specialists despite lack of widely accepted training or practice standards

1924: State certification of guidance counselors begins

Mental Health and Psychiatry

1920: Freud's ideas influence the development of mental health conceptualization

Vocational Development

1917: Federal government passed legislation that subsidized vocational education and teacher training (Smith-Hughes Act of 1917)

1925: Proctor suggests that students can make educational and vocational choices through guidance programming

Trait and Factor (Directive)

Student Centered (Non-directive)

Humanistic

Multiculturalistic

Student Personnel Administration

1920s: Student personnel administration model is applied to professional school counseling

Social Work

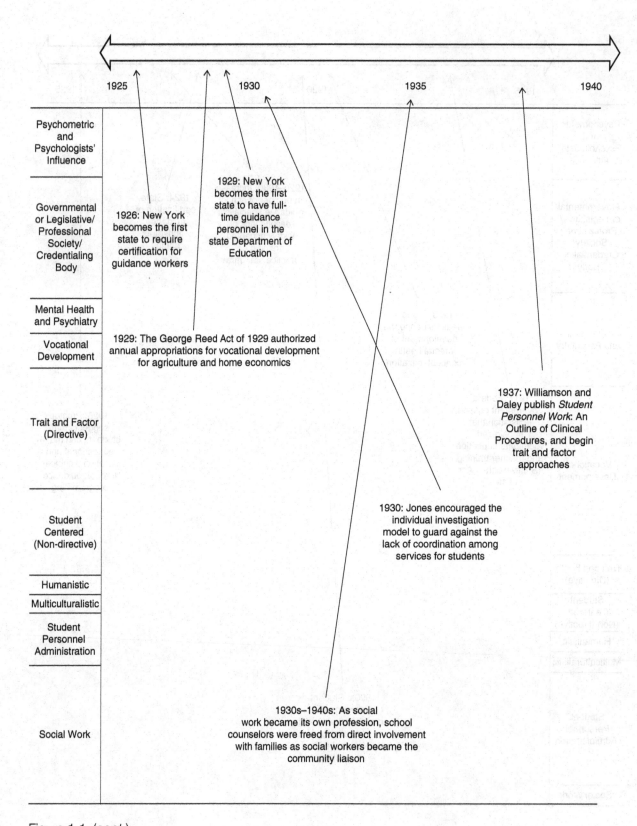

Figure 1.1 *(cont.)*

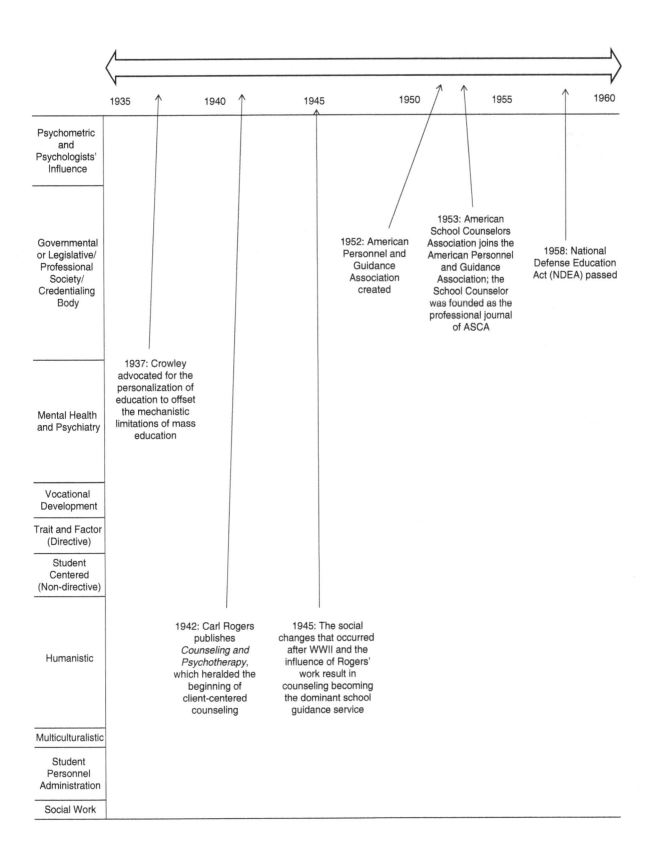

	1935		1940		1945	1950		1955		1960

Psychometric and Psychologists' Influence

Governmental or Legislative/ Professional Society/ Credentialing Body

1952: American Personnel and Guidance Association created

1953: American School Counselors Association joins the American Personnel and Guidance Association; the School Counselor was founded as the professional journal of ASCA

1958: National Defense Education Act (NDEA) passed

Mental Health and Psychiatry

1937: Crowley advocated for the personalization of education to offset the mechanistic limitations of mass education

Vocational Development

Trait and Factor (Directive)

Student Centered (Non-directive)

Humanistic

1942: Carl Rogers publishes *Counseling and Psychotherapy*, which heralded the beginning of client-centered counseling

1945: The social changes that occurred after WWII and the influence of Rogers' work result in counseling becoming the dominant school guidance service

Multiculturalistic

Student Personnel Administration

Social Work

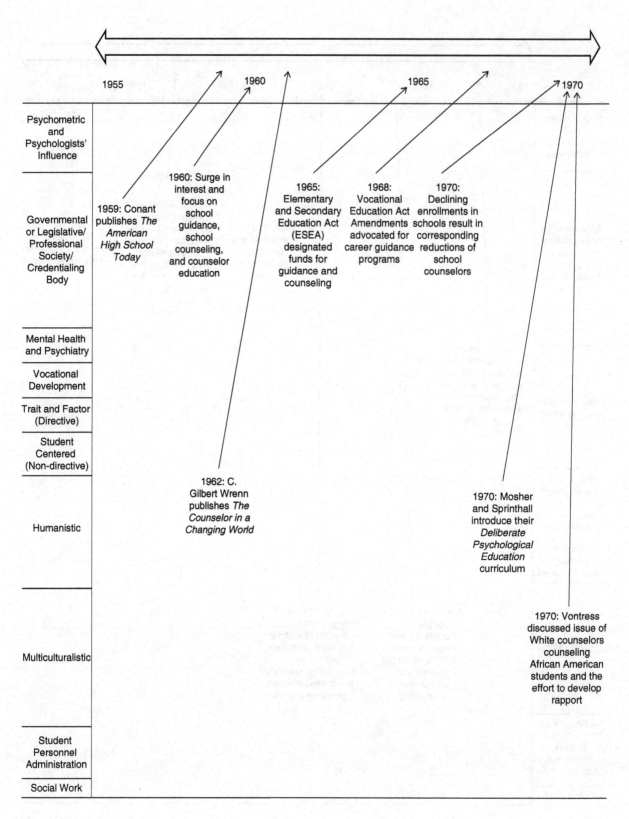

1955   1960   1965   1970

Psychometric and Psychologists' Influence

Governmental or Legislative/ Professional Society/ Credentialing Body

Mental Health and Psychiatry

Vocational Development

Trait and Factor (Directive)

Student Centered (Non-directive)

Humanistic

Multiculturalistic

Student Personnel Administration

Social Work

1959: Conant publishes *The American High School Today*

1960: Surge in interest and focus on school guidance, school counseling, and counselor education

1965: Elementary and Secondary Education Act (ESEA) designated funds for guidance and counseling

1968: Vocational Education Act Amendments advocated for career guidance programs

1970: Declining enrollments in schools result in corresponding reductions of school counselors

1962: C. Gilbert Wrenn publishes *The Counselor in a Changing World*

1970: Mosher and Sprinthall introduce their *Deliberate Psychological Education* curriculum

1970: Vontress discussed issue of White counselors counseling African American students and the effort to develop rapport

Figure 1.1 (*cont.*)

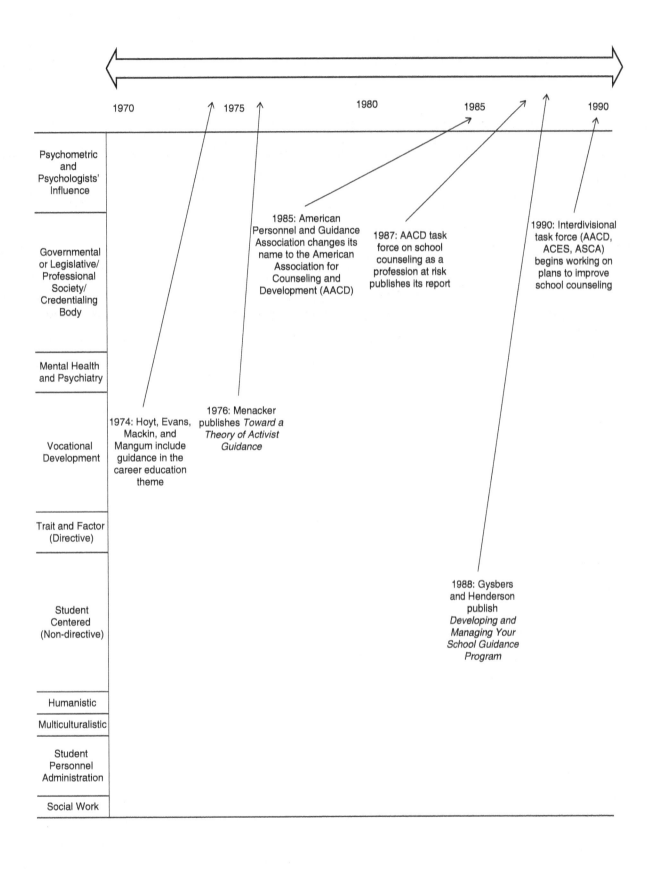

1970   1975   1980   1985   1990

Psychometric and Psychologists' Influence

Governmental or Legislative/ Professional Society/ Credentialing Body

1985: American Personnel and Guidance Association changes its name to the American Association for Counseling and Development (AACD)

1987: AACD task force on school counseling as a profession at risk publishes its report

1990: Interdivisional task force (AACD, ACES, ASCA) begins working on plans to improve school counseling

Mental Health and Psychiatry

Vocational Development

1974: Hoyt, Evans, Mackin, and Mangum include guidance in the career education theme

1976: Menacker publishes *Toward a Theory of Activist Guidance*

Trait and Factor (Directive)

Student Centered (Non-directive)

1988: Gysbers and Henderson publish *Developing and Managing Your School Guidance Program*

Humanistic

Multiculturalistic

Student Personnel Administration

Social Work

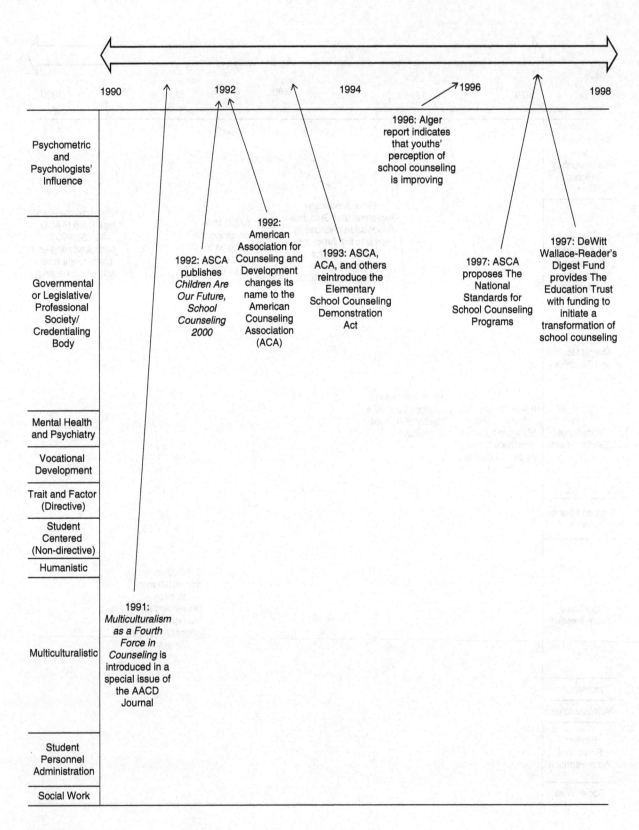

Figure 1.1 (cont.)

ever-improving ability to multiply the reach of the individual thereby reduced the unit cost; (3) The extension of vocational education, as options increased for measuring aptitude to direct individuals to appropriate postsecondary training; (4) Spread of modern forms of democracy, as individuals had options to pursue what they chose to do with their lives.

Similarly, Traxler and North (1966) traced the guidance movement in schools to five disparate philosophical, psychological, or sociological foundational advances: philanthropy or humanitarianism, religion, mental hygiene, social change, and the orientation to knowing students as individuals. Regardless of the background or contextual variables influencing the rise of school counseling at the end of the 19th and beginning of the 20th century, the beginnings of school counseling seemed to generally focus on vocational guidance. Additionally, there were concerns regarding the quality and utility of existing educational processes that also promoted the need for the field of school counseling. Moreover, the issue of individual choice and dignity appeared to be subsumed in both vocational guidance and educational reform. Herr and Erford (2007) posit that these three factors became entangled as philosophies and models of school guidance and counseling were then proposed by pioneers in the field.

Pioneers in the Profession

The unofficial introduction of school counseling was ushered in through the form of vocational guidance, which began in the late 1880s, with social reform initiatives and the political spread of democracy and immigration. In 1881, Lysander Richards was the first to present a model for career development, while in 1894, George Merrill advocated for exploratory classes in public education for students in order to develop their occupational interests. In 1907, Jesse Buttrick Davis, a principal in Michigan, initiated the first "school for systemic guidance" (Thompson, 2012, p. 4), maintaining that "students should be respected for their own abilities, interests, ideas, individual differences and cultural identity" (Davis, 1956, p. 176) in an effort to support all the students within the school setting. In order to incorporate school counseling classroom lessons into the general curriculum, Davis encouraged English teachers to take on the role of teaching guidance (as cited in Davis, 1956), which was the first time that teachers were encouraged to assume a counseling role.

The Vocationalists. George Merrill, a visionary in the conceptualization of the importance of vocational development, implemented the first systematic vocational guidance program in San Francisco (Herr & Erford, 2007). Richard Weaver, another pioneer in vocational awareness, developed one of the first publications regarding occupational information (Gysbers, 2010). He encouraged students to acquire a part-time summer job related to their educational plan, which can be regarded as an early form of job shadowing. Through this exhortation, Weaver is considered to be one of the early architects of the school counseling profession. However, Frank Parsons was graced with the title of "Father of Guidance" because he is considered to be the primary architect of vocational guidance in the US, based upon his advocacy work (Gysbers, 2010; Herr & Erford, 2007).

Parsons promoted the use of a more formal, scientific approach to career decision-making, recognizing this process as one of life's most important decisions, second only to choosing a spouse. Parsons (1909) promoted a formal position of guidance, indicating that "there is no part of life where the need for guidance is more emphatic than the transition from school to work" (p. 4). Parsons' Trait/Factor theory represented a three-step approach to vocational guidance: (1) finding your aptitudes, strengths, and interests; (2) developing knowledge of career choices and conditions for success; (3) understanding the relationship between the first two steps.

Parson's Trait/Factor theory was modified by E. G. Williamson, who is also recognized as a pioneer in the school counseling profession (Thompson, 2012). Williamson's book, *How to Counsel Students: A Manual of Techniques for Clinical Counselors* (1939), advocates for the use of empirical methods in assisting people to identify their abilities and aptitudes. He believed that people would be more satisfied in a career that was consistent with their aptitude. Williamson also wrote extensively about how overachievement, disabilities, and personality problems were related to learning and career development (Thompson, 2012).

The advocacy of these early pioneers resulted in the establishment of a national professional organization, the National Vocational Guidance Association (NVGA), which established an outline regarding the training emphases for school counseling professionals (Thompson, 2012). This organization also helped with the development of the American School Counselor Association (ASCA). In 1953, ASCA officially became a division of the American Personnel and Guidance Association (APGA), which is now referred to as the American Counseling Association (ACA).

The Humanists. Although Carl Rogers was not directly involved in advocating for the profession of school counseling, he was instrumental in influencing the approaches used by school counselors (Thompson, 2012). Rogers' concept of unconditional positive regard and his non-directive, person-centered approach has become a foundational competency for counselors in training. His theoretical premise of the self-determination of the client was extended by school counselors to students and resulted in school counselors seeing themselves as child and adolescent specialists.

The Integrators. A systemic approach to school counseling came about with Frank Wellman's identification of the school counseling profession's focus upon the three domains of educational, career, and social development, accompanied by operational objectives, and Gysbers and Myrick's advocacy for a comprehensive, standards-based, developmental school counseling curriculum in the 1980s and 1990s (Gysbers, 2010). Johnson and Johnson (1991) reinforced the need for a competency-based guidance program that sought to promote all students' acquisition of skills required for transitioning to post-secondary preparation. ASCA first published a model of school counseling in 1998, which was titled *Vision into Action* (Dahir, Sheldon, & Valiga, 1998). In 2003, ASCA replaced *Vision into Action* with a comprehensive, standards-based model, titled *The ASCA National Model: A Framework for School Counseling Programs*. This book references the third iteration of *the ASCA National Model®* (2012).

Evolution of Professional Identity

The focus of those who today are recognized as the founders of the school counseling profession was upon assisting students in understanding their career aspirations in a formalized and structured manner (Gysbers, 2010). Instead of allowing students to select careers without an informed selection process, the emphasis was upon "guiding" students through developmentally appropriate career decision-making. The term "vocopher," meaning those who helped individuals "bring order out of chaos and form or establish a system to enable a person to find the most fitting pursuit in which he can reap the greatest success" (Richards, 1881, p. iv), was used to refer to this orientation.

Box 1.3

Web connection: www.vocopher.com

Vocopher is the name of a free career collaborative effort that provides practitioners and researchers with instruments to assess different career-related issues (Glavin, 2015).

Although this term was eventually discarded, the focus on guiding students through a career decision-making process was maintained (Gysbers, 2010). Similarly, in the 1920s, the term "vocational guidance" began to decline in its use as this era was dominated by an emphasis on psychometrics.

In the mid-1930s, the professional identity of the school counselor shifted from a focus on the career development of students to that of assisting students with life adjustment, which included an emphasis on social and "mental adjustment" (Gysbers, 2010). The term "pupil personnel services," which was borrowed from the industrial organizations of that time, came into vogue. Schools were encouraged to make the pupil personnel services an integral part of the educational system, and this emphasis is still in existence today, as school counseling programs are expected to have a holistic view of student development. Within this new orientation, career guidance moved from a specific position in the education system to services provided in a framework of pupil personnel services. Gysbers (2010) describes Bell's (1939) assertion that counselors promoted student adjustment through personal contact and by focusing on educational and vocational development as being reflective of this era. Although "pupil personnel services" was the terminology used for the responsibilities of professional school counseling during the 1930s, the term "guidance" appeared occasionally, with a smattering of the term "counselor" being thrown into the lexicon.

The profession struggled with role confusion during the 1940s and 1950s (Gysbers, 2010). Indeed, the *National Vocational Guidance Association Yearbook* of 1948–49 showed 53 varying titles attributed to the school counseling profession (Gysbers, 2010). Some recommended that the term "counselor" be adopted to provide unity for the profession, as counseling services were identified as the "heart and core" of the guidance program. However, most of the counseling services provided within schools were practiced by teachers, administrators, and deans of students, as there were few full-time school counselors in existence. It was also common practice to have a guidance-teacher as opposed to a trained counselor. Career development and social-emotional learning activities were often provided in homeroom classes, and some schools began to deliver guidance activities to small groups. However, there were only a few post-baccalaureate programs offering coursework specific to the role of the school counselor.

In the 1960s and 1970s, new nomenclature such as "advisor," "human relations specialist," and "applied behavioral scientist" were bandied about in heated debates regarding whether or not the professional identity of school counselors should abide by the guidance educational model, or adhere to the psychologist model of counseling. While the argument escalated between those advocating for an educational focus and those advocating adoption of the psychological framework, because many graduate programs in school counseling emphasized a psychological orientation, some states began to eliminate the requirement of teaching experience for school counseling certification.

The debate about the title of "personnel worker" or "counselor" persisted during the 1980s and 1990s (Gysbers, 2010). Gradually, the term "counselor" achieved prominence while the term "guidance model" came to refer to the services provided by school counselors. In 1993, ASCA officially advocated for use of the terms "professional school counselor" and "comprehensive school counseling program." In 2009,

ASCA asserted that school counseling refers to a comprehensive and coordinated program rather than solely referring to the description of the position of school counselor.

Confusion and Diffusion of the Roles and Functions

Historically, there has been considerable confusion regarding the role of the school counselor. The use of visiting teachers, administrators, and deans of students as "guidance" educators in the school setting contributed to the ambiguity of the role of the school counselor from the onset of the profession. McCradie and Ferguson (1929) analyzed various positions in the school setting, differentiating the professional role of the school counselor from novice visiting teachers, school social workers, and other newly added educational positions. This initial attempt at role clarification resulted in the recommendation that the position of school counseling required post-baccalaureate training. The amount of time spent in scholarly preparation for the activities of the "guidance counselor," as such individuals were often called, became a means of role clarification.

Box 1.4

Did you know?

There is a substantial overlap between the roles of a mental health counselor and a clinical social worker. Both perform psychotherapy, but social workers tend to be more focused on modifying the environment to accommodate their clients, while counselors are more strongly oriented toward helping their clients adapt to the environments in which they function (Socialworklicensure.org, 2015).

Holbrook (1927) explained that the propensity for school counselors to often be promoted to an administrative role contributed to role confusion for the profession. Myers (1923) recognized the necessity for vocational guidance to be viewed as integral to the educational system and not as a nonessential add-on responsibility. He was one of the first to call for specialized training at the post-baccalaureate level and for unification and standardization of that training. Myers worried about the diffusion of the school counseling role, arguing against "the tendency for vocational guidance to be viewed as quasi-administration with non-counselor duties being piled on the counselor so no work of counseling is being done" (p. 140). This statement reflects prescience, as the same concerns are relevant today.

Higher standards for admission into the study of the profession of school counseling became common in an effort to increase the clarity and legitimacy of the field (Gysbers, 2010). Even though university coursework for "guidance services" began at Harvard as early as 1911, it was not until the 1920s that more courses specific to the profession of counseling were developed. In 1925, there were as many as 35 colleges offering coursework in vocational guidance, and this number increased to 70 colleges by 1928. Despite the growth of the school counseling profession during this time, some educators continued to suggest that all educators should be expected to provide guidance services, to which counselor educators responded by attempting to separate the role and training of school counselors from that of other educators.

The notion that school counselors were education specialists emerged during the political and economic turmoil of the 1930s (Gysbers, 2010). In an attempt to define the school counselor role, Reavis and Woellner (1930) identified three terms to describe the provision of guidance: educational, personal, and vocational. Gysbers (2010) points out that, interestingly, these domains seem similar to the domains of *the ASCA National Model®* (2012). A report published in 1941 revealed that the ratio of school counselor to students was 1:1,000, with only 16.4% of secondary schools even employing a qualified school counselor. This report attempted to legitimize the profession in its recommendation that guidance counselors complete at least 30 credits of graduate work and possess teacher certification. In 1948, the Division of Higher Education of the US Office of Education issued requirements for counselor education. Arnold (1949) conducted a study of school counseling activities, concluding that "more time and effort are being given to attendance, tardiness, discipline and school failure than are being given to counseling about vocational and educational plans and about personal, social and school problems" (p. 392).

Despite the efforts to legitimize the profession through post-baccalaureate training, and the number of research studies verifying the misdirection or misuse of professional skills, the lack of definition regarding the role of the school counselor persisted. Gysbers (2010) cites research published in the *California Guidance Newsletter* (1951) validating the misapplication of these professional skills, finding that as much as 80% of the school counselor's time was spent on clerical duties. Despite exhortations to the contrary, it appears that there was little difference between the early 1920s and early 1950s in terms of the activities of school counselors.

The 1950s witnessed continued debate regarding the appropriate role of school counselors (Gysbers, 2010). Conflict also emerged between those advocating for the retention of the vocational guidance concept and those advocating for the adoption of the use of psychological and personality development models. The widespread adoption of Rogers' non-directive approaches led many counselor preparation programs to deemphasize the traditional Trait/Factor theory in favor of approaches that emphasized the promotion of students' self-concept and social adjustment. This new movement pushed the topics of self-esteem and personality to the forefront of training, with the adjustment of the individual becoming the new goal of guidance and counseling. This shift moved the profession on from its vocational focus to the mental hygiene model of school counseling. With that shift came another change in title and function from guidance to pupil personnel services.

The new philosophical orientation of psychotherapeutic models served to add to the role confusion of the profession, yet again. However, the advocacy from the new professional organization, the American School Counselor Association (ASCA), a division of the American Personnel and Guidance Association (later American Counselor Association), brought new support and direction to the profession from its inception in 1953. The initial actions of the organization directed school counselors to vigorously advocate for their role and position while also turning to focus again on university training programs.

ASCA focused upon establishing a uniform curriculum for school counselors. This movement to standardize the curriculum of school counselors also instigated a debate regarding whether school counselors should have teaching experience. Research then and now supported the fact that both previous teachers and those with no teaching experience had a large learning curve when entering the school counseling field (e.g., Baker, 1994), causing many states to abandon the previous requisite of needing teaching experience to become a school counselor.

During the 1960s and 1970s another shift in the role of school counselors occurred (Gysbers, 2010). Organizational systems and preventive programming became the professional focus, advancing the school counselor as a change agent. To that end, Hatch (2008) purports that there are three theories that form the standards of professional legitimacy: organizational theory, institutional theory, and political theory, which are explained in Table 1.1. The following sections explore Hatch's perspective of how these theories of professional legitimacy elucidate some of the profession's challenges, and offer implications for establishing professional legitimacy.

Organizational theory. Organizational theory regards the effectiveness and efficiency of an organization in achieving its desired results (Hatch, 2008). Organizations develop formal structures, which

Table 1.1 Professional Challenges of School Counseling: Organizational, Institutional, and Political

Theoretical Construct	Professional Challenge Facing the School Counseling Profession	How is the Challenge Manifested?	How can the Challenge be Addressed?	Desired Outcome
Organizational	Effectiveness (predictive, desired and intended goals and outcomes are met)	Do not measure impact of activities and do not know whether they work or not	Evaluate the program	Measure results Know what works, and what does not work
	Internal efficiency (greatest output for the least energy and resources)	Status quo Inefficiency Random acts of guidance	Program improvement	Do more of what works, less of what does not work Program refinement Time efficiency
Institutional	Operational legitimacy	No structural elements institutionalized (rules, norms and routines, policies, procedures etc.) Unaware of standards or model	Reporting program results Social and cultural pressure Educate on standards and model programs	Indispensability Influence policy actors to create institutionalization of structural elements, laws, policies, handbooks, routines, and procedures reflecting appropriate role of school counselor
	Social legitimacy	Not involved in site leadership No legitimate voice in programs, or policies	Becoming involved in decision-making Systems change Student advocacy	Becoming a policy actor Influencing policy actors by contributing to the cultural pressure that leads to the creation of structures Partner with school leadership for systems change
Political	Value versus resources Social capital Political clout	Reduction in force Undervaluing profession Increase in non-school counseling responsibility	Reporting program results Marketing	Seen as integral Valued Performing school counseling activities

Note: Reprinted with permission from Hatch, T. A. (2008). Professional challenges in school counseling: Organizational, institutional and political. *Journal of School Counseling, 6,* 1–31.

includes the identification of members' roles, policies, and procedures, to evaluate both goal attainment and the efficiency of the formal structures in contributing to goal attainment. One of the historical challenges of the school counseling profession is that it has lacked formal structures, program definitions, or clear objectives. School counseling programs vary considerably between sites and districts, and there is little consistency regarding the role of the school counseling program and school counselor within the larger organization of the school. As a result, it is difficult to evaluate how the school counseling program contributes to the school's mission and the efficiency of the school counseling program's related services/functions. *The ASCA National Model*® (2012), first published in 2003, and which is discussed in considerable depth in Chapter 2, was developed to provide a consistent structure and methods of evaluation to enable school counselors and stakeholders to assess the effectiveness and efficiency of the school counseling program.

Institutional theory. Institutional theory concerns how organizations develop the formal structures and processes for establishing rules, policies, and procedures. Operational legitimacy is achieved within an organization when structural elements, including standards, policies, and processes, define norms and routines. Social legitimacy is established when organizational members contribute to objectives of the organization that resulted in the development of such structural elements, such as evaluation measures or role descriptions. Members are socially legitimate when they contribute to the decision/policy-making. School counselors often have not been part of the process of establishing the formal structures of schools. Rather, their role has often been defined by historical internal and external pressures. For example, upon being hired a school counselor is often informed of what duties he or she will have, not necessarily because the duties are defined in a formal job description or contribute to the school's efficiency, but rather because the previous school counselor performed the respective duties, or because school counselors in nearby schools do it this way. A graduate of the school counseling program in which the first author of this text taught was informed by the principal in her first school counseling position that she would be responsible for examining all of the students' heads for lice because that was a responsibility of the previous school counselor. The school counseling profession has also lacked operational legitimacy. The profession was not included in the development of the No Child Left Behind (NCLB: 2002) legislation, and in many states school counselors are not mandated nor do they have state guidelines. Many school districts do not have job descriptions, evaluation tools specific to school counselors, or policies and procedures manuals.

Institutional legitimacy is obtained by adopting the current societal values, norms, and procedures. Concern over the profession's exclusion from the NCLB and other educational reform movements resulted in ASCA seeking legitimacy through accepting the norms and values of the standards movement. ASCA created *the ASCA National Model*® (2012) and national standards for students, which closely resembled the form of similar student standards in education. Hatch (2008) urges school counselors to use the operational frameworks developed by ASCA to demonstrate to school personnel who are part of the policy-making process that they are essential contributors to student learning. This would increase the likelihood that school counselors will be invited to join the policy-making process. School counselors can educate stakeholders through brochures, handbooks, accreditation reports, etc. about the profession's operational frameworks, and can participate in efforts to reform state laws and education codes to reflect the new vision of school counseling.

Political theory. Political decisions concern the process by which finite resources are distributed, and often rest on the issue of value vs. resources. Programs that are highly valued have "social capital" and are likely to receive additional resources. Programs earn social capital by predicating and responding to the values and perceived needs of the organization.

Four levels of political influence are essential for the growth of the school counseling profession: site, district, state, and national. At the school level, school counselors must be valued by the administration to ensure the continuance of their programs and avoid the assignment of quasi-administrative and clerical duties. At the district level, the governing board must regard the school counseling program as vital. At the state level, the profession must influence state representatives who periodically receive pressure from various action groups pursuing school reform at the expense of eliminating school counseling programs. At the national level, school counselors must support the national professional organizations in their efforts to be part of the policy-making process.

One of the primary ways in which professional school counselors develop political clout is by evaluating and marketing the results of program initiatives. Evaluation indicates how program efforts can be improved to maximize efficiency, and informs stakeholders of the impact of the program. A school counseling student once remarked to the lead author of this text that she could not see how using data would be meaningful to her. While this may sound cynical, one can argue that the value of data is not so much of direct benefit to the school counselor, but rather, the benefit is to those who have political clout. It can be said that data is one of the "primary languages" through which we help others understand our impact and what we do.

Recent Efforts to Promote Unity within the Profession

The 1960s and 1970s encouraged individual school counselors to develop and define their own roles and responsibilities, based on the needs of each school. This individualized movement added fuel to the fire regarding the role confusion in the field of school counseling.

During the 1980s and 1990s, there was increased concern within the field of education regarding the achievement gap for children of color and those in poverty (Gysbers, 2010). Partially as a result of these concerns, school counselors were encouraged to focus more on prevention and providing developmental guidance than on conducting individual and group counseling with at-risk students. ASCA encouraged school counselors to dispute their assignment to activities that were not considered to be consistent with this prevention role.

A number of organizations, including ASCA, the Education Trust, and the College Board, became involved in an effort to transform and unify the school counseling profession (Gysbers, 2010). In addition, the writings and work of Myrick (1987), Gysbers (1990), and Johnson and Johnson (1982) were influential in defining school counseling as a program, which is developmental and comprehensive in nature, rather than a position. The focus shifted from the services provided by school counselors to viewing school counseling as an integral program that supports but is also distinct from the school's academic curriculum. There was also an increased emphasis upon the need for accountability and the collection of data to demonstrate the impact of the school counseling program.

While ASCA is a division of the American Counseling Association (ACA), and ASCA has actively promoted the use of the title "professional school counselor" vs. "guidance counselor," in the past decade there has been tension between ASCA and ACA. Whereas other divisions of ACA are required to join ACA, persons may become ASCA members without having to join ACA. In 2014, ACA, with the support of 29 other counseling organizations, adopted the following consensus definition: "Counseling is a professional relationship that empowers diverse individuals, families, and groups to accomplish mental health, wellness, education, and career goals" (Kaplan, Tarvydas, & Gladding, 2014, p. 366). However, ASCA did not endorse this definition, citing the fact that the definition did not distinguish counseling from other mental health professions and that the definition was not based on empirical support. The tension between ACA and ASCA may be partially due to the desire of ASCA to define the term professional school counselor as being more comprehensive in nature as opposed to focusing primarily on the mental health concerns of at-risk students, and this is discussed in greater length in Chapter 2. While ASCA defines professional school counselors primarily as educators, many counselor education programs have adopted ACA's recommendation that school counselors identify as counselors who work within an education setting.

Political and Social Impact on the School Counseling Profession

The school counseling profession has been redefined numerous times, and much of the role confusion inherent in the field can be attributed to the influence of political and social issues of the times. In the 1880s, social reform was the primary focus as a result of the working conditions of the Industrial Revolution. The Progressive Movement, which began at the turn of the century, sought to address demographic changes taking place at the time, which included the large increase in immigration and the nation's transition from largely an agrarian culture to an urban culture (Erford, 2004). The role of the school counselor became focused upon providing students with a more structured method of choosing postsecondary career options. Additionally, society's concern with mental illness, partially as a result of Clifford Beers' (1908) book, *A Mind That Found Itself*, in which he described the horrific conditions he experienced during his institutionalization in a mental hospital, resulted in calls for school counselors to work increasingly with the mental and social issues of children (Thompson, 2012).

Box 1.5

Did you know?

"The Army Alpha was a group-administered test that measured verbal ability, numerical ability, ability to follow directions, and knowledge of information. The Army Beta was a non-verbal counterpart to the Army Alpha. It was used to evaluate the aptitude of illiterate, unschooled, or non-English speaking draftees and volunteers" (ASVAB, 2015).

World War I had a significant impact upon the role of the school counselor. Standardized measurements, such as the Army's Alpha and Beta intelligence tests, were introduced to identify youth for armed services selection (Gysbers, 2010). During the war, school counselors focused upon identifying students for armed services selection, and students' vocational aspirations often represented a secondary interest. The psychometric movement inspired by World War I continued into the 1920s, and school counselors were heavily involved in the coordination of assessments for intelligence and vocational competencies. However, there was also considerable opposition to the psychometric movement, and many educators argued that the emphasis upon psychometrics failed to consider the "whole child." During this time, child clinics were established to help what were seen as problem children. As a consequence, school counselors began to focus more on children with social and emotional difficulties and assisting with the personal adjustment of students. The term "maladjusted child" became the new vernacular of the era (Johnson, 1972).

The 1930s brought the first recognition of the profession of school counseling "in the form of legislation and the creation of a national office in the federal government as well as state offices for guidance" (Gysbers, 2010, p. 42). School counselors returned to focusing upon vocational education. During Franklin D. Roosevelt's presidential administration, the Vocational Division of the US Office of Education was established. There was an effort to specialize the training of school counselors, to distinguish them from teachers, as well as to standardize the preparation curriculum.

In the subsequent decade, the passage of the Vocational Education Act of 1946, also known as the George Barden Act, provided federal funds for guidance program supervision, salaries of counselor-trainees and counselor supervisors, and research on the activities of school counselors (Gysbers, 2010). The political and monetary support helped to expand the profession in a dramatic fashion. A contributor to this professional momentum was the establishment of a standard curriculum by the National Vocational Guidance Association (NVGA) in 1948. Also in 1948, the National Conference of State Supervisors of Guidance Services and Counselor Trainers established certification regulations for school counselors.

Box 1.6

Did you know?

In addition to providing monetary support for the math and science aptitude testing of students, the Title V section of the National Defense Education Act provided funding for educational and career counseling to public high school students and the creation of guidance counselor training institutes. Guidance counseling preparation programs were encouraged to match students' abilities and courses of study and to assist qualified students to prepare for college education. The training institutes aimed to bolster the quality of the qualifications of those who provided counseling and guidance services for students in secondary schools (Flattau et al., 2006).

Interestingly, the National Defense Education Act (NDEA) of 1958 had a profound impact upon the school counseling profession (Gysbers, 2010). At this time, it was perceived that the defense of the nation was at risk because of the Union of Soviet Socialist Republics' launch of Sputnik and the escalation of the Cold War. The NDEA provided funds for the testing of students to identify students with aptitudes in math and science. The NDEA also provided funding for universities to train secondary school counselors, which resulted in the tripling of the number of school counselors nationwide between 1958 and 1967 (Thompson, 2012).

The political movements of the 1960s and 1970s, which included the Civil Rights, Feminist, and Peace movements, profoundly impacted the school counseling profession. Just as society was polarized in support or opposition to these movements, there was a division within the school counseling profession. School counselors were divided between those who identified primarily as educators versus those who classified themselves as human relations specialists. Also, some leaders within the profession wished to establish a guidance model that was a part of the educational system, whereas others wished to align school counseling with psychology.

The Vocational Education Act of 1963, the Vocational Education Amendments of 1968, and the Education Amendment of 1976 redirected the professional focus back to its origins of career awareness and career decision-making. These bills reflected the desire of Congress to ensure that the US remained a viable global competitor by encouraging students to pursue coursework and careers in math and the sciences. In contrast, the Elementary and Secondary Education Act of 1965 encouraged school counselors to address social issues, as the Act provided grants to local school districts to establish programs to prevent school dropout, particularly among the economically disadvantaged and students with disabilities (Erford, 2004).

The Elementary and Secondary Education Act also increased the number of elementary school counselors (Gysbers, 2010). While elementary school counselors were in existence as early as the 1920s, during the first several decades of their professional functioning, their positions were primarily viewed as educational and not therapeutic. Furthermore, the foundational guidance provided by elementary school counselors was seen as a vital component to the education of all students. However, gradually, there was an increasing overlap in the duties of school psychologists, school social workers, and school counselors. There was also debate regarding the relationship between elementary and secondary school counselors, with some arguing that elementary school counselors should seek to see themselves as distinct and separate from secondary school counselors. Dinkmeyer was a strong advocate for elementary school counselors at this time, asserting that the roles and functions of elementary school counselors should include consultation, counseling, school counseling classroom lessons, group guidance, and coordination of services.

Several social issues impacted the school counseling profession during the 1970s. Both an economic recession and a decline in the school population resulted in declining school budgets and the elimination of school counseling positions (Gysbers, 2010). There was a call for greater accountability for school counselors to identify their effectiveness and justify their positions. However, The Career Education Act of 1978 and the Carl Perkins Vocational Education Act of 1984 re-energized the school counseling profession (Erford, 2004). These acts supported school counselors' role in preparing students to enter the world of work, and provided federal funds for transition programs.

The Education for All Handicapped Children Act of 1975 and the Family Educational Rights and Privacy Act (FERPA) of 1974 expanded the professional focus of school counseling to include all students in the educational system, not just those who were college bound (Gysbers, 2010). These legislative initiatives provided legitimacy to school counselors being integral to the educational process, while maintaining the focus upon career decision-making and enhancing students' transitions from school to work.

During the 1980s and 1990s, there was a shift toward establishing a comprehensive, standards-based curriculum, based on the work of Gysbers, Myrick, and Johnson (Gysbers, 2010). ASCA supported this movement in the establishment of the *National Standards for School Counseling Programs* (Campbell & Dahir, 1997), and its companion, *Vision into Action: Implementing the National Standards for School Counseling Programs* (Dahir et al., 1998). Federal funding to support the school counseling profession's implementation of a comprehensive, standards-based curriculum was provided through the Elementary School Counseling Demonstration Act of 1995 and the Carl D. Perkins Vocational and Applied Technology Act of 1990 (Erford, 2004). However, the No Child Left Behind Act of 2001 (NCLB: 2002) represented a political setback for the school counseling profession as it was not included in the planning and development of this monumental legislative movement. This omission compelled ASCA, ACA, the Education Trust, and other professional advocates to develop initiatives to establish the legitimacy of the profession. In 2015 NCLB was replaced with the Every Student Succeeds Act (ESSA: US Department of Education, n.d.). ASCA (2015) issued a statement in support of ESSA, citing the legislation's emphasis on academic and career counseling, the importance of providing students with a well-rounded education, and improving the safety and health of school environments. In ESSA, the *Elementary and Secondary School Counseling Program* (ESSCP) grants were incorporated into a large block grant along with many other programs. This large block grant now explicitly lists school counselors as being eligible for federal professional development monies, which could result in increased funding for school counselors.

Professional Association Influences and Impact

The need for advocacy led by professional organizations is apparent in the evolution of the school counseling profession (Gysbers, 2010). The evolution of the professional organizations has closely mirrored changes in the school counseling profession. In the early 1920s, the National Education Association (NEA) created the Commission on the Reorganization of Secondary Education (CRSE), which directed public schools to incorporate vocational education throughout the educational process. Ironically, however, the CRSE did not include school counselors in their planning (Johnson, 1972).

The Occupational Information and Guidance Service (OIGS) of the late 1930s may have been the first official voice for the school counseling profession (Gysbers, 2010). This organization eventually became the National Association of Guidance Supervision and Counselor Trainers, currently known as the Association of Counselor Education and Supervision (ACES). Concerned with the lack of consistency in the education and training of school counselors, the OIGS collaborated with the Division of Higher Education of the US Office of Education. In 1948, the first National Conference of State Supervisors of Guidance Services and Counselor Trainers was held in Washington DC, and this conference ultimately resulted in the publication of the first manual on counselor preparation by the NVGA (Thompson, 2012). The American Personnel and Guidance Association (APGA) grew out of the NVGA, and eventually the APGA became the ACA. In 1952, the APGA (which is now ACA) created the American School Counselor Association (ASCA) division, which was the first organization specific to the profession of school counselors. From its inception, ASCA has sought to define, unify, and promote the school counseling professional through the publication of a professional journal, newsletters, professional position papers, etc.

In addition to ASCA, the Council for the Accreditation of Counseling and Related Educational Programs (CACREP) and the National Board of Certified Counselors (NBCC; Gysbers, 2010) have published preparation standards for school counselors. CACREP was formed in 1981 for the purpose of developing standards of preparation for all types of counseling professionals, including addictions counseling, clinical mental health counseling, and school counseling, to establish a standardized curriculum for the protection of the public welfare. NBCC was established in 1982 for the objective of developing a national credentialing exam that assesses students' mastery of CACREP's eight knowledge areas: human growth and development, social and cultural foundations, helping relationships, group counseling, career and lifestyle development, appraisal, research and program evaluation, program orientation, and ethics. NBCC issues a National Certified Counselor (NCC) certificate, and also issues certificates for specific types of counseling professionals, including the National Certified School Counselor (NCSC) designation. Some states and school systems offer increased salaries for NCSCs.

Summary

The evolution of school counseling has been more cyclical than linear. Initially, the profession's focus was upon vocational education. However, school counseling now emphasizes a more holistic view of students as reflected in *the ASCA National Model's*® (2012) prioritization of the career, personal/social, and academic domains. The pioneers of this profession began with the realization of the need for a structured process in which students could make effective career decisions. Assisting students in understanding their unique personal strengths, talents, interests, and abilities became the foundation of the profession. While the Trait/Factor Theory was the initial assessment method for career decision-making, new career theories, personality and ability assessments, and career portfolios now also contribute to students' career decision-making process.

The original focus of "guidance counseling" involved assessments for career decision-making; however, educators often presumed that the role of a school counselor was the coordinator of assessments related to learning. Ironically, this controversy continues to concern the profession, as the coordination of testing is a time-consuming responsibility of many school counselors. Although school counselors are trained in test preparation, the distribution, scheduling, and proctoring of tests is not considered by ASCA to be an effective use of the professional school counselor's time.

Through the evolution of the profession, many types of nomenclature have been used to explain the roles and functions of this education position. From vocational guidance to guidance services, pupil personnel services to guidance office, ASCA ultimately selected the term of professional school counselor. In the early years of the profession, utilizing the services of teachers and administrators to provide vocational guidance may have been a pragmatic measure. However, this decision may have also contributed to the role confusion within school counseling, as teaching credentials were considered to be a prerequisite for the school counseling position. Research has not supported the need for school counselors to have a teaching background, and thus the vast majority of states have eliminated this requirement.

The rigor of school counselors' preparation has been questioned at various times. Graduate courses specific to the occupational needs of a school counselor became necessary to legitimize the profession. The training of school counselors has been enhanced by CACREP's establishment of a standardized curriculum, and NBCC's standardized assessment criteria for the NCC and NCSC. The breadth of knowledge required of today's school counselors is considerable, as school counselors are expected to be able to effectively use both evidence-based prevention and intervention strategies to promote students' academic, social/emotional, and career development.

Many social and political issues have impacted the development of the school counseling profession. At times, school counselors have been expected to focus upon meeting the needs of at-risk students, whereas at other times school counselors were expected to focus upon the needs of all students by providing services or implementing programs that were infused into the school's curriculum. In response to the Soviet Union's launching of Sputnik, the NDEA of 1958 came about, offering federal funding for school counseling positions and professional education. In 1963, the Vocational Education Act redirected the focus of school counseling back to career decision-making as the threat of global competitiveness loomed. The Elementary and Secondary Education Act broadened the focus of school counseling from career information to include the social/emotional needs of students. However, the Carl Perkins Act brought the career focus back to the school counseling profession full circle.

Unfortunately, several educational reform efforts through the years have ignored the school counseling profession as an integral part of the discussions. No dismissal was more apparent than being left out of the NCLB educational reform legislation. Paradoxically, however, this rebuff propelled the school counseling profession and the professional organization into a new paradigm of educational collaboration. Prominent figures in this field began to advocate for a more proactive, developmental, standards-based approach to the school counseling profession.

This new realization highlighted the value of a comprehensive, standards-based, school counseling profession, which emerged during the 1980s and 1990s. This movement is seen as a turning point in the effort to establish legitimacy for the school counseling profession. *The ASCA National Model*® (2012) seeks to align school counseling with the mission of schools, ensuring that school counselors devote 80% of their time to provision of direct and indirect services to students, and promoting the utilization of strategies for management and accountability to ensure that school counselors impact the entire student population. Perhaps more importantly, the school counseling profession's commitment to a comprehensive, standards-based system of service delivery renders it less vulnerable to the reactionary responses of prevailing political and social issues.

The paradigm of the profession has been changed through viewing school counseling as an integral service in the educational system, and not merely as that which is provided by or to a few lone individuals within the school or district. In embracing this shift, the school counseling profession has taken the next step in its evolution. With legislative advocacy and proactive behaviors exhibited on the part of individual school counselors, state school counseling organizations, and national professional organizations, school counseling is poised to no longer be viewed as ancillary to the educational system, but rather as a service that ensures the holistic development of all students.

References

American School Counselor Association (2012). *The ASCA national model: A framework for school counseling programs* (3rd ed.). Alexandria, VA: Author.

American School Counselor Association (2015). *American School Counselor Association endorses Every Student Succeeds Act*. Available online at www.schoolcounselor.org/asca/media/asca/Press%20releases/ESSA.pdf (accessed January 14, 2016).

Armed Services Vocational Aptitude Battery (ASVAB) (2015). *History of military testing*. Available online at http://official-asvab.com/history_coun.htm (accessed January 24, 2015).

Arnold, D. L. (1949). Time spent by counselors and deans on various activities. *Occupations, 27,* 391–393.

Baker, S. B. (1994). Mandatory teaching experience for school counselors: An impediment to uniform certification standards for school counselors. *Counselor Education and Supervision, 33,* 314–326.

Baker, S. B. (1999). *School counseling for the twenty-first century* (3rd ed.). Upper Saddle River, NJ: Merrill.

Beers, C. (1908). *A mind that found itself.* New York: Longmans, Green & Company.

Bell, H. M. (1939). *Theory and practice of personal counseling.* Stanford, CA: Stanford University Press.

Brewer, J. M. (1942). *History of vocational guidance.* New York: Harper & Brothers Publisher.

California Guidance Newsletter (1951). Counselors revealed as clerical workers. *Occupations, 29,* 294.

Campbell, C., & Dahir, C. (1997). *The national standards for school counseling programs.* Alexandria, VA: American School Counselor Association.

Careers NZ (2015). *Parson's theory.* Available online at www.careers.govt.nz/educators-practitioners/career-practice/career-theory-models/parsons-theory/ (accessed January 24, 2015).

Dahir, C. A., Sheldon, C. B., & Valiga, M. J. (1998). *Vision into action.* Alexandria, VA: American School Counselor Association.

Davis, F. G. (1956). *The saga of a school master.* Boston, MA: Boston University Press.

Erford, B. T. (2004). *Professional school counseling: A handbook of theories, programs, and practices.* Austin, TX: Pro-Ed Publishing.

Flattau, P. E., Bracken, J., Van Atta, R., Bandeh-Ahmadi, A., de la Cruz, R., & Sullivan, K. (2006). *The National Defense Education Act of 1958: Selected outcomes* (IDA Document D-3306). Washington, DC: Institute for Defense Analyses Science and Technology Policy Institute.

Glavin, K. (2015). *Vocopher.* Available online at www.vocopher.com/GeneralHelp.cfm#WhyUseIt (accessed January 24, 2015).

Gysbers, N. C. (2010). *School counseling principles: Remembering the past, shaping the future. A history of school counseling.* Alexandria, VA: American School Counselor Association.

Gysbers, N. C., with Guidance Program Field Writers (1990). *Comprehensive guidance programs that work.* Ann Arbor, MI: ERIC Counseling and Personnel Services Clearinghouse.

Hatch, T. A. (2008). Professional challenges in school counseling: Organizational, institutional and political. *Journal of School Counseling, 6,* 1–31.

Herr, E. L., & Erford, B. T. (2007). Historical roots and future issues. In B. T. Erford (Ed.), *Transforming the school counseling profession* (2nd ed.; pp. 13–37). Upper Saddle River, NJ: Pearson.

Holbrook, H. L. (1927). In school administration. *The Vocational Guidance Magazine, 5,* 178–179.

Johnson, A. H. (1972). *Changing conceptions of vocational guidance and concomitant value-orientations, 1920–1930.* Unpublished doctoral dissertation. Indiana State University, Terre Haute, Indiana.

Johnson, C. D., & Johnson, S. K. (1982). Competency-based training of career development specialists or "let's get off the path". *Vocational Guidance Quarterly, 30,* 327–335.

Johnson, S., & Johnson, C. (1991). The NEW guidance: A systems approach to pupil personnel programs. *California Association for Counseling and Development Journal, 11*, 5–14.

Kaplan, D. M., Tarvydas, V. M., & Gladding, S. T. (2014). 20/20: A vision for the future of counseling: The new consensus definition of counseling. *Journal of Counseling & Development, 92*, 366–372.

McCradie, A., & Ferguson, B. (1929). A counselor and a visiting teacher describe their jobs. *The Vocational Guidance Magazine, 4*, 145–152.

Myers, G. E. (1923). A critical review of present developments in vocational guidance with special reference to future prospects. *The Vocational Guidance Magazine, 2*, 139–142.

Myrick, R. D. (1987). *Developmental guidance and counseling: A practical approach.* Toronto: Educational Media Corporation.

No Child Left Behind Act of 2001, Pub. L. No. 107–110 (2002).

Parsons, F. (1909). *Choosing a vocation.* Boston, MA: Houghton Mifflin.

Reavis, W. C., & Woellner, R. C. (1930). *Office practices in secondary schools.* Chicago, IL: Laidlaw Brothers.

Richards, L. (1881). *Vocophy: The new profession.* Washington, DC: Bratt Brothers, Steam Job Printers.

Socialworklicensure.org (2015). *Mental health: Social work vs. professional counseling.* Available online at www.socialworklicensure.org/articles/counseling-or-social-work.html (accessed January 24, 2015).

Thompson, R. A. (2012). *Professional school counseling: Best practices for working in the schools* (3rd ed.). New York: Routledge.

Traxler, A. E., & North, R. D. (1966). *Techniques of guidance* (3rd ed.). Oxford: Harper & Row.

Williamson, E. G. (1939). Training and selection of school counselors. *Occupations, 18*, 7–12.

Chapter Two
Professional Identity of School Counselors and *the American School Counselor Association National Model* (2012a)

Box 2.1

2016 CACREP School Counseling Specialty Area Standards

1.a History and development of school counseling

1.b Models of school counseling programs

2.a School counselor roles as leaders, advocates, and systems change agents in P-12 schools

2.c School counselor roles in relation to college and career readiness

2.d School counselor roles in school leadership and multidisciplinary teams

2.f Competencies to advocate for school counseling roles

2.l Professional organizations, preparation standards, and credentials relevant to the practice of school counseling

3.a Development of school counseling program mission statements and objectives

---

This chapter explores the professional identity of school counselors. An overview of the four components of *the ASCA National Model: A Framework for School Counseling Programs* (ASCA, 2012a), which include its foundation, management, delivery, and accountability, is provided. Much of the content of this specific chapter and this book in general are informed by the content of *the ASCA National Model*®. The Education Trust's Transforming School Counseling Initiative (TSCI; 2009) and the partnership between ASCA and the Education Trust are discussed. The impact of various educational reforms upon the role of the school counselor and school counseling program will be reviewed, including the No Child Left Behind (NCLB) Act (2002), the Every Student Succeeds Act (ESSA: US Department of Education, n.d.), Common Core State Standards (CCSS; National Governors Association and Council of Chief State School Officers, 2010), Response to Intervention (RtI), School-wide Positive Behavior and Intervention Supports (SWPBIS), and the Reach Higher Initiative. The chapter includes an overview of systems-ecological theory, which is either implicitly or explicitly identified in the various educational reforms previously referenced, together with the efforts made to transform the profession of school counseling. Finally, a discussion of

McMahon, Mason, Daluga-Guenther, and Ruiz's (2014) ecological model of professional school counseling is provided as a specific example of how school counselors can use a systems framework.

Professional Identity of School Counselors

The school counseling profession continues to pursue the long-sought objective of achieving a consistent identity. As an example of the problems associated with achieving this objective, the role of the school counselor often varies between districts and even between schools within the same district. In some schools, school counselors function in a manner similar to mental health therapists, providing individual counseling to at-risk students. In other schools, school counselors are heavily burdened with clerical duties, which may include registering and scheduling new students, coordinating the standardized test administrations, coordinating student study teams, maintaining attendance records, completing college applications, etc.

A new elementary school counselor recently complained to one of the authors that each principal of the three schools in which she worked had an entirely different view of her role. One principal wanted her to function as a crisis counselor, expecting her to constantly be on call to assist with students who had been removed from class for disciplinary reasons. Another principal requested that the school counselor primarily organize the administration of various standardized tests. Finally, her remaining principal wanted her to establish a comprehensive school counseling program, including the development of a school counseling curriculum; however, she found that her duties at her other schools interfered with her ability to implement such a program.

The effort to achieve a consistent identity is currently affected by the declining education budgets and the considerable emphasis on the accountability of educational institutions. School counselors are not mandated by law in many states and sometimes are among the first school personnel to be eliminated due to budget reductions. The increasing expectation is that schools and educators should be accountable for students' achievement or lack thereof, an expectation which is significantly represented in the No Child Left Behind (NCLB) Act (2002) and Every Student Succeeds Act (ESSA: US Department of Education, n.d.) of 2015. This has exerted pressure on the profession to identify how school counselors contribute to the academic mission of schools and to measure the impact of these contributions.

The school counseling profession must not only establish a niche within the education professions, but also must help the public understand their role and the positive impact of school counseling related programs in order to counter some of the common negative perceptions of school counselors. School counseling students may find that they receive interesting reactions when they reveal what they are studying to laypeople, and it is common for such individuals to complain that their school counselor only helped them with scheduling, and claimed that they would not amount to anything, etc. A national survey of recent high school graduates conducted in 2009 revealed that the students primarily gave their high school guidance counselors a fair or poor rating and viewed them as less helpful than teachers in providing career development support (Johnson, Rochkind, Ott, & DuPont, 2010). Moreover, 67% of respondents rated their school counselor as fair or poor for the assistance they provided in selecting a college, and 55% rated their school counselor as fair or poor in the assistance they provided with the college application process.

The ASCA National Model® (2012a) and Comprehensive School Counseling Programs

Thankfully, there appears to be progress in the development of a consistent and unique professional identity for school counselors. During the last few decades, ASCA and prominent school counselor

The ASCA National Model diamond graphic is a registered trademark of the American School Counselor Association and may not be reprinted or modified without permission.

Figure 2.1 *The ASCA National Model*® Diamond Graphic. Copyright American School Counselor Association (ASCA). Reprinted with kind permission.

educators have encouraged school counselors to work systematically and collaboratively to meet the developmental needs of all students through the design and implementation of what are referred to as comprehensive school counseling programs. A comprehensive school counseling program includes a school counseling curriculum that proactively addresses the academic, career, and personal/social needs of students. The curriculum is distinct from but supports the school's academic curriculum. Whereas in previous decades the profession focused upon the role of the school counselor and the services he or she provided, in the comprehensive school counseling program model, the emphasis is on the effectiveness of the program as opposed to the services provided by the school counselor. In this model, the school counselor is regarded as a coordinator or leader of the program and works collaboratively with other school personnel, including teachers and administrators, in delivering the curriculum. The curriculum is delivered through a variety of program components, including class-room lessons, individual student planning, individual and group counseling, crisis response, referrals, consultation, and collaboration.

The ASCA National Model® (2012a) is the predominant comprehensive school counseling program, and several chapters of this book are devoted to this Model in significant detail. *The ASCA National Model*® is comprised of four interrelated components: foundation, management, delivery, and accountability. The foundation concerns what the program is about – student knowledge, attitudes, and skills that the program seeks to promote – and the beliefs that will influence the activities used to facilitate the identified student competencies.

The International Model for School Counseling Programs (Fezler & Brown, 2011) is closely related to *the ASCA National Model*® (2012a) but was developed to allow school counselors to meet the specific needs of their school population.

Beliefs. One of the first steps in creating a comprehensive school counseling program is for the school counseling team, which should consist of the school counselor(s) and representatives of the various stakeholder groups, including administration, teachers, parents, and community members, to identify the beliefs that influence the team members' thinking about student development and the program. According to *the ASCA National Model*® (2012a), belief statements should reflect the fact that all students have the capacity to achieve at a high level, indicate how the school counseling program addresses students' developmental needs, emphasize that the school counselor is an advocate for all students, identify the persons involved in the creation and delivery of the program, describe how the data influence program decisions, and require that school counselors abide by ASCA's *Ethical Standards for School Counselors* (2010).

Box 2.3

Sample Belief Statement

The following is the belief statement (Lamberto, 2015) from Haine Elementary School in Cranberry, Pennsylvania, which became a Recognized ASCA Model Program (RAMP) in 2015.

- All students are our highest priority.
- All students are entitled to a safe, nurturing environment in order to help them achieve their highest potential.
- All students have the ability to learn and have the right to take advantage of quality educational opportunities provided.
- All students' ethnic, cultural, and racial differences and/or special needs are considered in planning and implementing the school counseling program.
- All students have the right to participate in a school counseling program that focuses on academic, career, and personal/social development with special attention to barriers that impede student learning.
- All students have the right to be served by a professional school counselor who is accessible, collaborates with other educators, families, and the community as an advocate for student success in a timely and effective manner.
- The Comprehensive School Counseling Program is for every student, and is developmental and comprehensive in scope and is proactive in design.
- The mandates and guidelines of the American School Counselor Association (ASCA) and the Pennsylvania School Counselors Association (PSCA) set the standards for the school counseling program.
- The Comprehensive School Counseling Program ensures a delivery system that provides school counseling core curriculum, individual student planning, responsive services, and system support.
- The Comprehensive School Counseling Program is driven by data through an ongoing review of service delivery, curriculum management, and ASCA Model results reports.

- The Comprehensive School Counseling Program is an integral part of the total educational program for each student's success.
- The Comprehensive School Counseling Program collects and shares process, perception and outcome data and analyzes critical elements of the data.
- The Professional School Counselor is the advocate and catalyst for the growth of and support for every student, fostering student connectedness with students, staff and families while creating the possibility for transformation and success.
- The Professional School Counselor collaborates with professional and support staff, families, and the community to remove educational barriers for all students.
- The Professional School Counselor abides by professional school counseling ethics promoted by the American School Counselor Association (ASCA).
- The Professional School Counselor regularly participates in professional development activities needed to maintain an excellent program consistent with the American School Counselor Association (ASCA) *National Model®*.
- The Professional School Counselor designs, implements, and evaluates the comprehensive school counseling program to ensure its alignment to Seneca Valley School District's strategic plan, Haine Elementary School's Improvement Plan and Report Card and Haine Elementary School's data profile.
- The Professional state-certified School Counselor plans and manages the comprehensive school counseling program in collaboration with the building administrators and in conjunction with the Pupil Services Director and the Seneca Valley School District's Elementary School Counseling Department and the Advisory Team of the Haine Elementary School's Counseling Program.

Vision statement. The foundation also includes a vision statement that is compatible with the school's and district's vision, and that reveals what the school counselors ideally wish the students and school community to attain or achieve in the future. The vision statement should indicate the best, but also achievable, outcomes for students within the next five to fifteen years, and depicts a future in which the goals of the school counseling program are being realized.

Box 2.4

Sample Vision Statement (Gordon, 2015)

Through the collective efforts of Blackhawk Intermediate School staff, families, and the community at large, the students at Blackhawk Intermediate School are educated in a positive, safe, and comfortable learning environment where they have opportunities to enrich their academic, career, and social/emotional development. Each student is supported, valued, and respected for his/her unique learning style to ensure overall success. Supported by the school counseling program, all students at Blackhawk Intermediate School participate in a curriculum that focuses on rigor, relevance and relationships. As students strive to become productive and confident citizens in the community, they are empowered to persevere, exhibit accountability for their actions, display respect, and demonstrate trustworthiness. As goal-oriented learners, our students continue to strengthen their skills necessary for a "college and career-ready" education.

Reprinted with permission.

Mission statement. The mission statement is also more concise than the vision statement, and identifies the specifics for achieving the depiction provided in the vision statement. The mission statement should be compatible with the school and district's mission, have students as the primary focus, advocate for equity and success for all students, and indicate the long-term goals for students.

Program goals. Program goals reflect how the vision and mission statement will be achieved, and direct the development of curriculum, small group, and closing-the-gap action plans. The program goals identify specific, measurable student outcomes in the academic, career, and social/emotional development domains. School data are used to identify the particular needs of the school, and often seek to address gaps between educational access, equity, and achievement between White students and typically disadvantaged groups of students. School data that are reviewed for disparities include the frequency of discipline referrals, enrollment patterns in rigorous courses, and student absences (e.g., Dimmitt, Carey, & Hatch, 2007). There is more discussion of the process of using data in the goal-setting process in Chapter 4: Management and Accountability. Examples of specific, measurable, and attainable goals may include the following:

- a 20% increase in attendance for the students who had ten or more absences the previous year;
- a 20% increase in the number of African American students enrolled in Advanced Placement courses;
- within two years, Latino American students' average gain in reaching achievement, as indicated by the state achievement test, will be 20% greater than the White students' gain scores.

ASCA Mindsets & Behaviors for Student Success (ASCA, 2014)

The ASCA Mindsets & Behaviors for Student Success (ASCA, 2014), which are available on the ASCA website, "describe the knowledge, skills and attitudes students need to achieve academic success, college and career readiness, and social/emotional development" (p. 1). They were developed based upon a review of the literature conducted by the University of Chicago Consortium on Chicago School Research concerning five categories of non-cognitive factors that are associated with student achievement (Farrington et al., 2012). These five categories include academic behaviors, academic perseverance, academic mindsets, learning strategies, and social skills. The 35 mindset and behavior standards identify the expected outcomes for the school counseling program (ASCA, 2014). School counselors identify the standards and behaviors that are addressed in classroom lessons and small groups. *The ASCA Mindsets & Behaviors* are comprised of three domains of academic, career, and personal/social development, and each of the 35 standards may be applied to any of the three domains. The Mindset Standards are comprised of six psychosocial attitudes students have about themselves regarding their learning. The Behavior Standards are grouped into three subcategories: learning strategies, self-management skills, and social skills. For example, the first mindset is "Belief in development of whole self, including a healthy balance of mental, social/

emotional, and physical well-being" (p. 2). Each of the subcategories of Behavior Standards has nine to ten more specific behaviors. For example, the Behavior Standard for learning strategies is "Demonstrate critical-thinking skills to make informed decisions" (p. 2).

ASCA *School Counselor Competencies* (ASCA, 2012b). The ASCA *School Counselor Competencies* (2012b), which can be found on the ASCA website, identify the knowledge, skills, and attitudes that are regarded as necessary for implementing a comprehensive school counseling program. School counselors may use the ASCA *School Counselor Competencies* for self-evaluation and identify potential areas for professional development.

Management, delivery, and accountability. The management component of *the ASCA National Model*® (2012a) is comprised of both organizational tools and assessments. The tools of the management component include: (1) an advisory council that coordinates the school counseling program; (2) annual agreements between the school counselor(s) and administration concerning the structure and goals of the school counseling programs; (3) curriculum, small group, and closing-the-gap action plans that identify the objectives for these activities and specify how they are measured; and (4) annual and weekly calendars to inform stakeholders of program activities. Using data is an explicit management component, and is an integral aspect of each of the organizational assessments that consist of school counselor competency and school counseling program assessments developed by ASCA, and audits to determine the time ratio in which school counselors are engaged with students.

The delivery system involves both direct and indirect student services. Direct student services are comprised of the school counseling core curriculum, which includes both classroom and group activities that support the school counseling program's curriculum, individual student planning, and responsive services, which are defined as individual and group counseling and crisis response. The delivery system also involves indirect services that may consist of providing referrals and consulting and collaborating with parents, school personnel, and community organizations. The last component of *the Model*, accountability, refers to the need to use data to assess the impact of the school counseling program upon student achievement and to inform revisions to the program. These three components of *the ASCA National Model*® (2012a) are reviewed in greater depth in various chapters of the book.

Recognized ASCA Model Program (RAMP) (ASCA, 2003). Schools may apply to ASCA for RAMP, the designation indicating that the school's counseling program is consistent with *the ASCA National Model*® (2012a) and is recognized by the professional community as following best practice. School counselors submit an application documenting the activities they used to create and establish a data-driven, comprehensive program designed to address the specific needs of the school. The application requires a narrative documenting the efforts in 12 areas, including the activities used to develop the school counseling program's philosophy, mission statement, goals, involvement of an advisory council, employment of outcomes-based classroom and small group programming, and what is referred to as "closing-the-gap" activities, which are defined as interventions intended to lessen the academic achievement gap between races or other specified category of difference (e.g., gender, SES, etc.). RAMP applications are reviewed by an independent panel of school counseling professionals who use a 28-page scoring document. RAMP status is maintained for five years, and schools may reapply for RAMP status at the end of the five-year term.

Box 2.6

Did you know?

Georgia, Indiana, North Carolina, and Virginia have a large number of schools that received RAMP status (ASCA, 2015a).

The Education Trust's Transforming School Counseling Initiative (TSCI)

The Education Trust (2009) is a nonprofit organization that seeks to reform education consistent with the primary aims of NCLB (2002), namely, promoting high levels of academic achievement for all students and closing the achievement gaps between Asian and White students and typically disadvantaged students, including low-income students and students of color. The Education Trust formed a subgroup called the National Center for Transforming School Counseling (NCTSC), which seeks to "prepare graduates [of school counseling programs] to serve as student advocates and academic advisors who demonstrate the belief that all students can achieve high levels on rigorous, challenging academic course content" (Martin, 2002, p. 148).

ASCA and NCTSC have worked to position the school counseling profession as a significant contributor to educational reform. ASCA developed the *ASCA National Model®* (2012a) and *Mindsets & Behaviors* (2014) to influence currently practicing school counselors. The Education Trust's Transforming School Counseling Initiative (TSCI) has primarily focused upon modifying the way in which school counselors are educated in graduate schools, providing grants to select universities to train students in a transformed model of school counseling, and encouraging state departments of education to adopt new standards for school counselor preparation (Perkins, Oescher, & Ballard, 2010). The TSCI vision for school counselors involves the following: (1) deemphasizing a mental health perspective in favor of an academic/student achievement focus; (2) adopting a whole school or systems perspective vs. focusing on individual student issues; (3) using data to effect change as opposed to school counselors simply being involved with data as part of record-keeping; and (4) serving as change agents to promote educational equity (Education Trust, 2009).

ASCA and TSCI have provided a framework for unifying the school counseling profession, but debate continues regarding the role of school counselors. A 2010 survey of elementary school counselors, elementary principals, elementary teachers, and school counselor educators revealed that each group identified the personal/social domain as being a more important focus for elementary school counselors than the academic and career domains (Perkins et al., 2010). This finding may indicate that elementary school counselors and their stakeholders may not have accepted the Education Trust's encouragement of school counselors to primarily adopt an academic focus in their role functioning.

The ASCA National Model® (2012a) Themes

The close partnership between ASCA and NCTSC is reflected in the *ASCA National Model's®* (2012a) four themes: leadership, advocacy, collaboration, and systemic change, which were part of the initial TSCI efforts. School counselors function as leaders in coordinating the school counseling program and promote systemic change by removing barriers and implementing programs that facilitate high levels of academic achievement for all students. TSCI and ASCA agree that school counselors must use data in advocating for the rights of all students to be taught at a high level. School counselors collaborate with other stakeholders, including administrators, teachers, parents, students, and community members in order to effect systemic change. Subsequent chapters of this book will explore *the Model* themes in greater detail.

Empirical Support for Comprehensive School Counseling Programs

Whereas past research in school counseling has primarily focused upon specific school counseling related interventions, such as career planning or social skills activities, there is emerging evidence for the effectiveness of school counseling programs as a whole (Wilkerson, Pérusse, & Hughes, 2013), particularly at the elementary level. Sink and Stroh (2003) found that, over time, students who attended elementary schools with comprehensive school counseling programs made greater gains in academic achievement than students who attended elementary schools that lacked comprehensive school counseling programs, although the difference in gains in academic achievement was not very large. Two studies found that elementary students at RAMP-designated schools had greater academic achievement than the state average (Ward, 2009) and control schools (Wilkerson et al., 2013). However, Wilkerson et al. (2013) revealed that RAMP schools at the middle and high school levels did not outperform non-RAMP schools.

Educational Reforms

Some have argued that one of the reasons why the school counseling profession has lacked a consistent identity is related to its little to no involvement in educational reform movements. As school districts look to eliminate personnel, the profession no longer has the luxury of watching educational reform from the sidelines. The ASCA has sought to be actively involved in the educational reforms that have had considerable impact on school operations within the past two decades. The rest of this chapter seeks to enhance school counseling students' understanding of current educational reforms and how these reforms impact the school counseling profession.

No Child Left Behind Act (NCLB). The NCLB Act of 2001 (2002) is probably considered as the most significant legislation to affect education within the past 30 years, and it will continue to impact education despite its replacement in 2015 with the Every Student Succeeds Act (ESSA: US Department of Education, n.d.). One of the primary aims of the NCLB Act was to increase schools' accountability for ensuring student achievement through the administration of statewide standardized tests.

The NCLB Act also strove to reduce the achievement gap between White and Asian students and historically disadvantaged groups, including Latino American, African American, and Native American students, economically disadvantaged students, students with disabilities, and students with limited English proficiency. NCLB mandated that states ensure that school districts collect such "disaggregated data" of subgroups (defined by gender, race, ethnicity, disability status, low-income status, English language proficiency, and migrant status), and implement corrective actions to address the needs of these subgroups. Whereas in the past, students were held liable for a lack of academic achievement, now teachers and school personnel are also deemed to be accountable for student achievement.

While NCLB (2002) did not explicitly identify the role of school counselors, the Act had an impact on the profession. A national survey of school counselors revealed that while 2.3% of the participants identified positive effects of NCLB upon the school counseling program's delivery system, 33.6% of the study participants identified negative impacts, including teachers being hesitant to yield class time to counseling or the developmental curriculum, testing responsibilities interfering with counseling students, and a decreased focus on the social and emotional needs of students (Dollarhide & Lemberger, 2006). Although 25.1% of the school counselors indicated that they were engaging in activities related to testing processes that are considered to be appropriate within *the ASCA National Model*® (2012a), such as interpreting tests and counseling students about test anxiety, the majority of school counselors identified that they were having to engage in testing activities that are not considered appropriate by ASCA. Inappropriate activities included functioning as the building test coordinator, proctoring tests and conducting make-up tests, ensuring the implementation of test accommodations for students with disabilities, and providing academic remediation. Dollarhide and Lemberger (2006) concluded that NCLB high-stakes testing has reinforced the perception that school counselors function as test administrators. In order to counter this perception, these authors recommend that school counselors use data to advocate the need for students' holistic development.

Accountability was also emphasized within NCLB (2002) through the expectation that schools rely upon scientifically based research for teaching methods, which has resulted in an effort within the school counseling profession to increase the rigor of studies evaluating the impact of school counseling related programs and interventions. Prior to NCLB, evaluation studies yielded support for the effectiveness of a variety of school counseling interventions, including providing group, peer, and individual counseling, and conducting school counseling classroom lessons (McGannon, Carey, & Dimmitt, 2005). However, much of this research did not employ an experimental design and thus does not qualify as scientifically based according to the definitions used by NCLB. Consequently, the Center for School Counseling Outcome Research and Evaluation (CSCORE) established the National Panel for School Counseling Evidence-Based Practice to develop the research base required for evidence-based practice (Carey, Dimmitt, Hatch, Lapan, & Whiston, 2008). The Panel developed a standardized method for evaluating school counseling interventions, using the categories of strong, promising, and weak evidence, and has begun to evaluate common school counseling programs.

NCLB (2002) was comprehensive and was designed to impact various aspects of education, including activities that historically have been associated with the role of school counselors. For example, it mandated that schools regularly provide parents and the public with data regarding students' achievement and create programs that involve parents in meaningful ways. The "Safe and Drug-Free Schools" provision of NCLB required that state departments of education identify schools that are unsafe. Schools that have consistently high levels of violent behavior for two years are designated "persistently dangerous" and suffer penalties such as voluntary student transfers.

Every Student Succeeds Act (ESSA: US Department of Education, n.d.) of 2015. ESSA represents a significant shift from NCLB. School districts are still required to assess students' learning in the form of standardized testing in reading and math in grades 3–8 and once in high school (Education Week, 2015). However, ESSA reduces the emphasis on standardized testing in several major respects, which are listed below:

- the NCLB requirement that schools demonstrate adequate yearly progress (AYP) toward achieving 100% proficiency in reading and math was replaced with the requirement that states must establish long-term achievement goals with measures of interim progress;
- federal funding is provided to states to develop alternative assessments that will reduce duplication of assessments;
- high schools may apply to use another nationally recognized assessment, such as the ACT (2016), instead of the state assessment test;
- states may establish a cap limiting the amount of time students engage in test-taking;
- parents have the right to opt children out of state assessments where local and state policies allow them to do so;
- elementary and middle schools may use a measure of student growth or another academic indicator to assess differences among student groups.

ESSA maintains NCLB's emphasis on reducing the achievement gap, but uses different indicators to identify struggling schools and different interventions to support those schools (US Department of Education, n.d.). Whereas NCLB required that all schools which failed to meet AYP for several years provide students the option of transferring to other schools and required the restructuring of the school's leadership and staff, ESSA uses different indicators to identify struggling schools. In ESSA, states would have to identify and provide assistance to schools which are in the bottom 5% in terms of performance, schools which have a graduation rate below 67%, and schools which have subgroups (e.g., race, gender, special education) who are struggling. Under ESSA, schools identified in need of support must implement evidence-based, locally determined interventions, and for schools which have a low performing subgroup, the school must identify in their improvement plan resource inequities that likely contribute to the underperformance of the subgroup. ESSA indicates that schools may but are not required to permit students to transfer to another school. School counselors were explicitly identified as professionals who should have an input to the required improvement plan for struggling schools (ASCA, 2015a).

It is unclear how ESSA will impact the school counseling profession, but there are aspects of the legislation that appear to provide hope for an expanded role for school counselors.

With the increased emphasis on graduation rates ushered in by ESSA, it is possible that high school counselors may be seen as key contributors in efforts to promote enhanced graduation rates given that historically this has been an area of focus for high school counselors. States must require elementary and middle schools to include at least four indicators in their accountability systems, and may include various kinds of assessments such as student and teacher engagement, postsecondary readiness, access and completion of advanced coursework, and school climate/safety (Education Week, 2015). The opportunity to use more varied forms of indicators may lead to an increased emphasis on career and personal/social development, which have been traditionally associated with the school counseling program.

Common Core State Standards (CCSS) (National Governors Association and Council of Chief State Schools Officers, 2010). The CCSS are an initiative by states to use universal standards in English and mathematics (Rothman, 2012). The CCSS were developed by the states to address some of the perceived limitations of NCLB (2002). NCLB sought to increase standardization within education by requiring states to establish academic standards and corresponding assessments. NCLB left it up to the individual states to define proficiency, and research indicated that state definitions of proficiency varied widely. Another common concern is that the NCLB's focus on proficiency meant that state assessments were designed to measure a low to moderate level of knowledge and skills. The CCSS initiative intended to develop a higher level of standards that are based on the skills necessary for postsecondary success. Students would be required to understand content at a deep level and be able to apply the content to problem-solving and reason from evidence, as these skills were deemed to be required to succeed in college. Although most states had indicated a commitment to adopt the CCSS, many states have rescinded their commitment. ESSA requires that states adopt "challenging" academic standards, but explicitly states that they do not have to adopt the CCSS (Education Week, 2015).

Box 2.7

Achieve (2013) and several other educational organizations that support the CCSS developed a position paper outlining how school counselors can collaborate with other school personnel in order to promote the CCSS. Their recommendations for school counselors can be summarized as follows:

- become familiar with the math and literacy standards;
- join the school leadership teams to advocate for increased academic rigor;
- gather and analyze data to identify patterns of student performance;
- develop strategies for addressing math and literacy standards as part of the comprehensive school counseling curriculum;
- maintain and analyze data concerning the number of students who are on target for college and career readiness, including at the elementary level;
- review the school's curriculum to ensure that all have access to higher-level mathematics courses;

- establish dual and concurrent enrollment options with local colleges;
- assess the impact of Tier 2 and Tier 3 interventions;
- create and update a six-year individual education plan for students;
- develop and implement lesson plans that are aligned with CCSS college and career readiness standards;
- incorporate career and college readiness principles in the philosophy, vision, and mission statements of the school counseling program;
- create a college-going culture through the use of visual displays depicting college and scholarship information, announcing upcoming opportunities concerning college, celebrating academic achievements, and infusing a high level of rigor throughout the academic curriculum.

Response to Intervention (RtI). Another major trend impacting education and school counseling programs has been the emergence of tiered intervention approaches such as RtI and School-wide Positive Behavioral Intervention and Support (SWPBIS). RtI uses data-driven decision-making and a multi-tiered approach for the dual purposes of reforming general education and assisting struggling learners (Buffum, Mattos, & Weber, 2009). The 2004 reauthorization of the Individuals with Disabilities Education Act (IDEA) allowed schools to use RtI as an alternative to the traditional discrepancy model for determining whether a child has a specific learning disability (P.L. No 108–446). The federal government permitted this alternative for identification of a learning disability partly as a means to address the over-representation of minority students in special education (Buffum et al., 2009). RtI is also designed to improve the core curriculum and provide a framework for providing increasing levels of differentiation to students within the regulation education setting in order to reduce inappropriate referrals to special education.

RtI models vary in implementation, but they typically have three tiers of increasing instructional intensity. Tier 1 refers to the core curriculum. RtI emphasizes the need to ensure the effectiveness of the core curriculum through the use of empirically supported practices that are implemented with treatment fidelity, which means that the practice was applied in a manner that is consistent with the protocol. The model expects that 80–85% of students will respond positively to the core curriculum. Failure of more than 20% of the students to achieve benchmarks results in a review and possible modification of the core curriculum. The 15–20% of students who fail to demonstrate expected levels of progress receive Tier 2 intervention, which consists of small group intervention, typically involving three to five group sessions of up to 30 minutes per week. Lack of response to Tier 2 intervention results in the application of Tier 3 intervention, which often consists of individualized instruction. It is estimated that 3–5% of students may require Tier 3 intervention if the model is being effectively implemented. In some states failure of a student to respond to Tier 3 intervention automatically results in assessment for special education services, whereas in others the student would automatically receive special education services without a disability assessment.

RtI uses data-driven decision-making, which involves "a continuous process of regularly collecting, summarizing, and analyzing information to guide development, implementation, and evaluation" (Buffum et al., 2009, p. 206). Universal screens are typically used at the beginning, middle, and end of each academic year to assess student performance in comparison to benchmarks and learning standards. With each level of instruction, there is an increase in how frequently student performance is assessed. For example, at Tier 2, progress monitoring of a student's reading achievement may occur twice a month. At Tier 3, a student's progress may be assessed on a weekly or even daily basis.

ASCA's (2008) position statement regarding RtI is that school counselors are "stakeholders" (p. 34) in the design and implementation of RtI and vital contributors in meeting students' academic and behavioral concerns through the implementation of comprehensive school counseling programs. Ockerman, Mason, and Hollenbeck (2010) assert that RtI and comprehensive school counseling programs have important similarities, in that they can be characterized as collaborative, proactive, data-driven, multi-tiered, and advocating for holistic development and educational equity. Both RtI and comprehensive school counseling programs emphasize increased attention to Tier 1 interventions, given that they are the most efficient way to serve the majority of students. Tier 1 or school-wide interventions within the comprehensive school counseling programs could be considered to include lessons that support the school counseling core curriculum, substance abuse prevention activities, career development events such as career days, and academic incentive programs. Tier 2 interventions could involve group counseling and peer support services such as peer mentoring on tutoring. Tier 3 interventions represent the most intensive and individualized level of service, which for school counselors could involve individual counseling, behavior or academic improvement plans, repeated parent consultation, or community referral.

The limited research available concerning school counselors' involvement with RtI indicates that some school counselors coordinate the Student Support Team, which may also be called the Child Study Team, Behavior Intervention Team, or RtI Team (Ockerman et al., 2012). In their role as team coordinator, some school counselors monitor and analyze the data for both academic and behavioral interventions for each tier of RtI. Ockerman et al. (2012) recommend that school counselors seek to achieve a balance between serving a supportive role as an RtI team member and an active role as an intervention provider. School counselors can make significant contributions to the RtI team, sharing their knowledge of the connections between the academic, social/emotional, and career development of students, expertise in the use of data, their knowledge, prevention and intervention strategies, and facilitating constructive collaboration between school personnel and family members. However, they should avoid serving as the RtI team coordinator as the considerable coordination duties may interfere with their ability to coordinate the comprehensive school counseling program. Ryan, Kaffenberger, and Carroll (2011) provide an example in which a school counselor coordinated the screening and placement of students within the tiers and evaluated the impact of the RtI program on student achievement, but also infused personal/social and career objectives into the academic curriculum objectives. A survey of teachers revealed that they positively viewed the school counselor's contributions to the program.

School-wide Positive Behavioral Interventions and Supports (SWPBIS). SWPBIS is a universal, behavioral theory-based prevention and intervention program that is employed by many schools that use RtI to focus specifically upon students who exhibit behavioral and mental health issues. SWPBIS, encouraged by the US Department of Education and several state departments of education, similar to RtI, uses a three-tiered model to address disruptive behavior (Bradshaw, Mitchell, & Leaf, 2010). Whereas traditionally, school-based behavioral interventions primarily focused upon the individual student, SWPBIS and other types of "proactive classroom management" programs seek to alter the school environment through the universal application of principles of behavioral theory. At the Tier 1 level, students are taught and positively reinforced for demonstrating school-wide behavioral expectations. Data are used at all levels to establish the behavioral expectations, evaluate the effectiveness of tiered interventions, and identify students in need of an increased intensity of intervention. Research suggests that when implemented with fidelity, 80–85% of students positively respond to Tier 1 interventions.

The second tier is intended to assist the 10–15% of students who tend to not positively respond to Tier 1 interventions. Common examples of Tier 2 interventions include social skill and academic instruction groups, and Check-In/Check-Out (CICO). Tier 3 interventions are individualized for the 3–5% of students who fail to respond to both Tier 1 and 2 interventions. Common Tier 3 interventions are assigning an adult mentor, social skills training, behavioral modification, and self-monitoring. Research indicates that the implementation of SWPBIS has resulted in reduced student suspensions, office discipline referrals (e.g., Bradshaw et al., 2010), and increased student perceptions of safety at school (Horner et al., 2009).

Data-driven decision-making is used within the various tiers of SWPBIS. A variety of universal screening instruments are used to identity students at risk for emotional and behavioral difficulties, including Systematic Screening for Behavioral Disorders (Albers, Glover, & Kratochwill, 2007), the Student Risk Screening Scale (Drummond, 1994), Behavioral Assessment for Children-2 (BASC-2) (Reynolds & Kamphaus, 2004), and the Strengths and Difficulties Questionnaire (Goodman, Meltzer, & Bailey, 1998). The universal screening instruments use a multiple gating procedure, which typically involves having teachers rank in order which students they consider to be at risk as indicated by observable behaviors, followed by the teacher completing a standardized assessment for the identified students. Students who are identified as at risk through both procedures are referred to Tier 2 intervention. Other forms of data used to identify behaviorally and emotionally at-risk students include office discipline referrals (ODR) and the students' attendance/tardy rates. The effectiveness of Tier 2 interventions may be assessed through a daily progress report that indicates students' progress in meeting individualized behavioral expectations. At Tier 3, a functional behavioral assessment (FBA) and functional assessment interview are often conducted to identify hypotheses regarding the function of the student's behavior and to develop a more comprehensive behavioral modification plan. Some states use universal screens to identify students who are at risk for mental health issues, including depression and suicide among adolescents. Students who are identified as having an elevated risk for depression and suicide may receive services from mental health professionals in the community or within the schools. Clearly, school counselors are likely to play a significant role in administering and interpreting data concerning behavioral and emotional functioning, providing services to such students, and collaborating with mental health professionals for students receiving Tier 3 interventions.

School counselors are likely to be an integral member of the school committee coordinating SWPBIS, given their background in data-driven decision-making, and the fact that students who require increased levels of support are more likely to qualify for a mental health diagnosis (Martens & Andreen, 2013). Martens and Andreen (2013) encourage school counselors to collaborate with other school staff in implementing Check-In/Check-Out (CICO). CICO uses a structured routine in which an identified student meets with a school staff member to review the student's progress in meeting targeted behavioral expectations. Students carry a daily report card throughout the school day on which teachers rate students' exhibited targeted behaviors using a Likert-type scale. In demonstrating progress, students receive positive reinforcement that is uniquely developed for the individual child, and students' progress is regularly shared with both the students' teachers and parents/guardian. Research indicates that CICO is effective in reducing problematic behavior and is one of the few Tier 2 interventions to be considered worthwhile by school personnel. Martens and Andreen believe that CICO enables school counselors to positively impact a group of students through individualized interventions, and is consistent with *the ASCA National Model's*® (2012a) emphasis on data-driven decision-making. School counselors can use their knowledge of mental health issues and principles of behavioral modification in constructing students' behavioral expectations and in consulting with school personnel who are involved in the CICO process.

Reach Higher Initiative. The Reach Higher Initiative is Michele Obama's agenda to encourage all students to pursue postsecondary education and/or training (ASCA, 2015c). The First Lady has partnered with ASCA to increase students' exposure to college and career opportunities, knowledge of the availability of financial aid, academic planning, and summer learning opportunities. ASCA's partnership with the First Lady has resulted in greater public exposure for the profession, as the 2014 and 2015 School Counselor of the Year award ceremonies were conducted at the White House. In a related effort, the former Secretary of Education, Arne Duncan, published guidelines for school administrators to devote financial resources to the professional development of school counselors, and identified sources of federal funding for this pursuit.

Systems-Ecological Theory

A prevailing theme found within recent educational reforms, and efforts to transform the school counseling profession, is the need for school personnel to adopt a broader, comprehensive perspective of students. The following statement by Dr. Peggy Hines, who has served as Director of TSCI, succinctly states the need for systemic change:

> The idea is that it's not always the students that are broken; sometimes it's the system or the school that is broken. If school counselors can get schools to change policy and practice, and support those kinds of systemic interventions for students, then that's going to be a lot more effective than trying to change kids one at a time.
>
> (Pérusse & Colbert, 2007, p. 478)

Much of ASCA's efforts in the past few decades emphasize the need for school counselors to implement and support programs that promote all students' achievement by enhancing the environments in which students function. The trends in educational reform, and as a consequence, the transformation of the school counseling profession, are reflective of the emergence of an ecological perspective of student achievement.

The systems-ecological framework represents an alternative scheme for understanding children's behavior in contrast to the traditional linear model of cause and effect. We are using the term "systems-ecological" to refer to two similar theories: general systems theory (von Bertalanffy, 1968) and social ecology theory (Bronfenbrenner, 1979). The main assumption of the systems-ecological framework is that children's functioning and development is the result of the interaction between the child and the environment. General systems theory represents a paradigm shift in that it rejects the traditional linear causal perspective of Western science and the medical model, which conceptualizes behavior as being the result of a single cause or chain of causes that occur within the child. In contrast, general systems theory posits a circular causal perspective in which a child's behavior instead is believed to be a function of numerous interacting variables that reciprocally influence each other.

Parents, teachers, and peers are seen as potentially impacting a child's behavior, and in turn, being impacted by the child in question. No one person or environmental context is regarded as causative; persons and contexts are seen as potential contributors to children's development. Bronfenbrenner's (1979) theory of social ecology shares some of the basic principles of systems theory, including the importance of reciprocal interaction, but is broader in scope than systems theory. Whereas systems theory tends to focus upon the interactions within a system, particularly the family system, Bronfenbrenner claimed that the multiple embedded systems in which the child exists, which include the peer group, family, school, community, and cultural environments, may be equally as important in promoting children's development. Children do not develop in isolation but instead are influenced by various contexts (e.g., society, peers, family, etc.) in which they interact. Although not as intensely researched as traditional, linear behavioral models, some studies have directly evaluated systems-ecological models for childhood issues, providing empirical support for the model's application to school violence (Khoury-Kassabri, Benbenishty, Astor, & Zeira, 2004) and bullying (Espelage, Rao, & De La Rue, 2013). Indeed, Henggeler et al.'s (1996) review of the research literature revealed that "serious antisocial behavior is multidetermined by the reciprocal interplay of characteristics of the individual youth and the key social systems in which youths are embedded (i.e., family, peer, social, neighborhood, and community)" (pp. 6–7).

Systems-ecological theory offers significant advantages over the traditional, linear model for identifying implications for intervention and prevention with children. In the traditional, linear model, school personnel have a tendency to become overly focused upon the individual child, often resulting in thinking about the child's deficits and their causes, such as biological deficiencies, lack of student motivation, etc. This tends to lead to what has been referred to as a "blame game," in which teachers overly focus upon the deficiencies of the student, parents, or previous teachers, and parents focus on the school's inadequacies. The systems-ecological theory provides practitioners with a framework that is more complex, in terms of encouraging them to think about various variables and their interactions, which most likely is a more realistic view of behavior and child development, and more conducive to self-reflection by school personnel. School personnel can consider the school- and community-based factors that may contribute to a student's lack of achievement, implications for modifying the larger environment, or what might be referred to as prevention. In terms of intervention, school personnel can examine how their instruction of a child or their relationship with a child may possibly contribute to the issue, or how family factors may contribute, or even how the relationship between the family and the school could be enhanced. It can be argued that NCLB, RtI, and SWPBS were instituted in order to create such a paradigm shift in encouraging school personnel to assume more ownership for student achievement.

Ecological Model of Professional School Counseling

McMahon et al. (2014) presented an ecological model of professional school counseling which they developed to support *the ASCA National Model*® (2012a) by providing a theoretical/conceptual foundation for the atheoretical structural model of *the ASCA National Model*®. This model was also developed as a framework for guiding comprehensive interventions, in contrast to the more individualistic counseling theories that have traditionally informed the work of school counselors. McMahon et al. (2014) present a number of basic assumptions for their ecological model of professional school counseling. The core assumption from which all of their other assumptions derive is that schools are ecosystems. As ecosystems, schools are comprised of numerous subsystems (e.g., classrooms, grade levels, clubs, cliques), and are part of larger systems, or a "suprasystem" (e.g., school districts, community, state). The school, its subsystems, and the suprasystems in which the school is embedded are interconnected in various ways, and changes within any of these levels can affect each other.

Another principle of the Model is that well-functioning schools are dynamic, balanced, and flexible. Schools function as a network of interdependently related components that are continually undergoing change but also strive to achieve a healthy balance within the face of change. They require semipermeable boundaries that permit the distinction of clear subgroups (e.g., teachers, students, administrators), but are also flexible enough to allow for healthy connections between the groups. In schools that achieve this balance, members comprehend the roles and expectations to be part of the system and any subsystems with which they might identify. Well-functioning schools are also more likely to be diverse. A diverse faculty can promote academic achievement, as students are more likely to identify with school personnel who are similar to them in terms of race and/or ethnicity. A diverse peer group provides students with enhanced perspective-taking by being exposed to different forms and styles of communication. Exposure to such diversity increases the likelihood that graduates will more readily adapt to changes within the larger society.

Similar to a family system, schools use feedback to identify and manage emerging issues (McMahon et al., 2014). Ecosystems must have mechanisms, referred to as feedback loops, to address imbalances in the system. When ecosystems become unbalanced, either toward too much structure, meaning they are rigid in the face of change, or too much change, in which members lack clear expectations regarding their roles and the rules of the organization, new structures or patterns will spontaneously develop within the ecosystem in an effort to find order within the system. Intentional feedback loops used in schools include the use of data for decision-making and strategic planning. However, as with all ecosystems, schools also have feedback loops that emerge spontaneously, often among students who have less officially sanctioned power. McMahon et al. (2014) present the examples of absenteeism and gangs as indicators that the ecosystem is not addressing the needs of the members, but which are often perceived by school personnel as problems that must be eradicated as opposed to a need for redress of the ecosystem.

McMahon and colleagues' (2014) ecological model of professional school counseling postulates that meaning is both constructed and experienced within schools and their subsystems. Meaning-making is an essential aspect of the human condition, and people constantly make meaning of their experiences that occur within an environmental context. McMahon et al. (2014) identify two main implications of the meaning-making process. One is that the school must provide a process in which members of both the school and its various subsystems define the identity and purpose of the respective systems for that particular time. The other implication is that meaning-making is derived from feedback that is received by the school-as-system. The feedback is received through both through formal processes, such as school outcome data, and informal processes, such as off-hand complaints by parents about teachers. These data do not reveal objective truth; rather, they are interpreted differently based on the unique perspectives of the viewer and his or her context.

The final principle of McMahon et al.'s (2014) model is that healthy schools are sustainable. The organisms and subsystems contribute in their unique way to the functioning of the system, and the school has a reciprocal relationship with the community in which it is embedded. An effective reciprocal relationship between the school and community involves the production of graduates who are to fulfill the various jobs and functions of the community, including the teaching, parenting, and mentoring of the new generation of students who will comprise the school community. The implication is that schools should keep at the forefront its mission of preparing graduates to meet the needs of the community.

ASCA and TSCI urge school counselors to adopt such a systems-ecological perspective. ASCA incorporated TSCI's emphasis on systemic change, which is one of the four *ASCA National Model®* themes. The description of systemic change within *the ASCA National Model®* indicates that a school functions much like a family system in that the various components or members reciprocally influence each other. *The ASCA National Model®* (2012a) and *the ASCA Mindsets & Behaviors for Student Success* (2014) provide school counselors with models to promote all students' academic, personal/social, and career development, thus providing students with the skills to negotiate developmental challenges, as opposed to school counselors primarily focusing upon remediating the problems of at-risk students. TSCI calls for school counselors to contribute to increases in the rigor and effectiveness of the academic curriculum in promoting college and career readiness. The systems-ecological perspective has significant implications for the way in which school counselors intervene with individual students and expands intervention options. School counselors can conduct brief individual counseling with students, but can also consider consulting with teachers and parents to assist them in more effectively responding to a student's needs. School counselors need to consider what intervention with whom is most likely to be successful and which is the most time-efficient. Talking with a teacher or parent for 20 minutes may be more effective than conducting three individual sessions with a child. In consulting with parents and teachers, school counselors can use a systems-ecological perspective to identify how the patterns between the child and the teacher or parent may contribute to the respective issue, or even how the relationship between the parents and the teacher may be modified.

The phenomenon of bullying can be used as a case illustration of the systems-ecological approach. Espelage et al.'s (2013) review of the literature found support for the contention that bullying behaviors are influenced by characteristics of the individual, family, and school environments. In terms of individual characteristics, perpetrators of bullying are more likely to be male, physically larger than their peers, and be enrolled in special education. Victims tend to be less popular and have lower social status than their peers. The parents of perpetrators are more likely than the parents of non-perpetrators to provide inadequate supervision, be less involved in their children's lives, and encourage aggression and retaliation. The parents of victims of bullying are more likely than the parents of non-victims to be abusive or inconsistent, while victims of bullying who have nurturing relationships with their families have more positive outcomes. Classrooms that are less democratic and have larger disparities in social power are associated with greater bullying. In schools which have higher rates of bullying, students are less likely to seek assistance from teachers and staff, and perpetrators are more likely than victims to have high social status.

The complex nature of bullying and the fact that it is influenced by contextual variables appears to be recognized in the comprehensive approach used by many bullying prevention programs. For example, the *Olweus Bullying Prevention Program* (OBPP; Olweus & Limber, 2010) seeks to modify the school's environment through the implementation of rules and sanctions for bullying, increased supervision of identified high frequency areas for bullying, and classroom lessons that define bullying and provide bystanders and victims with strategies to address bullying. A meta-analytic study, which involves aggregating the results of various studies, revealed that on average, programs reduce bullying by 20–23%, and that many of the program components that are associated with effectiveness are comprehensive in nature (Ttofi & Farrington, 2011). Having a whole-school anti-bullying policy, classroom rules, teacher training, classroom management, firm disciplinary methods, improved playground supervision, and parent training/ meetings were associated with effectiveness in reducing bullying. In contrast, the researchers did not find evidence to support individual approaches with victims and perpetrators of bullying.

These findings have implications for school counselors' roles in bullying prevention, and illustrate the need for school counselors to think comprehensively. Within the mental health model, in which school counselors were trained in previous decades, the school counselor might tend to focus upon providing individual counseling to victims and perpetrators of bullying. However, the data do not appear to support such an approach. Certainly, school counselors should consider providing counseling to students in need, but they should simultaneously consider programmatic/systemic interventions that seek to alter the school and community environment that support bullying behaviors. School counselors can advocate for the need for a bullying prevention program, and lobby the state and federal government for legislation and funding for bullying prevention programs. School counselors can collaborate with teachers, administrators, and parents in creating and coordinating a bullying prevention program. School counselors can lead training sessions for parents and teachers. For individual victims and perpetrators, school counselors might most effectively intervene by consulting with their parents. School counselors have erroneously equated systems theory with conducting family counseling. Rather, systems-ecological theory provides a way of thinking about issues that enables practitioners to consider the larger framework of contextual variables and their implications for working with the specific needs of an individual student.

Summary

School counselors must understand the reforms that are reshaping the US educational system in order to remain relevant in an era of accountability and shrinking budgets. ASCA and TSCI provide school counselors with a framework for contributing to the academic mission of schools while simultaneously developing a distinct identity. School counselors are encouraged to understand systems-ecological theory and the implications it has for prevention and intervention at multiple levels. The chapters that follow will examine many of these issues in greater depth and provide applied examples.

References

Achieve, National Association of Secondary Schools, & National Association of Elementary Schools (2013). *Implementing the Common Core state standards: The role of the school counselor.* Available online at www.achieve.org/files/RevisedCounselorActionBrief_Final_Feb.pdf (accessed March 2, 2016).

ACT, Inc. (2016). *The ACT Test for Students.* Available online at www.actstudent.org/ (accessed January 15, 2016).

Albers, C. A., Glover, T. A., & Kratochwill, T. R. (2007). Where are we, and where do we go now? Universal screening for enhanced educational and mental health outcomes. *Journal of School Psychology, 45,* 257–263.

American School Counselor Association (2003). *Learn about RAMP.* Available online at http://ascamodel.timberlakepublishing.com/content.asp?pl=11@contentid=11 (accessed November 7, 2015).

American School Counselor Association (2008). *The professional school counselor and response to intervention.* Available online at http://asca2.timberlakepublishing.com//files/PS_Intervention.pdf (accessed December 1, 2014).

American School Counselor Association (2010). *Ethical standards for school counselors.* Available online at www.schoolcounselor.org/files/EthicalStandards2010.pdf (accessed December 10, 2014).

American School Counselor Association (2012a). *The ASCA national model: A framework for school counseling programs* (3rd ed.). Alexandria, VA: Author.

American School Counselor Association (2012b). *ASCA school counselor competencies.* Alexandria, VA: Author.

American School Counselor Association (2014). *Mindsets & behaviors for student success: K-12 college- and career-readiness standards for every student.* Alexandria, VA: Author.

American School Counselor Association (2015a). *Every Student Succeeds Act.* Available online at www.schoolcounselor.org/school-counselors-members/legislative-affairs (accessed January 14, 2016).

American School Counselor Association (2015b). *RAMP recipients.* Available online at www.schoolcounselor.org/school-counselors-members/recognized-asca-model-program-(ramp)/past-ramp-recipients (accessed September 1, 2015).

American School Counselor Association (2015c). *ASCA and reach higher.* Available online at www.schoolcounselor.org/school-counselors-members/legislative-affairs/asca-and-reach-higher (accessed May 11, 2015).

Bradshaw, C. P., Mitchell, M. M., & Leaf, P. J. (2010). Examining the effects of schoolwide positive behavioral interventions and supports on student outcomes: Results from a randomized controlled effectiveness trial in elementary schools. *Journal of Positive Behavioral Interventions, 12,* 133–148.

Bronfenbrenner, U. (1979). *The ecology of human development: Experiments by nature and design.* Cambridge, MA: Harvard University Press.

Buffum, A., Mattos, M., & Weber, C. (2009). *Pyramid response to intervention: RTI, professional learning communities, and how to respond when kids don't learn.* Bloomington, IN: Solution Tree Press.

Carey, J. C., Dimmitt, C., Hatch, T. A., Lapan, R. T., & Whiston, S. C. (2008). Report of the National Panel for Evidence-Based School Counseling: Outcome research coding protocol and evaluation of Student Success Skills and Second Step. *Professional School Counseling, 11,* 197–206.

Dimmitt, C., Carey, J. C., & Hatch, T. (2007). *Evidence-based school counseling: Making a difference with data-driven practices.* Thousand Oaks, CA: Corwin Press.

Dollarhide, C., & Lemberger, M. (2006). No Child Left Behind: Implications for school counselors. *Professional School Counseling, 9,* 295–304.

Drummond, T. (1994). *The Student Risk Screening Scale (SRSS).* Grants Pass, OR: Josephine County Mental Health Program.

Education Trust (2009). *National Center for Transforming School Counseling at the Education Trust.* Available online at https://edtrust.org/resource/the-new-vision-for-school-counselors-scope-of-the-work/ (accessed March 3, 2016).

Education Week (2015, December 9). The Every Student Succeeds Act: Explained. *Education Week*. Available online at http://www.edweek.org/ew/articles/2015/12/07/the-every-student-succeeds-act-explained.html (accessed December 29, 2015).

Espelage, D. L., Rao, M. A., & De La Rue, L. (2013). Current research on school-based bullying: A social-ecological perspective. *Journal of Social Distress and the Homeless*, *22*, 7–21.

Farrington, C. A., Roderick, M., Allensworth, E., Nagaoka, J., Keyes, T. S., Johnson, D. W., & Beechum, N. O. (2012). *Teaching adolescents to become learners: The role of noncognitive factors in shaping school performance: A critical literature review*. Chicago, IL: Consortium on Chicago School Research.

Fezler, B., & Brown, C. (2011). *The international model for school counseling programs*. Available online at www.aassa.com/uploaded/Educational_Research/US_Department_of_State/Counseling_Standards/International_Counseling_Model_Handbook.pdf (accessed September 1, 2015).

Goodman, R., Meltzer, H., & Bailey, V. (1998). The Strengths and Difficulties Questionnaire: A pilot study on the validity of the self-report version. *European Child & Adolescent Psychiatry*, *7*, 125–130.

Gordon, G. (2015). *The vision statement for Blackhawk Intermediate School's counseling program*. Unpublished document.

Henggeler, S. W., Schoenwald, S. K., Borduin, C. M., Rowland, M. D., & Cunningham, P. B. (1996). *Multisystemic treatment of antisocial behavior in children and adolescents*. New York: Guilford Press.

Horner, R. H., Sugai, G., Smolkowski, K., Eber, L., Nakasato, J., Todd, A. W., & Esperanza, J. (2009). A randomized, wait-list controlled effectiveness trial assessing school-wide positive behavior support in elementary schools. *Journal of Positive Behavior*, *11*, 133–144.

Individuals with Disabilities Education Improvement Act (2004). Public Law 108–446 (20 U.S.C. 1400 et seq.).

Johnson, J., Rochkind, J., Ott, A. N., & DuPont, S. (2010). *Can I get a little advice here? How an overstretched high school guidance system is undermining students' college aspirations*. Bill & Melinda Gates Foundation. Available online at http://www.publicagenda.org/files/can-i-get-a-little-advice-here.pdf (accessed April 29, 2016).

Khoury-Kassabri, M., Benbenishty, R., Astor, R. A., & Zeira, A. (2004). The contributions of community, family, and school variables to student victimization. *American Journal of Community Psychology*, *34*, 187–204.

Lamberto, R. (2015). *The belief statement for Haine Elementary School's counseling program*. Unpublished document.

Martens, K., & Andreen, K. (2013). School counselors' involvement with a School-wide Positive Behavior Support Intervention: Addressing student behavior issues in a proactive and positive manner. *Professional School Counseling*, *16*, 313–322.

Martin, P. (2002). Transforming school counseling: A national perspective. *Theory into Practice*, *41*, 148–155.

McGannon, W., Carey, J., & Dimmitt, C. (2005). *The current status of school counseling outcome research* (Research Monograph No. 2). Amherst, MA: University of Massachusetts, School of Education.

McMahon, H. G., Mason, E. C. M., Daluga-Guenther, N., & Ruiz, A. (2014). An ecological model of professional school counseling. *Journal of Counseling & Development*, *92*, 459–471.

National Governors Association and Council of Chief State School Officers (2010). *Common core state standards initiative*. Available online at www.corestandards.org (accessed June 11, 2015).

No Child Left Behind Act of 2001, Pub. L. No. 107–110 (2002).

Ockerman, M. S., Mason, E. C. M., & Hollenbeck, A. F. (2012). Integrating RTI with school counseling programs: Being a proactive professional school counselor. *Journal of School Counseling*, *10*, 1–37. Available online at http://eric.ed.gov/?id=EJ978870 (accessed December 20, 2014).

Olweus, D., & Limber, S. P. (2010). Bullying in school: Evaluation and dissemination of the Olweus Bullying Prevention Program. *American Journal of Orthopsychiatry*, *80*, 124–134.

Perkins, G., Oescher, J., & Ballard, M. B. (2010). The evolving identity of school counselors as defined by the stakeholders. *Journal of School Counseling*, *8*, 1–28.

Pérusse, R., & Colbert, R. D. (2007). The last word: An interview with Peggy Hines, director of the Education Trust's National Center for Transforming School Counseling. *Journal of Advanced Academics*, *18*, 477–487.

Reynolds, C. R., & Kamphaus, R. W. (2004). *Behavior assessment for children* (2nd ed.). Circle Pines, MN: AGS Publishing.

Rothman, R. (2012). Laying a common foundation for success. *Phi Delta Kappan*, *94*, 57–61.

Ryan, T., Kaffenberger, C. J., & Carroll, A. G. (2011). Response to intervention: An opportunity for school counselor leadership. *Professional School Counseling, 14*, 211–221.

Sink, C. A., & Stroh, H. R. (2003). Raising achievement test scores of early elementary school students through comprehensive school counseling programs. *Professional School Counseling, 6*, 350–354.

Ttofi, M. M., & Farrington, D. P. (2011). Effectiveness of school-based programs to reduce bullying: A systematic and meta-analytic review. *Journal of Experimental Criminology, 7*, 27–56.

US Department of Education (n.d.). Every Student Succeeds Act. Available online at www.ed.gov/essa (accessed March 3, 2016).

von Bertalanffy, L. (1968). *General systems theory: Foundation, development, applications.* New York: Braziller.

Ward, C. A. (2009). *An examination of the impact of the ASCA National Model on student achievement at recognized ASCA Model Program (RAMP) elementary schools.* PhD Dissertation. Corpus Christi, TX: Texas A&M University. Retrieved from ProQuest (ED515238).

Wilkerson, K., Pérusse, R., & Hughes, A. (2013). Comprehensive school counseling programs and student achievement outcomes: A comparative analysis of RAMP vs. non-RAMP schools. *Professional School Counseling, 16*, 172–184.

Chapter Three
Social Justice, Advocacy, Collaboration, Leadership, and Systemic Change

---

Box 3.1

2016 CACREP School Counseling Specialty Area Standards

1.d Models of school-based collaboration and consultation
2.a School counselor roles as leaders, advocates, and systems change agents in P-12 schools
2.d School counselor roles in school leadership and multidisciplinary teams
2.f Competencies to advocate for school counseling roles
2.j Qualities and styles of effective leadership in schools
3.k Strategies to promote equity in student achievement and college access

---

According to *the ASCA National Model®* (2012), school counselors pursue socially just outcomes by infusing their school counseling program with the four themes of leadership, advocacy, collaboration, and systemic change. These roles are considered necessary in order to ensure that all students achieve college readiness by the completion of high school. The four themes each imply the need for school counselors to implement and support programs that enhance the environments in which students function, reflect the school counseling profession's desire to distance itself from a responsive model, and, instead, emphasize providing services to at-risk students, and implement comprehensive interventions that result in systemic change. We provide practical and specific examples of the way in which school counselors use *the ASCA National Model's®* themes of advocacy, collaboration, and leadership toward systemic change to promote minority students' achievement. We also identify school counselors' use of direct services, including small- and large-group instruction and counseling, which incorporate a social justice focus.

Achievement Gap

The two primary objectives of the No Child Left Behind (NCLB; 2002) Act and the Every Student Succeeds Act (ESSA: US Department of Education, n.d.), which replaced NCLB in 2015, are to raise academic achievement for all students and to decrease the racial achievement gap, which is defined as the gap in academic performance between Asian and White students on the one hand, and Latino and African American students on the other hand.

Box 3.2

Achievement Gap – a term used to describe the sizable differences between African American and White, Latino and White, and recent immigrant and White students on both standardized testing scores and overall academic achievement nationwide (Ladson-Billings, 2006).

Despite the implementation of these educational reform legislative acts, there remain considerable racial disparities in educational achievement. In 2012, the school dropout rate for Whites was 4%, 8% for African Americans, and 13% for Latinos (US Department of Education, 2014). The National Assessment of Educational Progress (NAEP, 2013) revealed that among high school seniors, the White-African American gap in math and reading scores was 30 points, and the White-Latino gap was 22 points in reading and 21 points in math. In 2011, 72% of White high school graduates enrolled in college that same year, whereas the rate for African American students was 44%, and 50% for Latino students (US Department of Education, 2011). Despite federal and state efforts to increase minority students' participation and achievement in classes in science, technology, engineering, and mathematics (commonly referred to as STEM subjects), in 2013, African American and Latino students were significantly less likely than Whites and Asians to both take and pass STEM-related Advanced Placement (AP) tests (College Board, 2013).

Causes of the Achievement Gap

According to Chambers (2009), initiatives in the 1960s and 1970s to reduce the racial achievement gap primarily focused on addressing the perceived cultural deficits and intrapsychic issues of African Americans and Hispanics, which implied that the problem resided within minority students' ability to achieve. It is now commonly understood that the issue of racial disparities in education is complex and multifaceted and cannot be explained in terms of individual deficits of minority students. Researchers have identified a number of environmental variables that are associated with the racial achievement gap, although the research literature is not always conclusive regarding which variables are most strongly related to the racial achievement gap. For example, the extant literature base concerning whether teacher-student ratios are associated with the racial achievement gap is mixed (Rowley & Wright, 2011).

Box 3.3

Historically, there have been two types of theories as to what has caused the achievement gap:

- **Cultural or intrapsychic deficit** – minority groups have some internal issue or inherent skill deficit that causes them to be less likely to achieve
- **Environmental deficit** – problems with the environment that minority students are more likely to be exposed to causes them to be less likely to achieve.

Figure 3.1 Picture of Four Children Holding the American Flag. Copyright: www.istockphoto.com.

McKown's (2013) review of the research literature identified a number of factors that appear to contribute to the White-African American achievement gap. Racial-ethnic differences in parenting practices appear to account for a substantial portion of the White-African American achievement gap even after controlling for socioeconomic status. This is demonstrated through findings suggesting that White parents are more likely than African American parents to engage in practices that are associated with academic achievement, including such practices as warmth, sensitivity, involvement in school activities, monitoring, and involving children in decision-making. White students are also more likely than African American students to receive high-quality instruction, in that they often are taught by better teachers, are exposed to a more challenging curriculum, and have better relationships with teachers than their African American peers with comparable records of achievement.

McKown concluded that the extant research supports the contention that racism contributes to the racial achievement gap as African American students receive direct and indirect messages from society and teachers that their race is considered inadequate in comparison to Whites. For example, African American students are likely to interpret lower teacher expectations as an indicator of being less competent than White students. Similarly, studies have found that higher rates of disciplinary referrals for African American and Latino students are associated with minority students perceiving school personnel as unfair, and may be interpreted by minority students as indicating that they are less valued, which is likely to negatively impact their academic achievement.

Peer and neighborhood influences are also likely to partially explain the White-African American achievement gap, although McKown indicated that the empirical support for their role is not as strong as it is for family factors and high-quality instruction. Some studies have found that the stigma related to academic achievement and its association with White culture, which has been referred to as stereotype threat, contributes to the underachievement of African American students. The level of cohesion and social support within a community, which may be considered as protective factors when strong, also may contribute to the academic achievement of African American students when lacking.

Segregation and tracking, such as scheduling students in classes with fewer academic demands, also appear to contribute to the racial achievement gap. In one of the most comprehensive studies conducted to date, Condron, Tope, Steidl, and Freeman (2013) found that school segregation between schools was a small but statistically significant contributor to increases in the White-African American achievement gaps in math and reading. However, increases in the exposure of African American to White students resulted in small but statistically significant reductions in the achievement gaps. Segregation within schools also appears to contribute to the racial achievement gap. Berends, Lucas, and Penaloza (2008) found that the percentage of African American students who reported being enrolled in a college track placement in high school increased between 1972 and 2004, and that this increase was associated with a considerable decrease in the White-African American gap in mathematics test scores during this time period.

Despite the increase in the number of African American students who reported being in a college track placement, many minority students appear to believe that postsecondary degrees are not within their reach. This is thought to lead them to disengage from an educational setting that they do not perceive to be encouraging their aspirations (Herring & Salazar, 2002).

Box 3.4

While formal segregation has been famously outlawed (e.g., *Brown v. Board of Education*), research suggests that minority students still experience educational segregation as minority students often attend neighborhood schools with high minority populations and are also less likely to be placed in college preparatory tracks in an integrated high school compared to their White peers.

It has been proposed that between-school segregation and within-school segregation, or tracking, increases racial stratification by creating richer educational environments for White students, which further exacerbates the unequal access to resources that Whites have outside of schools (Condron et al., 2013). In summary, it appears that non-school factors (e.g., parenting practices, socioeconomic status, neighborhood cohesion), between-school factors (e.g., racial segregation), and within-school factors (e.g., curriculum differentiation/tracking) all contribute to the racial achievement gap.

Educators' Negative Contributions to the Achievement Gap

As mentioned earlier, McKown's (2013) review of the research literature indicated that teachers' racism and their differential approaches toward White and African American students appears to contribute to the White-African American achievement gap. McKown (2013) concludes that the racial achievement gap is likely to be reduced by emphasizing strong instruction for all students, promoting positive teacher-child relationships, and training school personnel to reduce stereotyping of students. Many educational experts have written about the need for training to help school personnel learn about how their frequently unconscious assumptions about minority students and their learning negatively impacts minority students.

Stephens and Lindsey (2011) assert that education is permeated by the values and assumptions of the dominant White majority culture with the simultaneous denial that culture and heritage are not an inherent part of the learning process. They argue that teachers who identify with the dominant group perspective merely tolerate minority students whom they regard as problematic because of their underperformance.

Stephens and Lindsey (2011) have several terms to characterize such educators. *Cultural destructiveness* is defined as the desire to eliminate any mention of cultures other than the dominant, majority culture within the school setting. Educators who are culturally destructive might issue such statements as "I don't see why we have to have Black History month, we don't have a White History month," or "I am here to teach students math, I'm not here to babysit."

Cultural incapacity involves demeaning other cultures and persons from lower socioeconomic statuses, often characterizing them as deficient. Educators who are culturally incapable might make such statements as "They just need to pull themselves up by their bootstraps," "I don't see why they keep bringing up slavery, I never owned slaves," or "Their problem is that they don't care about education."

Cultural blindness refers to the failure to recognize the culture and socioeconomic status of others. Educators with such a perspective might be heard to utter "I don't see color, I only see individuals." Or, such teachers might assert that the racial achievement gap is about socioeconomic status rather than race or ethnicity, implying that a student's cultural background is not important to consider in relating to and teaching students. Stephens and Lindsey (2011) assert that some educators are resistant to change, believing that persons from other cultures should change by adapting to the dominant, majority culture. Some educators even deny the existence of both oppression and the privileges enjoyed by the White, middle class that are not available to members of traditionally disadvantaged groups.

Box 3.5

Cultural Destructiveness – the desire to eliminate any mention of culture, other than the dominant culture.

Cultural Incapacity – demeaning persons from other cultures or socioeconomic statuses as deficient.

Cultural Blindness – the failure to recognize the culture and/or socioeconomic status of others.

Stephens and Lindsey (2011) also identify several types of barriers to cultural proficiency that are often displayed by educators. One barrier is being resistant to change. Educators may believe that others, but not them, are responsible for making changes. Another barrier is failing to acknowledge that systems of oppression, including classism, racism, sexism, and ethnocentrism, are real. Finally, Stephens and Lindsey (2011) state that educators may deny the notion of privilege, meaning that they fail to recognize that certain groups receive more benefits than others simply because of their race, gender, sexual orientation, or socioeconomic status.

Social Justice and School Counselors

The disparities in achievement between racial groups and the role of the environment in contributing to the gap highlight the need for school counselors to demonstrate a commitment to social justice. Social justice counseling has been defined as intentional efforts to remove systems of oppression, inequity, inequality, or exploitation of traditionally marginalized groups in order to promote equity and participation (Constantine, Hage, Kindaichi, & Bryant, 2007). During the past decade, the school counseling literature has increasingly focused upon the need for school counselors to engage in advocacy and leadership in order to address educational inequalities by removing institutional barriers to student achievement. It has been argued that school counselors, for a variety of reasons, are in a unique position to assume a leadership position to advocate for persons from marginalized groups in order to promote systemic change and thereby social justice.

Box 3.6

Social Justice Counseling – intentional efforts to remove systems of oppression, inequity, inequality, or exploitation of traditionally marginalized groups in order to promote equity and participation.

First of all, school counselors have traditionally been expected to fix the "underachieving students," who Stephens and Lindsey (2011) argue should more rightly be referred to as "underserved students." In contrast, as the school counseling profession seeks to move away from primarily being identified as working with solely at-risk students, they have the challenge articulated in *the ASCA National Model®* (2012) of meeting the needs of the entire student population. Such a commitment requires a broad perspective and a focus on comprehensive interventions.

School counselors also have unique access to both formal data, such as school-wide data regarding academic achievement, attendance, and disciplinary reports, and informal data, in the form of their interactions of with the diverse array of students and parents. Additionally, school counselors' training in multiculturalism, human relations, change processes, group work, learning theories, and program evaluation sets them apart from other school personnel, providing school counselors with the skills to promote collaboration among school personnel and to serve as the liaison between families and the school (Borders & Shoffner, 2003).

The school counseling profession rightly recognizes that the achievement gap should not be conceptualized merely from an intrapsychic model, which emphasizes individual student deficits. *The ASCA National Model®* (2012), through the four themes, emphasizes the need for school counselors to think comprehensively to promote equity and educational achievement for all students. As discussed in depth in Chapter 1, the systems-ecological perspective provides professional school counselors with a framework for thinking comprehensively in regards to addressing environmental issues that have contributed to the achievement gap. The recognition that social justice is a moral imperative is also reflected in ASCA's *Ethical Standards for School Counselors* (2010). In the preamble, professional school counselors are called on to be advocates, leaders, collaborators, and consultants in creating an equitable educational environment that promotes access and success for all students.

> Each person has the right to be respected, be treated with dignity and have access to a comprehensive school counseling program that advocates for and affirms all students from diverse populations including: ethnic/racial identity, age, economic status, abilities/disabilities, language, immigration status, sexual orientation, gender identity/expression, family type, religious/spiritual identity and appearance.
>
> (ASCA, 2010, p. 1).

The school counseling profession appears to be in the process of developing evidence-based approaches that require school counselors to play a significant role in reducing the racial achievement gap. Therefore, the remainder of this chapter examines models and interventions available in the literature that concern school counselors' role in this process. Research clearly indicates that the racial achievement gap is related to factors that are embedded within society, communities, and the culture of the school. Thus, school counselors must have a broad perspective in order to implement interventions that impact the larger systems, as well as thinking about how to help individual teachers, students, and parents.

Singh, Urbano, Haston, and McMahon (2010) identified seven overarching strategies used by sixteen school counselors who identify as social justice change agents. *Political Savvy* refers to knowing how to intervene in a manner that strikes an appropriate balance between being a supportive counselor and an aggressive change agent by delivering information that can be heard, and knowing when or with whom to intervene. In other words, the school counselor must understand who has power in particular situations, or who are the key players, and how to communicate in a way that is likely to influence the persons with power. *Consciousness Raising* is defined as the intent of advocacy conducted by school counselors, meaning that school counselors' use of advocacy is a tactic for increasing educational personnel's understanding of the needs of diverse students. *Initiating Difficult Dialogues* refers to the fact that school counselors who are identified as social change agents typically feel discomfort in discussing topics that they recognize will likely result in other school personnel feeling defensive. *Building Intentional Relationships* is indicative of the fact that nearly all of the school counselors who are identified as change agents indicate that they intentionally sought to develop allies from various groups, including students, parents, administrators, teachers, and school support staff (e.g., custodians) in order to create broad coalitions. Each of the participating school counselors identified the importance of *Teaching Students Self-Advocacy Skills*. Examples of this skill include teaching low-income students how to use the Internet to identify college scholarships, how to navigate the college admissions process, and providing students with the vocabulary and skills necessary to understand complex situations. *Using Data for Marketing* refers to all but one of the school counselors who claimed to be a social justice change agent asserting that they used data to increase the consciousness of their school-based colleagues. *Educating Others About School Counselors' Role as Advocate* reflects that most of the school counselors identified the importance of educating others about their specific social justice interventions.

Box 3.7

School counselors who desire to be social justice change agents should be able to:

- demonstrate political savvy
- raise consciousness
- initiate difficult dialogues
- build intentional relationships
- teach students self-advocacy skills
- use data for marketing
- educate others about school counselors' role as advocate.

Advocacy and School Counselors

Advocacy is one of the four themes within *the ASCA National Model®* (2012), and advocating for the academic achievement of all students is considered to be an essential role of school counselors and a way in which school counselors can assume a leadership position in promoting school reform. The American Counseling Association's (ACA) Advocacy Competencies (2003) were adapted for school counselors by Ratts, DeKruyf, and Chen-Hayes (2007), and are included in *the ASCA National Model®* (2012). The advocacy competencies include strategies concerning student empowerment, student advocacy, school/community collaboration, systems advocacy, public information advocacy, and social/political advocacy.

Student empowerment is defined as efforts to increase students' awareness of how disparate power and privilege impacts their self-concept, worldview, and opportunities, and to provide students with the self-advocacy skills to address barriers to their access to educational resources.

Box 3.8

"Student Empowerment – school counselors' efforts to increase students' awareness of how disparate power and privilege impact students' skills, opportunities, and well-being"(ASCA, 2012, p. 5).

Within *the ASCA National Model®* (2012), school counselors promote student empowerment through the school counseling core curriculum, individual student planning, and responsive services (i.e., counseling and crisis response). At the elementary level, school counselors can use multicultural children's literature in small- and large-group instruction to facilitate students' understanding of their own culture and those of others (Singer & Smith, 2003). At the secondary level, small- and large-group instruction can be used to enhance students' awareness of their culture by helping them to write about their cultural biography (Singer & Smith, 2003).

Astramovich and Harris (2007) recommend the use of bibliotherapy to increase students' awareness of prejudice and its impact upon victims and society. They recommend Tatum's (1997) book, *Why are all the black kids sitting together in the cafeteria? And other conversations about race*, to help students comprehend the history of oppression in the school system. Small- and large-group instruction can be used at both levels to teach students how to talk with members of their family and community about prejudice, and to promote assertiveness and communication skills. Small group instruction can be also used with victims of bullying and in peer mediation (Ratts et al., 2007), and to help minority students network with each other (Singer & Smith, 2003). School counselors may use individual counseling to help victims of bullying identify strategies for self-protection and for obtaining assistance from adults (Ratts et al., 2007).

Student advocacy refers to when school counselors directly intervene on the behalf of a student by identifying allies and implementing a plan. School counselors engage in student advocacy through the indirect services of referral, consultation, and collaboration, through the program management activities of creating a school data profile, which provides a review of the school's key achievement and behavioral data in a disaggregated fashion, and through closing-the-gap and small-group action plans, which identify activities intended to reduce behavioral or academic achievement gaps. Ratts et al. (2007) provide an example of a school counselor helping a student who wishes to communicate with a teacher or a more powerful student. In such a case, the school counselor can function like a mediator, establishing the ground rules for the interaction. School counselors can advocate for activities or opportunities that may promote the career and college readiness of impoverished students (Ratts et al., 2007). Such students may not have the career developmental opportunities typically afforded to the children of middle-class parents. School counselors may find that they can address this disparity by providing job shadowing opportunities, mentoring, and providing assistance with applying for colleges and pursuing financial aid, to name just a few of the potential opportunities for student advocacy.

School counselors can also engage in *school/community collaboration* to coordinate resources and strategies with allies within the community, and the program management activities of the advisory council, program goals, and curriculum action plan are reflective of collaboration with the community.

Systems advocacy involves the identification of a systemic barrier to achievement that requires intervention at a systems level. Systems advocacy may involve indirect services of consultation and collaboration, and a number of program management activities. These activities may include data collection and analysis tools, such as needs assessments, school data profile analysis, results reports analysis, program assessment analysis, program goal analysis, and program management activities that seek to instill change at a systems level, which include annual agreements and action plans. Ratts et al. (2007) suggest that school counselors might be simply able to effect change by highlighting racial disparities revealed through data analysis, such as a school where 40% of the student population is Latino and yet the 10% of the students in Advanced Placement calculus are Latino. School counselors may become aware of systemic issues through simply noting a number of students dealing with similar issues. For example, if the school counselor notices that he or she has a number of lesbian, gay, bisexual, or transgender (LGBT) students who are experiencing harassment, the school counselor may wish to initiate the formation of a Gay-Straight Alliance (GSA), conduct classroom lessons on harassment, and collaborate with the administration in providing in-service training for the staff on identifying and responding to harassment.

The types of advocacy strategies identified within *the ASCA National Model*® (2012) heretofore mentioned are referred to as micro-level interventions, as they are aimed at invoking change within an individual or particular school. In contrast, macro-level advocacy strategies seek to affect the community external to the particular school.

Public information advocacy involves a school counselor's efforts to collaborate with the community to inform the public about issues relevant to social justice. Such advocacy efforts may be included in such school counseling program management activities as the belief, vision, and mission statements, results reports, and such indirect services as collaboration with community groups and service on school committees. *Social/political advocacy* seeks to redress student issues through changes to policy or legislation, which may require the school counselor to participate in district committees, conduct school board presentations, be involved with state and national professional associations, and engage in efforts to influence legislation.

For example, two of the authors of this text, Drs. Crothers and Kolbert, have collaborated with a number of community organizations, including an agency that provides mental health services to the LGBT community, the local chapters of the Parents and Friends of Lesbians and Gays (PFLAG), and the Gay, Lesbian & Straight Education Network (GLSEN), to increase the safety of LGBT students in Allegheny County, Pennsylvania.

The respective authors surveyed teachers within the county, LGBT students, and LGBT parents to obtain their perceptions regarding the bullying experiences of LGBT students. Interestingly, the data revealed that while most teachers perceive that schools and staff members are supportive of LGBT students, LGBT students and teachers find schools and school staff as less encouraging toward LGBT students. The respective authors have presented these results at community forums and state professional associations, for the purposes of encouraging school districts and the Commonwealth to adopt policies and procedures that offer increased protection for LGBT students. One school district modified their anti-bullying policies, naming LBGT students as a specifically protected group, along with other traditionally marginalized groups (Buzgon et al., 2014).

Collaboration and School Counselors

Historically, school counselors were not included as contributors to major educational reform initiatives and the services they provided were often seen as ancillary to the mission of schools. However, with the declining funding available to schools and the increased call for social justice, school counselors must collaborate with various stakeholders, including teachers, administrators, parents, and students, in order to achieve systemic change. The following section provides an overview of Schulz, Hurt, and Lindo's (2014) model for school counselors' use of collaborative strategies to promote cultural responsiveness. We also discuss other examples found in the literature of school counselors using collaboration to promote systemic change.

Schulz et al.'s (2014) Collaborative Strategies for Promoting Cultural Responsiveness. Educators have been urged to adopt culturally responsive teaching (CRT) strategies as a means to reduce the achievement gap. Gay (2006) asserts that CRT teaches through the strengths of diverse students by using the strengths of their culture, their prior experiences, and their performance styles to make learning more relevant and interesting for them, thereby establishing a bridge between diverse students' home and school lives.

Box 3.12

Culturally Responsive Teaching (CRT) – teachers utilizing the strengths of diverse students' cultures, prior experiences, and performance styles to make learning more relevant and interesting.

Schultz et al. use this bridge metaphor, asserting that school counselors' role in cultural responsiveness is to create a bridge between teachers and students. Table 3.1 presents Schulz et al.'s model of how school counselors can collaborate with teachers and other adults in order to promote cultural responsiveness within schools. The examples of collaboration are divided into three levels of intervention. The first level, *Faculty Development*, includes strategies that can be implemented with entire faculties. The next level,

Table 3.1 Culturally Responsive Strategies

Level of Implementation	Examples
1. Faculty Development	(a) Workshops focused on building cultural competence and culturally responsive philosophy, teacher characteristics, curriculum, instructional strategies, and assessments (b) Guest speakers to address special topics (c) Vision/mission building sessions (d) Inventory of current building and classroom practices
2. Small Group Development	(a) Departmental task-focused group to build philosophy, curriculum, instructional practices, and assessments (b) Interdisciplinary group focused on inter- and intrapersonal skill building (c) Focus groups read a book together to promote cultural responsiveness and discuss relevance to own practice (i.e., Tatum, 1997) (d) Peer coaching teams to practice and evaluate culturally responsive approaches
3. Individual Development	(a) Counselor/Teacher collaboration focused on development of teacher's multicultural awareness (b) Regular consultation on implementation and practice (c) Team teaching using standards blending approach (d) Individual and small group discussion inclusion interventions (see Clark & Breman, 2009)

Source: Adapted from Schulz, L. L., Hurt, K., & Lindo, N. (2014). My name is not Michael: Strategies for promoting cultural responsiveness in schools. *Journal of School Counseling, 12*, 1–35. Reprinted with permission from Mark Nelson and the *Journal of School Counseling*.

Small Group Development, provides examples of strategies that can be used with small groups of teachers, administrators, and staff. The third level, *Individual Development*, is comprised of strategies that can be used with individual adults within the school system.

Faculty development. School counselors can assume a leadership role by collaborating with teachers in planning in-service and professional development opportunities that are already required of teachers by nearly all states. Schulz et al. (2014) recommend that school counselors use such workshops to help teachers identify their own cultural backgrounds and how these backgrounds influence their perspectives of diverse students. Ford (2010) asserts that teacher training programs typically do not require future teachers to examine their cultural biases and assumptions, nor do they teach future teachers how to tailor teaching strategies to meet the needs of diverse students.

The multicultural competencies for counselors, which are divided into personal awareness, knowledge of diverse groups, and the acquisition of skills for working with diverse groups, can serve as a framework for training teachers in diversity (Schulz et al., 2014). School counselors can use the preparation they received in multiculturalism in training teachers to become aware of their cultural assumptions and biases, and increase teachers' understanding of the strengths and worldview of specific diverse groups.

School counselors could teach DuPraw and Axner's (1997) six fundamental ways in which cultures tend to differ from each other, which include communication style, attitudes toward conflict, approaches to task completion, decision-making styles, attitudes toward disclosure, and approaches to knowing. Such information can help teachers in empathizing and developing rapport with students from diverse backgrounds, consulting/conferencing with parents of diverse backgrounds, and using different ways of knowing in their teaching. For example, Gay (2006) asserts that most teachers use deductive reasoning in the classroom, by focusing on specific details which are then generalized to identify the whole. However, many African American, Latino, and Asian American students tend to prefer a more constructivist style of learning in which information is related to existing cognitive structures. Teaching methods that are considered to be more compatible with a constructivist approach have been given such titles as inquiry learning, discovery learning, and project-based learning. There is also some research suggesting that while White students tend to prefer independent and competitive forms of learning, in which individual achievement is highlighted, Asian American, African American, and Latino students perform better in educational environments that use cooperative and collaborative approaches to learning (e.g., Chizhik, 2001). Training in diversity for teachers can also be enhanced through multimedia exposure utilizing videos, contemporary films for starting conversations about unfamiliar social contexts, and experiences promoting a more personal connection with poverty and diversity have been shown to be effective in developing cultural competence (Cholewa & West-Olatunji, 2008). Also, teachers can be asked to participate in cultural events, community meetings, and a variety of religious experiences, which may be helpful in increasing connections with their students.

One form of resistance to cultural proficiency that some teachers will display is overt or covert challenges to the school counselor's expertise regarding pedagogy, given that many school counselors do not possess teacher certification, or are no longer in the role of teacher and thus cannot truly understand what it is like to "be in the trenches" (Stephens & Lindsey, 2011). In such situations, school counselors are encouraged to align themselves with influential teachers who can take the lead in helping their colleagues to understand how to incorporate the strengths and worldviews of diverse groups into the classroom, and learn to incorporate more constructivist style teaching strategies. By teaming with influential teachers to increase the cultural responsiveness of the staff in this manner, the school counselor is using some of the strategies that Singh et al. (2010) found to be used by school counselors who identify as change agents. The school counselor is being *Politically Savvy* by recognizing who has power within the school and is *Intentionally Building Relationships* with those who have power in order to *Initiate Difficult Dialogues and Raise Consciousness*.

Small group development. Schulz et al. (2014) assert that small group development is sometimes preferable to large-group learning experiences in that small group development can provide greater depth of exploration. The school counselor can assist subject departments (e.g., Social Studies, Science) in generating vision and mission statements that incorporate cultural responsiveness. School counselors can also help departments identify professional development needs that are specific to their department. Schulz et al. (2014) provide the example of assisting a mathematics department in revising their assessments to be more culturally fair/responsive. Schulz et al. (2014) established voluntary reading groups to discuss a chapter of Tatum's (1997) *Why are all the black kids sitting together in the cafeteria? And other conversations about race*, and had teachers discuss their personal reactions to the book, followed by an exploration of how their new understandings influenced their approach to teaching diverse students.

Individual development. School counselors can also use consultation to increase teachers' cultural proficiency as, unfortunately, didactic training is not always sufficient to address the barriers to cultural proficiency. Rather, many people also learn cultural proficiency through experience in interacting with people who are different from themselves. School counselors often have access to information from various stakeholders, such as students and parents, who approach them with concerns about teachers or administrators and may confide in the school counselor about issues with teachers. It is not unusual for teachers to mistrust school counselors because of teachers' awareness that school counselors receive such information. Singh et al. (2010) found that school counselors who identify as change agents are very purposeful in how they approach teachers about their potential lack of cultural proficiency in order to increase the likelihood that teachers can hear such messages. This is also related to Singh et al.'s (2010) counselor competency of *Initiating Difficult Dialogues*.

The school counselor may want to first consult with the teacher alone, sharing with them that a number of students and/or parents have expressed concern about the teacher's responsiveness. The school counselor should allow the teacher to defend him- or herself and use active listening skills to indicate that they hear the teacher's perspective. The use of active listening skills typically decreases the teacher's emotional intensity, whereupon the school counselor can ask questions to increase the teacher's understanding of diverse groups. For example, the school counselor can ask the teacher about what he or she thinks the student's and/or parent's perspective may be.

A common complaint of less culturally proficient teachers is that minority students and their parents do not value education. As such, teachers can misread the behaviors of minority students. By using questions, the school counselor can assist such a teacher in understanding that the student and parents indeed do value education, but that they display this value in a different manner, or they can help the teacher to realize that the parent and child value different kinds of learning experiences. This can begin to help such a teacher understand that the student's/parent's behaviors of concern may reflect a healthy mistrust of the educational system which historically has been unresponsive to their needs. Through such a manner, the school counselor is attempting to "normalize" the student's mistrust. The school counselor can then ask the teacher how he or she might approach the student in a different manner, or ask the teacher about times when he or she has related more effectively to the student in question, or when he or she has related effectively to other minority students. By asking such questions, the school counselor is "framing" the issue as being about how the teacher relates to minority students. The use of data also serves to help teachers develop a more objective perspective about how they are impacting students from diverse groups.

It is not uncommon for minority students to claim that a teacher is prejudiced, which many teachers vociferously deny. However, school counselors can help teachers in consultation and training realize their prejudices and stereotypes as products of a prejudiced society. Only by increasing awareness of one's prejudices in a non-defensive manner can a person learn how to not act upon them.

Schulz et al. (2014) provide an example of a school counselor who, upon noticing that 64% of the freshmen earned either a "D" or "F" grade in their science class, approached two science teachers separately, offering the teachers her support in her role as counselor. Through multiple discussions focusing upon the teachers' personal world and their classroom management and teaching philosophy, the school counselor assisted the teachers in developing more effective ways of both relating to and teaching students, which resulted in a significant decrease in the number of students who earned a "D" or "F" in the next academic year.

Dowden's example of collaboration and action research. Dowden (2010) discusses her experience of using collaboration, consultation, and counseling to promote social justice as a high school counselor in a southeastern college town. She utilized Kolb's (1984) Action Research model, which involves identifying a problem, collecting and analyzing data to develop a plan, implementing a plan, observing the results of the plan by gathering and interpreting outcome data, and reflecting upon the results. The problem she identified was the apparent existence of a school within a school, where the advanced curriculum courses were comprised mostly of White, middle- and upper middle-class students, while the African American students were mostly enrolled in "regular" level courses, and the Latino students were mostly enrolled in English as a Second Language (ESL) courses. Dowden (2010) reports that the administrators and other school counselors were indifferent to this disparity.

The first part of Dowden's plan was to inform parents, students, and school staff about these inequities and how they resulted in unequal educational opportunities. She used individual and group counseling to encourage minority students to challenge themselves by taking more advanced courses, encouraged minority students to assume leadership roles within the school, and prompted these students to join academic organizations such as the math club. Dowden used the College Board's Advanced Placement (AP) Potential program (College Board, 2010), which is a web-based tool that identifies students who have potential to succeed in an AP course based upon Practice Scholastic Assessment Test (PSAT) scores. She supported students who accepted the challenge by assuring them that she would advocate for them if necessary, providing them with a mentor, and exposing them to the Advancement Via Individual Determination (AVID) program, which offers curriculum instruction and foundational academic skills, such as note-taking. Dowden collaborated with a nearby university to recruit African American male students who exposed their mentees to the college through joint participation in campus events. Dowden also established an after-school program in which student discussion forums were created to enable students who had been successful in overcoming social barriers to share their experiences with their peers. Dowden recruited motivational speakers from the local churches to come and speak to the students in the after-school program about self-determination, motivation, and persistence. Parent meetings were also held to inform parents of their options. Dowden (2010) also directly challenged school personnel whom she believed were serving as barriers to equity. She suggested to an art and band teacher who appeared to discourage minority students from enrolling in their courses through the use of high financial fees for associated activities that the required fees could be raised by a booster club.

In order to evaluate the effectiveness of these efforts on minority student engagement and achievement, Dowden first approached the school's principal about conducting a survey of students' perceptions of the school's level of inequities. Despite all the support Dowden had gained through the implementation of the discussed programs and changes, her request to conduct the survey was denied by the principal. Instead, she collected and disseminated disaggregated data on student test scores, course enrollment, and attendance and suspension rates, and the data revealed that there was a gradual improvement in the academic achievement of minority students during her three-year tenure at the school.

Leadership and School Counselors

Advocacy, collaboration, and systemic change all require leadership, and thus leadership can be regarded as the foundation of the skills required for implementing a school counseling program (Mason & McMahon, 2009). While there are various models of leadership for educational systems, the ASCA National Model® (2012) references the research of Bolman and Deal (2008), who identified four types of leadership: structural, human resources, political, and symbolic. Structural leadership refers to efforts made to develop an organization, which for school counselors involves the creation and implementation of a comprehensive school counseling program. According to Dollarhide (2003), who adapted Bolman and Deal's forms of leadership for the school counseling profession, school counselors must establish the foundation of the school counseling program through mastery of the various tools delineated in the ASCA National Model® (2012), including development of the program's beliefs, vision, mission, etc., and the various tools for collecting and analyzing data.

Human resource leadership concerns empowering and inspiring others. School counselors embody human leadership in conveying the expectation that all students can achieve at a high level, and by removing barriers to student achievement, including enhancing colleagues' awareness of how their negative view of the capabilities of minority students tends to be filtered through a White privileged perspective.

Structural Leadership – school counselors' efforts to develop and implement a comprehensive school counseling program (ASCA, 2012).

Human Resource Leadership – school counselors' efforts to empower and inspire others (ASCA, 2012).

The visibility of the school counseling program can be enhanced by increasing stakeholders' awareness of the program's vision and mission statements, and publicizing the activities of the school counseling program through annual and weekly calendars and newsletters.

Political leadership involves the use of interpersonal and organizational power. School counselors demonstrate political leadership in leading the school counseling program's advisory council and building relationships with stakeholders and administrators. Research reveals that the support of the school principal regarding the maintenance of a school counseling program is essential (e.g., Lambie & Williamson, 2004). School counselors must make principals aware of *the ASCA National Model®* (2012) and the evidence supporting its contribution to student success.

Symbolic leadership refers to the exhibition of a commitment to change and development. School counselors demonstrate such a commitment in developing a school counseling program that addresses the needs of students and the community, as indicated by data providing direct services that address such needs, regularly evaluating and revising the school counseling program, and exhibiting a high degree of integrity by following ASCA's *Ethical Standards for School Counselors* (2010; Dollarhide, 2003).

Political Leadership – school counselors' use of interpersonal and organizational power (ASCA, 2012).

Symbolic Leadership – school counselors' exhibition of a commitment to change and development (ASCA, 2012).

Militello, Schweid, and Carey (2008) provide an example of the distributive leadership model in promoting college readiness through advising in an urban high school situated in a low socioeconomic status neighborhood. The high school established a new graduation requirement of having to submit two college applications to the principal. Obtaining approval of the school's parent-teacher association (PTA), school counselors and math teachers required students to submit their parents' financial data in completing the Free Application for Federal Student Aid (FAFSA). The language arts teachers assisted students in writing their personal statements for college applications. The school counselor, the PTA, and the assistant principal collaborated in obtaining funding for the college application for students in need. In this example, the school counselors demonstrated leadership through collaborative practices, while transforming the school by enhancing the college-going culture.

Young, Millard, and Kneale (2013) recommend the formation of school counseling collaborative teams (SCCT) to serve as a structure through which school counselors may collaborate and provide instructional leadership. Members of the SCCT share a goal or vision, and are committed to the use of collective inquiry and a results orientation, meaning that there is a continuous cycle of questioning the status, strategy experimentation, and use of data. The initial meetings seek to achieve a consensus regarding the team's goals, which can use the SMART goal practice, meaning that the goals are specific, measurable, attainable, results-oriented, and time-bound. Once consensus is achieved regarding the goals, members can construct an action plan for each goal.

Box 3.15

SMART Goals are:

- Specific
- Measurable
- Attainable
- Results-oriented
- Time-bound

The team engages in inquiry and data collection to determine why students are not achieving the respective goal, and this may involve the formation of a focus group of students, and implementation of needs assessments or surveys on students, parents, and/or teachers. Team members should review the professional literature to identify evidence-based interventions. The concluding step in the process is the evaluation of various types of data to determine whether students have achieved the identified learning outcome.

Young et al. (2013) provide an example of the use of an SCCT to address an achievement gap. After two years of implementation, a middle-school based SCCT had been successful in decreasing the number of students receiving "Ds" and "Fs" and increasing the proficiency rates in math and reading. In the third year, the SCCT identified a racial achievement gap in honors courses. The percentage of African American and Latino students in honors classes represented the school's composition of minority students, but they were not passing the reading and math state assessment tests at the same rate as White and Asian American students, and they had an average grade of "C" in the honors courses. The SCCT members collaborated with teachers in delivering a *Success Prep curriculum*, which included fostering healthy relationships, improving organization and study skills, identification of learning styles, self-advocacy, using formative and summative assessment strategies, and setting SMART goals. The intervention resulted in 90% of students passing state assessment tests and the average grade for African American and Latino students increased to a "B."

Standards Blending to Promote Social Justice

Standards blending, which involves the integration of specific core academic standards with *the ASCA Mindsets & Behaviors for Student Success* (ASCA, 2014) in a culturally competent manner, has received considerable attention within the school counseling literature as a practice to promote social justice (Schellenberg, 2008). Standards blending uses a student-centered approach in that it draws upon students' previous knowledge and encourages them to personalize the material. Students are provided opportunities to socially interact with their peers and teachers in small learning communities, where the respective material is examined and resolved. Schellenberg recommends that language arts and mathematics standards should be the focus in standards blending, versus other core academic standards, because these academic areas serve as the foundation for the other core academic areas. Examples of standards blending are provided in the following paragraphs.

Standards Blending – the integration of specific core academic standards with school counseling mindsets in a culturally competent manner.

Schellenberg (2008) provides an example of the use of standards blending in eighth grade school counseling classroom lessons to address career development standards from the school counseling program's curriculum, the language arts curriculum's standard of interviewing techniques to acquire information, and the math standards of estimating, data analysis and conjectures, and determining means. The school counseling curriculum standard regarded learning how to research different careers by gaining and interpreting information. Students also learned how to conduct informational interviews, and explored how this form of information gathering compared to techniques they had used in the past to obtain information.

In order to demonstrate their knowledge, students conducted an informational interview (language arts competency) to engage in career exploration (school counseling competency). Each student constructed ten questions for their interview (language arts competency), and at least five of the questions had to include proportions such as scaling questions (math competency). Students role-played the interview with the school counselor and other students, recording the responses (language arts competency). Students had to use a table or graph to present the results of the scaled responses, and identify patterns and similarities within their results and compare their results to their classmates' (math competency). The entire class discussed the inferences of their findings (math competency), and the effectiveness of the interviews (language arts competency) for career exploration (school counseling competency), and the usefulness of interviews for their personal, academic, and professional lives.

Schellenberg and Grothaus (2011) used standards blending while conducting a large-group intervention with four classes of diverse public high school students. Analysis of the school's outcome data revealed that a disproportionate number of students of color and students receiving special education services were not achieving success in language arts and were also not meeting positive behavioral expectations in career and technical education (CTE) classes. The CTE faculty and school counselor decided to implement a Tier 2 response. The lead author conducted four one-hour, large-group lessons that sought to promote the students' employability skills as well as selected language arts and school counseling curriculum standards. Use of paired sample t-tests revealed that the post-test scores were significantly higher than the scores for both the language and school counseling content areas. African American and Latino students made statistically significant gains in both content areas while the students receiving special education services exhibited statistically significant gains for the school counseling curriculum items.

Schellenberg and Grothaus (2009) applied standards blending to a school-based counseling group for six low-achieving third grade African American males in an urban public elementary school. The *"Me I Wanna Be" group* sought to promote participants' self-esteem and identification of cultural strengths to empower the participants and thus facilitate their academic achievement. The group was comprised of four 30-minute sessions. Session 1 involved assigning students into pairs who interviewed each other, and then presented a brief biography of their partner following a discussion of the characteristics of biographies and autobiographies (language arts competency). There was also discussion regarding the importance of friendship and positive relations. The objectives of session 2 were to promote participants' sense of individualism while in connection with others. Participants spent 5–10 minutes talking to each other to acquire information regarding how each student is different and alike. Following the information gathering, students reflected upon the information obtained, comparing and contrasting themselves in relation to the other student, and reported their findings to the group. The goals of session 3 were to increase students' problem-solving skills. They were instructed to select one of three goals listed on the board to accomplish during the session. The goals were to: (1) say something positive to a group member, (2) say something positive to the school counselor, and (3) ask someone for help during the session.

Students were asked to select from a deck of cards, each of which had a goal on one side and the corresponding steps on the other side. They then took turns in sharing the goal and asking group members to identify possible steps to achieve the goal. The cards were pre-selected by the group leader to illustrate the mathematical concept of inverse operations (math competency). The goals of the final session were to teach students how to modify their internal dialogue to enhance their self-efficacy. This internal dialogue, or self-talk, was defined and modeled. The impact of positive vs. negative self-talk was discussed and examples were indicated on 20 individual strips of paper. The strips of paper were described as consisting of a whole and then divided in order to illustrate fractions (math competency). The results indicated that all six students exhibited knowledge development related to both the academic curriculum and school counseling content, and the self-reported self-esteem of the participants increased by 72% from the beginning to the completion of the group.

Schellenberg (2008) argues that standards blending enables school counselors to develop and implement programming which leads them to be viewed by educational personnel as valuable partners in closing the achievement gap and promoting academic achievement, while simultaneously maintaining their unique role of an educational specialist who is also committed to promoting students' personal/social and career development. Schellenberg and Grothaus (2009) suggest that school counselors can train teachers to use standards blending by incorporating students' cultural knowledge and strengths.

Small- and Large-Group Interventions to Promote Social Justice

Many of the responsive interventions conducted by school counselors to reduce the racial achievement gap that can be found in the research literature have involved large-group or group counseling interventions seeking to promote the study skills of minority students. Bruce, Getch, and Ziomek-Daigle (2009) found that eight sessions of a study-skill counseling group with 15 African American eleventh grade students resulted in a reduction in the gap in the pass rate between White students and African American students as well as an overall increase in the pass rate for African American students on the Georgia High School Graduation Tests. The researchers suggest that a group counseling format may be culturally responsive for African American students as it is consistent with the African American community's shared value of connectedness. A group setting may also provide African American students with an opportunity to bond and discuss personal issues while also working toward a shared goal.

Leon, Villares, Brigman, Webb, and Peluso (2011) evaluated the impact of the *Spanish Cultural Translation of Student Success Skills* (SCT-SSS). *Student Success Skills* (SSS) is a study skills program that seeks to provide students with cognitive, social, and self-management skills that the research literature indicates are associated with increased student achievement (Carey, Dimmitt, Hatch, Lapan, & Whiston, 2008). Studies suggest that SSS promotes students' academic achievement, as measured by state achievement tests, but there are questions as to whether students retain the skills promoted within SSS. Five Spanish-speaking school counselors from different countries in Latin America adapted the SSS to match both the language and culture of different Latin American nations. Two bilingual school counselors implemented the SCT-SSS intervention with 62 fourth and fifth grade Latino students in two schools, conducting five SCT-SSS 45-minute classroom lessons once per week for five consecutive weeks, followed by three 45-minute booster sessions in three consecutive months. The results revealed that the students who received the treatment had significantly greater increases in math and reading, as measured by Florida's state achievement test, than a comparison group of fourth and fifth grade Latino students who did not receive the intervention. The effect size for both the math and reading gains was 0.37, which is generally considered to be a small to moderate intervention impact.

Dowden (2009) used a five-session psychoeducational group to teach self-advocacy skills to six African American adolescents attending a large suburban high school in the Southeast, in order to enhance their self-concept and academic motivation. One of the group sessions sought to enhance students' understanding of cultural power and privilege. Students discussed their reactions to portrayals from the media which depicted minority populations in a negative fashion, shared personal experiences of discrimination, and received feedback from group members regarding how they managed the discrimination. In the third group session, the group discussed the components of self-determination, including effective and ineffective ways students could demonstrate self-determination. In the fourth group session, members identified examples of social injustice within their school, and developed plans for addressing the inequity they identified. Follow-up evaluation of the group members revealed that five of the six students exhibited decreases in truancy and behavior problems, and four of the six students passed all of their semester academic classes.

Summary

The school counseling profession has made a clear commitment to advocating for social justice. The examples of social justice interventions involving school counselors provided in this chapter indicate that school counselors contribute to systemic change by collaborating with various stakeholders. It is important for school counselors to recognize that their training in human relations, multiculturalism, group work, etc. possibly situates them as the educational professional best prepared to invoke such systemic interventions. A consistent theme indicated in the professional school counseling literature is that school counselors need to recognize that some people will be resistant to such a challenge to the status quo. School counselors must understand that social justice advocacy requires a long-term commitment.

References

Advancement Via Individual Determination (AVID) (2010). *AVID*. Available online at www.avid.org/ (accessed December 10, 2014).

American Counseling Association (2003). *Advocacy competencies*. Available online at www.counseling.org/docs/competencies/advocacy_competencies.pdf?sfvrsn=3 (accessed December 8, 2014).

American School Counselor Association (2010). *Ethical standards for school counselors*. Available online at www.schoolcounselor.org/files/EthicalStandards2010.pdf (accessed December 10, 2014).

American School Counselor Association (2012). *The ASCA national model: A framework for for school counseling programs* (3rd ed.). Alexandria, VA: Author.

American School Counselor Association (2014). *Mindsets & behaviors for student success: K-12 college- and career-readiness standards for every student*. Alexandria, VA: Author.

Astramovich, R. L., & Harris, K. R. (2007). Promoting self-advocacy among minority students in school counseling. *Journal of Counseling & Development, 85*, 269–276.

Berends, M., Lucas, S. R., & Penaloza, R. V. (2008). How changes in families and schools are related to trends in black-white test scores. *Sociology of Education, 81*, 313–344.

Bolman, L. G., & Deal, T. E. (2008). *Reframing organizations: Artistry, choice, and leadership* (4th ed.). San Francisco: Jossey-Bass.

Borders, L. D., & Shoffner, J. F. (2003). School counselors: Leadership opportunities and challenges in the schools. In J. D. West, C. J. Osborn, & D. L. Bubenzer (Eds.), *Leaders and legacies: Contributions to the profession of counseling* (pp. 51–64). New York: Brunner-Routledge.

Bruce, A. M., Getch, Y. Q., & Ziomek-Daigle, J. (2009). Closing the gap: A group counseling approach to improve test performance of African American students. *Professional School Counseling, 12*, 450–457.

Buzgon, J. W., Wells, D. S., Stephenson, E. R., Berbary, C., Nesson, L., Griffin, A., Crothers, L. M., & Kolbert, J. B. (2014). *Bullying of LGBTQ students in southwestern Pennsylvania.* Poster presented at the Association of School Psychologists of Pennsylvania Fall Conference, State College, PA.

Carey, J. C., Dimmitt, C., Hatch, T. A., Lapan, R. T., & Whiston, S. C. (2008). Report of the National Panel for Evidence-Based School Counseling: Outcome research coding protocol and evaluation of Student Success Skills and Second Step. *Professional School Counseling, 11*, 197–206.

Chambers, T. V. (2009). The "Receivement Gap": School tracking policies and the fallacy of the "Achievement Gap". *Journal of Negro Education, 78*, 417–431.

Chizhik, A. W. (2001). Equity and status in group collaboration: Learning through explanations depends on task characteristics. *Social Psychology of Education, 5*, 179–200.

Cholewa, V., & West-Olatunji, C. (2008). Exploring the relationship among cultural discontinuity, psychological distress, and academic achievement outcomes for low-income, culturally diverse students. *Professional School Counseling, 12*, 54–61.

Clark, M. A., & Breman, J. C. (2009). School counselor inclusion: A collaborative model to provide Academic and social-emotional support in the classroom setting. *Journal of Counseling & Development, 87*(1), 6–11.

College Board (2010). *AP Potential.* Available online at https://appotential.collegeboard.com/welcome.do (accessed December 11, 2014).

College Board (2013). *Program facts: Overview of the AP program.* Available online at http://apreport.collegeboard.org/ap-program-facts (accessed March 15, 2015).

Condron, D. J., Tope, D., Steidl, C. R., & Freeman, K. J. (2013). Racial segregation and the black/white achievement gap, 1992 to 2009. *The Sociological Quarterly, 54*, 130–157.

Constantine, M. G., Hage, S. M., Kindaichi, M. M., & Bryant, R. M. (2007). Social justice and multicultural issues: Implications for the practice and training of counselors and counseling psychologists. *Journal of Counseling & Development, 85*, 24–29.

Dollarhide, C. T. (2003). School counselors as program leaders: Applying leadership contexts to school counseling. *Professional School Counseling, 6*, 304–308.

Dowden, A. R. (2009). Implementing self-advocacy training within a brief psychoeducational group to improve the academic motivation of black adolescents. *The Journal for Specialists in Group Work, 34*, 118–136.

Dowden, A. R. (2010). A personal journey in promoting social justice as a school counselor: An action research approach. *Journal of School Counseling, 8*, 1–23. Available online at http://eric.ed.gov/?id=EJ895901 (accessed October 23, 2015).

DuPraw, M. E., & Axner, M. (1997). Working on common cross-cultural communication challenges. *Toward a more perfect union in age of diversity: A guide to building stronger communities through public dialog.* Study Circles Resource Center. Available online at www.pbs.org/ampu/crosscult.html (accessed December 3, 2014).

Ford, D. Y. (2010). Culturally responsive classrooms: Affirming culturally different gifted students. *Gifted Child Today, 33*, 50–53.

Gay, G. (2006). Connections between classroom management and culturally responsive teaching. In C. M. Everston & C. S. Weinstein (Eds.), *Handbook of classroom management: Research practice and contemporary issues* (pp. 343–370). Mahwah, NJ: Erlbaum.

Herring, R. D., & Salazar, C. (2002). Non-western helping modalities. In J. Trusty, E. J. Looly, & D. S. Sandhu (Eds.), *Multicultural counseling: Context, theory and practice, and competence* (pp. 283–318). New York: NOVA Science Publishers, Inc.

Kolb, D. (1984). *Experiential learning: Experience as the source of learning and development.* Englewood Cliffs, NJ: Prentice Hall.

Ladson-Billings, G. (2006). From achievement gap to the education debt: Understanding achievement in US schools. *Educational Researcher, 35,* 3–12. doi:10.3102/0013189X035007003

Lambie, G. W., & Williamson, L. L. (2004). The challenge to change from guidance counseling to professional school counseling: A historical proposition. *Professional School Counseling, 8,* 124–131.

Leon, A., Villares, E., Brigman, G., Webb, L., & Peluso, P. (2011). Closing the achievement gap of Latina/Latino students: A school counseling response. *Counseling Outcome Research and Evaluation, 2,* 73–86.

Mason, E. C., & McMahon, H. G. (2009). Leadership practices of school counselors. *Professional School Counseling, 13,* 107–115.

McKown, C. (2013). Social equity theory and racial-ethnic achievement gaps. *Child Development, 84,* 1120–1136.

Militello, M., Schweid, J., & Carey, J. C. (2008). *Si se puedes! How educators engage in open, collaborative systems of practice to affect college placement rates of low-income students.* Paper presented at the meeting of the American Educational Research Association, New York.

National Assessment of Educational Progress (NAEP) (2013). *The nation's report card: A first look: 2013 mathematics and reading.* Available online at http://nces.ed.gov/nationsreportcard/pubs/main2013/2014451.aspx#section3 (accessed December 18, 2014).

No Child Left Behind Act of 2001, Pub. L. No. 107–110 (2002).

Ratts, M. J., DeKruyf, L., & Chen-Hayes, S. F. (2007). The ACA advocacy competencies: A social justice advocacy framework for professional school counselors. *Professional School Counseling, 11,* 90–97.

Rowley, R. L., & Wright, D. W. (2011). No "White" child left behind: The academic achievement gap between Black and White students. *The Journal of Negro Education, 80,* 93–107.

Schellenberg, R. (2008). *The new school counselor: Strategies for universal academic achievement.* New York: Rowman & Littlefield Education.

Schellenberg, R., & Grothaus, T. (2009). Promoting cultural responsiveness and closing the academic achievement gap with standards blending. *Professional School Counseling, 12,* 440–449.

Schellenberg, R., & Grothaus, T. (2011). Using culturally competent responsive services to improve student achievement and behavior. *Professional School Counseling, 14,* 222–230.

Schulz, L. L., Hurt, K., & Lindo, N. (2014). My name is not Michael: Strategies for promoting cultural responsiveness in schools. *Journal of School Counseling, 12,* 1–35. Available online at http://eric.ed.gov/?id=EJ1034778 (accessed November 18, 2015).

Singer, J. Y., & Smith, S. A. (2003). The potential of multicultural literature: Changing understanding of self and others. *Multicultural Perspectives, 5,* 17–23.

Singh, A. A., Urbano, A., Haston, M., & McMahon, E. (2010). School counselors' strategies for social justice change: A grounded theory of what works in the real world. *Professional School Counseling, 13,* 135–145.

Stephens, D. L., & Lindsey, R. B. (2011). *Culturally proficient collaboration: Use and misuse of school counselors.* Thousand Oaks, CA: Corwin.

Tatum, B. (1997). *Why are all the Black kids sitting together in the cafeteria? And other conversations about race: A psychologist explains the development of racial identity.* New York: Basic Books.

US Department of Education (2014). *The condition of education 2013.* Available online at http://nces.ed.gov/pubs2013/2013037.pdf (accessed July 9, 2015).

US Department of Education, National Center for Education Statistics (2011). *The condition of education 2011* (NCES 2011–033), Indicator 21.

Young, A. A., Millard, T., & Kneale, M. M. (2013). Enhancing school counselor instructional leadership through collaborative teaming: Implications for principals. *National Association of Secondary School Principals, 97,* 253–269.

Chapter Four
Management and Accountability

Box 4.1

2016 CACREP School Counseling Specialty Area Standards

1.d Models of school-based collaboration and consultation

1.e Assessment specific to P-12 education

2.a School counselor roles as leaders, advocates, and systems change agents in P-12 schools

2.d School counselor roles in school leadership and multidisciplinary teams

3.b Design and evaluation of school counseling programs

3.n Use of accountability data to inform decision-making

3.o Use of data to advocate for programs and students

Accountability has become a major emphasis within primary education over the past several decades. Although the No Child Left Behind (NCLB; 2002) Act has been replaced by the Every Student Succeeds Act (ESSA; US Department of Education, n.d.), the increased emphasis of accountability through assessment instituted by NCLB remains within ESSA and will likely continue. State departments of education are still required to develop "challenging" standards of learning and standardized measurements to assess students' achievement of the standards. Schools must publically report achievement results. There are sanctions for schools that do not meet achievement targets. Schools must continue to evaluate and implement evidence-based interventions for academically underperforming subgroups of students, such as minority or special education students. Many states require that students pass a test to graduate from high school, and a few states even require passing a test in order to be promoted to the next grade level.

The school counseling profession has been significantly impacted by this emphasis on accountability, as the profession seeks to play a more significant role in educational reform and to demonstrate the impact of school counseling-related activities and programs. Whereas in the past, school counselors' use of data was often limited to documenting the number of students or stakeholders who participated in school counseling related activities, the ASCA and the Education Trust's Transforming the School Counseling

The term "principles of scientific research" means the use of rigorous, systematic, and objective methodologies to obtain reliable and valid knowledge. Specifically, such research requires:

A. development of a logical, evidence-based chain of reasoning;
B. methods appropriate to the questions posed;
C. observational or experimental designs and instruments that provide reliable and generalizable findings;
D. data and analysis adequate to support findings;
E. explication of procedures and results clearly and in detail, including specification of the population to which the findings can be generalized;
F. adherence to professional norms of peer review;
G. dissemination of findings to contribute to scientific knowledge; and
H. access to data for reanalysis, replication, and the opportunity to build on findings.

The examination of causal questions requires experimental designs using random assignment or quasi-experimental or other designs that substantially reduce plausible competing explanations for the obtained results. These include, but are not limited to, longitudinal designs, case control methods, statistical matching, or time series analyses. This standard applies especially to studies evaluating the impacts of policies and programs on educational outcomes.

The term "scientifically based research" includes basic research, applied research, and evaluation research in which the rationale, design, and interpretation are developed in accordance with the scientific principles laid out above. The term applies to all mechanisms of federal research support, whether field-initiated or directed.

Figure 4.1 Alternative Definition of Scientifically Based Research (SBR) Supported by AERA Council, July 11, 2008. Copyright 2008 by the American Educational Research Association; reproduced with permission of the publisher (AERA, 2015).

Initiative (TSCI) encourage school counselors to collect data that helps to answer the question, "How are students different as a result of the school counseling program?" The use of data is an integral component of all four components of *the ASCA National Model®* (2012), and even more so for the management and accountability components of *the Model*.

Scientific Based Research

The expectations of accountability for educators can be divided into two primary types: (1) use of Scientific Based Research (SBR) practices, and (2) the use of evaluation. Obviously, there is overlap between these accountability emphases, but there are some important differences as well. NCLB (2002) requires that schools use SBR methods. Although consensus has not yet been reached regarding the procedure for determining what is considered an SBR method, there appears to be general agreement that the process of identifying an educational intervention as SBR involves the use of either randomized experiments or quasi-experiments (Beghetto, 2003). True experimental designs within an educational context involves randomly assigning students, schools, or districts to a group that receives a particular intervention and to a group that either receives a different intervention (comparison group), or no intervention (control group).

Furthermore, to be considered an SBR method, the practice must be replicated in other settings (Beghetto, 2003). NCLB has been criticized as using a narrow definition of SBR, as several forms of qualitative research are not recognized as SBR, including case studies, ethnographies, and action research. Qualitative research methods may be used to develop hypotheses regarding what components of programs are contributing to a program's effectiveness or why a program is working or not working, but they are not considered sufficient for determining whether a program is effective. Other organizations, such as the American Educational Research Association (AERA), have also published descriptions of SBR, which may assist in interpreting the definition of the term (see Figure 4.1).

Box 4.2

Opportunistic Experiment

Did you know?

An opportunistic experiment is a kind of randomized controlled trial that allows the researcher to study the effects of an intervention or policy change with little additional disruption and cost (Resch, Berk, & Akers, 2014).

Experimental research within an educational context seeks to identify a causal relationship, meaning that an intervention was alone responsible for an increase in student achievement (Carey, Dimmitt, Hatch, Lapan, & Whiston, 2008). This involves ruling out plausible explanations as to why the increase occurred, and thus requires "controlling" or keeping constant other variables. There are considerable challenges to conducting experimental research within school settings, as random assignment of subjects to conditions is typically not feasible. Comparison schools/groups will always differ in ways that may potentially impact the outcome measure(s), and also may be reluctant to engage to participate in a research study. Replication is difficult, as teachers and schools are likely to vary in their use of the intervention. It is also cumbersome to use blind conditions given that use of parent and teacher ratings introduces the potential for subjectivity. Finally, the school counseling profession is increasingly emphasizing the use of systemic and comprehensive interventions that seek to impact the school environment as a whole, but it is difficult to control for the variables involved in such all-encompassing interventions.

SBR and School Counseling Interventions

Although much of the research in school counseling does not meet NCLB's definition of research, the profession is making progress in developing evidence-based practices. As discussed in Chapter 1, the Center for School Counseling Outcome Research and Evaluation (CSCORE) formed the National Panel for School Counseling Evidence-Based Practice to increase the research base in the school counseling profession through the establishment of a method for evaluating and identifying practices that are consistent with the NCLB standards for evidence-based practice (Carey et al., 2008). The National Panel concluded that there is strong empirical support for the *Second Step Violence Prevention Curriculum* (Committee for Children, 2004), which is designed to decrease violence through enhanced empathy and social skills and through decreases in aggressive behaviors. Furthermore, the Panel deemed the evidence to be promising for *Student Success Skills* (Brigman & Webb, 2004), which is a group and school counseling lesson approach to promoting metacognitive, social, and self-management skills (Carey et al., 2008).

There is empirical support for common school counselor-led interventions. Whiston, Tai, Rahardja, and Eder (2011) conducted a meta-analytic study of the school counseling intervention literature. Meta-analysis involves aggregating the results of various previous studies by estimating and combining the magnitude of the effect of the intervention, which is referred to as the effect size, in order to identify patterns among study results. The results revealed that, on average, school counseling interventions produced an effect size of 0.30, which is considered to be small to moderate. School counseling lessons, responsive services, small group counseling, and individual planning also yielded small to moderate effect sizes. Parent workshops were found to yield a high effect size, while individual counseling only had a small effect size, but the authors cautioned that there were not enough studies in the literature to reach a firm conclusion regarding the empirical support for these types of school counseling interventions. School counseling interventions appeared to increase students' problem-solving, attendance, and social skills, and resulted in reduced discipline problems and physical aggression, but only had a small impact upon self-esteem. Finally, school counseling interventions yielded a small but significant impact on grade point average and achievement tests, and the authors noted that school counseling interventions are not likely to have a large impact on academic achievement given the large caseloads of school counselors.

A major challenge of the school counseling profession is the need to evaluate the effectiveness of broader, systemic interventions such as *the ASCA National Model®* (2012). Most likely, the school counseling profession will never be able to achieve NCLB's definition of SBR given the near impossibility of using random assignment for school-wide initiatives. However, several studies have used research design methods other than random assignment to control for extraneous variables. Wilkerson, Pérusse, and Hughes (2013) compared schools that had a Recognized ASCA Model Program (RAMP) vs. a randomly selected control group of non-RAMP schools over a four-year period. They found that RAMP schools at the elementary level outperformed the control group on state proficiency scores for math and language arts, but there were no statistically significant differences between RAMP and non-RAMP schools at the middle and high school levels. Furthermore, the longitudinal analysis revealed that the school-wide proficiency scores did not significantly increase or decrease in both RAMP and control schools.

Sink and Stroh (2003) compared elementary school counseling that had comprehensive school counseling programs to a randomly selected control group of elementary schools that lacked comprehensive school counseling programs. These authors found that while the elementary school counselors without comprehensive school counseling had significantly higher achievement test scores than the schools with comprehensive school counseling programs at pre-test, the achievement gap between these groups significantly declined over a period of two to three years. Sink and Stroh (2003) noted that while the magnitude of the impact of comprehensive school counseling programs at the elementary level was not large, the results suggest that comprehensive school programs can significantly increase achievement test scores.

Evaluation

Accountability is not only demonstrated through the use of SBR methods, but is also demonstrated through the use of evaluation. Evaluation has been defined as "the purposeful and systemic collection and analysis of data or information for the purpose of documenting the effectiveness, impact, and outcomes of programs, establishing accountability, and identifying areas needing change and improvement" (Dimmitt, 2009, p. 396). Evaluation and research are similar in that both use the scientific method by establishing a question, developing a hypothesis, analyzing data related to the hypothesis, and forming conclusions from the data. However, evaluation and research differ in terms of the scope of the question being explored, and the sophistication of the methods used to answer the question. Research seeks to establish a universal rule; that an intervention would yield similar results if applied to similar children and settings.

Box 4.3

Evaluations Tell You Whether the Program or Intervention Worked

Questions Answered by an Impact Evaluation

- Did the program accomplish its goals?
- What are the results?
- Is the program or intervention effective in addressing the problem as intended?
- How did the problem improve?
- How did the program or intervention bring about this improvement?

(Paulsen & Dailey, 2002, pp. 2–3)

An example of a research question might be "Is individual planning using Super's Theory of Career Development effective at increasing career decision self-efficacy?" In contrast, evaluation seeks to assess the impact of a program or intervention on students in a particular setting and is not intended to generalize the findings beyond that setting or group of students. An example of a question used in evaluation might be "Is an anger management group conducted by the school counselor in Liberty Middle School effective for a group of six students with externalizing behaviors (e.g., physical and verbal aggression, defiance)?" Because there is no attempt to extend the findings of evaluation beyond the particular setting, evaluation typically does not use some of the design methods associated with research, such as random assignment, follow-up testing, numerous measurements of outcomes, and use of valid and reliable measurements. As well-stated by Dimmitt (2009), evaluation seeks to answer "Did this program or intervention make a difference for these kids in this setting?" (p. 398).

Data-Driven Decision-Making

Data-driven decision-making is related to the concept of evaluation but also has some important differences. Evaluation, for example, can help determine the impact of an intervention, which is sometimes referred to as summative or outcome evaluation (e.g., Dimmitt, 2009). In contrast, data-driven decision-making encompasses this function of evaluation but also involves the use of data to identify the current and future needs of students, assess the differential impact of interventions on different types of students, and offer possible reasons for the causes of problems. Whereas evaluation provides data regarding the effectiveness of an intervention, data-driven decision-making can be used in the planning stage to make more informed decisions about what types of activities to implement, with whom, and how, and also can be used during the process of implementation to make mid-course corrections. Using data to design and modify an intervention during the process of implementing the intervention is commonly referred to as formative evaluation.

The ASCA National Model® (2012) and Evaluation

It can be argued that one of the most significant changes in the school counseling profession in the most recent decades is the increased emphasis on using data. All four components of the ASCA National Model® (2012) emphasize the use of data. While school counselor educators have been collaborating with school counseling practitioners in evaluating the empirical support for school counseling-related activities and the ASCA National Model® (2012), the type of data required of school counseling practitioners following the ASCA National Model® (2012) involves the use of evaluation and data-driven decision making. While the effort to conduct SBR involves the use of complex research designs and inferential statistics, such as Analysis of Variance (ANOVA), required for generalization, data-driven decision-making and evaluation conducted by school counseling practitioners is primarily comprised of descriptive data analysis, such as computing averages, frequencies, percentages, etc.

Use of Data

Within the ASCA National Model® (2012), the use of data is listed as a management tool. School counselors use data for a variety of purposes, including: tracking student progress, identifying students who are having academic or behavior difficulties, evaluating the effectiveness of the components of the school counseling program, changing or modifying the services provided to students, informing stakeholders about the effectiveness and potential of the school counseling program, and providing guidance and justification for additional resources.

Following NCLB's (2002) mandate, school counselors examine disaggregated data to identify potential barriers to learning, including access and equity issues, and to decrease achievement and opportunity gaps. Disaggregated data involves comparing groups of students on a data indicator. For example, a school counselor might compare the percentages of students by race, gender, or socioeconomic (SES) status that are enrolled in Advanced Placement courses to determine if there are inequities in opportunities. School counselors may examine state achievement test data to determine if there are achievement gaps by gender, race, SES status, or language spoken at home. School counselors may also analyze behavioral data to explore whether there are differences between groups in rates of attendance, suspension, discipline, substance use violations, homework completion, and extracurricular participation.

School Data Profile

The School Data Profile is a tool within the Management component of *the ASCA National Model®* (2012). The School Data Profile template identifies for school counselors the important categories of data to collect, as schools may not report in an organized fashion a wide array of data that is most relevant for the school counseling program. For achievement indicators, school counselors are encouraged to collect disaggregated data on rates of graduation, promotion and retention, and dropouts. Standardized test data often includes the proficiency levels for the state achievement tests by subject area (e.g., reading, math, science, etc.), the number of students at or above grade level for achievement tests (e.g., *Iowa Test of Basic Skills*), and SAT/ACT and Advanced Placement (AP) exam scores. Other academic indicators could be grade point average and enrollment in advanced courses (e.g., AP, honors, International Baccalaureate, college preparation).

The School Data Profile also includes behavioral data for indicators that research has identified as being related to academic achievement, which include the rates of discipline referrals, suspension, substance use violations, attendance, course enrollment, postsecondary education, homework completion, etc. Analysis of behavioral data may identity possible reasons for low academic achievement or gaps in academic achievement. For example, a high number of discipline referrals may indicate poor teacher-student relations, or gaps between racial groups in terms of the number of discipline referrals may indicate a need for enhanced training of staff. Low attendance or gaps between groups in attendance could be due to various reasons, including difficulties in transportation, students' difficulty in seeing the importance of school for their future, etc. In summary, analysis of behavioral data can help school counselors develop hypotheses regarding the reasons for low academic achievement.

Collection of additional data can help further explore the likelihood of hypotheses. School counselors can collect and analyze data concerning the types of issues for which students were referred for discipline. School counselors may conduct focus groups with teachers, students, and additional stakeholders to obtain their perceptions and suggestions for enhancing the functioning of the school. Whereas in past decades school counselors would often conduct needs assessments, which involved surveying students, teachers, parents, and other stakeholders regarding the focus of the school counseling program and the services provided, today, the development of a school counseling program also includes academic and behavioral data. The School Data Profile can identify potential areas for intervention, and analysis of the data collected for the profile over time can be used to identify the impact of the school counseling program.

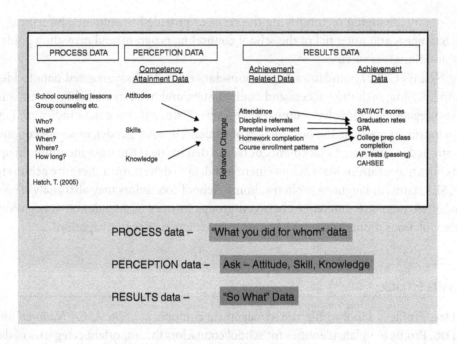

Figure 4.2 Review of ASCA Model's Types of Data. Reprinted with permission from ASCA. ASCA Working Group (2012). *ASCA model and creating pre-post surveys to measure perception data (ASK)*. Available online at www.slideshare.net/shashley14/asca-perception-data-surveys.

Types of Data Within *the ASCA National Model®* (2012)

The ASCA National Model® (2012) requires school counselors to collect three types of data: process, perception, and outcome data, to evaluate the impact of the school counseling program (see Figure 4.2). Process data involves a description of the types of activities provided to whom. Examples of process data include:

- all the sixth grade students received four 45-minute classroom lessons on anger management;
- twenty parents of eleventh grade students attended an hour-long presentation regarding financial aid options;
- fifteen ninth grade students who failed two or more academic subjects in the preceding marking period participated in a study skills group comprised of six 45-minute sessions.

Process data is generally considered a necessary but insufficient form of data because it does not indicate how such activities impacted the participants.

Perception data refers to identifying how participants believe they have been impacted by a school counseling activity. Perception data may take various forms. School counselors may conduct pre- and post-tests of students receiving school counseling classroom lessons and small group counseling sessions to assess changes in participants' competencies, attitudes or beliefs, or knowledge. Assessing changes in students' perceived competence may include comparing the average number of strategies student participants identified prior to the start of a small group or series of school counseling classroom lessons on such topics as study skills, conflict resolution, anger management, and bullying to the average number of strategies identified by participating students upon completion of the school counseling activity.

Other variables that may be assessed in this fashion include the average number of variables considered in exploring a college/university, opportunities for financial aid, the number of careers within a career cluster, etc. An example of how the school counselor could report such a finding would be: "Before the implementation of the classroom lessons concerning selecting a college, students on average identified 1.4 variables they were considering, whereas at post-test, the average number of variables identified by participating students was 3.4." Student competency may also be assessed in terms of self-efficacy, which refers to students' degree of confidence in completing a respective task/issue. Bandura (2006), who created the term "self-efficacy," identified a variety of self-efficacy beliefs related to adolescents' confidence in using social resources (e.g., "Get teachers to help me when I get stuck on schoolwork"), engaging in self-regulated learning (e.g., "Get myself to study when there are other interesting things to do"), relating to peers (e.g., "Work well in a group"), and self-assertion (e.g., "Stand up for myself when I feel I am being treated unfairly"). His assessment involves asking students to rate their confidence on a 100-point scale in engaging in such tasks. Bandura's self-efficacy scale could be used as both a screener to identify students in need of more intensive services, and as an indicator of change/progress.

School counselors can also measure students' actual competencies, as opposed to students' perceived competencies. For example, a school counselor might instruct eleventh grade students in job interviewing skills in small group counseling sessions. The school counselor could have the participating students conduct a simulated role-play of a job interview, and could assess the students' use of the job interview skills either by observing the simulation or even analyzing a video of the simulation. The results could be reported as, "80% of the eleventh grade students effectively used at least four of the job interview skills taught at least at a standard level of performance within the mock job interview." This example implies that the school counselor developed a rubric that provided an explicit description of performance at the standard and below the standard level (a rubric for a mock job interview is provided in the below section on Authentic/performance assessment). Other examples of what is referred to as performance-based assessments include assessing students' mastery of conflict resolution skills, using a college search tool such as the College Board, use of a particular study skills method, and so forth.

Gains in knowledge can either include a pre-post assessment comparison or an assessment at the completion of a school counseling activity. An example of a change in knowledge using a pre- and post-assessment is: "Prior to the beginning of the three classroom lessons on conflict resolution, 42% of the seventh grade students were able to identify at least two strategies for effectively managing conflict, whereas at the completion of the lessons, 81% of the participating students were able to identify at least two strategies for effectively managing conflict." An example of just using a post-assessment of knowledge is: "At the completion of the six-session study skills group, 75% of students were able to correctly identify the terms of the SQ3R reading method."

Outcome data may be considered a more valid form of assessment by stakeholders because it indicates how students' participation in school counseling-related activities (process data), and changes in attitudes, competencies, and knowledge (perception data), impact performance on standardized achievement tests and behavioral indicators. The ASCA National Model® (2012) distinguishes between outcome data related to achievement, attendance, and behaviors; all three types of outcome data can be reported in various forms. For example, Cook and Kaffenberger (2003) analyzed the impact of a counseling group that used solution-focused theory with academically at-risk students by indicating the percentage of participating students whose grade point average (GPA) decreased, remained the same, or improved following the implementation of the group. Changes in the graduation rate for an entire grade may be reported, or the graduation rate of students participating in a school counseling-related activity, such as a group, can be compared to the graduation rate for the rest of the grade.

The impact of school counseling activities on standardized tests, such as respective state assessment tests or other standardized achievement tests, can be reported in terms of changes in the average score or the percentage of students who achieved a rating at the proficient or advanced levels. Some school counselors will track the progress of students for whom they provided individual and group counseling, and compare their scores on standardized achievement tests with those of students who did not receive school counseling-related services. For example, a school counselor could compare the changes in the percentile rank (the percentage of scores in its frequency distribution that are the same or lower) for students participating in a school counseling-led study skills group versus the rest of the students in the grade. Such a comparison could be reported in the following manner:

> The average percentile rank for the reading scale of the *Iowa Test of Basic Skills (ITBS)* for the 16 students who participated in the eight-session study skills group increased from the 38th percentile rank to the 44th percentile rank between grades 7 and 8, whereas the rest of the grade decreased one percentile rank between grades 7 and 8.

Rates of attendance and discipline referrals can also be evaluated in terms of the changes in their percentages for the entire grade, or changes in students who participated in a school counseling-related program. Such changes can then be compared to the rest of the grade. While the collection of data may at first appear to be time-consuming, much of the standardized data is available to school counselors in the school's student information system.

In summary, while process and perception data may prove to be useful to school counselors in assessing the impact of school counseling-related activities, stakeholders are more likely to evaluate the school counseling program as a whole in terms of its ability to impact outcome data. School counselors should use process and perception data to modify school counseling activities, but should be mindful of the greater importance of implementing activities that are likely to impact the outcome data.

Accountability Identification and Reporting

The *ASCA National Model*® (2012) has three types of results reports: curriculum, small-group, and closing-the-gap. The *ASCA National Model*® (2012) identifies guiding questions that assist school counselors in analyzing the results of these three types of action plans. The next step in the accountability process is to share the results of the data analysis to stakeholders in a manner that enables them to understand the impact of the school counseling program. There are a number of different evaluation programs available to school counselors for sharing results with stakeholders. MEASURE is one of the most common approaches used by school counselors to analyze and disseminate the results of school counseling activities (Stone & Dahir, 2010). This six-step process stands for: Mission, Elements, Analyze, Stakeholders-Unite, Results, and Educate. One of the examples we will use to elucidate the MEASURE process is an intervention to improve students' scores on a state's academic achievement tests.

Step 1 – Mission. The goals and activities of the school counseling program should readily relate to the academic mission of the school (Stone & Dahir, 2010). Academic outcome indicators may include the following:

- scores on standardized tests such as the state achievement tests, SAT, or ACT;
- grades for a marking period or number of subjects passed; enrollment patterns in Advanced Placement (AP), International Baccalaureate (IB), and/or honors classes;
- rates regarding graduation, retention, promotion/dropout; acceptance to postsecondary institutions; number of visits to postsecondary institutions;
- the number of variables identified in exploring a career/college.

School counseling activities/interventions that are not necessarily concerned with promoting an academic behavior, such as in the case of a social skills group or series of lessons on bullying prevention, should still use academic outcome indicators, in addition to indicators that are more directly linked to the objectives of the activity. Outcome indicators that may be relevant for school counseling-related interventions that concern social/emotional development include:

- discipline referrals
- suspension rates
- attendance patterns
- participation rates in mediation
- extracurricular activity participation
- standardized measurements assessing a psychological construct, such as self-esteem, self-efficacy, emotional intelligence, attitudes toward the use of violence, depression, anxiety, happiness, etc.

Career-oriented activities could include such outcome indicators as:

- the number of variables students consider in selecting a career
- the ability to identify career clusters
- patterns in the use of a school's career resource center, and standardized measures of career maturity.

Step 2 – Elements. School improvement plan committees identify data elements that can be analyzed to indicate areas for improvement, and one way school counselors can demonstrate leadership is through participation in the school's improvement plan (Stone & Dahir, 2010). Important data elements can often be found on the district's or school's report card, which are coordinated by the state as part of the requirements of the NCLB (2002). Furthermore, school systems also collect and house academic and demographic data, and often school counselors have ready access to such data as attendance/tardies, discipline referrals, etc. Analysis of the data must include disaggregation of a variety of categories that are required by NCLB (2002), which include, among other variables, race, gender, economic disadvantage, special education, English as a Second Language (ESL) learners, etc.

Step 3 – Analyze. This step involves analyzing the data elements to identify which areas are in need of redress. A review of the disaggregated data may reveal gaps between respective groups, thus indicating which group may require targeting in order to increase the respective indicator. Table 4.1 provides the percentage of students at a fictitious school who scored either at the advanced or proficiency level of a state's achievement test in math and reading.

In Table 4.1, there are achievement gaps between White and Black students, and between grade levels. Data only provides a picture of what is occurring, but does not explain the why, meaning the variables that may contribute to the achievement gap. Often, contextual variables are important in helping to identify potential causes for such gaps. In other words, the school counselor can ask herself or himself, what is it about the school environment that may contribute to the existence of such disparities? For example, helpful questions may include: Is there a lack of understanding of multiculturalism among the staff? Are there differences in how staff relate to White vs. Black students? Are there differences between the level of parental involvement between White and Black parents? The identification of gaps often reveals that additional information may need to be collected and analyzed. For example, the school counselor could attempt to determine if there are differential patterns in discipline referrals between White and Black students, or in the involvement of White vs. Black parents, etc.

Table 4.1 Percentage of Students Scoring at the Proficient and Advanced Levels for Math and Reading on the State Achievement Test at Jane Doe Elementary School

Grade	Group	Number of Students	% Advanced & Proficient in Math	% Advanced or Proficient in Reading
3	All students	70	71.4	68.6
3	Economically disadvantaged	58	70.0	67.1
3	Male	36	80.5	69.4
3	Female	34	61.8	67.7
3	White	22	86.4	86.4
3	Black	40	67.5	75.0
4	All students	72	75.0	58.3
4	Economically disadvantaged	57	71.9	54.4
4	Male	35	71.4	57.2
4	Female	37	78.3	59.4
4	White	19	84.2	68.4
4	Black	46	67.3	47.9
5	All students	71	63.4	71.8
5	Economically disadvantaged	53	60.3	66.0
5	Male	37	67.5	70.3
5	Female	34	58.8	73.5
5	White	28	67.8	71.4
5	Black	36	52.8	72.2

While much of the statistical analysis conducted by school counselors can be done through Microsoft Excel, there are a number of commercially available statistical programs designed for school counselors. *EZAnalyze* enhances the capabilities of Microsoft Excel through "point and click" functionality to determine percentage change and percentile rank, and to disaggregate data. The *Time Elapsed Analysis & Reporting System (TEARS)* is a Microsoft Excel add-in that automatically calculates the total amount of time school counselors devote to particular activities, and the *School Counselor Use of Time Analysis (SCUTA)* is a smartphone app that provides the same purpose.

Step 4 – Stakeholders-Unite. This step involves identifying stakeholders with whom to collaborate in addressing the critical data elements, including both internal community members (e.g., administrators, teachers, school board members), and external community members (e.g., parents, faith-based groups). If possible, an existing school committee should be used, such as the school improvement team, data team, grade team, etc. In collaborating with the team of stakeholders, an action plan for improving the selected data elements should be developed. The plan should include strategies, a timeline, and responsibilities for achieving a selected target. A targeted goal of the data presented in Table 4.2 could be to increase by four percentile points the number of Black students who achieve proficiency or advanced levels for the state's math and reading achievement tests.

Step 5 – Results. This step involves refining the action plan and strategies developed to achieve the goal. The stakeholders must reconvene to identify what aspects of the plan they believe were effective, based on analysis of the data, which interventions appear to be effective, which require modification, and which should be discarded.

Step 6 – Educate. It is crucial that schools educate both internal and external stakeholders about the results of school counseling-related activities in order to demonstrate that school counselors and the school counseling program are vital contributors to the school's educational mission and to exhibit accountability. School counselors should use visual depictions of data in the form of graphs and charts to clearly indicate the impact of initiatives. For example, Figure 4.3 illustrates how the school counselor in

Table 4.2 Stakeholders-Unite Plan to Develop Strategies to Increase the State Achievement Test Scores of All Students and Reduce the Achievement Gap between Black and White Students

Start Date:	September
End Date:	June
Stakeholders	Strategies
School Counselors	– Implemented the *Student Success Skills* curriculum (Brigman & Webb, 2004) in group counseling sessions to all fourth and fifth grade students who did not achieve advanced or proficient levels in either math or reading the previous year
	– Arranged for presentations by community members, including African American members, regarding how education assists them in their postsecondary training and their current occupation
	– Coordinated college pride week in which teachers and community volunteers wore the t-shirts and baseball caps of their college in order to help students understand the relationship between academic achievement and college readiness
	– Provided training for teachers in using solution-focused strategies in consulting parents, including discussion of how to develop rapport with African American parents, during in-service day
	– Coordinated a mentoring/tutoring program with local colleges and universities, training the mentors in active listening and tutoring skills
Teachers	– Used standards-based instructional practices to improve skill attainment, including inquiry and problem-solving, collaborative learning, continual assessment embedded in instruction, and higher order questioning (March, 2003)
	– Used improvement-focused teacher evaluation systems, including measuring effective teaching (setting expectations, using multiple measures, and giving 33 to 50% of decision-making weight to student achievement measures), ensuring high-quality data (monitoring validity, ensuring reliability, and assuring accuracy), and investing in improvement (making meaningful decisions, prioritizing support and feedback, and using data for decisions at all levels; Bill and Melinda Gates Foundation, 2013)
Administrators	– Provided funding for training for the mentoring/tutoring program
	– Reorganized several consultation rooms to provide space for the mentoring/tutoring activities
Clerical Staff	– Assisted in the scheduling of the mentoring/tutoring program
Business Partners	– Served as speakers regarding the importance of education for postsecondary training and occupations
Colleges and Universities	– Hosted "College for a Day" programs for fifth grade students
	– Provide mentors for African American students

the scenario depicted in Tables 4.4 and 4.5 could use a bar graph to inform stakeholders of the results of one of the school counseling activities identified in the Stakeholders-Unite Plan.

As Figure 4.3 reveals, the hypothetical application of the *Student Success Skills* (SSS) curriculum to the fourth and fifth grade students who did not achieve a passing score on either of the state's math or reading achievement tests during the previous year appeared to have a positive impact on the students' scores. The school counselor in this hypothetical situation could have also elected to report the mean of the student scores or the total percentage of the grade who achieved a passing score. The results of such programs should be listed on the school counseling program's webpage, and may also be disseminated at public forums such as school board and parent-teacher association (PTA) meetings and newsletters.

Measuring the Impact of School Counseling Activities

As previously mentioned, *the ASCA National Model*® (2012) recommends that school counselors use three types of data to measure the impact of school counseling activities: process, perception, and outcome. With the advent of NCLB (2002), there are many forms of outcome data that are available in schools, including standardized test scores, attendance and graduation rates, and behavioral data, such as office discipline referrals and suspensions. Outcome data is considered to be the most valid form of

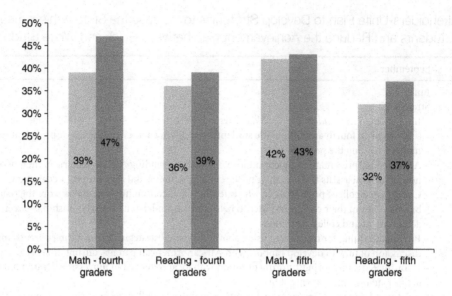

Figure 4.3 Graph Showing the Change in the Percentile Rank on the Math and Reading State Achievement Tests for the Fourth and Fifth Grade Students Who Received the *Student Success Skills* (SSS) Curriculum (Brigman & Webb, 2004).

data and is thus the most likely to influence stakeholders. School counselors should always attempt to use outcome data as indicators for school counseling-related activities.

Outcome data can be regarded as summative data in that it is an indicator of the overall impact of a school counseling-related activity. However, educators also may wish to have more immediate feedback to determine the effectiveness of a single lesson or a group counseling session. Perception data, which in *the ASCA National Model®* (2012) is defined as people's perceptions regarding what they know or can do, can be seen as a type of formative data in that it provides school counselors with information immediately following a school counseling activity. School counselors can use perception data as an indicator of the effectiveness of a school counseling activity, and can also use the data to make mid-course adjustments. For example, if a school counselor is conducting three lessons on career development with ninth grade students and after the first lesson determines that only 32% of the students can name more than one career cluster, the school counselor can cover the material in greater depth and use different and more effective instructional activities for the next lesson. If a school counselor is conducting a group on social skills, analysis of questions regarding the content knowledge students received is likely to be more helpful in modifying the intervention.

Establishing Objectives

The first step of assessment is determining the objectives. Dimmitt, Carey, and Hatch (2007) outline a series of questions that guide the development of objectives. The first question is: What do we want students to know or be able to do following the school counseling activity? The learning outcomes should be connected to ASCA's *Mindsets & Behaviors for Student Success* (2014) and state curriculum standards for academic content areas. Students should be informed of the learning outcomes. The second question determines how students' learning can be measured. What do students currently know? Is there data in the system that helps us determine what students know? What method(s) of assessment should be used to indicate learning?

Common Methods of Assessment used by School Counselors

There are many methods that can be used to measure student learning. This section explores some of the more common methods used by school counselors.

Existing assessment tools. Increasingly, commercially available curricula include assessments, but they are not necessarily well developed and may need to be revised to match the developmental level and/or language capabilities of the students (Dimmitt et al., 2007). Although many school counselors do not currently use standardized measurements, other than the academic and behavioral measurements that are used by schools, the increased emphasis on accountability suggests that at some point, standard practice will involve the more frequent use of objective measurements for school counseling-specific activities. For example, school counselors may regularly use a standardized measurement of career development, such as the *Career Decision-Making System-Revised* (O'Shea & Harrington, 2003), or the *Young Adult Social Behavior Scale* (*YASB*; Crothers, Schreiber, Field, & Kolbert, 2009) to measure changes in students' use of social and relational aggression.

Scales. Likert-type scales, which assess agreement (5 = strongly agree) or disagreement (1 = strongly disagree) on a 4- or 5-point scale, are commonly used.

Box 4.4

Did you know?

The Likert scale is named after its inventor, Rensis Likert, who developed it during his doctoral research. Likert demonstrated, with empirical comparisons, that his "much simpler method (asking the respondent to place himself on a scale of favor/disfavor with a neutral midpoint) gave results very similar to those of the much more cumbersome (though more theoretically elegant) Thurstone procedure (based on the psychophysical method of equal-appearing intervals)" (Kish, 1982, p. 124).

Bandura (2006) recommends the measurement of self-efficacy, which refers to people's perceptions of their ability to perform a task, as self-efficacy has been found to be a fairly reliable indicator of performance. Bandura (2006) has developed self-efficacy questions for a variety of domains, and Likert-scale questions can be used to assess these self-efficacy domains. One domain is self-efficacy for self-regulated learning, which has such assessments as, "I feel confident that I can finish my homework assignment by the deadline," and, "I feel confident that I can arrange a place to study without distractions." Example questions for the domain of social self-efficacy include, "I feel confident that I can work well in a group," and, "I feel confident that I can make and keep friends of the opposite sex."

A different type of scale is response choice, in which the scale items include all of the possible range of answers. Dimmitt et al. (2007) provide the following example of a response choice question: "How much time, on average, do you spend on homework every day?" (p. 122). The choices for this question include: "1: More than 2 hours," "2: Between 1–2 hours," "3: Between 30 minutes and 1 hour," "4: Less than 30 minutes, more than none," and "5: none" (p. 122).

Some important guidelines should be used when developing surveys that employ scales. In order to maintain students' attention and increase the likelihood that they will complete the survey and future surveys, surveys should use the least number of questions to obtain the information that is sought. The questions must be age-appropriate. Surveys for kindergarten through second grade students should use a two- or three-point scale involving visuals for the response choices: a frowning face for no, a smiling face for yes, and a confused face for not sure. Surveys should use parallel language and response choices as much as possible. Other common problems in survey construction involve questions that include more than two issues, which are referred to as "double-barreled questions." The following is an example of a double-barreled question: Identify if you agree or disagree with the following statement: "My friends and I have an equal amount of control in our relationships. I sometimes talk about other people when I'm angry with them but that doesn't happen often." This question should be separated to make two questions. Survey designers should have colleagues and students of the age group who will receive the survey review it to assess the reading level and clarity of the questions.

Authentic/performance assessment. Authentic or performance-based assessments involve having students apply acquired knowledge, often referred to as skill development (Dimmitt et al., 2007). It can be argued that having students apply knowledge is a more valid form of assessment than assessments that merely ask students to identify a correct answer or assess students' ability in using newly acquired knowledge. Dimmitt et al. (2007) provide the following examples of skill-based assessment that may be relevant for school counseling activities: completing a job application, financial aid form, or a four-year plan of study; calculating grade point average, portfolios, PowerPoint or audiovisual presentations of information students have learned in their career exploration; and using their assignment/agenda planner. Other authentic assessments include various types of role-playing (e.g., job interview, using communication skills for negotiating conflict) and uses of technology (e.g., using at least three variables in a search engine to learn about colleges, etc.). The difficulty with authentic assessments is that student performance must be rated, typically through the use of a rubric, and the rating process and the development of the rubric require a significant time investment. Table 4.3 provides an example of a rubric for a performance assessment of responding to job interview questions.

Multiple-choice questions. The advantages of using multiple-choice questions are that they are easy to score and they allow for ready pre-post-test comparisons. However, one of the challenges with constructing multiple-choice questions that are to be used for measuring change between the pre- and post-test is achieving an appropriate level of difficulty. The questions should not be so obvious as to enable most students to answer the question correctly prior to the lesson. The questions must also be directly connected to the instruction. Multiple-choice questions can be designed to assess factual knowledge or the ability to apply knowledge. An example of a factual-based multiple-choice question would be asking students to identify how many credits they need to graduate from high school, the different types of financial aid available for postsecondary education, or the definition of what constitutes a college preparatory course (Dimmitt et al., 2007). While performance-authentic based assessment may be a more valid way to measure students' mastery of a skill, multiple-choice questions can also attempt to assess students' ability to recognize the accurate application of concepts, skills, etc. Examples of application-based multiple-choice questions include identifying an example of the use of a particular study skill or anger management technique. Application-based multiple-choice questions do not ensure that the student will use the skill or method but at least they assess students' ability to identify accurate examples of the application of the skill or method. In Table 4.4, sample learning goals, the related Behavior Standards from *ASCA's Mindsets & Behaviors* (2014), and corresponding pre- and post-test questions are provided.

The School Counselor's Role in Accountability within School-wide Positive Behavioral Intervention and Support (SWPBIS)

As discussed in Chapter 1: History and Trends in the School Counseling Profession and Chapter 12: Helping Students with Exceptionalities, schools are increasingly implementing Response to Intervention (RtI) to identify and remediate academic and behavioral deficits. While the role of school counselors in addressing

Table 4.3 Rubric for Job Interview Performance

Question/Indicator	Below the standard	Approaching the standard	Meets the standard	Exceeds the standard
Talks about strengths and interests	Does not mention any strengths/interests	Mentions several strengths/interests but they are not directly related to the job/duty	Mentions at least two strengths/interests and they are related to the job/duty	Mentions at least two strengths/interests that are related to the job/duty and provides examples of strengths/interests
Explains how they would deal with customers	Fails to answer the question	Identifies a strategy/approach but they are not appropriate to the job/duty	Identifies at least two strategies/approaches that are appropriate to the job/duty	Identifies at least two relevant strategies/approaches and provides an example of how they would apply
Gives an example of a time they worked well with others/ "team player"	Fails to answer the question	Example provided is not highly related to job/duty	Provides at least two relevant examples	Provides at least two relevant examples and relates the examples to strengths/interests
Communication skills	Failed to use oral communication skills (e.g., clear speech) or effective body language (e.g., intermittent eye contact, faced interviewer, appropriate posture)	Used effective communication skills (e.g., clear speech) or effective body language (e.g., intermittent eye contact, faced interviewer, appropriate posture)	Used effective communication skills (e.g., clear speech) and effective body language (e.g., intermittent eye contact, faced interviewer, appropriate posture)	Used effective communication skills (e.g., clear speech) or effective body language (e.g., intermittent eye contact, faced interviewer, appropriate posture) and also demonstrated active listening skills (e.g., paraphrased interview, asked open-ended questions)

academic deficits in the RtI model is unclear, it is evident that school counselors can play a vital role in the behavioral domain of RtI. The behavioral component of RtI is referred to as SWPBIS. In order to be viewed as valuable members of the school behavior team, school counselors must use data to contribute to the data-driven decision-making process in RtI and SWPBIS (Gruman & Hoelzen, 2011). This section examines some of the different approaches for school counselors in collecting student behavioral data.

Universal Screens

In SWPBIS, data must be collected at the universal level in order to determine the effectiveness of the school's approach to ensuring that students meet behavioral expectations, and to identify students who may be in need of additional services. Some commonly used assessment methods at the universal level include office discipline referrals (ODRs) and multiple-gate screening systems (Kalberg, Lane, & Menzies, 2010).

Office discipline referrals (ODRs). An ODR is a checklist of behavioral concerns that school personnel use to refer a student for violation of a school's code of conduct. Many schools input ODR information into the student information system, which a school counselor can access to determine which students have been receiving a large number of infractions (Gruman & Hoelzen, 2011). The data can be useful for

Table 4.4 Sample Learning Goals and Related Pre- and Post-questions

1. Learning Goal (sixth grade)	Students will understand the strategies of effective communication in working as a group member.
ASCA Behavior Standard	Uses effective oral and written communication skills and listening skills. (SS-1)
Question	Which of the following is the correct definition of paraphrasing? a. Apologizing b. Telling a person how to think/feel about something c. Stating back to another person in your own words what you believe another person has said*
2. Learning Goal (eighth grade)	Students will learn the SSCD method of learning new vocabulary while reading.
ASCA Behavior Standard	Use time-management, organization, and study skills (LS-3)
Question	When encountering a new word, Jennifer attempts to understand the meaning of the word by looking for clues in the surrounding passages. In the Sound, Structure, Context, and Dictionary (SSCD) method of learning new vocabulary while reading, this is an example of which of the following? a. Sound b. Structure c. Context* d. Dictionary
3. Learning Goal (sixth grade)	Students will learn to use the SMART goal format in setting goals.
ASCA Behavior Standard	Identify long- and short-term academic, career and social/emotional goals (LS-7)
Question	Which of the following is an example of a goal that is specific, measurable, attainable, realistic, and timely (SMART)? a. I will increase my grade in Language Arts from an "C" to a "B" for the next marking period.* b. I will get better grades. c. All my grades will increase from "Ds" to "As" for the next marking period.
4. Learning Goal (ninth grade)	Students will know how to think rationally to manage their anger.
ASCA Behavior Standard	Demonstrate self-discipline and self-control (SMS-2)
Question	Which of the following is an example of replacing self-talk with more rational self-talk? a. I cannot believe my sister, she always takes my clothes, and never thinks of what I want. b. My mother needs to solve this problem for us. c. I am angry at my sister. I wish she did not borrow my shirt when I planned to wear it today. I wonder if she is mad about me borrowing her shirt last week?* d. My sister needs to never come in my room again.
5. Learning Goal (ninth grade)	Students will learn cognitive and behavioral self-motivation strategies.
ASCA Behavior Standard	Demonstrate ability to delay immediate gratification for long-term rewards
Question	Which of the following is an example of the use of a self-reinforcement strategy? a. Miguel helps Jennifer with her homework. b. Miguel always completes his homework at the library. c. Miguel starts his homework after watching television for several hours. d. After Miguel completes his math homework, he responds to texts for 15 minutes before starting his foreign language homework.*

developing a list for the school behavioral team and identifying systems-wide trends. However, ODRs are not used to monitor individual student progress for several reasons. First, ODRs generally do not have a high degree of reliability, as teachers often have different expectations for student behavior, refer students inconsistently, and their referrals may be influenced by cultural bias (Shores, 2009). Second, while ODRs have been found to be a reliable indicator of externalizing problem behaviors (McIntosh, Campbell, Carter, Russell, & Zumbo, 2009), defined as disruptive, aggressive, and defiant behaviors, they are not effective in identifying students who may be experiencing internalizing behaviors, which include extreme shyness, anxiety, withdrawal, and depressive symptoms.

Multiple-gate universal screening. Multiple-gate universal screening involves several steps of assessments. The first step in the assessment process is the use of a broad screener to identify at-risk students, whether it be for academic, behavioral, or emotional difficulties. Those students who are identified as being at risk then receive a more intensive, reliable assessment. There are a number of commercially available multiple-gate universal screening programs that are considered psychometrically sound. At the elementary and middle/junior high school levels, screening programs are typically used to identify students who exhibit internalizing and externalizing behaviors (Kalberg et al., 2010). At the high school level, screening procedures such as *Signs of Suicide* (Aseltine & DeMartino, 2004) have been used to identify suicide risk.

Maloney's (2015) use of a multiple-gate screening procedure in the four elementary schools in Hempfield Area School District (Pennsylvania) will be described as an example of the multiple-gate assessment process and the role of school counselors in providing services to students who are identified through this process. In the first stage of the assessment process, teachers use the *Systematic Screening for Behavior Disorders* (SSBD; Walker & Severson, 1992) to rank all students for internalizing and externalizing behaviors. The behavior of the three students who receive the highest ratings for internalizing and externalizing behaviors are then measured using the *Walker Assessment Scale/Walker Survey Instrument* (WAS/WSI; Walker & McConnell, 1988). The third gate in the Hempfield Area School District involves a review of data in the following areas over a nine-week period: office disciplinary referrals (two or more), non-emergency visits to the nurse (four or more), attendance (six or more absences), and behavior grades on the most recent report card (25% of scores indicate "needs improvement"). Students who receive the threshold score on the WAS/WSI, and who meet at least one other of the criteria listed above, are then referred to Tier 2 intervention.

If the parent provided consent, students in the Tier 2 intervention participated in the *Behavior Education Program* (BEP), which is also known as Check-In/Check-Out (CICO). In CICO, students receive daily monitoring and feedback through the use of a daily behavior report card (DBRC) to assess students' progress in meeting the school-wide expectations for Tier 1. Each morning, the student "checks-in" with his or her assigned adult facilitator, then takes the DBRC to each class and receives feedback and reinforcement from the teacher using a point system. At the conclusion of the school day, the student "checks-out" with his or her adult facilitator and takes the form home to be reviewed by a parent/guardian (Crone, Hawken, & Horner, 2010). In the Hempfield Area School District elementary schools, the school counselor is the students' assigned CICO adult facilitator.

Maloney (2015) conducted a study comparing the effectiveness of BEP/CICO to small group social skills training, which is another commonly used Tier 2 intervention for students exhibiting behavioral deficits. Students who were identified through the multiple-gate screening procedure were randomly assigned to either the BEP/CICO program or a social skills training group that used the *Strong Kids Curriculum* (Merrell, Carrizales, Feuerborn, Gueldner, & Tran, 2007). The *Strong Kids Curriculum* is designed to promote students' social and emotional competence, and the topics of the curriculum include: understanding feelings, managing anger and stress, understanding others' feelings, clear and positive thinking, problem-solving. The students assigned to the *Strong Kids Curriculum* met once a week with their school counselor for thirty-minute sessions over an eight-week period. In each session, previous skills were reviewed, after which the students role-played new skills.

Students in both the BEP/CICO group and the *Strong Kids Curriculum* social skills training group showed significant behavioral improvements upon completion of the program (Maloney, 2015). At a four-month follow-up, students who received the social skills training showed continued improvement from the post-test, and outperformed the students who received the BEP/CICO, whose behavioral gains were maintained but did not increase from the initial post-test. Students who were identified as those with externalizing behavior problems exhibited greater behavioral gains than those with internalizing behavior problems at the four-month follow-up point. The school counselors reported that they perceived the BEP/CICO and *Strong Kids Curriculum* social skills training group to be programs that could be feasibly implemented within the school setting and were within the scope of their role as school counselors. For the BEP/CICO, the four school counselors achieved an average fidelity rating of 84.5%, with 80% being considered an acceptable rating (Horner et al., 2004). For the *Strong Kids Curriculum*, the school counselors averaged a 95.4% satisfaction rating, again compared to an 80% target.

Observation Methods

Gruman and Hoelzen (2011) encourage school counselors to use behavioral observations to determine the effectiveness of services provided within SWPBIS. Anecdotal and interval observations can be used to identify the severity of a child's problem; communicate with school personnel, parents, and any external professionals assisting the child; and assess changes following the implementation of an intervention.

Anecdotal observations. In anecdotal observations of behavior, an observer records all the behaviors and interactions that occur during a specified period of time. A "time-stamp" is used to note behavioral changes by the student or environment changes.

Box 4.5

Anecdotal observations

8:45 Listening attentively to other students as they presented their book reports.

9:20 Talked out ("This sucks") while doing morning seat work in which there was no clear purpose to the seat work. John's friend Tom laughed. John was verbally redirected by the teacher, and then received a warning that he would receive a time out if he continued the behavior.

9:55 Shouted out to his classmate Mike while lining up for the next class, which got Mike's attention. He was verbally redirected by the teacher.

10:10 Fell out of his chair while doing seat work. Mike looked over at him. He was verbally redirected by the teacher and the teacher stood by him for five minutes reading with him and going over the directions.

10:20 The class started a reading assignment, but he refused. His peers and the teacher ignored him.

10:30 He dumped his books on the floor and swore. Tom looked over at John. He received a time out for five minutes.

10:45 Paying attention while teacher showed a video on dinosaurs.

Anecdotal observations are used in Functional Behavioral Analysis (FBA) to identify the Antecedent-Behavior-Consequence (ABC) links associated with a child's behavior, which may indicate environmental contributions of peers or a teacher to a child's problematic behavior. Limitations of anecdotal observations include difficulty in quantifying and sharing the data with others, and time-intensiveness.

Interval observations. Interval observations assess the frequency of specific student behaviors associated with academic achievement (e.g., inattention, disorganization, attention-seeking). Interval observations are objective and more readily understood by parents, teachers, etc. In order to conduct an interval observation, the observer chooses times when the class will be involved in individual or small group tasks. The observer tallies behavior for the target student and a same-gender peer on an established interval schedule. At each time point, the observer selects behaviors from an established list of behaviors (e.g., on-task, off-task, out-of-seat,

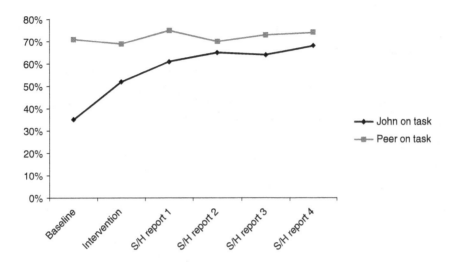

Figure 4.4 Interval Observation Data Comparing John's On-Task Behavior to a Composite of Selected Peers' On-Task Behavior Measured at Different Points in the Intervention Process. Each Data Point Represents 120 Intervals Collected in 20 Minutes of Classroom Observations. Intervention = Behavioural Modification Point Card Implemented; S/H Report = School-Home Report Intervention.

talk out). Usually, several observations are conducted and data are analyzed to determine the behavioral "average." For example, if an observer uses a twenty-second interval and records data for ten minutes for four different observations, the data set would yield 120 data points for both the target and comparison students. The data points are then graphed and percentages can be shared with team members (see Figure 4.4).

Summary

The use of data-driven decision-making to demonstrate accountability has irrevocably modified education. Historically, school counselors have avoided measuring the impact of their activities and programs, often due to a belief that the multifaceted and ambiguous role of the school counselor did not lend itself to program evaluation. However, as politicians and the public challenge educators to demonstrate the impact of their efforts, school counselors no longer have the luxury of standing along the sidelines. School counselors must understand and meet these new expectations head on.

Recently, a school counselor explained to one of the authors his belief that *the ASCA National Model*® (2012) was unrealistic. This school counselor stated that his job is to have an open door policy, in which he is always available for any student's immediate need. He proudly recounted how he had helped a boy find his retainer, which he had accidentally discarded. He also appeared to be proud of the fact that he did not collect or analyze data. While the school counselor's retelling of helping the boy find his retainer may appear compelling, school counselors must understand that such stories are not likely to have much impact if the school board is seeking to reduce the district budget by trimming school personnel who do not have a clear record of effectiveness.

References

AERA (2015, May 8). *AERA offers definition of scientifically based research*. Available online at www.aera.net/AboutAERA/ KeyPrograms/EducationResearchandResearchPolicy/AERAOffersDefinitionofScientificallyBasedRes/tabid/10877/ Default.aspx (accessed January 10, 2015).

American School Counselor Association (2012). *The ASCA national model: A framework for school counseling programs* (3rd ed.). Alexandria, VA: Author.

American School Counselor Association (2014). *Mindsets & behaviors for student success: K-12 college- and career-readiness standards for every Student.* Alexandria, VA: Author.

ASCA Working Group (2012). *ASCA model and creating pre-post surveys to measure perception data (ASK).* Available online at www.slideshare.net/shashley14/asca-perception-data-surveys (accessed January 15, 2015).

Aseltine, R. H., & DeMartino, R. (2004). An outcome evaluation of SOS Suicide Prevention Program. *American Journal of Public Health, 94,* 446–451.

Bandura, A. (2006). *Self-efficacy beliefs for adolescents.* Charlotte, NC: Information Age Publications.

Beghetto, R. (2003). *Scientifically based research.* ERIC Clearinghouse on Educational Management. Available online at http://eric.ed.gov/?id=ED474304 (accessed December 17, 2013).

Bill and Melinda Gates Foundation (2013). *Feedback for better teaching: Nine principles for using measures of effective teaching.* MET Project: Author.

Brigman, G., & Webb, L. (2004). *Student Success Skills: Classroom manual.* Boca Raton, FL: Atlantic Education Consultants.

Carey, J. C., Dimmitt, C., Hatch, T. A., Lapan, R. T., & Whiston, S. C. (2008). Report of the National Panel for Evidence-Based School Counseling: Outcome research coding protocol and evaluation of Student Success Skills and Second Step. *Professional School Counseling, 11,* 197–206.

Committee for Children (2004). *Knowledge assessment for Second Step: A violence prevention curriculum.* Seattle, WA: Author.

Cook, J. B., & Kaffenberger, C. J. (2003). Solution shop: A solution-focused counseling and study skills program for middle school. *Professional School Counseling, 7,* 116–123.

Crone, D. A., Hawken, L. S., & Horner, R. H. (2010). *Responding to problem behavior in schools* (2nd ed.). New York: Guilford Press.

Crothers, L. M., Schreiber, J. B., Field, J. E., & Kolbert, J. B. (2009). Development and measurement through confirmatory factor analysis of the Young Adult Social Behavior Scale (YASB): An assessment of relational aggression in adolescence and young adulthood. *Journal of Psychoeducational Assessment, 27,* 17–28.

Dimmitt, C. (2009). Why evaluation matters: Determining effective school counseling practices. *Professional School Counseling, 12,* 395–399.

Dimmitt, C., Carey, J. C., & Hatch, T. (2007). *Evidence-based school counseling.* Thousand Oaks, CA: Corwin.

Gruman, D. H., & Hoelzen, B. (2011). Determining responsiveness to school counseling interventions using behavioral observations. *Professional School Counseling, 14,* 183–190.

Horner, R. H., Todd, A. W., Lewis-Palmer, T., Irwin, L. K., Sugai, G., & Boland, J. B. (2004). The school-wide evaluation tool (SET): A research instrument for assessing school-wide positive behavior support. *Journal of Positive Behavior Interventions, 6,* 3–12.

Kalberg, J. R., Lane, K. L., & Menzies, H. M. (2010). Using systematic screening procedures to identify students who are nonresponsive to primary prevention efforts: Integrating academic and behavioral measures. *Education & Treatment of Children, 33,* 561–584.

Kish, L. (1982). Rensis Likert (1903–1981). *The American Statistician, 36,* 124–125.

Maloney, L. A. (2015). *A comparison of two interventions in a Response to Intervention (RtI) framework across student problem type.* Unpublished doctoral dissertation. Duquesne University, Pittsburgh, Pennsylvania.

March, T. (2003). The learning power of webquests. *Educational Leadership, 61,* 42–47. Available online at http://tommarch.com/writings/ascdwebquests (accessed March 15, 2015).

McIntosh, K., Campbell, A., Carter, D., Russell, D., & Zumbo, B. (2009). Concurrent validity of office discipline referrals and cut points used in schoolwide positive behavior support. *Behavioral Disorders, 32,* 100–113.

Merrell, K. W., Carrizales, D., Feuerborn, L., Gueldner, B. A., & Tran, O. K. (2007). *Strong Kids 3–5: A social & emotional curriculum.* Baltimore: Paul H. Brookes Publishing Co.

No Child Left Behind Act of 2001, Pub. L. No. 107–110 (2002).

O'Shea, A. J., & Harrington, T. F. (2003). Using the Career Decision-Making System-Revised to enhance students' career development. *Professional School Counseling, 6,* 280–286.

Paulsen, C. A., & Dailey, D. (2002). *A guide for education personnel: Evaluating a program or intervention.* Washington, DC: PhD Elementary and Middle Schools Technical Assistance Center (EMSTAC) American Institutes for Research.

Resch, A., Berk, J., & Akers, L. (2014). *Recognizing and conducting opportunistic experiments in education: A guide for policymakers and researchers* (REL 2014–037). Washington, DC: US Department of Education, Institute of Education Sciences, National Center for Education Evaluation and Regional Assistance, Analytic Technical Assistance and Development. Available online at http://ies.ed.gov/ncee/edlabs (accessed February 28, 2015).

Shores, C. (2009). *A comprehensive RTI model: Integrating behavioral and academic interventions.* Thousand Oaks, CA: Corwin.

Sink, C. A., & Stroh, H. R. (2003). Raising achievement test scores of early elementary school students through comprehensive school counseling programs. *Professional School Counseling, 6,* 350–364.

Stone, C. B., & Dahir, C. A. (2010). *School counselor accountability. A MEASURE for student success* (3rd ed.). Upper Saddle River, NJ: Prentice Hall.

US Department of Education (n.d.). Every Student Succeeds Act. Available online at www.ed.gov/essa (accessed March 3, 2016).

Walker, H. M., & McConnell, S. R. (1988). *The Walker-McConnell Scale of Social Competence and Adjustment.* Austin, TX: PRO-ED.

Walker, H. M., & Severson, H. H. (1992). *Systematic Screening for Behavior Disorders* (2nd ed.). Longmont, CO: Sopris West.

Whiston, S. C., Tai, W. L., Rahardja, D., & Eder, K. (2011). School counseling outcome: A meta-analytic examination of interventions. *Journal of Counseling & Development, 89,* 37–55.

Wilkerson, K., Pérusse, R., & Hughes, A. (2013). Comprehensive school counseling programs and student achievement outcomes: A comparative analysis of RAMP vs. non-RAMP schools. *Professional School Counseling, 16,* 172–184.

Chapter Five
School Counseling Core Curriculum

Box 5.1

2016 CACREP School Counseling Specialty Area Standards

3.b Design and evaluation of school counseling programs

3.c Core curriculum design, lesson plan development, classroom management strategies, and differentiated instructional strategies

3.d Interventions to promote academic development

3.l Techniques to foster collaboration within schools

3.n Use of accountability data to inform decision-making

The ASCA National Model® (2012) encourages school counselors to utilize the classroom as an effective and time-efficient method of delivery for a comprehensive, developmental school-counseling curriculum. A school counselor who teaches school counseling curriculum lessons assists the teacher in classroom management, helps to enhance social skills in students, delivers information to promote students' career and college readiness, and encourages the use of learning strategies to improve students' academic achievement (Akos, Cockman, & Strickland, 2007).

Obtaining proficiency in conducting school counseling lessons is a difficult, developmental process, as there are many layers of competence, from curriculum development to classroom management, which are necessary for successful teaching of these skills. In this chapter, a review of the literature regarding school counseling curricula and the value of this type of curriculum delivery will be provided. The creation of a developmentally appropriate school counseling curriculum will be discussed with consideration to the scope and sequence of lessons, the vertical and horizontal articulation of the curriculum, and differentiated classroom strategies. Teaching skills and strategies for planning and developing goals and objectives for lesson plans will be offered along with classroom management techniques, methods for collaboration with teachers, and examples of a developmental curriculum. Marzano's (2007) high-yield instructional strategies will also be explored.

Referring to Chapter 1, in which we discussed the history of school counseling, it is clear that the roots of school counseling developed from the teaching profession. The establishment of the school counseling profession owes much to the teachers who were asked to expand their classroom services to deliver vocational and career guidance to their students. However, it soon became apparent that removing teachers from the classroom to deliver vocational and career information was neither effective for the students nor an appropriate use of teachers' time in light of the competing tasks required for completion. Furthermore, the need for more intensive professional training beyond vocational knowledge for school counseling became more evident as the value of this position was realized.

Despite the beginnings of school counseling, which relied on teachers for service delivery, the profession has moved away from requiring a teaching certification as a prerequisite to the Master's-level training in school counseling. Currently, only seven states continue to mandate prior teaching experience as a condition for school counseling certification (ASCA, 2014a).

Box 5.2

Did you know?

As of 2015, the states that still require teacher certification are Kansas, Kentucky, Louisiana, Nebraska, North Dakota, Oregon, and Texas.

Much of the research on prior teaching experience as a necessity for a school counseling certification suggests that having teaching experience neither helps nor hinders the effectiveness of a professional school counselor (Peterson, Goodman, Keller, & McCauley, 2004; Stein & DeBerard, 2010). Interestingly, Baker (1994) found that teaching experience may actually be a detriment to becoming an effective school counselor because of the potential preconceived and entrenched mindsets of those with teaching experience.

Despite the fact that prior teaching experience does not appear to be associated with performance as a school counselor, all school counselors need to be adept in delivering the school counseling curriculum, developing effective curricula, and evaluating the results of prevention or intervention approaches. "It is widely accepted that school counseling classroom lessons remains critical for a developmental, sequential and systemic school counseling program. An implicit assumption of school counseling classroom lessons has been that it is an effective way to impact student development" (Akos et al., 2007, p. 445).

Benefits of School Counseling Core Curriculum

Currently, the amount of empirical research regarding the effectiveness of the school counseling core curriculum is relatively small, but the obligation to effectively and efficiently meet the needs of students in the academic, career, and social/emotional domains persists. Therefore, despite the paucity of empirical endorsement for the effectiveness of the school counseling core curriculum, school counselors must be able to deliver such lessons. Whiston, Tai, Rahardja, and Eder's (2011) meta-analysis of school counseling outcome research revealed that school counseling curriculum lessons had a statistically significant and small to moderate impact on students, and that there was some evidence that school counseling lessons yielded a larger effect than did responsive services, which includes individual and group counseling and crisis response.

Lapan, Gysbers, Hughey, and Arni (1993) found that schools with a fully implemented school counseling program, including school counseling lessons, demonstrated higher grades, a more positive school climate, and better preparation of its students for the future. Sink (2005) asserts that school counseling lessons provide students with a number of opportunities for social development, as students hear others' opinions and learn to problem-solve and experiment with new behaviors. "Large group guidance is one way to provide opportunities for students to participate meaningfully in discussion about important life skills and for counselors to model caring relationships and to demonstrate that they expect students to achieve and succeed" (Sink, 2005, p. 194).

With the many documented positive influences from school counseling lessons, it may be hard to imagine why more school counselors do not take advantage of this efficient way of delivering prevention and intervention curricula. Reportedly, one of the major impediments to delivering a school counseling curriculum is the prodigious focus upon teacher accountability from the state and nationally required assessments. Instructional time has become increasingly precious; the No Child Left Behind (NCLB) Act (2002) and other state and national assessments contribute to teachers' reluctance to lose any of their instructional time with their students. However, with the inception of the Common Core Student Standards (National Governors Association and Council of Chief State School Officers, 2010), school counselors have a renewed opportunity to become active members in this curriculum integration as *the ASCA Mindsets & Behaviors for Student Success* (2014b) is aligned with the Common Core standards.

This "crosswalking" of standards may aid in the collaboration efforts between classroom teachers and school counselors. An example of such integration could include a collaborative activity with the English teacher who uses Shakespeare's *Romeo and Juliet* in his or her curriculum. The classroom teacher might explain the content of the literature, while the school counselor teaches conflict mediation between the two warring families of this story. Another collaborative endeavor with the English department might include a school counseling curriculum lesson about peer pressure when reading the novel, *Lord of the Flies*. Yet another example is when the social studies teacher discusses Thomas Jefferson, the school counselor can introduce the university system and how postsecondary choices apply to the students. While there are multiple examples of teaching/counseling collaboration, school counselors must actively cultivate such relationships with teachers. Teachers are much less likely to refuse a school counseling curriculum lesson by the school counselors if the information can be tied to their academic standards.

Marzano's (2007) Evidence-based Teaching Strategies

A major initiative of the educational reform movement of the past several decades has been the identification and proliferation of evidence-based strategies in teaching. Although many school counselors do not receive intensive training in providing instruction given that they do not provide subject-based instruction, we urge school counselors to be familiar with the research literature regarding evidence-based instructional strategies to be better prepared to collaborate with educators and provide sound instruction. Through meta-analytic procedures (an aggregation of multiple studies to identify an average effect size, quantifying the magnitude of impact), Marzano (2007) identified high impact teaching strategies. In the section that follows, Marzano's (2007) high-yield instructional strategies are listed in order from the strongest to the weakest in terms of their impact on students' academic achievement. School counselors are not likely to use all of these instructional strategies in a single lesson, but will likely find that effective incorporation of at least several of the strategies will enhance their instructional effectiveness.

Identifying similarities and differences. This strategy includes comparing, classifying, creating metaphors, and creating analogies. Providing students with the opportunity to divide a concept into its similar and dissimilar characteristics enables them to analyze and solve complex problems by approaching them in a simpler way. An example of the way in which a school counselor could incorporate this instructional strategy in delivering the school counseling core curriculum is providing students with examples and non-examples of the characteristics of effective goal setting while having the students develop hypotheses about what principles are unique to the examples presented.

Summarizing and note-taking. This strategy involves teaching students how to engage in effective summarization/note-taking, which involves eliminating unnecessary information, replacing some information, rewriting, and analyzing information (please see Chapter 9: Academic Development for further discussion regarding this topic). Summarization and note-taking have been shown to increase student recall and are believed to contribute to students' deeper understanding of concepts. While school counselors typically do not emphasize the use of note-taking given that they do not provide subject instruction, they may utilize this strategy in asking students to consider what they learned from the school counseling curriculum lesson, or asking them to name one thing they are likely to use or do within the next week.

Reinforcing effort and providing recognition. Reinforcing effort refers to enhancing students' awareness that learning is difficult and requires sustained and active effort on the part of the learner. Surprisingly, many younger students, who are more likely to have an external locus of control, do not attribute learning to their own efforts. Instead, they see the instructor as the person responsible for their learning. School counselors can help students explore times that they have been successful and help them identify the various thoughts, feelings, and behaviors they had that were associated with their success. Providing recognition for these successes involves giving students symbolic or tangible rewards for achievement. School counselors may provide students with tangible rewards for completing activities associated with a lesson. For example, the school counselor could provide students with a reward for completing a journal worksheet identifying how they replaced irrational beliefs with more positive or rational beliefs. Also, school counselors can integrate both of these instructional strategies by teaching students to recognize and praise themselves for their effort and achievements, which promotes students' intrinsic motivation.

Homework and practice. Homework and practice provide students with the opportunity to apply their learning, which is associated with deeper understanding. An example of how a school counselor might utilize homework is provided in the discussion of the previous instructional strategy. School counselors should always seek to provide opportunities for practice when conducting school counseling lessons. For example, for a lesson on communication skills, the school counselor could model the use of assertive talking and listening, and then have students pair up and practice the specific assertiveness skills taught. One student could be asked to think of a time when he or she was really angry with someone, and practice communicating his or her anger in a respectful and assertive manner. Correspondingly, the listener might play the person with whom the student is angry, and focus on using paraphrasing to identify the student's anger in a non-defensive manner.

Nonlinguistic presentations. This includes the use of graphic presentations, mental pictures, drawings, pictography, and kinesthetic activities. The use of nonlinguistic presentations has been associated with increased brain activity. School counselors can incorporate nonlinguistic activities in school counseling lessons by incorporating visuals in PowerPoint presentations, having students create a picture or symbol of their understanding of the material, and through the use of applied activities in the form of role-playing, group problem-solving, etc.

Cooperative learning. The school counseling profession acknowledges the importance of social interactions through the profession's emphasis on social/emotional development. School counselors can include cooperative learning in a variety of ways. They can divide the class into small groups to work on scenario-based issues. For example, for a lesson in which the school counselor seeks to promote rational thinking, students can be assigned to small groups to identify the likely irrational thoughts of a depiction of a similar-aged student and construct relevant positive or rational replacement thoughts. Students could be assigned to role-play a job interview in which one student functions as the interviewer, one the interviewee, and another student serves as an observer who evaluates the interviewees' ability to use specified interview skills. Importantly, the extant research suggests that when creating groups, it is important to instruct students regarding the expected roles of group members and the expectations of the group work.

Setting objectives and providing feedback. Student achievement is enhanced when students understand the objectives of the lesson, and school counselors should also explain how the objectives are relevant for students' development. Feedback from school counselors varies somewhat from teacher feedback in that school counselors do not typically provide formal grades. Rather, school counselor feedback is more likely to be connected to a specific learning activity, and in such cases, the focus of feedback should be on the student's mastery of a task, such as communication skills, the use of the career search engine to locate relevant information, etc. One school counselor developed a comprehensive way in which to provide feedback through a Likert-scale rubric to assess students' videotaped role-play of a job interview. As is the case with all kinds of feedback, such information should be provided to students in a timely and constructive manner.

Generating and testing hypotheses. The generation and testing of hypotheses involves the use of inductive and deductive reasoning through problem-solving. An example of a school counselor's use of this instructional strategy is helping students identify a social problem, research the various causes of the social problem, and implement an applied project to address one of the causes of the identified social problem. Given the long-term nature of this instructional strategy, it may not be as applicable for school counselors, who are not likely to conduct a long series of lessons.

Cues, questions, and advanced organizers. Cues may include identifying the objectives for the lesson, emphasizing the most essential information, questions that help students identify what they already know about the topic, and advanced organizers that help students relate new information to what they already know. School counselors can incorporate these strategies by asking students early in a lesson about their understanding and experiences of a topic. For example, when teaching a lesson on assertive communication, a school counselor may ask students about their experiences in receiving or eliciting poor communication skills and what strategies they have developed for maintaining good relationships with peers and family members.

Curriculum Development

Needs assessments. The curriculum for a school counseling program can be developed through a number of ways, but the first step is to gear the lessons toward an identified target based on the needs of the students. Asking for access to teachers' classrooms should be supported with data from a needs assessment. Gysbers and Henderson (2000) recommend the delivery of a formalized needs assessment at the start of a comprehensive program implementation. Not only will the needs assessment inform the school counselor about what may be most helpful from the perception of the students, but it can also effectively incorporate the perceptions of the parents and teachers. Alternative methods of assessing needs in developing the school counseling core curriculum include examining easily accessible data such as discipline referrals, attendance, and any type of archival data (Sink, 2005). Additionally, Goodnough, Pérusse, and Erford (2007) suggest that the school counseling core curriculum should be aligned with the school counseling program's vision and goals and should receive "the active commitment and involvement of administrators and teachers" (p. 151).

The initial needs assessment should be comprehensive so that the school counseling core curriculum may seek to address the needs of the entire student population. However, ongoing, albeit less formal, assessments should also be conducted. Although the needs of the parents, students, and faculty are of the upmost importance in program development, the national, state, and local directives must also be considered in the implementation process. For example, many states require that schools include bullying prevention programming, and in many schools, the school counselor(s) coordinate this programming. The needs assessment provides the baseline information as the school counseling program is developed, but the next consideration concerns the continuity and articulation of the program from one grade to the next.

Scope and sequence articulation. School counselors must also attend to the content of this curriculum. Although there are many types of commercial curricula available, school administrators increasingly expect school counselors to show that the curriculum they implement has empirical support. It is also important to implement a curriculum that matches the school's culture. Issues such as the cost of the curriculum, materials needed, necessary training for delivery, effectiveness for the largest number of students, and evaluation are additional considerations for a curriculum selection process. Conversely, there are advantages to designing your own curriculum. Developing a curriculum may more effectively match the needs of the particular classroom and teachers' styles. It is particularly important for self-designed curricula to be evaluated given their lack of empirical support.

The breadth and depth of a curriculum is called the scope or horizontal articulation (Goodnough et al., 2007; Sink, 2005). "Horizontal articulation establishes the connection between the content of the counseling curriculum and content in other subject areas" (Goodnough et al., 2007, p. 154). The sequence, or vertical articulation, is described as the connection of information from one grade level to the next, so that all standards are addressed at various and developmentally appropriate grade levels without redundancy or gaps in the curriculum (Goodnough et al., 2007). When developing curricula, consideration must be given to the learning profiles of the students, differentiation techniques for effective learning, types of grouping, cultural awareness and sensitivity, and methods of evaluation (Akos et al., 2007; Tomlinson, 2005).

The school counseling core curriculum should also be based in developmental theories, such as Piaget's theory of cognitive development, Kohlberg's theory of moral development, Erikson's theory of psychosocial development, and Super's career developmental theory, to name only a few. Developmental theories identify the likely developmental challenges and issues confronting students at a particular age. As stated by Havighurst (1972):

A developmental task is a task which arises at or about a certain period in the life of the individual, successful achievement of which leads to his or her happiness and to success with later tasks, while failure leads to unhappiness in the individual, disapproval by the society and difficulty with later tasks.

(Sink, 2005, p. 192)

For example, in terms of career development, elementary-age students are just learning about the world of work that exists outside of their family and school life, and school counselors promote elementary students' awareness of the various careers that exist in society. In contrast, in early adolescence, many students are developing the capacity for formal operational thinking, and can begin to think more abstractly about who they are and their interests and abilities. School counselors assist early adolescents with career development by encouraging them to learn more about themselves and relate their growing self-awareness to possible careers, which is referred to as career exploration. High school students are confronted with the task of developing a program of study that corresponds with their career goals. This is referred to as career planning, which school counselors facilitate by helping high school students learn about their postsecondary career and educational options, creating a program of study that supports their future goals, and identifying resources, such as financial aid, that will assist them in achieving their career goals.

Another developmental issue that may be identified as the result of conducting a needs assessment is the issue of sexual harassment. If the school counselor is using a developmental approach, it would not be appropriate to present the issues of sexual assault and dating violence to sixth graders. Rather, it would be age-appropriate to teach sixth grade students the definition of sexual harassment, which includes the use of derogatory slurs toward other students such as "gay," "fag," "slut," and "ho." For seventh graders, school counseling lessons about the difference between flirting and hurting would be age-appropriate, while eighth grade students would benefit from a lesson on dating violence and the dating bill of rights (Williams & Riedo, 2008).

Curriculum development also includes how the school counseling lessons will be delivered (Akos et al., 2007). The level of effectiveness of a school counseling curriculum lesson is only as good as the method of delivery of the information to the students. Goodnough et al. (2007) identify three basic methods of delivery and their advantages and disadvantages (see Box 5.3).

Box 5.3

Goodnough et al.'s (2007) Three Basic Methods of Delivery and their Advantages and Disadvantages

1. *School counselor delivery*
   (a) Disadvantages: time-consuming for school counselor; school counselor may lack confidence in teaching skills.
   (b) Advantages: research and information are conveyed with passion and knowledge of the subject matter by the school counselor; assessment and delivery of information is standardized for each class; students get to know the school counselor.
2. *Classroom teacher delivery*
   (a) Disadvantages: consumes precious classroom time; may not be delivered with the passion and urgency that would be provided by the school counselor; may not be a priority for the teacher.
   (b) Advantages: saves the counselor time; information is provided by someone the students know.
3. *Collaboration between both counseling and teacher delivery*
   (a) Disadvantages: both education professionals are tied up at the same time.
   (b) Advantages: students see collaboration being modeled; students understand the importance of the message.

Differentiation

Differentiation is the intentional planning for effective school counseling lessons that incorporate students' cognitive strengths and challenges (Goodnough et al., 2007; Tomlinson & Imbeau, 2012). Learning styles, cultural diversity, English proficiency, economic backgrounds, and individual students' learning challenges must all be factored into an effective classroom presentation; thus, there is a need for differentiated instruction (Akos et al., 2007; Tomlinson & Imbeau, 2012). Differentiation is a pedagogical philosophy that promotes a focus on the educational needs of the individual student. Incorporating the strengths of students' learning profiles, and using those strengths to engage and inspire students to learn new materials can accomplish this.

> Differentiation is an instructional approach and does not dictate curricula...The primary goal of differentiation...is to help teachers develop and use multiple pathways for students to learn whatever they teach, including content standards.
>
> (Tomlinson & Imbeau, 2012, p. 2)

Akos et al. (2007) suggest that the basic tenants of differentiation are to focus on addressing the learning needs of all students using a variety of learning strategies. These tenants of differentiation are remarkably similar to the core beliefs of the school counseling profession. Differentiated school counseling lessons operate within the belief that the variety of interests, learning profiles, and readiness levels of the learners must be addressed for a more equitable and effective delivery of the information. When developing school counseling curriculum lessons, one strategy for the school counselor to employ is classroom observation prior to the lesson, in order to assess the learning readiness and needs of the students. The differentiated strategies for school counseling lessons are factored into the lesson planning.

Assessment and evaluation. School counselors must evaluate the impact of lessons or the series of lessons, which is commonly referred to as the unit, and such data should be used for program improvement (Sink, 2005). Such evaluation has unfortunately been met with resistance by many school counselors, as some argue that the type of soft skills frequently focused upon in school counseling lessons are difficult to assess. However, Goodnough et al. (2007) proclaim that this is an errant belief and arguably one of the causes for professional school counselors often being excluded from important educational decisions.

The assessment of classroom school counseling lessons should be driven by the following principles:

- Tied to your stance on education: What importance does this lesson have for students' behavior or performance?
- Driven by learning goals: Is what you are teaching consistent with what the students learned?
- Systematic: Are you gathering data in a way that is accurate, fair, logical, and equitable?
- Tied to instruction: Work should begin at the planning stage as objectives are developed and standards are addressed.
- Inclusive of the learner: This should be done *with* students not *to* students in an effort to reflect on their own learning.
- Integrated into a manageable system: A method of collection should be implemented that allows you to focus on student learning.

(Guillaume, 2008)

Types of assessments for a school counseling curriculum lesson or unit may include the following: a web-based assessment tool such as Poll Everywhere; a round, asking each student to respond to a particular question or asking each student to say something new that he or she learned; a brief written response to a question as an exit ticket from the classroom; a board blitz, in which students come to the board and write the answers to the questions; a gallery tour, where all the work done by the students is presented around the room; role plays demonstrating the skills learned; journaling; and classroom students' presentations (Guillaume, 2008; Williams, Lantz, & Noorulamin, 2008).

Planning. Thorough lesson planning should be based on the data collected from the needs assessment. If the data indicate a need for a prevention or intervention strategy that would best be delivered through the school counseling core curriculum, the school counselor should first review the literature to determine if there exists an evidence-based program for the topic. The Center for School Counseling Outcome Research and Evaluation (CSCORE), What Works Clearinghouse, and the Substance Abuse and Mental Health Services Administration (SAMSHA) list on their websites the school-based programs that they have identified as having empirical support. The ASCA website has a resource center with a multitude of ideas and information. CSCORE concluded that there is strong empirical support for the *Second Step Violence Prevention Curriculum* (Committee for Children, 1997), which is designed to decrease violence through enhanced empathy and social skills and through decreases in aggressive behaviors. The Panel deemed the evidence to be promising for the *Student Success Skills* (SSS) curriculum (Brigman & Webb, 2005), which is a group and school counseling curriculum approach to promoting metacognitive social skills, and self-management skills. While there are many other resources that can provide excellent school counseling lessons and curricula, the most important component of any selection made by the school counselor is the evidence supporting the curriculum. If there is not a lot of evidence, then develop an assessment tool and collect your own data. It is important that school counselors can validate the impact of the school counseling core curriculum.

Box 5.4

Suggested Proposal Planning Format

1. Identify the local and national data that indicate the need for the intervention.
2. Review and document the research literature that identifies effective interventions.
3. Crosswalk and align *the ASCA Mindsets & Behaviors* (2014) with the educational course in which this intervention might be presented.
4. Develop overarching unit goals and objectives.
5. Identify the baseline data that will be used to assess the lesson's/unit's effectiveness.
6. Present the proposal to the necessary stakeholders, advisory council, administrators, and teachers for approval.

Developing goals and objectives for each lesson. Upon approval of the proposal for the lessons, the school counselor will develop the specific goals and objectives for each lesson. When the school counselor enters the classroom, it is of the upmost importance that he or she has a plan for what students should know when they leave the classroom. These are known as goals and objectives. Involving the classroom teacher in the development of the goals and objectives can provide school counselors with valuable insights into this process. The overarching goal for the entire unit, developed in the proposal, will be based on what the school counselors want the students to know, to be able to do, and the behaviors that will be demonstrated following the implementation of the unit. The goal development is framed around the data from which the proposal was derived, and drives the long-term planning of the lesson. Moreover, goals are typically divided into three domains: cognitive, affective, and psychomotor (Guillaume, 2008).

Based on Bloom's taxonomy, each domain has developmental levels:

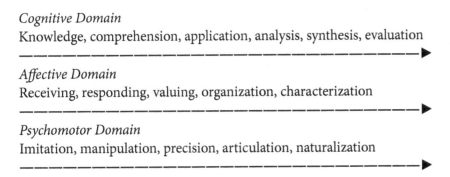

Cognitive Domain
Knowledge, comprehension, application, analysis, synthesis, evaluation

Affective Domain
Receiving, responding, valuing, organization, characterization

Psychomotor Domain
Imitation, manipulation, precision, articulation, naturalization

Goals are intended to be broad and general. These lofty aspirations which drive the long-term planning, unlike objectives, are not intended to be measurable (Guillaume, 2008). A suggestion for goal development from *K-12 Classroom Guidance: A Primer for New Professionals* (Guillaume, 2008) includes:

> Think about the broader contexts and issues; analyze what is already known by the students; what are the hopes you have for the students; review standards in consideration of the students; check vertical articulations and what is being currently taught; examine materials.
>
> (Guillaume, 2008, p. 84)

An example of a goal: Students will value the importance of preventing sexual harassment.

The next level of lesson planning involves the development of the objectives or the "doing" part of the goals. Mager (1997) explains that learning objectives help with the selection of activities and procedures, achieving results, and in using time effectively. The objectives state the outcome of the lessons, or as Mager (1997) puts it, "where you want the students to end up." An ABCD model of writing objectives has been developed by Erford and McKechnie (2004). These authors integrated several different models of objective writing in this ABCD model, which includes:

A) Audience; most objectives for school counselors will be directed toward the students, so the objective will begin: "Students will…"
B) Behavior; what one expects the student to engage in or be able to think, solve, or do.
C) Conditions; explains when and how the behavior will be measured. For example, "After watching a series of role plays, the students will be able to…"
D) Description of expected performance; the criterion for expected performance, or the level of acceptable performance.

(Erford & McKechnie, 2004, p. 276)

When writing objectives, Guillaume (2008) suggests that the author should remain focused on the intended outcomes and stay attuned to the skill or concept the students should achieve, not the technique used to teach it. Additionally, Guillaume (2008) encourages that "only the criteria and conditions that you will actually use" (p. 101) be included in the writing of the objective. An example of an objective for the above-mentioned goal on sexual harassment might be: After participating in a Hurting vs. Flirting activity, students will be able to name two reasons a behavior might be considered sexual harassment.

Selection of curriculum or activities. The selection of the curriculum and activities should be connected to the strengths and learning readiness of the students. Lesson materials are based on "understanding the learners' interests, abilities, and needs, and based on high expectations you place upon students to master the content – search out the resources that will push all of your students forward" (Guillaume,

2008, p. 85). Using a variety of differentiated learning strategies allows for all students to be able to learn in a way that fits their learning style and helps keep them engaged. One way to differentiate instructional activities is to incorporate various learning styles. A meta-analysis of interventions using the Dunn and Dunn (1999) Learning Style Model, which is the most researched learning style model, found that matching students' learning style preferences results in a moderate to large effect upon academic achievement and student attitudes toward learning (Lovelace, 2005). See Box 5.5 for a description of Dunn and Dunn's Learning Style Model. The *Learning Style Inventory* has been found to be a reliable and valid instrument for assessing students' learning styles (Dunn, Dunn, & Price, 2003).

Box 5.5

Dunn and Dunn's (1999) Learning Style Model

1. Environmental characteristics (preferences for sounds vs. quiet, warm vs. low temperatures, low vs. bright light, and formal vs. informal seating).
2. Emotional characteristics (need for breaks vs. persistence, high vs. low academic motivation, conformity vs. non-conformity, internal vs. external need for structure).
3. Sociological preferences (working alone vs. in pairs or part of a team, with either an authoritative or collegial adult).
4. Physiological characteristics (perceptual strengths [auditory, visual, tactual and kinesthetic], time-of-day energy levels, and the need for nutrition and mobility).
5. Processing preferences (global/analytic, right/left, impulsive/reflective).

Dahir and Stone (2012) provide an example of a school counselor who, in collaboration with a teacher, used activities to match several learning styles in conducting a lesson on Harriet Tubman and the Underground Railroad during Black History Month. For students with a visual learning style, diagrams of the various paths for the Underground Railroad were provided. To match students with a kinesthetic learning style, students worked together in creating a skit of slaves escaping to the north. The school counselor used a familiar example of the slaves' wish to move to the north for a better life to the situation faced by the many of the families from the Caribbean nations that comprise the primary demographics of the respective school. The school counselor shared the results of his administration of the *Learning Style Inventory* (Dunn et al., 2003) to a group of sixth grade students with the students' parents and teachers who collaborated in developing teaching strategies to match the students' learning styles. Most of the teachers and parents agreed to develop a personalized student plan, and the teachers reported improved academic achievement within several weeks.

School counselors should be thoughtful about planning instruction to accommodate the strengths and needs of students with learning, emotional, or behavioral disabilities in the classroom. Intervention practices that are associated with positive effects upon learning include direct instruction, learning strategy instruction, and the use of a sequential, simultaneous structured multi-sensory approach (Learning Disabilities Association of America, n.d.). In using such interventions, some strategies that school counselors may find to be useful in developing classroom lessons include repetition of information; chunking information into smaller amounts; frequent probes to assess learning; timely, meaningful feedback; the use of pictorial representations of information (e.g., graphics and diagrams); well-designed intensive independent practice; modeling and prompting; and the use of process questions such as, "Is this strategy helpful? Where else might you be able to use it?" (Learning Disabilities Association of America, n.d.).

An overall approach that seems to be effective with diverse learners is the use of scaffolding. The school counselor can begin a lesson using explicit instruction, in which he or she is extensively directing the course and pace of instruction, and gradually encouraging students to acquire the skill, increasingly approaching the goal of student-mediated instruction (Learning Disabilities Association of America, n.d.). As students become more comfortable with the learning concepts, the school counselor can urge them to become more independent and self-directed in their learning. An example of this may be in teaching students to use study skills to improve their performance in assessments of their learning. The school counselor can begin by explicitly teaching mnemonic strategies in memorizing, for example, the cranial nerves, giving the students a sentence that represents each nerve's first initial (e.g., "OOOTTAFVGVAH" is "Oh, oh, oh, to touch and feel very good velvet…ah, heaven" (Wang, Mukhtar, & Saenz, 2005). After the students have understood the principle being used, they can be encouraged to develop mnemonics for other hard-to-remember facts, such as the capital of each of the 50 states or the periodic table of elements.

Lesson materials. Materials necessary for the delivery of the curriculum must be cost-efficient and readily available for the lesson. These necessary materials should be assembled prior to the lesson and not left to chance. For example, it is not a good use of educational time to cut paper or manipulate some type of preparation for the lesson that could have been done in advance. It is also not a wise practice to expect the teacher to have the materials for the lesson, unless this was prearranged.

Lesson development. Before beginning the first lesson, the school counselor needs to know the students' current knowledge about the respective subject. This information can be gleaned from a formalized pre-test, or it can be done through a classroom observation prior to the lessons being taught, or teacher report. A pre-assessment can be done informally by asking students questions or it can be done in a fun and inviting way by using technology such as Poll Everywhere (www.polleverywhere.com), clickers, or some other technology-based information source. Basing the lesson plan on what the students already know will allow for more effective lesson delivery, will guide the lesson planning, and will help keep students more engaged.

Walking into the classroom to tell students why they need to know this information will not promote enthusiasm or engagement from the students. An attention-grabbing introduction to the lesson or unit will be a valuable part of the first session. Students need to understand why this information is being presented and how it will be applicable to them. A creative introduction will help students engage in the lesson and minimize negative behaviors. Suggestions include using music the students listen to, a story that catches their attention, or a role-play that will be a model for students' learning. An introduction to the sexual harassment unit might be: "Why should students and faculty care about what sexual harassment is?" After several answers, all of which may be correct, the school counselor can indicate that the main reason is that sexual harassment is illegal! Statistics and percentages of girls and boys who are sexually harassed daily will surprise the learners and help them to gain interest in the topic. This introduction can include a guessing game comparing the percentage of girls vs. boys of the respective age group who report having been sexually harassed. The real answers are often surprising and alarming to the students and promotes their interest in the topic.

After conducting an activity that captures students' attention, the objectives and agenda should be shared with them. Listing the objectives of the lesson on the board or reciting them to the students reinforces the intent of the lesson and how it will be measured. Reviewing the agenda for the lesson helps students know what to prepare for and often reduces their anxiety. As Dollarhide and Saginak (2012) suggest, a description of what the lesson will entail also demonstrates respect for the learner. This informs the students about the lesson so they can determine the amount of investment they will commit to it. This is another reason why an engaging and interesting introduction to the unit or lesson is so important. "Getting their agreement up front that what you're presenting is meaningful, interesting, or important will increase their attention and decrease distracting classroom behavior" (Dollarhide & Saginak, 2012, p. 152).

The activities for the lesson should be thoroughly developed since students will often sense an ill-prepared endeavor. Thorough development of the activities also assists more novice school counselors to manage their understandable anxiety about presenting to a class. School counselors may develop a script to organize their thinking and approach to the lesson, but they should avoid reading from a script, as this may suggest to students that the school counselor is anxious and may result in off-task behaviors. When developing step-by-step delivery of the lesson, consider the small details. Planning of the simple details can make or break a lesson, even how the school counselor assigns students to groups should be considered beforehand. School counselors who have not decided upon how they will group students may find that the most disruptive students wind up in the same group. Be creative and unpredictable in the pairing or grouping, introductions, and assessments. An example of pairing up students might be: Line up according to your birthday in one straight line and take the first six students into one group, etc. Another aspect of the lesson delivery is the arrangement of the room. School counselors must consider the type of arrangement that would work best for the respective activity, the time necessary to arrange the room in the preferred manner, and should also obtain the approval of the classroom teacher to make such arrangements.

Activity selection. No matter the age of the students or audience, most learners do not appreciate long "sit and get" methods of teaching, and this type of instruction is not associated with student retention of information (Williams & Riedo, 2008). While lecture-style instruction may be time-efficient and easier for the presenter, it also encourages passive learning. A more interactive and inductive method of teaching engages the learner and allows for more self-discovery. People typically learn best by doing (Kovalik & Olsen, 2005), rather than being directly told the information. Experiential learning has a longer effect on information retention. The developmental skills of the learners are important to consider in lesson planning. Consider: Are the students developmentally capable of doing what is asked of them? Are the students capable of success with the selected activity? Time is another consideration. Is there enough time for the planned activities and for effective processing of the activities?

Debrief the activity. The point of an activity is not in the doing of the activity but in the processing of what happened in the activity, the purpose of the activity, and the application to real life (Williams & Riedo, 2008). Such processing increases the likelihood that students will engage in transfer of learning, meaning that they will develop the skills, attitudes, and/or behaviors that they can apply to real-world contexts. Be sure to carefully plan the debriefing questions in advance. This will help to alleviate the spontaneous and distracting on-the-fly questions that may not promote the objective of the activity.

Furthermore, readers are encouraged to follow the debriefing process outlined in Chapter 7: Group Counseling. There are three main types of debriefing questions. The WHAT questions ask about the immediate experience: What just happened? Additionally, the SO WHAT questions ask about the purpose of the activity: Why do you think we did this activity? Finally, the NOW WHAT questions are about application and tying the activity to the students' own lives: How does the learning you just had in this activity apply to your daily life? (Williams, Lantz, & Noorulamin, 2008). Each question may elicit a number of responses.

Evaluation and assessment. There are many essential steps in lesson planning but the core of the lesson is in the evaluation process. "Assessment supports us in our serious responsibility to help all students learn rigorous content" (Guillaume, 2008, p. 174). This component of lesson planning is vital for many reasons; not only does it allow for feedback about the lesson but it also offers information about the effectiveness of the lesson or unit. The evaluation informs the next steps and necessary accommodations for subsequent lessons.

Unfortunately, many school counselors are reluctant to evaluate their programs because of the perception that the lessons taught by school counselors are "soft skills," such as self-esteem, motivation, team-building, communication, and success, and are thus too hard to measure. However, Erford and McKechnie (2004) admonish school counselors who argue this stance; this conviction only serves to discredit the impact that school counseling programs have on student success. Erford and McKechnie (2004) suggest that "the answer to this dilemma, of course, is to teach what can be mastered and write the learning objective in a way that mastery can be determined" (p. 275). While school counselors may not be able to measure how students are motivated, they can measure the students' ability to name three ways to enhance their motivation.

At the conclusion of the lesson, the school counselor must assess the impact of the lesson. This evaluation can include all three types of data collection identified in *the ASCA National Model®* (2012). The school counselor can utilize *process data*, by documenting how many students were involved in the lesson, the grade level, the length of the session, etc. *Perception data* can be assessed through a survey either at the end of a single lesson or at the end of the unit. An example of perception data includes the percentage of students who report that they understand the definition of sexual harassment. *The ASCA National Model®* (2012) identifies three types of *outcome data*: short-term, intermediate, and long-term. An example of short-term outcome data for the sexual harassment lesson may be the change in the percentage of students who successfully identified an example of sexual harassment at pre- to post-test. The number of sexual harassment cases that have been reported a month or more after the lessons would be considered intermediate outcome data. Long-term outcome data could be noted through sexual harassment cases that occurred in the semester following the implementation of the lessons.

There is a tendency for school counselors to experience frustration if data does not indicate that the lesson/unit resulted in change. However, such a finding may not be a cause for disappointment. A small adjustment to the lessons may be all that is required to change the outcomes. The time of day that the lesson was delivered, or the age of the students it was delivered to, may have an impact on the data. The emphasis is on the use of data-driven decision-making for improvement of services and the program.

Table 5.1 Lesson Plan Example Format

Grade Level	Indicate the grade of the class.
Classroom Delivered	Indicate the teacher's class.
Title of Lesson	Indicate the title of the lesson.
Goal	What is the overarching intent of the lesson/unit?
Objectives	2–3 items of what you want the students to be able to do at the end of the lesson.
Standards	Identify the standards being addressed and crosswalk the standards with the subject standards if possible.
Materials	What is needed for a successful lesson?
Introduction	– Create a novel way in which to introduce this lesson. Get the students interested. – Review previous lesson if this is following the first lesson. – Use some type of check-in procedure with the students, depending on the time allotted.
Lesson Information	Detailed description of what is in the lesson and how it will be delivered will enhance the learning experience.
Activity/Experiential Component to the Lesson	Learning by doing increases the students' learning and allows for the students to apply the activity to their own lives.
Debrief Questions	– Well-planned questions will draw the students to their own conclusions and help them assess their own learning. – "What?" – immediate questions – "So what?" – purpose questions – "Now what?" – application to life questions
Summarization and Closure	Review the lesson information and interest the students with the next lesson.
Differentiation	Plan in advance the learning strategies necessary for all students in the class.
Evaluation	What type of evaluation process will address the question of effectiveness?
Data Collection	Indicate the procedures for collecting process, perception, and outcome data.
Process Data	How many students, grade level, etc.
Perception Data	Exit ticket survey as students leave.
Outcome Data	How are students different as a result of this information?

Classroom Management

Many school counselors attempt to avoid the difficult dual relationship of disciplinarian and counselor. As a classroom instructor, it is important that the school counselor has some training, awareness, and skills in handling disruptions in the classroom. In the school counseling lesson venue, it is important for the school counselor to support the classroom teacher's rules, but equally important is developing an approach for managing students' off-task behaviors while preserving their relationship with students.

> Professional school counselors need to behave in such a way as to help students understand that the responsibility for the classroom's environment belongs to the students, and the professional school counselors are not police officers present to enforce oppressive rule.
>
> (Goodnough et al., 2007, p. 150)

Interestingly, the primary difference between successful and unsuccessful behavior managers is not the manner in which they handle discipline problems, but instead the number of discipline problems they encounter, with the successful managers creating a structured environment and managing behavioral antecedents to diminish the likelihood of behavior problems ever occurring (Elliott, Witt, Kratochwill, & Stoiber, 2002). In an effort to avoid potential behavior problems, one of the first considerations is developing procedures, which are essentially a way to accomplish an action. Each time you want to accomplish something, there should be a procedure or set of procedures to achieve it (Wong, Wong, Jondahl, & Ferguson, 2014). For elementary school counselors, this could be something like:

Box 5.6

Getting Ready for our Counseling Corner

1. Put away our books.
2. Get out our counseling folders.
3. Come to the carpet quietly.

Middle and high school counselors may also use procedures, but they should be tailored to the developmental levels of the students. An example might be a PowerPoint slide that precedes a counseling session:

Box 5.7

Procedures for Counseling Exercises

1. If you are finished with your work, submit it to your teacher.
2. On your laptop, go to the district's school counseling webpage.
3. Login and answer the warm-up question.

Wong and colleagues (2014) suggest that it is necessary for students to understand that classroom procedures are used to make their days flow more efficiently and peacefully. Procedures function as a way of eliminating confusion, establishing a routine, and enabling the students' focus to be on the work of the lesson (Wong et al., 2014). Students should practice these procedures until they demonstrate mastery.

In order to diminish the opportunity for talking and misbehavior that a transition point may imply, having students complete planned work, such as a warm-up activity, is often beneficial. The school counselor can post a question to ascertain students' prior knowledge, or ask them to respond to a quotation about the topic that will be presented. For elementary school students, having them draw a picture that shows a particular behavior, for example, may maintain their interest and bridge the time between the previous instructional activity and the counseling session scheduled for the day. Similarly, ending the session with a routine wrap-up activity, such as, "this week, I am going to use _____ that I learned today" may reduce a tendency to become inattentive or disruptive as the class returns to their instructional activities (Wong et al., 2014).

Expectations for students should be communicated proactively, with active strategies used to help maintain student behaviors. These active strategies may include both nonverbal and verbal interventions. Nonverbal interventions include such techniques as planned ignoring, proximity control, and signal interference, while verbal interventions may include verbal redirection, contingent praise, and tension reduction. While these techniques are helpful in managing unwanted behavior, the most effective method of encouraging desired behavior is reinforcement. Reinforcement increases the probability that a behavior will be demonstrated, either through positive reinforcement, in which the behavior is followed by a preferred stimulus or negative reinforcement, in which an adverse stimulus is removed after the desired behavior has occurred (Shepherd & Linn, 2015).

The delicate balance between being a disciplinarian in the classroom or allowing an "anything goes" approach takes time for school counselors to develop. Use of the authoritarian approach by school counselors often leads students to distance themselves from the counselor, and gives the student yet another negative experience with an adult. On the other hand, the passive school counselor, who does not respond to negative behaviors, sends a message of powerlessness of the adult and undermines the students' respect, which can ultimately render the lesson ineffective (Goodnough et al., 2007).

Responding to inappropriate behavior during school counseling curriculum lessons or group activities requires finesse and strategies. Power struggles only tend to escalate behaviors rather than mitigate them. Modeling self-control is the premier teaching moment for a school counselor. Yet, some negative behaviors may be attributed to a poorly planned or ineffectively delivered classroom lesson. This speaks to why it is so important for school counselors to be intentional in the planning of their presentations. Gordon (1997) recommends five strategies for connecting with students, which include: understand the culture of the students and of the school; validate the students' experiences; relate your lesson to the students' world as in music, videos, movies; be able to name the students and understand their social connections; and be "real" with the students as deemed appropriate.

Many suggestions have been offered for handling difficult behaviors (e.g., Dollarhide & Saginak, 2012; Guillaume, 2008; Williams, Lantz, & Noorulamin, 2008). Through the use of various tools and strategies, the basic rules that may help the school counselor develop a respectful and productive classroom environment include:

1. Treat all learners with dignity and respect.
   Strategies: Utilize listening skills, I-statements, private correction, hints, humor, or emotional control.
2. Actively prevent misbehavior.
   Strategies: Develop a meaningful curriculum, consider developmental age, use appropriate power, develop clear expectations, anticipate what is the worst that could happen, approach the situation from the positive, and utilize the power of nonverbal communication.

3. View discipline as an opportunity to help students gain independence and responsibility.
   Strategies: Use learning moments, establish boundaries, encourage choices, be consistent, and use natural consequences.
4. Address discipline issues in many ways and on multiple levels.
   Strategies: Consider group size using hand motions, lights off and on, and noise signals. Overlapping, which includes addressing behavior without stopping the lesson, will diminish time for acting-out behaviors. Consider the intensity of your response and the motivation of the behavior, as well as how to redirect the students.

(Guillaume, 2008, pp. 243–267)

One important component in school counseling curriculum lessons and management that is often overlooked is the cultural awareness of the students who comprise the class. Not all students come from the same socioeconomic status or cultural experiences; however, educators seldom take the time to learn from the students about their individual cultures. Given that cultural issues are also a part of the students' experiences and that cultural awareness is a contributing factor in the achievement gap, it is imperative that school counselors be more aware of this dynamic.

Summary

The school counseling core curriculum can have a powerful impact on students within the school system. Research indicates that not only is this type of school counseling programming an efficient delivery method, but when delivered effectively, it can impact all three domains of the school counseling program: academic, career, and social/emotional. Collaborating with the teacher in whose class the school counseling curriculum lesson will be presented regarding the goals and objectives aids in the educational alliance. It is also critical to align *the ASCA Mindsets & Behaviors* (2014b) with the Common Core Standards (National Governors Association and Council of Chief State School Officers, 2010) of the subject of the class.

A thorough proposal for the school counseling curriculum can help teachers understand the importance of the lessons and the scope and sequence of the unit being developed. Aside from the curriculum used, one of the keys to effective school counseling lessons is how well it is delivered. It is important for school counselors to develop effective teaching strategies as well as being able to deal with classroom management issues that may arise. With proper and intentional planning of the lessons and the pedagogy, school counseling lessons can be fun and informational for both the students and the school counselor, while impacting the school climate in a positive way.

References

Akos, P., Cockman, C. R., & Strickland, C. A. (2007). Differentiating classroom guidance. *Professional School Counseling, 10*, 455–463.

American School Counselor Association (2012). *The ASCA national model: A framework for for school counseling programs* (3rd ed.). Alexandria, VA: Author.

American School Counselor Association (2014a). *State certification requirements*. Available online at www.school-counselor.org/school-counselors-members/careers-roles/state-certification-requirements (accessed April 3, 2015).

American School Counselor Association (2014b). *ASCA mindsets & behaviors for student success: K-12 college- and career-readiness standards for every student*. Alexandria, VA: Author.

Baker, S. B. (1994). Mandatory teaching experience for school counselors: An impediment to uniform certification standards for school counselors. *Counselor Education & Supervision, 33,* 314–326.

Brigman, G., & Webb, L. (2005). *Student Success Skills: Classroom manual.* Boca Raton, FL: Atlantic Education Consultants.

Committee for Children (1997). *Second Step: A violence prevention curriculum, grades 1–3* (2nd ed.). Seattle, WA: Author.

Dahir, C. A., & Stone, C. B. (2012). *The transformed school counselor* (2nd ed.). Belmont, CA: Brooks/Cole.

Dollarhide, C. T., & Saginak, K. A. (2012). *Comprehensive school counseling programs.* Boston, MA: Pearson Education, Inc.

Dunn, R., & Dunn, K. (1999). *The complete guide to the learning styles inservice system.* Boston, MA: Allyn & Bacon.

Dunn, R., Dunn, K., & Price, G. E. (1989). *Learning style inventory (LSI).* Lawrence, KS: Price Systems.

Elliott, S. N., Witt, J. C., Kratochwill, T. R., & Stoiber, K. C. (2002). Selecting and evaluating classroom interventions. In M. A. Shinn, H. M. Walker, & G. Stoner (Eds.), *Interventions for academic and behavior problems II: Preventive and remedial approaches* (pp. 243–294). Bethesda, MD: National Association of School Psychologists.

Erford, B. T., & McKechnie J. A. (2004). How to write learning objectives. In B. T. Erford (Ed.), *Professional school counseling: A handbook of theories, programs, and practices* (pp. 273–301). Austin, TX: Pro-ed Publishing.

Goodnough, G. E., Pérusse, R., & Erford, B. T. (2007). Developmental classroom guidance. In B. T. Erford (Ed.), *Transforming the school counseling profession* (2nd ed.; pp. 142–165). Upper Saddle River, NJ: Pearson Education.

Gordon, R. L. (1997). How novice teachers can succeed with adolescents. *Educational Leadership, 54,* 56–58.

Guillaume, A. M. (2008). *K-12 Classroom teaching: A primer for new professionals* (3rd ed.). Upper Saddle River, NJ: Pearson Education Inc.

Gysbers, N. C., & Henderson, P. (2000). *Developing and managing your school guidance program* (3rd ed.). Alexandria, VA: American Counseling Association.

Havighurst, R. J. (1972). *Developmental tasks and education* (3rd ed.). New York: David McKay.

Kovalik, S. J., & Olsen, K. D. (2005). *Exceeding expectations: A user's guide to implementing brain research in the classroom* (3rd ed.). Federal Way, WA: Author.

Lapan, R. T., Gysbers, N.C., Hughey, K., & Arni, T. J. (1993). Evaluating a guidance and language arts unit for high school juniors. *Journal of Counseling & Development, 71,* 444–451.

Learning Disabilities Association of America (n.d.). *Adult literacy, pre-k thru high school for educators.* Available online at http://ldaamerica.org/successful-strategies-for-teaching-students-with-learning-disabilities/ (accessed May 19, 2015).

Lovelace, M. K. (2005). Meta-analysis of experimental research based on the Dunn and Dunn Model. *Journal of Educational Research, 98,* 176–183.

Mager, R. F. (1997). *Preparing instructional objectives: A critical tool in the development of effective instruction* (3rd ed.). Atlanta, GA: The Center for Effective Performance.

Marzano, R. J. (2007). *The art and science of teaching: A comprehensive framework for effective instruction.* Alexandria, VA: Association for Curriculum and Supervision Development.

National Governors Association and Council of Chief State School Officers (2010). *Common core state standards initiative.* Available online at www.corestandards.org (accessed May 11, 2015).

No Child Left Behind Act of 2001, Pub. L. No. 107–110 (2002).

Peterson, J. S., Goodman, R., Keller, T., & McCauley, A. (2004). Teachers and nonteachers as school counselors: Reflections on the internship experience. *Professional School Counseling, 7,* 246–255.

Shepherd, T. L., & Linn, D. (2015). *Behavior and classroom management in the multicultural classroom: Proactive, active, and reactive strategies.* Los Angeles, CA: Sage.

Sink, C. (2005). *Contemporary school counseling: Theory, research and practice.* Boston, MA: Routledge.

Stein, D. M., & DeBerard, S. (2010). Does holding a teacher education degree make a difference in school counselors' job performance? *Journal of School Counseling, 8,* 1–26.

Tomlinson, C. T. (2005). Quality curriculum and instruction for highly able students. *Theory into Practice, 44,* 160–166.

Tomlinson, C. A., & Imbeau, M. B. (2012). Common sticking points about differentiation. *School Administrator*, *69*, 18–22.

Wang, K. C., Mukhtar, R. A., & Saenz, R. E. (2005). *Hardcore neuroscience*. Philadelphia, PA: Lippincott, Williams, & Wilkins.

Whiston, S. C., Tai, W. L., Rahardja, D., & Eder, K. (2011). School counseling outcome: A meta-analytic examination of interventions. *Journal of Counseling & Development, 89*, 37–55.

Williams, R. L., & Riedo, S. (2008). *A handbook for leading positive youth development programs*. Denver, CO: Smart-Girl.

Williams, R. L., Lantz, A., & Noorulamin, S. (2008). *Making smart choices: Social and emotional skills for adolescent girls*. Alexandria VA: American School Counselor Association.

Wong, H. K., Wong, R. T., Jondahl, S. F., & Ferguson, O. F. (2014). *The classroom management book*. Mountain View, CA: Harry K. Wong Publications, Inc.

Chapter Six
Individual Counseling

In *the ASCA National Model®* (2012), individual counseling, along with group counseling and crisis response, is categorized as a responsive service, which is defined as "activities designed to meet students' immediate needs and concerns" (p. 86). These services are steeped in the history of schools, where interventions were directed toward individual children who required support after showing distress. However, as the school counseling profession has moved away from the student services model, which focused more upon meeting the needs of at-risk students, and toward models that emphasize impacting the entire student population through comprehensive programming, school counselors have been encouraged to spend less time providing individual counseling.

This philosophical shift in *the ASCA National Model®* (2012) has brought into focus a long-standing controversy within counselor education programs in which school counselors often comprise a plurality of the student body and yet the majority of the backgrounds of most of the faculty are clinical in nature. Such a faculty may fail to demonstrate an understanding of the educational context where services are delivered. As such, these faculty members tend to train school counselors to function as mental health therapists who apply their skills in the school setting. However, *the ASCA National Model®* (2012) explicitly states that "School counselors do not provide therapy or long-term counseling in schools to address psychological disorders" (p. 86). In contrast to therapy, *the Model* indicates that counseling is planned, goal-focused, and short-term, and is used to address issues that hinder achievement. Accordingly, this chapter will identify and describe theories, techniques, and frameworks that are relevant to school counselors in providing individual, brief counseling within an educational context.

School counselors must use brief approaches in providing individual counseling. It is essential to remember the primary mission of the school is promoting academic success – interventions that remove children from the classroom potentially interfere with this mission. School counselors should attempt to minimize students' removal from the classroom by scheduling individual counseling sessions during less instructionally intensive times, such as during homeroom, study halls, elective classes, lunch periods, etc. Individual counseling conducted within school settings must be time limited. Individual sessions typically run from 10–30 minutes, and the amount of time is often dictated by the school's schedule. For example, when a student seeks to talk with the school counselor, the school counselor often seeks to attempt to assist the student with his or her issue, helping the student to construct an approach to the issue, by the end of the period or before the next important school activity, such as an exam or the start of a lesson. Thus, he or she may only have 10 minutes to assist the student with the issue. As he or she listens to the student and gathers information about the issue, he or she must assess the time and number of sessions it may take to assist the student with his or her issue, or whether the student should be referred outside of the school. The school counselor seeks to instill a sense of empowerment in the student, providing the message that the student possesses the resources to address whatever issue he or she is presenting, and avoids implying that meeting with the school counselor again is essential for addressing the issue. However, if the student and school counselor agree to meet again, the school counselor should ask the student to identify times for future meetings which are less likely to interfere with the student's academics.

Another reason why school counselors must use brief approaches in individual counseling is that it may not be an efficient use of time in comparison to the time spent in group counseling and school counseling classroom lessons. School counselors who primarily use individual counseling are not likely to impact the entire student population and thus may not be regarded as valuable members of the school staff. *The Model* states that students who require long-term therapy should be referred to relevant community resources.

Although school counselors are encouraged by *the ASCA National Model®* (2012) to provide individual counseling in a brief format, this does not diminish the importance of this service. Studies comparing brief counseling to long-term therapy have revealed no difference in effectiveness (e.g., Brown & Minami, 2010). Furthermore, while *the ASCA National Model®* (2012) recommends that school counselors refer students who require long-term therapy to community resources, only a small number of families follow through on a school counselor's referral to mental health services outside the school system. Thus, the brief counseling provided is often the only therapy the child will receive. In recognition of this, it is imperative that school counselors work to improve their effectiveness in providing brief counseling.

Effectiveness of Individual Counseling with Children

The research literature regarding positive responses to counseling services shows that counseling is effective and results in fairly large benefits for both adults (e.g., Wampold, 2010) and children (Kelley, Bickman, & Norwood, 2010). The research also seems to indicate that a variety of counseling theories/approaches are equally effective, and there are factors that are common to all counseling approaches, which are responsible for facilitating positive outcomes; this is referred to as the common factors model. Lambert's (1992) analysis of the research literature indicated that client factors account for 40% of the change shown in response to the counseling provided. Client factors associated with change include their strengths, severity of the disturbance, capacity to relate to others, psychological mindedness, ability to identity particular goals, and motivation. An additional 30% of client change is predicted by client-counselor relationship factors such as the ability to build and maintain rapport and effective communications. Fifteen percent of client change is accounted for by the client's hopefulness, meaning their expectation that counseling will benefit him or her. Finally, 15% of client change is attributed to the specific counseling model or technique. In summary, the research seems to indicate that counselors should primarily seek to develop a caring and genuine relationship with students as it is the factor under the control of the counselor which has the strongest relationship to positive outcomes for students.

It is understood that in most programs students will complete a course of counseling theories and techniques. The intent of this chapter is to provide a review of several counseling theories that have particular relevance for conducting brief, individual counseling in a school setting. Counseling theories that are reviewed include person-centered, reality, solution-focused, and cognitive-behavioral. Motivational interviewing is discussed in Chapter 9: Academic Development. Adler's individual psychology and narrative theory are two other counseling theories which are commonly used by school counselors, but due to space limitations, are not reviewed in this chapter.

Person-Centered Theory

Nearly all counseling theories emphasize the need for counselors to establish a positive relationship with students. However, it can be argued that Rogers' person-centered theory (Raskin, Rogers, & Witty, 2011) is the only major theory that claims that the relationship is in itself necessary *and* sufficient for producing client growth, and thus speaks most directly about the nature of the client-counselor relationship. Rogers believed that people are inherently oriented toward growth but become maladjusted when they deny or distort aspects of their experience. People often deny experiences in order to maintain an ideal image of themselves. For example, men and boys are often fearful of appearing weak and thus may deny or distort negative feelings as sadness, hurt, rejection, etc. that they believe imply vulnerability and weakness to others. The incongruence enables the male to maintain the ideal image but at the cost of failing to symbolize or integrate aspects of his experience, eventually leading to more significant maladjustment.

Box 6.2

Did you know?

Carl Rogers committed the latter part of his life to applying his theories to national social conflict and political oppression, working in Northern Ireland, South Africa, Brazil, and the Soviet Union (Raskin, Rogers, & Witty, 2011).

The person-centered counselor facilitates a caring, democratic, non-judgmental, non-directive environment that enables the student to become more fully aware of various aspects of his or her experience, thus activating the student's innate tendency toward growth.

Box 6.3

Person-centered theory – popularized by Carl Rogers and theorizes that the client-counselor relationship is both necessary *and* sufficient for producing client growth.

Within this theoretical framework, the role of the counselor can be likened to that of a facilitator who provides the conditions for change, rather than being responsible for directing the helpee's change. The conditions that the counselor provides are congruence, unconditional positive regard, and empathic understanding of the helpee's internal frame of reference. The counselor himself or herself must be congruent, meaning that he or she can assimilate and integrate various aspects of his or her own experience. In other words, the counselor should be psychologically mature, self-aware, and open and accepting of himself or herself and others.

Also, the counselor must demonstrate an unconditional positive regard for the student, accepting without judging the student's thoughts, feelings, motivations, etc. Accepting the student without judgment is meant to enable the student to identify and integrate aspects of his or her experience that he or she has been denying or distorting.

Box 6.4

Necessary Aspects of Person-Centered Theory:

- Counselor must be *congruent* and assimilate various aspects of their own experience.
- Counselor must demonstrate *unconditional positive regard* toward the student.
- Counselor must demonstrate *empathic understanding* of the helpee's internal frame of reference.

Students often enter counseling through the urging of parents, teachers, and administrators who want the student to change in some fashion, and at the beginning of the relationship with the counselor, students often repeatedly defend their views and positions. However, the non-judgmental position of the counselor often enables students to eventually examine aspects of themselves that heretofore they have been unwilling to consider. Some school counselors may struggle to accept aspects of students, parents, or teachers which they consider abhorrent and problematic. A perspective that is often helpful when viewing persons counselors are seeking to assist is the view that in the vast majority of situations people have good intensions and are doing the best that they can. Problematic behaviors often do make sense from their point of view.

The last condition the school counselor is responsible for providing is empathic understanding of the helpee's frame of reference. The counselor seeks to enter and understand the worldview of the student at a deep level, paraphrasing the student's implied thoughts, feelings, goals, and values, which is referred to as advanced empathy. By paraphrasing the student's implicit communications, the student gains self-awareness as he or she is presented with his or her thoughts and feelings with which he or she is struggling to better understand and assimilate. The establishment of these conditions helps students develop an expanded view of themselves, clarify their goals and values, and enhance confidence in their decision-making.

The research literature clearly demonstrates the importance of the helper-helpee relationship, and school counselors may wish to consider using Roger's person-centered theory as the foundation for their work with students. Indeed, strengthening positive adult-child relationships is the hallmark of good work in the school context. However, there are some myths about why a school counselor may object to using person-centered theory; each of these is considered below.

As indicated within *the ASCA National Model®* (2012), school counselors provide counseling rather than therapy, and as a result, the school counselor's use of a theoretical orientation may be regarded as "therapy." This argument can be rejected on several grounds. First, the distinction between "counseling" and "therapy" is not clear. For some, the distinction between the two appears to be in terms of length, but as discussed earlier, the length of the relationship does not necessarily appear to be a predictor of effectiveness. Although counseling theories do not appear to be substantially different in terms of their effectiveness, it can be argued that the failure to base one's work in a counseling theory increases the likelihood that the school counselor will impose his or her values, and thus increase the probability of causing harm. School counselors are particularly vulnerable to imposing values on others because rules governing a child's behavior are implied within the school context; unchecked advice-giving about behavior expectations can devolve into dogmatic judgments. School counselors often find a balance by avoiding the use of terms and language with parents and administrators that imply they are providing "therapy." Instead, school counselors describe their counseling work as an "approach" or "framework" in order to capture the benefits of counseling, but also remain less intrusive.

Another common criticism of person-centered theory is its lack of effectiveness with less abstract and expressive students, but later in this chapter we discuss how school counselors should select counseling theories that are consistent with the student's developmental level. As such, this criticism is not unique to a person-centered approach. A related criticism of person-centered theory suggests the non-directive stance is not well-suited for the brief time available within schools. Although the person-centered school counselor assumes a non-directive stance with students, since he or she believes in the capability of the student to generate his or her own solutions, this does not mean that the school counselor cannot be structured in his or her approach. In the following section, we describe how the person-centered approach, and other counseling theories for that matter, can be integrated with Ivey, Ivey, and Zalaquett's (2010) five stages of the well-formed interview to produce an approach that fosters students' own problem-solving, while at the same time providing a framework that assists the students in progressing through a structured problem-solving sequence.

Basic Listening Sequence. Ivey et al.'s (2010) stages of the well-formed interview, or the Basic Listening Sequence, provides school counselors with a logical, sequential framework where they can use active listening skills to guide students through the process of problem-solving. It is particularly relevant for early concrete operational and formal operational students who have, or are at the beginning of acquiring, the capacity for their own sequential reasoning. School counselors using the well-formed interview stages assist students in exploring their thoughts and feelings but do so in a focused, purposeful manner so that the exploration is related to a particular goal or outcome. This structured focus is particularly relevant to the brief nature of individual counseling conducted within a school context. The basic listening skills can be integrated with any counseling theory.

Box 6.5

Basic Listening Sequence – a logical, sequential framework that counselors can use to guide students through the process of problem-solving.

Relationship stage. In the first stage of the Basic Listening Sequence, the primary functions are to establish a positive relationship and explain the process of counseling (Ivey et al., 2010). Children vary considerably in the amount of time needed for counselors to establish trust, which is necessary for students to share thoughts and feelings. Younger children and children who are not self-referred are often reluctant to self-disclose. School counselors can increase students' comfort by explaining the counseling process. Children often are not familiar with counseling and may require explanation, in language that is at their level, about the purpose of counseling and what is expected of the school and the student. The following summary from the counselor may be helpful:

> "Students often talk with me when they are having big feelings, such as when they are angry, upset, or confused, or if they have a goal in mind like getting better grades, or making more friends. I help students better understand their thoughts and feelings, their goals, and together we can help you develop a plan to achieve your goals."

For children who are not self-referred, a somewhat common mistake for beginning school counselors is to fail to discuss why they are meeting with the child. That is, counselors sometimes assume the child is aware of the adults' concerns about the child's behavior or academic progress. In situations when a child is meeting with the school counselor at the urging of an adult, it is best for the school counselor to obtain the permission of the adult to share, in general terms, why the adult encouraged the child to meet with him or her. Honest and direct communications are likely to decrease the child's suspicions and defensiveness, thus helping to develop the child's trust. In such a situation, the school counselor might say, "Your dad called because he was concerned about your grades and he thought I might be able to help."

The school counselor can also increase the child's comfort by first engaging in safe activities, or discussing issues that are not emotionally charged. For example, after explaining the process of counseling, the school counselor might say, "I know we only met at the beginning of the school year and I was hoping to get to know you a little better. What do you like to do when you are not here in school?" Other safe activities include games like Jenga and Connect Four, playing with stress balls, shooting baskets, coloring, etc. Activities that facilitate child-counselor interactions are especially helpful. That is, watching the child color is less engaging than coloring together. Counselors can use the child's preferences as the basis for selecting safe activities.

Story and strengths stage. In this stage, the primary functions are to gather data by exploring the student's perspective, thoughts, feelings, and strengths/resources. During this stage, the school counselor is particularly non-directive, and should mainly use open-ended questions, paraphrases, or reflection of feelings as the student shares his or her perspective on the issue that led him or her to seek counseling, or led an adult to encourage the student to seek counseling. The counselor seeks to understand the student's explicit statements, and implied thoughts, feelings, meanings, motivations, and solutions, which when reflected back to the student may help him or her develop a deeper understanding of his or her perspective of the situation. Person-centered theory believes in the student's ability to generate his or her own solutions, and often during this stage, the student will imply solutions for his or her situation depending upon how he or she discusses an issue. For example, a student who is unhappy with a recent grade in a class may talk about how he or she does not like the teacher, which some may regard as the student disowning responsibility. Although that may be the case, it may also imply that he or she views their relationship with the teacher as part of the problem, and thus possibly as part of the solution.

Goals stage. In this stage, the school counselor formally clarifies the student's goal. After collecting data in the story and strengths stage, the school counselor should summarize the student's perspective, and then ask the student: "We've been talking for a while, let me ask you, what do want in this situation?" It is a mistake for the school counselor to assume that he or she knows the student's goal, as often the exploration that occurred in the story and strengths stage has helped to clarify and thus slightly change the student's goal. The school counselor can follow up this initial question with an exploration of the student's vision of the goal, meaning what the student thinks he or she may gain by accomplishing the described goal. The school counselor can encourage the student to define the goal in specific terms, asking, "So what specifically are the types of grades you want to have by the end of the marking period?"

Restory stage. The primary function of this stage may be seen as developing solutions or perspectives that may assist with achievement of the student's goal. The school counselor can maintain a non-directive stance by exploring the student's ideas for achieving his or her goals. For example, the school counselor might say, "You mentioned that you have thought about talking with your friend about your belief that she spread a rumor about you, but you also said that you are not sure if you want to do this."

This example reflects another function of this interview stage, which is to explore the student's incongruities or dilemma. In this example, the student's dilemma is that on the one hand she wants to talk with her friend, but on the other hand she is reluctant to do so. Often, students have generated options, but they are concerned about carrying out an option, and the active listening provided by the school counselor enables the student to examine his or her concerns about the various options, which often helps them with decision-making. For situations that involve the potential of communicating with someone else, whether it be a peer, teacher, or parent, the school counselor can help the student examine what he or she believes is the other person's perspective. This process may help the student develop insight regarding his or her contribution to the situation, and how to explore how the other person might respond if the student was to approach him or her.

During this stage, the school counselor can also highlight strengths or resources that the student mentioned or implied in a previous stage, which may be relevant to the student's achievement of his or her goal. Solution-focused theory, which will later be discussed in greater detail, uses the techniques of exception seeking to explore times when the goal in question has been realized or when the problem does not exist. For example, the student might be asked to explore when he or she has been successful at earning good grades, motivating himself or herself to do something that he or she did not want to do, managing conflict with a peer or adult, managing his or her emotions, etc., which the school counselor follows up by exploring how the skills or techniques that enabled him or her to achieve past success can be modified or used in the current situation.

Action stage. In the last stage, the school counselor helps the student transfer the information discussed, gained, or clarified in the previous stages by exploring what the student plans to do with the information. The emphasis is on helping the student develop a concrete plan of action to implement.

Box 6.6

Stages of the Basic Listening Sequence:

- *Relationship stage* = building trust and explaining expectations.
- *Story and strengths stage* = exploring the student's thoughts, feelings, and strengths/resources.
- *Goal stage* = clarification of the student's goals.
- *Restory stage* = development of solutions or perspectives that may help the student achieve their goal.
- *Action stage* = helping the student transfer previously discussed information or strategies into concrete action steps.

Given that school counselors are typically limited to anywhere from one to three individual meetings with a student, the school counselor wants the student to leave even a first session with a specific plan of action. In order to increase the likelihood the student will engage in transfer of learning, the school counselor should examine with the student the what, who, when, where, and how of their plan. For example, for a student who has decided that he wants to increase the amount of time he studies for a subject, the school counselor can help him consider how much time he will spend studying, what he will focus upon, where he studies best, and who might assist him in realizing his plan. For situations in which the student is leaning toward communicating with another person, the school counselor might suggest that they role-play the potential interaction. The school counselor can end the individual meeting by summarizing the student's intended plan, asking the child if he or she would like to meet again, and if the student would like the school counselor to ask him or her when they next encounter each other how the plan worked out.

Developmental Approach to Individual Counseling

One of the most challenging aspects of providing counseling to children is that they vary widely in terms of their socio-emotional and cognitive development. A number of counseling developmental theorists, such as D'Andrea (1988), assert that counseling theories vary in their applicability to the developmental stages, and that the task of the counselor is to identify the child's developmental level and apply the counseling theory that is relevant to his or her level of cognitive complexity. These counseling developmental theories are based on Jean Piaget's cognitive developmental theory, which asserts that there are specific cognitive tools or "operations" associated with each stage of cognitive development. According to D'Andrea (1988), counseling theories vary in the degree to which they match the cognitive complexity of the various stages of development of the child.

Cognitive developmental stages. At the preoperational level, in which children are typically between infancy and 7 years of age, children are learning to use symbols such as words and images to understand how the world operates, and they tend to express themselves in terms of physiological sensations and actions and often talk in a random and disorganized fashion (Ivey et al., 2010). At this developmental level, the child lacks control of his or her thoughts, feelings, and impulses because he or she lacks the ability to reflect upon the source of the psychological phenomena.

Children usually function within the concrete operational stage between the ages of 7–11. The advantage of concrete operations is that the child can reason logically – in contrast to the preoperational child who tends to base their logic on appearance (e.g., concrete, observable events) and thus fails to consider cause and effect or sequential transformations. Children within this developmental stage tend to focus upon linear, sequential details regarding social interactions and events, and they struggle to understand the perspective of others and how their actions may have contributed to events. In other words, the child is learning to think in a sequential, logical manner, but is not yet able to do so.

Children may acquire the capacity for formal operational thinking around the age of 11. Formal operational thinkers are capable of deductive reasoning, enabling them to examine various solutions and options, understand abstract concepts such as justice, democracy, love, etc., and identify behavioral patterns and reflect upon their meaning. They are able to "think about their thinking."

Individual counseling with preoperational children. Because of preoperational children's limited capacity for self-awareness, school counselors can use behavior theory to teach the child specific behavioral skills, through the use of modeling, practice/role-playing, and either tangible or verbal reinforcement. There are a limitless number of behavioral skills that school counselors may teach children and the child's specific needs can be determined through the use of observation and consultation with the children's teachers and parents. Commonly taught behavioral skills include anger management, conflict resolution, anxiety management, social skills, attending, organization, etc. Such behavioral skills can also be taught within the context of structured play approaches, in which the school counselor acts out through puppets, stuffed animals, etc. the various components of a behavioral skill. Counselors help children use games they play during recess for the skills they need in the classroom. For example, games like red light/green light and Simon Says are particularly useful in teaching children listening skills, physiological control, and how these skill sets are coordinated. Both games teach children what to listen for (i.e., green light) and how to act when you do hear the cue compared to when you do not. Classrooms that use visual prompts (green, yellow, and red lights) to prompt behavioral expectations and control can capitalize on the similarities of these games. Teachers that reinforce attentive listening through games (e.g., staying in your seat, lining up when asked) are especially effective. Researchers have shown that teaching children behavioral self-regulation also improves academic readiness skills (Tominey & McClelland, 2011).

Counseling children at this developmental level should also include a psychoeducational component such that the school counselor can help the child begin to develop the language to identify and express his or her thoughts, feelings, and physiological sensations. With this knowledge comes the understanding that such development will, in the future, increase the child's capacity to reflect upon and manage these psychological phenomena. It is useful, for example, to help children begin to differentiate between thoughts, feelings, and behavior. A counselor could ask the child: "Tell me three happy thoughts." Here, counselors are helping children find positive associations. Once mastered, a counselor may ask, "Tell me three things you did that worked out well," which helps to promote a focus upon cause and effect. In developmental order, the counselor wants to help children distinguish between thoughts and feelings and then move to how the child can affect outcomes through actions. Counselors may point out, "Because you studied you got a good grade, because you showed good effort your teacher was happy with your project, because you listened to your classmate she said you were a good friend."

However, many children at this age may not understand the extent to which behavioral outcomes are under their control. Accordingly, the next task is to ask the same questions about others: "Tell me something that worked out well for someone else" and then "Tell me what they did to make it work out well." With these basic questions, the school counselor can help children to understand cause and effect and whose actions led to the outcome. This is a critical skill, because young children often confuse the cause and effect of their problems (e.g., my parents are divorcing because I didn't clean my room).

Box 6.7

Development-related Goals of Counseling with Preoperational Children:

- Improve language skills related to thoughts, feelings, and physiological sensations.
- Differentiate between thoughts, feelings, and behavior.
- Help foster cause and effect thinking and understanding of child's own thoughts and feelings.
- Help foster cause and effect thinking and understanding of other's thoughts and feelings.

Furthermore, we want students to appropriately connect their efforts with their outcomes; otherwise it is difficult for them to detect how they might be able to influence the outcomes they desire.

Individual counseling with concrete operational children. Students in the concrete operational stage are beginning to understand logical sequences, but are not yet ready for hypothetical thinking or inferences. They do understand an object can be round and green and small but will miss more complex logic; if the bird is bigger than the cat and the cat is bigger than the dog, then the dog, by definition, is also smaller than the bird. Concrete operational children are most likely to benefit from counseling that assists such children in expanding their thinking in a logical, sequential manner, which includes reality therapy, solution-focused theory, certain techniques of behavioral theory, and structured cognitive theory approaches such as those developed by Kendall (2011).

Reality therapy. Choice theory, a major tenant of reality therapy, asserts that the brain functions like a thermostat, in that it regulates behavior in order to change the environment to meet our five basic needs, which are belonging, power, freedom, fun, and survival (Wubbolding, 2010). Reality therapy includes a psychoeducational aspect, in that students can be taught about these basic needs and be helped in determining which of their needs are currently satisfied and which of their needs they wish to pursue.

Box 6.8

Reality therapy – counseling technique that teaches students how to recognize which of their basic needs are currently met and which should be pursued.

Students are taught the WDEP system in which W stands for Wants, D is concerned with Direction and Doing, E regards Evaluation, and P is for Planning. The WDEP system is essentially a method of problem-solving and students can be taught these steps using WDEP as a mnemonic device.

Box 6.9

Did you know?

William Glasser, the founder of reality therapy and choice theory, was a psychiatrist. However, many psychiatrists considered Dr. Glasser's theories to be controversial as Dr. Glasser was very critical of modern psychiatry and what he considered to be an excessive emphasis on diagnosis and use of psychotropic medications (Wubbolding, 2010).

First, the school counselor helps a student identify their *Wants* by accessing their "Quality World," which consists of the student's ideals. A counselor helps the student generate or describe his or her Quality World through guided imagery, exploring an ideal day, or a situation in which the student would feel a sense of pride. Helpful questions include "If you could wave a magic wand and get whatever you want, what it would be," or "When have you gotten part of what you wanted?" Upon identifying the student's desires or wants, the school counselor can help the student identify what he or she believes would be the advantages of achieving his or her goal, which often leads to further exploration of their priorities. The school counselor can use a scaling question to have the student rate his or her level of commitment to achieving the goal, posing the following type of question: "On a scale of 1–10, with 10 being the thing you want the most and 1 being not that important, how important is it for you to increase your grades to at least all 'Cs?'"

Assessing the student's level of commitment enhances his or her self-awareness and helps the school counselor understand the degree to which a topic should be focused upon in the counseling session. Next, the school counselor has the student identify his or her *Direction* or *Doings*, meaning the various thoughts and behaviors related to the issue. The school counselor can use an element of brainstorming during this phase, in which he or she can have the student write down his or her thoughts and behaviors about his or her goals/wants, or have the student generate a list of his or her daily activities that will ultimately be compared to how he or she relates to a desired goal.

In the next phase, the school counselor has the student *Evaluate* the degree to which he or she thinks the various behaviors and thoughts he or she identified are either "helping" or "hindering" the process of achieving his or her goal, which enables the student to identify which behaviors and thoughts he or she wants to increase or decrease or eliminate altogether. The school counselor should refrain from providing advice, regardless of the immaturity of the student's ideas, but should perceive his or her role as facilitating the student's problem-solving.

For example, it is not uncommon for male students to first identify violence as an option for achieving their goal, and the school counselor should refrain from immediately rejecting this option, but should instead assist them in exploring the potential consequences of using aggression. In this manner, the school counselor hopes to help the student learn to "think through the consequences of his or her actions." It is tempting to tell the child what to do; however, people are more likely to engage in options which they have generated, and the objective of this process is to help the child learn the process of problem-solving rather than solving a particular problem/issue in a manner preferred by the adult. Usually students have thought about various aspects of the problem/goal, and if the school counselor is patient, often the student will share the variety of options he or she has generated, and his or her preferences for various perspectives about the problem/goal. The task of the school counselor then becomes one of helping the student sort through the potential positive and negative consequences of his or her various ideas.

During the *Planning* phase, the school counselor assists the student in organizing his or her goals and ideas identified through brainstorming to develop a plan for achieving the goal. The school counselor can teach the student about the characteristics of effective planning through the SAMIC acronym: (S)imple, (a)ttainable, (m)easurable, (i)mmediate, (c)ontrolled, (c)ommitted, and (c)onsistent. Subsequent meetings involve reviewing the student's implementation of his or her plan or lack thereof. Lack of progress may be due to lack of commitment on the student's part to which the school counselor can respond by exploring the student's ambivalence, identifying other goals that he or she would be more interested in pursuing, or exploring the potential consequence of not making progress.

For example, if the student is receiving pressure from teachers or parents to improve his or her performance, the school counselor may help the student guess how his or her parents or teachers might respond to his or her lack of progress, and then the student can consider his or her willingness to accept the consequences. Lack of progress may also indicate that the student's goal is unrealistic. For example, some students, without explicitly saying so, want to be popular but that student's level of status may be very resistant to change; the school counselor may lead the student to redefine the goal of popularity as developing a friend, or making the effort to connect with others while focusing less on whether others actually respond.

Box 6.10

Phases of Reality Therapy:

(W)ants
(D)irection and Doing
(E)valuation
(P)lanning

Finally, a common reason for lack of progress is related to an inadequate or underdeveloped plan; in this case the school counselor use the same WDEP phases to help the child revise his or her plan.

Reality therapy case study. Reality therapy was used with Brandy, an African American, seventh grade student, who sought out the school counselor after receiving detention from her math teacher, Mr. Johnson, for what he identified as her "poor attitude." Brandy was angry with Mr. Johnson, explaining that she did not think that he was an effective teacher as it was her perception that he used a lot of worksheets, did not respond adequately to students' questions, and seemed to favor certain students in the class. Previously, the school counselor had developed a good relationship with Brandy as he had helped her resolve a conflict through mediation with one of her cousins who was also in seventh grade. The school counselor's perspective was that Brandy had a number of strong leadership characteristics in that she could be very assertive and compassionate, but some of the seventh grade teachers, including Mr. Johnson, appeared to regard Brandy as verbally aggressive.

After using active listening skills to identify Brandy's thoughts and feelings, the school counselor asked Brandy what she was hoping to get out the situation. Brandy indicated that she wanted to be removed from Mr. Johnson's class, but the school counselor explained that the administration did not permit such schedule changes two months into the school year. Brandy expressed anger that she could not change her math teacher, but eventually she identified her goal of improving her math grade, as she knew her mother would be unhappy if she received another "C" in math for the next marking period.

Next, the school counselor assisted Brandy in identifying her various thoughts and behaviors related to her performance in her math class and evaluating whether they were helping or hindering her in achieving her goal. Through this exploration, Brandy indicated that she was engaging in a number of behaviors that were not helping her, including choosing to sit in the back of the math class with a friend with whom she often talked while she was supposed to be working on worksheets, and not asking Mr. Johnson for help because she did not like him. The school counselor and Brandy also identified her strengths/assets for achieving her goal, which included her independence and outspokenness. The school counselor provided two reframes, stating that maybe Brandy's challenge was to learn to use her strength of outspokenness in a way that Mr. Johnson could hear, and learn to work with someone she did not like, which unfortunately is part of getting older, and these reframes appeared to resonate with Brandy.

With Brandy's consent, the school counselor and Brandy proceeded to role-play how to approach Mr. Johnson for help, with Brandy playing herself, and the school counselor playing Mr. Johnson. Following the role-play, the school counselor asked Brandy to evaluate her performance, and the school counselor provided his feedback as well, commending her on the polite way she approached the pretend Mr. Johnson. Several weeks later, when questioned in the hallway by the school counselor, Brandy indicated that she had developed a better relationship with Mr. Johnson and that her scores on recent quizzes had improved.

Solution-focused theory. Solution-focused theory can be effectively applied with both concrete and formal operational children. Solution-focused theory is widely used by school counselors for both counseling and consultation, as it is designed to be brief, and it emphasizes students' strengths. Solution-focused theory is similar to person-centered theory in that it assumes that people are growth-oriented and proactive self-healers (Murphy, 2008). A basic tenet of solution-focused theory is that people have their own resources to achieve their goals and these resources lie within their personal histories.

Solution-focused theory is influenced by the theory of social constructivism, which asserts that people actively construct their reality through the use of language, as opposed to there being an objective reality. The primary task of the school counselor is to expand a student's perception of a problem or issue, which the school counselor accomplishes by encouraging the student to change the way he or she talks about the problem or him or herself.

Students often enter counseling with what solution-focused theorists refer to as a "problem-saturated perspective." According to Taylor (2005), people often begin a counseling relationship with a focus on what they do not want, when things go wrong, aspects of the situation they cannot change, when they have not been successful in addressing the issue, and are pessimistic about the future. The task of the counselor is to shift the conversation and the student's language to discuss what the student wants, explore times when he or she has been successful, or at least partially successful, and aspects of the situation that the student can change.

Similar to person-centered theory, the school counselor initially seeks to understand the student's world-view, listening intently to the student, looking to emphasize or reinforce the student's communications that imply positive possibilities. The counselor eventually uses a number of questions or techniques that are designed to help shift the student's perspective (Murphy, 2008). Exception-seeking questions involve asking the student to identify times when he or she has been successful in dealing with the respective issue. For example, the school counselor may ask the student to describe a time when he or she believed he or she had effectively managed anger, resolved a conflict with a peer or adult, was assertive, completed homework, performed well on a test, etc. Exception-seeking questions are followed up with "not-knowing questions," in which the school counselor helps the student to minutely analyze the things he or she did to be successful, exploring the specific thoughts, behaviors, steps, motivations, etc., he or she used.

Scaling questions involve having the student rate his or her success regarding an issue. For example, the school counselor might ask, "On a scale of 1–10, with 10 being managing your anger extremely well, and 1 being not handling your anger well at all, what number would you currently give yourself in managing your anger?" Students typically respond with a rating of anywhere from 3–7, and regardless of the number the student identifies, the school counselor explores with the student what he or she did positively to get to a 3, once again minutely analyzing the various thoughts and behaviors that helped him or her achieve that positive number. This is followed by asking the student what he or she would be doing when he or she is at the next number or half-numbered step. This question helps the student to see the small things he or she needs to do in order to make progress, rather than overly focusing on the large, often unrealistic goal of fully achieving the goal. Scaling questions can also be used to explore times when the student believes he or she had a higher rate of success.

In the miracle question, the school counselor instructs the student to imagine that the problem has been resolved overnight, and then has the student explore as concretely as possible how things would be different, asking the student to identify how he or she would feel, think, behave, what he or she would do during that day, what would he or she do next, and what would friends, parents, and teachers notice about him or her.

Box 6.13

Types of Questions Used During Solution-Focused Theory Sessions:

- *Exception seeking* – student identifies a time when a problem was handled effectively.
- *Scaling* – student labels his or her level of skill or distress on a scale of 1–10 which can lead to discussions of how to move higher along the scale.
- *Miracle* – student describes how his or her life would be different if the problem were to vanish overnight.

The miracle question helps the student move beyond a problem-saturated perspective which may help the student see himself or herself and the situation in a different light, and may generate new thoughts, feelings, and ideas that are helpful for making progress.

Cognitive-behavioral theory. The structured cognitive-behavioral approach used by Kendall (2011) highlights the connections between the body's responses to anxiety-provoking situations and how the student's thinking about those feelings can increase or decrease his or her ability to cope.

Box 6.14

Cognitive-behavioral theory – focuses on the relationship between thoughts, feelings, and behaviors and promotes skills acquisition through modeling and practice sessions.

Kendall's approach has two primary segments; the first is a focus on skills training, and the second focuses on skills practice. During skills training, a counselor reviews the body's anxiety reactions (e.g., heart racing, quick breathing, sweating, skin turning red and feeling hot, feeling sick to your stomach, tightness around your ribcage, fearfulness, etc.), including those experienced by most people, those the student reports, and those the counselor has had. The message here is that it is normal for the body to respond to anxiety-provoking situations and it is important to notice your own patterns. The counselor should highlight that physical feelings are cues from the body to let us know that we need to help our body relax. Catching on to the cues early can help us manage our feelings before they spiral out of control.

In the skills practice section, counselors begin by helping students to identify their own fears and expectations about a specific situation. Identifying the student's self-talk (e.g., what he or she says to himself or herself) about the situation and his or her own reactions allows the student to modify his or her expectations. Next, the counselor helps the student to problem-solve about which attitudes or actions would be more effective. Finally, the student should evaluate if his or her efforts have been effective in helping them cope and feel better. If so, he or she should reward his or her own success.

The FEAR plan is used to counsel students exhibiting anxiety. F stands for "Feeling Frightened?" and reminds students to be aware of their physical feelings of anxiety. E stands for "Expecting bad things to happen?" and asks students to recognize their own self-talk. A stands for "Attitudes and Actions?" and reminds students to use previously identified behaviors and self-talk that will manage or decrease feelings of anxiety. R stands for "Results and Rewards?" and reminds students to consider the usefulness of their response to anxious feelings and to reward themselves for success.

Kendall and his colleagues are credited with establishing the effectiveness of manualized treatment – a treatment plan used in a predetermined order – for children and adolescents reporting feelings of anxiety. His work, the *Coping Cat Program*, is widely used and routinely updated (Kendall, 2011). Students reporting relatively minor disruptions, as well as those identified with clinical disturbances, have shown improvement after participating in the *Coping Cat Program*. Counselors are on safe ground identifying this program as an evidence-based practice when required to do so in their school districts.

Individual counseling with formal operational children. During formal operational thought, students can make decisions based on prior experiences and think logically about abstract concepts. Not only can students recognize patterns in their own behaviors, but they can also identify causality between their emotions and behaviors. As reviewed above, there can be some crossover in working with concrete operational and formal operational students. However, once formal operations are well established, person-centered and structured cognitive-behavioral approaches that are frequently used with adults are useful. Primarily, the difference between those approaches when used with students who are now in the formal operational stage is the degree of emphasis on individual choice and insight. That is, as students age, free choice and responsibility are highlighted, whereas psychoeducational information sharing is emphasized for students in the concrete operational stages. As students age, it is expected that the sources of their distress (e.g., insight) become more apparent to them and thus are available for student-driven efforts.

Person-centered theory. Person-centered theory can be considered to be the preferred approach in working with formal operational adolescents, as such youths have the capacity for problem-solving and developing complex understandings of their self-concept, values, and patterns regarding how they relate to others. The role of the school counselor using this approach is that of a facilitator, who helps the student enhance their meaning-making by providing them with a safe environment in which to explore their various thoughts and feelings, and to enhance the clarity of their perspective.

Person-centered theory case study. Jodi, a 15-year-old, ninth grade student, sought assistance from the school counselor, reporting that she was experiencing difficulty "controlling my emotions." Jodi explained that she often would "tear up" in class, meaning that she would begin to cry for no apparent reason.

Jodi moved back to the school district in the middle of her eighth grade year. She had attended elementary school in the district, but moved in fifth grade to another state when her parents separated and her mother remarried a man whom Jodi believes her mother had been having an affair with for several years. Jodi reported that her mother's new husband sexually abused her on several occasions. Jodi reported that when she informed her mother of the abuse her mother became "depressed" and felt betrayed. Jodi's mother initiated steps to separate from Jodi's stepfather, but her mother ultimately decided that it would be best for Jodi to return to live with her father. Jodi reported that she had not seen her mother or her older sister for over a year, and that her mother did not seem very interested when they talked sporadically on the phone. Jodi's mother sought counseling for Jodi, but Jodi stopped attending when she resisted the counselor's suggestion that she attempt to re-experience the sexual abuse in order to reduce her emotional intensity connected to the event.

Jodi reported being fearful and angry with her father. Her dad allegedly had been quite physically punitive with her when she was younger, and he had been investigated by Child Protective Services. She had not wanted to return to live with her father, and tried to keep her distance from him. Jodi also had "crying spells" at home to which her father would become agitated, telling her that she needed to get over it. She also saw her father as dictatorial and controlling, and said that much of their interactions involved him telling her that she needed to assume more responsibility for cleaning the home, doing dishes, etc.

Jodi had frequent altercations with other girls, often leading to her being referred to the school counselors for mediation or to the principal's office. During such a mediation, the school counselor observed that Jodi would be quite verbally aggressive, telling other girls that they had better shut up or she would make them.

Jodi began dating a boy named Mike, who was a junior at the school she attended, shortly after she returned to live with her father. She described their relationship as chaotic in that they frequently verbally argued and she worried that either he or she would eventually escalate the argument to physical aggression. She saw Mike as controlling in that he did not want her to spend time with her group of friends. She considered breaking up with Mike, and did for a short time when he confirmed that he had slept with another girl, as she feared losing her independence.

Jodi was unsure about her goals for the future. In eighth grade she received an overall score of 110 on a group intelligence test. She received mostly "B's" and "C's" in her academic subjects and was not taking any advanced academic classes. She had not given much thought to a career or post-high school plans.

The school counselor used a non-directive approach in counseling Jodi, meeting with her once a week for 6 weeks. By reflecting Jodi's implicit thoughts and feelings, the school counselor helped her to identify important themes in her worldview and patterns in her life. The school counselor affirmed Jodi's ambivalent feelings about her mother and stepfather, as well as her anger regarding her mother's apparent decision to choose Jodi's stepfather by sending Jodi to live with her father. The school counselor helped Jodi to recognize how her relationships with her parents influenced her current relationships. For example, Jodi offered the view that her tendency to become angry quickly with both female and male peers was related to her high level of anger over the past years of her life, and the school counselor and Jodi explored what she regarded as positive mechanisms for managing her feelings. Jodi gradually expressed ambivalence about her relationship with her boyfriend and men in general in that she longed for closeness, and yet was terrified by it as well.

The school counselor helped Jodi recognize that her current conflicted feelings were normal, and were also related to her past. Eventually, the school counselor helped Jodi to explore her anxiety about relating to her father in a more mature way, and Jodi reported some success in developing a closer relationship with her father. The school counselor assumed a slightly more directive approach by asking Jodi about her goals for the future. The school counselor helped Jodi to identify her personal strengths and how they could apply to the world of work. Jodi appeared to engage in more serious explorations of who she was and what she wanted for herself.

Cognitive-behavioral theory. As cognition becomes well developed in the formal operational stage, cognitive-behavioral counseling emphasizes the freedom of the individual to accept or reject his or her problematic thinking. The assumption is that problematic thinking precedes and results in problematic emotions or behaviors; by changing one's thinking – or one's perceptions of the problematic thinking – a person will change his or her feelings and/or behaviors. Some counselors following the work of Beck (Beck & Weishaar, 2014) and his colleagues have applied his cognitive approach to working with youths (e.g., Friedberg, McClure, & Garcia, 2009), and emphasize how an individual's distorted thinking (e.g., because you made one error means you will never be successful) is the primary target area. Others following the work of Ellis (Ellis & Ellis, 2014) point out irrational thinking/beliefs (e.g., one must be perfect to be loved) as the primary target area. These traditions almost exclusively assert that cognitions are the focus of counseling sessions. Other counselors are known to emphasize behavioral practices in cognitive therapy, such as stress inoculation (e.g., exposure to a perceived stressful event and re-conceptualizing the stress response) pioneered by Meichenbaum (1977). Visual imagery, rather than real life practice, may be used to "prepare" for stressful situations.

Box. 6.15

Did you know?

Aaron Beck (Beck & Weishaar, 2014) and Albert Ellis (Ellis & Ellis, 2014), whom some consider to be co-founders of cognitive-behavioral theory, were both originally trained as psychoanalysts.

In practice, counselors often use a variety of techniques to best match the needs of the individual. Further, individual responsibility is emphasized via homework assignments, in which cognitive or behavioral skills are practiced outside of the counseling sessions. Indeed, as children age into adulthood, there are specific generational assumptions and family roles that counselors will take into account in addressing problematic cognitions. Cognitive-behavioral counseling is a highly engaging process whereby both the counselor and individual participate actively to set goals, evaluate successes, modify approaches, and reward successes. Demonstrating its usefulness is often very compelling to students across the life span.

In addition to the counseling approaches described, school counselors are also encouraged to use the school's curriculum to support student cognitive development, which ultimately supports children's overall skill set. Regardless of the student's level of skill development, counselors can reference curricular experiences in which students are engaged to help their thinking about their current behaviors. For example, the counselor may reference a persuasive writing assignment an eighth grader is completing in language arts, where he is assigned the prompt: "Write for 15 minutes about something you wish someone had told you earlier!" The counselor may ask about his point of view to the question: "Write for 15 minutes about something you wish someone had told you earlier about feelings of anxiety!" That is, by using a similar prompt to the classroom activity, the student can capitalize on a practiced skill set to answer a question that can help change his thinking, and thus his behavior. Counselors in school are advantaged by the opportunity to coordinate readings and reflections already occurring within the curriculum to maximize a particular student's perspective on the life events with which he or she is struggling. Counselors who are aware of the planned curriculum can place well-timed experiences to help each student in his or her development. Working with parents around school activities is very helpful in encouraging family support as well.

Summary

School counselors are not likely to provide long-term individual counseling to students. Students and families requiring long-term clinical care are likely to receive those services through other professionals in the building (e.g., social workers or school psychologists), or they will be referred to community-based facilities. However, school counselors do need to have clinical skills. Counselors will be called upon to help school teams understand and promote behavioral change so that students may benefit from their educational environment and advance in their academic skills. Short-term counseling is routinely required for students in crisis, acute distress (e.g., peer rejection), and to promote stalled or uneven social-emotional development. Understanding the usefulness of specific therapies and being able to apply those therapies with appropriate age groups to facilitate academic and social-emotional development is a critical skill for school counselors.

References

American School Counselor Association (2012). *The ASCA national model: A framework for for school counseling programs* (3rd ed.). Alexandria, VA: Author.

Beck, A. T., & Weishaar, M. E. (2014). Cognitive therapy. In D. Wedding & R. J. Corsini (Eds.), *Current psychotherapies* (10th ed.; pp. 231–264). Belmont, CA: Brooks/Cole.

Brown, G. S., & Minami, T. (2010). Outcomes management, reimbursement, and the future of psychotherapy. In B. L. Duncan, S. D. Miller, B. E. Wampold, & M.A. Hubble (Eds.), *The heart and soul of change: Delivering what works in therapy* (2nd ed.; pp. 267–297). Washington, DC: American Psychological Association.

D'Andrea, M. (1988). The counselor as pacer: A model for the revitalization of the counseling profession. In R. Hayes & R. Aubrey (Eds.), *New directions for counseling and development* (pp. 22–44). Denver, CO: Love Publishing.

Ellis, A., & Ellis, D. J. (2014). Rational emotive behavior therapy. In D. Wedding & R. J. Corsini (Eds.), *Current psychotherapies* (10th ed.; pp. 151–189). Belmont, CA: Brooks/Cole.

Friedberg, R. D., McClure, J. M., & Garcia, J. H. (2009). *Cognitive therapy techniques for children and adolescents: Tools for enhancing practice.* New York: Guilford.

Ivey, A. E., Ivey, M. B., & Zalaquett, C. P. (2010). *Intentional interviewing and counseling: Facilitating client development in a multicultural society* (7th ed.). Belmont, CA: Brooks/Cole.

Kelley, S. D., Bickman, L., & Norwood, E. (2010). Evidence-based treatments and common factors in youth psychotherapy. In B. L. Duncan, S. D. Miller, B. E. Wampold, & M.A. Hubble (Eds.), *The heart and soul of change: Delivering what works in therapy* (2nd ed.; pp. 325–355). Washington, DC: American Psychological Association.

Kendall, P. C. (Ed.) (2011). *Child and adolescent therapy: Cognitive-behavioral procedures* (4th ed.). New York: Guilford Press.

Lambert, M. J. (1992). Implications of outcome research for psychotherapy integration. In J. C. Norcross & M. R. Goldfried (Eds.), *Handbook of psychotherapy integration* (pp. 94–129). New York: Basic Books.

Meichenbaum, D. (1977). *Cognitive-behavior modification: An integrative approach.* New York: Springer.

Murphy, J. J. (2008). *Solution-focused counseling in schools* (2nd ed.). Alexandria, VA: American Counseling Association.

Raskin, N. J., Rogers, C. R., & Witty, M. C. (2011). Client-centered therapy. In R. J. Corsini & D. Wedding (Eds.), *Current psychotherapies* (9th ed.; pp. 149–195). Belmont, CA: Brooks/Cole.

Taylor, L. (2005). A thumbnail map for solution-focused brief therapy. *Journal of Family Psychotherapy, 16,* 27–33.

Tominey, S. L., & McClelland, M. M. (2011). Red light, purple light: Findings from a randomized trial using circle time games to improve behavioral self-regulation in preschool. *Early Education & Development, 22,* 489–519.

Wampold, B. E. (2010). The research evidence for the common factors models: A historically situated perspective. In B. L. Duncan, S. D. Miller, B. E. Wampold, & M. A. Hubble (Eds.), *The heart and soul of change: Delivering what works in therapy* (2nd ed.; pp. 49–70). Washington, DC: American Psychological Association.

Wubbolding, R. E. (2010). *Reality therapy: Theories of psychotherapy.* Washington, DC: American Psychological Association.

Chapter Seven
Group Counseling

Box 7.1

2016 CACREP School Counseling Specialty Area Standards

3.c Core curriculum design, lesson plan development, classroom management strategies, and differentiated instructional strategies

3.d Interventions to promote academic development

3.f Techniques of personal/social counseling in school settings

3.l Techniques to foster collaboration within schools

3.m Strategies for implementing and coordinating peer intervention programs

---

Meeting the needs of students drives school counselors' work and vision. School counselors use group counseling interventions to promote students' academic, career, and personal/social development through the application of developmentally based approaches. This chapter will explore the school counselor's role of group facilitator, and discuss some of the relevant issues for conducting group counseling in the school setting. The availability of groups for students in schools is crucial to their overall development, and has been an integral part of *ASCA School Counselor Competencies* (ASCA, 2012). Providing students with the opportunity to come together and learn about themselves and others allows space to address *the ASCA Mindsets & Behaviors* (ASCA, 2014) as well.

According to Erford (2011), school counselors are called to bridge the achievement gap through culturally competent interventions aimed at improving students' personal, social and emotional, and career concerns. Pérusse, Goodnough, and Lee (2009) posited that group work is an effective way of providing opportunities for students to develop social skills and foster peer acceptance. Through group work, students may experience a stable environment in which it is deemed safe to express difficult feelings (Veach & Gladding, 2007). Research indicates that group counseling interventions can increase students' achievement and effectively address students' emotional and behavioral issues (Bemak, Chung, & Siroskey-Sabdo, 2005; Corey & Corey, 2006; Steen & Kaffenberger, 2007), and increase school attendance

Figure 7.1 Group Counseling Session. Copyright: www.istockphoto.com.

and work habits (Paisley & Milsom, 2007). Bailey and Bradbury-Bailey (2007) also reported that group participation allows members to bond and feel safe in sharing their experience, while working toward a shared goal. This also helps to satisfy the needs of adolescents to be socially accepted and belong to a group as well as to find their place in the world.

Professional school counselors are called to perform many group tasks throughout the course of an average day. Those groups will vary in length and level of intensity, from Response to Intervention (RtI) groups, to grief and loss groups with students, to meeting with groups of teachers for professional development training. Professional school counselors wear many group facilitator hats as part of their role in delivering a comprehensive, developmental, equitable, school counseling program. Irvin Yalom has been instrumental in influencing the group work processes of counselors for over 40 years.

Box 7.2

Did you know?

Irvin Yalom is a psychiatrist and is considered one of the foremost authorities in group counseling and existential psychotherapy.

He believed that to be an effective group facilitator, one needed to consistently demonstrate care and concern for the members of the group, while being present and emotionally available to them (Lieberman, Yalom, & Miles, 1973). Others agreed, and decades of research and practice provide support for group counseling in schools. Researchers and school counselors determined that group counseling is effective for many reasons, including:

- school counselors can see many students at one time;
- from a developmental and pedagogical perspective, students often learn best from each other (due to shared feelings and experiences);

- groups provide an excellent forum for students to experience this student-to-student learning process (mentoring, supporting, understanding, empathizing);
- groups are a microcosm of society and as such provide real-life settings in which students can work out issues and problems.

(Bruce, Getch, & Ziomek-Diagle, 2009; Gladding, 2008; Pérusse et al., 2009)

Within *the ASCA National Model®* (2012), group counseling is categorized as a direct student service that may be used to deliver the school counseling core curriculum, provide individual student planning, or for responsive services. Professional school counselors are expected to provide group counseling interventions to all students in the school community. This task can be challenging, especially in schools where large student-to-counselor ratios exist and space to conduct groups is limited. However, even in the toughest of circumstances, school counselors offer an array of group topics for students to explore, learn, and grow. While developing an equitable program serving all students, school counselors must be purposeful in their planning and preparation. Being aware of the details for each and every group will allow the counselor to facilitate each group with confidence.

Box 7.3

Important Questions in Creating School-based Counseling Groups

Answering these questions might prove helpful in establishing an effective group program.

- Why is this group relevant to students?
- Who is this group meant to serve (ages, grade level, issues addressed, and number of students)?
- Will this be a homogeneous or heterogeneous group, based on what criteria?
- How will you recruit members?
- How will you screen for appropriate fit of members for the group?
- How often will the group meet and for what period of time (six weeks, twelve weeks, etc.)?
- What will be the location of the group?
- What will be the structure of the group meetings?
- How will you evaluate the group's effectiveness?

Ethical Considerations Regarding Groups

One of the most time-efficient and effective counseling program components is offering small group counseling (ASCA, 2012). However, there are several ethical concerns to be considered when establishing small group counseling into the program. These ethical concerns encompass group participant screening, informed consent for students and parents, confidentiality, school counselor group facilitation competency, and cultural awareness in the group setting. All of these topics are explicitly addressed in *ASCA's Ethical Standards for School Counselors* (2010).

Group Screening

Section A.6 of *ASCA's Ethical Standards for School Counselors* (2010) directly discusses group work in the school setting, which is markedly different from group work conducted in a clinical venue. The first ethical concern addressed in the A.6.a subsection is the selection and screening process of student participants. As stated, "The school counselor takes reasonable precautions to protect members from physical and psychological harm resulting from interaction within the group" (ASCA *Ethical Standards*, 2010, A.6.a). This necessary precaution considers students in conflict or students with severe behavioral problems. While these issues may interfere with the progression of the group, the biggest ethical concern is that they may also cause damage to individual group members. Questions to consider in the screening process might include: Does this student work well in groups? Are they capable of understanding the material covered? Do the direction, intention, and goals of this group work for this student? Not all students necessarily benefit from small group processes, as their social skills may not be up for the challenges of group dynamics. This screening is also an opportunity to evaluate whether the individual student's needs may be effectively addressed through the group process. The success and effectiveness of the group can be sabotaged by lack of screening.

Informed Consent

At the time of the screening process the informed consent can be obtained from the potential participants. A.2 of the ASCA *Ethical Standards* (2010) suggests that in both individual and small group counseling, it is important for the practitioner to inform participants of the purpose, goals, and techniques that will be used in the sessions. This informed consent should be provided in a developmentally appropriate and meaningful manner, inclusive of a check for understanding. Additional information that should be presented to students in a developmentally appropriate manner includes how they were selected for the group, what they will get out of the group, techniques and theoretical approaches, and what they can expect regarding confidentiality.

Confidentiality

Confidentiality is the cornerstone of school counseling (Kaplan, 1995); however, in working with minors and groups there are some intrinsic limits to confidentiality. The informed consent process educates participants about the limitations to confidentiality within the group (ASCA *Ethical Standards* 2010, A.2.a). Although the importance of confidentiality must be presented in the early stages of the group's development, it is equally important to reinforce the importance of confidentiality and its limitations throughout the group process. The school counselor should explain to students that he or she is required to violate confidentiality in situations in which a student is a threat to him/herself or another, and if the school counselor suspects that a student is being harmed. As stated by Stone (2013), "School counselors must establish clear expectations in the group setting and clearly state that confidentiality in group counseling cannot be guaranteed" (p. 248). Despite the limitations of confidentiality, the school counselor can reiterate the value and respect that confidentiality offers for effective group work. However, parents must also understand the role of confidentiality.

Parental Permission

Best ethical practice seeks parental/guardian permission for their child's participation in group sessions. While the school counselor's primary obligation is to the student as stated in A.1.a, it is important to seek parents' support. A.2.d of the ASCA *Ethical Standards* (2010) recognizes that parents/guardians should be regarded as the voice of their children. The practitioner is encouraged to develop a collaborative relationship with the parents and should respect their rights to help their child make value-laden decisions (ASCA *Ethical Standards*, Section B, 2010). Likewise, parents have the right to family privacy, which may be counterintuitive in a group setting. Utilizing a parent permission form is, on the other hand, a good opportunity to build parent relations with the school counselor. This is especially true when initiative is taken to help parents understand the group process and how it could help their children develop social intelligence and strengthen academic success (Malekoff, 2004). Appendices A and B are parental consent letters, one in English, one in Spanish.

Group Facilitation Competency of the School Counselor

Professional school counselors may be compelled to offer groups based on data from a needs assessment or requests from teachers, administrators, or parents. However, when implementing a group, the professional competency of the group facilitator is an ethical consideration. In a recent professional survey by Kozlowski and Stone (2013), 79% of the respondents said they felt confident or very confident in implementing counseling strategies such as leading small groups. Although this survey supports the fact that the majority of school counselors feel competent in their group facilitation skills, Section E of the ASCA *Ethical Standards* (2010) is directive regarding professional competency. It stresses that the school counselor must function within the boundaries of their competence and must take responsibility to seek professional development for skills necessary to maintain that competency, including group facilitation skills.

Not only is competency for group facilitation a professional skill necessary for the school counselor, but also knowledge and competency of some intense topics are crucial. Serious topics such as incest, eating disorders, trauma, self-mutilation, to name a few, are topics that require specialized training. These subjects of such a grave nature may best be implemented in a clinical setting rather than an academic venue. Because it is important to have specific training in some of these difficult topics, and because the ethical standards of both ASCA and ACA caution us to do no harm, it is incumbent upon the school counselor to be trained in the areas in which they are practicing. It may be more practical, not to mention ethical, for school counselors to implement more generic groups, such as leadership groups (Stone, 2013). While difficult subjects may arise in leadership groups, the life skills taught in such groups is relevant to the growth, productivity, and academic success of all students. Additionally, leadership skill development is more palatable to parents when parental permission is sought for students' participation.

Cultural Awareness in Groups

An additional ethical layer for effective group counseling encourages the cultural awareness of the school counselor.

> In any group, the unique experiences, personalities and backgrounds of individuals and their interactions affect the way the group will work. Understanding that these differences and similarities exist and knowing how this can affect the group is crucial to being a successful group leader.
>
> (Williams, Lantz, & Noorulamin, 2008, p. 14)

The culturally sensitive school counselor will promote social justice and equity within the group as well as within the school. As small groups are developed, the school counselor considers the cultural implications within the group. Section E.2 encourages the professional school counselor to "monitor and expand personal multicultural and social justice advocacy awareness, knowledge and skills. School counselors strive for exemplary cultural competence by ensuring personal beliefs or values are not imposed on students or other stakeholders" (ASCA, 2010, p. 5). The conscious cultural awareness within a group may impact the entire school if done well. When diverse groups come together, contact hypothesis predicts that prejudice is reduced and respect for everyone is valued (Williams et al., 2008).

The ethical issues of small group counseling in an educational setting are very different from the clinical setting. However, the value and effectiveness of the group learning and group process far outweigh any concerns, so long as the school counselor remains vigilant about the ethical implications of group counseling.

Ages and Stages of Groups

Groups may vary in size, depending on the purpose and scope. Counseling groups, such as those which help students with personal struggles to belong at school, may include between two and ten members, while psychoeducational groups performed in a classroom setting (also known as school counseling classroom lessons) may include an entire class of 25 to 30 students. The school counselor's preparedness to facilitate the group may have a significant impact on the group's outcome (Hess, Magnuson, & Beeler, 2011). It is important that the school counselor follows developmental cues when providing group guidance to students, paying special attention as the group is created.

Box 7.4

Important Aspects of Group Planning

Needs: the concerns and issues specific to the group and individual participants.
Purpose: the focus and intentions of the group function.
Composition: the members participating in the group and the group facilitator.
Structure: inclusive of not only the logistics of time and place for the group, but also considering the physical and emotional safety of the group.
Content and Curriculum: the means to achieve the purpose.
Screening Process: the preliminary evaluation and invitation of potential participants.
Context: the culture and climate within the group.

The manner in which a group is conducted may be as important as the participants themselves. The facilitator must take great care in designing an appropriate group counseling program plan, but also develop the skills, knowledge, and awareness to conduct the groups effectively. When a group facilitator does not allow for participants to solve their own problems, the group may struggle to stay connected, and eventually the members will lose interest (Steen & Bemak, 2008).

Throughout the group process, members become fluid in their development, and the group takes on characteristics that resemble unique stages that are achieved as the members collectively process information and demonstrate characteristics that Corey (2015) described as *Formation, Orientation, Transition, Working,* and *Consolidation.* Within each stage of group development, members maintain growth from the previous stage and build on the knowledge and coping skills from the stage achieved. Corey described the stages as:

Formation – identifies the initial process members go through at the onset of the group, and is characterized by group members' anxiety, curiosity, and feeling of hope as they learn about the purpose and objectives of the group process. The facilitator takes care of the logistical aspect of the group formation, by setting up the meeting times and location, inviting and screening potential members, obtaining consent for participation if working with students, and planning each session (as needed, depending on the type of group) so members are aware of any curriculum plan for the group meetings.

Orientation – involves the members moving into a deeper level of understanding regarding the group process, as feelings of distrust, anxiety, and skepticism surface. The facilitator is responsible for creating a safe and welcoming environment in which the members will work. An effective facilitator will allow for members to introduce themselves in a way that connects one to another, and will make the group goals known to the group (either through collaborative development or sharing of predetermined goals). This is also a time for members and facilitators to voice concerns and expectations for group participation. The facilitator will also address specific needs and concerns of the group members, in order to cultivate trust and support open communication.

Transition – is the phase where members become less willing to share emotional burdens with the group, for fear of over-disclosing or retribution by the facilitator or other members. The group begins to experience conflict among members that prompts members to resort to a "fight or flight" stance on issues they deem uncomfortable to discuss openly. The facilitator's role in this stage is to validate and provide support for members' feelings of anxiety. Normalizing feelings, while acknowledging strong emotional responses, will help build trust among the group members. It is important for the facilitator to remain objective and not personalize the potentially strong reactions members may have to conflict in the group. By acknowledging the conflict among members as part of the group process, and as something to be expected not feared, members may begin to let go of anxiety and irritation toward one another and begin to practice the coping skills that the facilitator has demonstrated for them during this phase.

Working – can be recognized by the group facilitator when members appear to be connected and freely interact with one another without being prompted. They demonstrate a shared commitment to the group and each other. This stage is marked by members challenging each other to work on individual goals, while recognizing each member's contribution to the group as a whole. The facilitator continues to model appropriate coping skills, as members begin to practice these skills within and outside of the group. Collaboration and openness to feedback are also seen at this stage in the process, whereas some members will spend an entire group session working on a personal issue with the support of the others. Many groups stay in this stage for long periods of time without disruption, others will begin working and suffer a setback in which they regress back to the transition stage. This is common and not something that should be feared. All groups have a personality of their own and if the facilitator can remain objective and allow the group room to grow, the outcome will be much richer than if the facilitator attempts to control the movement of the group in and out of the stages.

Consolidation – is characterized by the ending of the group process and termination of group meetings. Many members will reflect on their accomplishments and satisfaction of their goals, while others will shy away from ending the group because of the feelings of loss that might accompany it. Some members might feel ambivalent toward the group terminating, and these feelings should be normalized. Each member will react to the consolidation process differently. While some will want to celebrate accomplishments, others will feel sad and lonely at the thought of something ending in their life. The facilitator supports this closure by providing each member the opportunity to talk about what the group meant to them, what they gained, what they might be looking forward to doing with their new-found skills, and what they will do to prevent relapse. The facilitator also offers information about upcoming groups or other resources within the community that might be of benefit to the members.

Types of Groups

Developmental

Developmental counseling groups are created to provide students with a specific set of interventions, based on need. The students are recruited and placed in groups based on their specific educational, social, or future-oriented challenges. There are three types of developmental groups that are found in schools, including:

- *Groups for Academic Development:* Issues addressed include, but are not limited to, time management, study skills, test-taking strategies, and institutional transition issues (middle to high school, high school to college).
- *Career Development Groups:* Issues addressed include goal setting and decision-making, transitioning into postsecondary life, exploration of options, financial literacy, and college planning.
- *Social/Emotional Groups:* Issues addressed include, but are not limited to, grief and loss, fears and anxiety, building healthy friendships, self-esteem, dealing with relational aggression, dating relationships, sexual identity, personal empowerment, accepting a newborn sibling, or dealing with divorce or separation from parents (incarceration, hospitalization, etc.).

While academic groups are designed to provide psychoeducational materials and support for students experiencing mild anxiety while attempting to meet their educational goals, career development groups provide information and support specific to graduating from high school and transitioning to adulthood. Personal/social groups provide support for students with a multitude of interpersonal challenges with the intent of awakening their awareness and providing support for individual growth. Brigman and Campbell (2003) reported that achievement and behavior are positively impacted by group counseling interventions that focus on the social and emotional issues of the group participants. School counselors are in the unique position of providing group counseling support for all students as part of their comprehensive, developmental, inclusive, school counseling program. With a clean structure and common understanding as to the role of the school counselor, the above groups would be effective in promoting a healthy school climate and have a tremendous impact on the school community.

Remedial or RtI Groups

RtI groups may provide students with the opportunity to share their feelings on topics that impair their learning or development, both in and outside of the school community. The group process may involve helping students learn to cope with specific issues that relate to potential learning disabilities, while establishing the use of innovative methods for gathering data on students within contextualized environments (Hamayan, Marler, Sanchez-Lopez, & Damico, 2013). While confidentiality is a concern, the group facilitator may report to the RtI team the general progress of students attending the group. This would enable the team to establish a comprehensive picture of the students' coping skills and ability to engage in support services.

The premise of RtI groups is to help students develop coping skills in order to assist them in facing challenging personal and social issues, while helping them recognize the need to engage in the learning process. Such groups might focus on issues surrounding divorce, deployment of a parent(s), substance use/abuse, healing from the impact of substance use/abuse of a family member, incarcerated parent(s), grief and loss, anger management, conflict resolution, depression, disordered eating behaviors, and issues related to adoption (Pérusse et al., 2009). These groups are psychoeducational in nature, and provide age-appropriate information to ultimately enhance academic success. For example, students who are grieving a loss need to be taught about the grieving process and stages of healing in order to understand the process they are going through and the support that is available to them. Another example would be a conflict resolution group, where strategies are taught to students so they may solve their own problems as they arise. With an effective group counseling program in place, all students have the opportunity to learn new, useful information as they move through the K-12 system.

Culture and Climate Groups

According to Koth, Bradshaw, and Leaf (2008), students' perceptions of their "school climate" were positively correlated to their academic achievement, issues of adjustment, and social and personal attitudes toward others. Through the use of group counseling interventions, students may learn to become more culturally aware of the challenges others face. This could lead to a reduction in biases and prejudices that impact students' day-to-day interactions, leading to an increased level of respect for themselves and one another (Nikels, Mims, & Mims, 2007). By engaging students in a dialogue regarding the cultural and institutional barriers some students face, a more tolerant, supportive school climate may emerge. Students facing daily harassment for being viewed as different (LGBTQQI, race, ethnicity, ability, religion, SES, etc.) face many more challenges than students who perceive themselves as part of the majority culture.

Box 7.5

Did you know?

Bruce et al. (2009) suggest that a group counseling format may be culturally responsive for African American students as it is consistent with the African American community's shared value on connectedness. A group setting may also provide African American students with an opportunity to bond and discuss personal issues while also working toward a shared goal.

Group counseling interventions designed to provide minority students with the opportunity to gain a voice regarding social issues may contribute to their feelings of connectedness to their school and how they perceive themselves within the context of the school environment. Sharing these thoughts and feelings regarding their personal development is necessary in order to understand systemic issues they face (decreasing feelings of alienation, increasing feelings of hope, and increasing positive coping and social skills). By providing an outlet to talk about concerns, find common interests and values, and promote equitable learning environments, school counselors can become significant change agents within the school (Lee, 2005; Pérusse et al., 2009).

Another type of group that has large cultural implications for a school would be those involving a crisis, such as a terrorist attack, an incident of school violence, the sudden death of a student or school personnel, or a natural disaster that impacts the local school community. By providing an immediate, safe place for students to come and debrief their feelings of fear, anger, hope, and remembrance, the climate of the school may become one of love and acceptance, instead of fear and division. School counselors must display confident leadership skills and model appropriate boundaries for students and faculty during a time of crisis. Projecting a calm and safe demeanor to students and other school/community stakeholders helps the school counselor to be viewed as a person who can be counted on in a time of crisis, and one who can keep others safe as well. This supports the school counselor's role as a member of the leadership team of the school, and a district resource for others in crisis.

Group Formation

Homogeneous and Heterogeneous

When looking at the make-up of a group it is prudent to decide the characteristics you would like to include. There are two types of groups, those that contain members with similar challenges, and those experiencing different challenges, but who are able to learn coping skills to tackle a wide range of student concerns. The facilitator is tasked with deciding which type of group to create and how members will be selected. Once that decision is made, members may be recruited based on needs and appropriateness for each group.

A homogeneous group is comprised of students who are struggling with similar issues. By grouping students together that have a common interest in a particular subject (i.e., grief, loss, substance abuse, social issues, divorce, dating violence), the counselor brings students that might not connect with each other into the same room. Students are able to identify with one another, whereas someone without knowledge of the issue may not understand. Students may feel less alone or isolated in this type of group, where members may offer support to one another. According to Yalom (1995), this idea of "universality" is what makes groups successful. Participants learn that they are not alone and engage with others on a level of common understanding.

Heterogeneous groups form around a common means for solving a problem, with specific psychoeducational information provided (i.e., solution-focused problem solving, or choice theory) as a means of working with all members. Within heterogeneous groups, individual student concerns may vary. Some students may have challenges in certain areas of their lives, but still serve as a model for others within the group, providing examples of healthy responses to stressful situations. With these student-models as guides, other members are encouraged to test out new, healthy behaviors within and outside of the group. This process works best if not all students lack the coping skills the facilitator hopes they each develop. The facilitator may also model certain behaviors as a means of reinforcing psychoeducational material presented.

Leadership Groups

Bemak et al. (2005) developed the Empowerment Groups for Academic Success (EGAS) approach for use with high school students. This group approach boasted no set curriculum, but had "clearly defined goals for academic achievement" (Steen & Bemak, 2008, p. 338). The authors believed that the students' improved school performance was due to the processing of group dynamics and addressing individual issues that arose during the group session. Bauer, Sapp, and Johnson (2000) demonstrated a "supportive view" that group counseling can also be an "educational experience" where students can learn and practice positive interactions that will assist them in higher performance in school. This supports the idea that empowerment within groups creates positive outcomes within the school environment. By encouraging group participation, students will develop a greater understanding of themselves in relation to others. This avenue toward more effective self-reflection carries students toward roles as leaders and decreases the likelihood that they will engage in at-risk behaviors.

Effective Group Facilitation

Group Leadership Skills

When implementing group work in a school setting, many people think about the activities and curriculum first and often miss other essential aspects of creating effective groups. Actually, the most important component that makes groups work is the quality and skills of the facilitator (Brown, 2009). As a facilitator, the school counselor not only brings their skills and techniques but also their personality, including playfulness and supportiveness (Corey, Corey, Callanan, & Russell, 2004). The authenticity and uniqueness of the group facilitator can make or break a group. Brown (2009) avows that "effectiveness is tied to the groups' perceptions of what you demonstrate rather than what you say. Who you are ends up being more influential on group members than your actions or your words" (p. 4). The group's progress can be based on the authenticity of the facilitator. Depending on only techniques and curriculum forces the facilitator to become mechanical (Brown, 2009). While many experienced group leaders caution that there is no "right" way to facilitate, Corey et al. (2004) warn that the primary goal of good facilitation is being "*with* the group members and understanding their subjective world" (p. 25).

The facilitator serves as a guide, model, instructor, mediator, mentor, coach, cheerleader, and architect, whose responsibility it is to structure the framework in which the group will operate (Brown, 2009). Malekoff (2004) suggests that group leaders embrace the beauty, fluidity, and the uncertainty of groups while maintaining a sense of humor and checking your ego at the door. In addition to those skills the group facilitator must be flexible and willing to handle novelty and uncertainty. Malekoff (2004, p. 24) states that "to look with planned emptiness is to hold to a position of uncertainty, to be willing to learn from the inside-out, and to enable oneself to weather the sometimes disorienting qualities of a group in motion." These skills and traits are without merit, however, if the most crucial effective facilitation skill cannot be met, which is being able to develop relationships. Competency for group work requires a leader's ability to connect with group members, developing a trusting environment in which students can be themselves and feel safe participating in the activities.

The leader's skills and personality are balanced with the complexities of the multitasking skills of facilitation. Group facilitation requires a focus on the whole of the group, which is a change from the individual counseling perspective. Additional suggested perception shifts (Brown, 2009; Corey et al., 2004) for effective group leading include:

- Observing and understanding interactions among and between members – which are often projections, transference, and a reflection of their daily interactions.
- Being honest with the group members regarding observations and feedback in a way that can be understood by them without provoking defensiveness.
- Identifying similarities among members – offering an understanding of universality, which impacts feelings of separation.
- Using group dynamics effectively – which is a major source of information about group members' responses, offering insight into potential intervention strategies.
- Making group process commentary – revealing negative and positive group interactions is a primary responsibility of the group facilitator.
- Demonstrating acceptance of all participants in the group and not labeling or judging individuals.
- Recognizing the impact of the various cultural and diversity factors which are presented in the group even when all members appear to be from the same culture or diversity.
- Detecting the facilitator's own countertransference reactions, misusing leadership power, and attempting to meet the group leader's own needs at the expense of the members'.

Group Planning

Group counseling is inherently more challenging than individual counseling because there are many moving parts. It offers more professional growth for the facilitator and arguably more personal growth for the participants. Group counseling gives a view of the individual's microcosm while exposing macrocosmic aspects of the group interaction. Allowing this flow to occur requires the three P's of group development. Planning, performing, and processing constitute the best practice framework for group facilitation as determined by the Association for Specialists in Group Work (Thomas & Pender, 2008).

Planning. The planning stage refers to all the preparatory aspects of setting up a group. This may include a needs assessment for what types of groups to offer, group curriculum and design, time and site logistics, identification of group members, and parent permission (Conyne, Crowell, & Newmyer, 2008). This portion of the group planning process has often been a neglected area. Frequently, the success or failure of a group is attributed to unmotivated participants, inadequate curriculum, or parental interference, when, instead, it may ultimately lie at the door of poor or negligent planning (Malekoff, 2004). In order to effectively determine a plan for your group, keeping in mind ecological impact factors, the areas in Box 7.6 should be addressed.

Box 7.6

Conyne et al. (2008) suggest using the Purposeful Group Techniques Model (PGTM) that includes five steps:

1. *Identify* the group type and purpose, the relevant best practice area, and the developmental stage that it may be in at the present time.
2. *Analyze* the presenting group's situation by applying ecological concepts of context, interconnection, collaboration, social system, meaning-making, and sustainability.
3. *Review* possible group techniques, considering focus and level.
4. *Select* a best-fit technique for that situation that holds promise for success.
5. *Implement and evaluate* how well the technique worked.

Intentional Techniques

Another aspect of effective group facilitation is intentional planning of techniques and activities. Conyne et al. (2008, p. 8) define techniques as "the interventions ('tools of the trade') that are used by group leaders – and sometimes by group members – to focus group processes, try out behavior, accentuate thoughts and feelings, and provide opportunities for learning." Some facilitators choose to use a "canned" curriculum of techniques, while others develop their own. It may be easiest to follow an established curriculum, but if it doesn't meet the conceptual framework of the group (Conyne et al., 2008), or the group goals, nor does it address the dynamics of the members, then the curriculum will fail.

Adult groups may benefit from a discussion-based format; however, talk groups do not fit well with the developmental needs of the younger group participants (Conyne et al., 2008; Corey et al., 2004; Malekoff, 2004). Talk groups are also more difficult to facilitate with younger participants. Adolescents and children learn best by doing, thus experiential activities actually teach lifelong learning skills. In planning for this type of experiential learning and choosing activities, the facilitator must first assess which techniques will best serve the interactions of each particular group.

Box 7.7

Cooley's (2009) Recommendations for how Group Facilitators Demonstrate Effective Leadership Skills:

- Express concern regarding the members' behavior without calling names or labeling.
- Resist the urge to address a sarcastic remark with sarcasm.
- Be open about how the group process works and answer questions as they arise.
- Address members' feelings of resistance in the moment.
- Describe disruptive behavior without labeling, criticizing, or condemning the member involved. Model the effective use of "I" statements.
- When expressing hunches or observations, avoid generalizations and provide specific examples that lead to your discovery.

After the decision on activities has been made, an effective group leader must carefully consider three main components of every activity: concept introduction, the activity, and debrief (Williams et al., 2008).

Concept introduction – How will the group leader get the group members to buy in to the activity? Just as a paper is written with an introduction, a body of information, and a conclusion, the facilitator must follow the same pattern with an experiential activity. So to encourage engagement and enthusiasm, the facilitator develops a creative method of introducing the concept in the activity. In addition, it is important to keep in mind the objective for the activity.

Conduct the activity – Experiencing the experience is when the actual learning occurs for the participants, if facilitation is done well. Conducting the activity includes attaining the necessary materials needed and prioritizing the physical and emotional safety of all the group members. After the directions of the activity are given and questions are answered, the role of the facilitator shifts to that of an observer. Facilitators do not solve the problem for the participants but allow for exploration within the group, and encourage effective communication, teambuilding and problem-solving without rescuing the participants (MacIver & McCarroll, 1999).

> Whether as a [group leader] who facilitates discussions, or as an enforcer of rules for the safety of participants, or as a leader who models appropriate behavior, the role of the facilitator should remain fluid in function as the dynamics of group change.
>
> (MacIver & McCarroll, 1999, p. 10)

Debrief the activity – The third, and most valuable, component of facilitation is processing the experience. No activity should be done unless there is time to debrief the experience, which is where the intention of an activity comes to fruition (Williams et al., 2008). Done immediately following an activity, the facilitator structures the debrief so individuals are encouraged to reflect on how the group planned, how the members interacted, analyze the communication, and transfer meaning to the group learning that just occurred (MacIver & McCarroll, 1999). There are many suggested processing structures; however, the one that seems most concise and meaningful is the reflective model presented by Rolfe, Freshwater, and Jasper (2001). This technique consists of asking three basic questions: "What?", "So what?", and "What now?"

"What" Questions: This line of questioning is about the immediate response of the group members regarding the activity. Examples: So what just happened? What was that activity like for you? It encourages the group to reflect on the immediate feelings that occurred during the activity. These questions can refer to actions, attitudes, and behaviors of the group or individuals.

"So What" Questions: These questions ask about the purpose of the activity. Examples: Why do you think we did this? What was the point of this activity? These questions are intended to draw conclusions about the actions of the group and success of the strategies employed by the group. This portion of the debrief process allows for group members to consider actions that worked well and consider changing actions that were not successful.

"Now What" Questions: The final level of debrief questions are about the real life application or meaning of the experience for each person. Example: What did you learn about yourself in this activity? What are the behaviors you brought to this activity that helped with the groups' success? The purpose of these application questions is to increase the likelihood that group members develop self-awareness and apply the learning to their own lives.

Encouragement to utilize activities and techniques comes with the caution of balance. Be intentional in your planning and purpose. As stated by Malekoff (2004, p. 166), "Activity is more than a 'tool,' more than programmed content, more than 'canned' exercises and more than a mechanistic means to an end." Ideally, the means to the end is obtaining new personal awareness and more effective behaviors. It is the essence of experiential learning. But this does not occur by coincidence. Simply doing an activity does not give meaning and application to the participants. It is through the processing of the activity that meaning is attached and learning occurs (Williams et al., 2008).

Assessing Group Functioning

- Causes members to be reliant on others.
- Outcomes of experience cannot be totally predictable.
- Possibility to learn from natural consequences, mistakes, and/or success.
- Provides opportunities for learning and experiencing in a unique and physical setting – Kinesthetic learning.
- Holistic, involving all senses, using a variety of learning styles.
- Immediate feedback on performance.
- Activities are novel and multi-dimensional.
- Educators recognize spontaneous opportunities for learning.
- Learning is personal and a basis for future learning.
- Relationships are developed.
- An activity that is structured to encourage individuals to plan, reflect, describe, analyze, and communicate about experiences.
- Can be used to:
    - Help individuals focus awareness on issues
    - Facilitate awareness to promote change
    - Reflect, analyze, describe, or discuss
    - Reinforce perceptions of change and promote integration

When group members engage in the assessment process, reflection and understanding become part of their awareness. Without this necessary function, members may not fully understand the depths to which they have connected with others in the group, or with the group facilitator. While this process relies mostly on the work of the members, the facilitator has an obligation to provide the structure necessary for members to engage in meaningful ways. The skills needed by the facilitator vary, depending on the overall development of the members, but having adequate training is a must for those who hope to engage in group work with students.

Group Dynamics

Leading a counseling group within a school is considered by Lee and Goodnough (2007) to be a highly specialized skill, requiring specific training in how to facilitate groups. Group facilitators also need to be grounded in counseling theory and practice in order to be effective (Pérusse et al., 2009). When students apply what they learn in the group setting to their own lives, they come back to the group to share their experiences. This sharing may open students up to emotional risk. Encouraging students to maintain confidentiality supports the notion that the group is a safe place to experience emotional growth, promote trust among members, and develop a sense of inclusion (Pérusse et al., 2009). Group facilitators help students understand that they are not alone by connecting students to each other in meaningful ways. This is used to promote healing by allowing students to share their personal experiences in a supportive environment.

Structure of a Group

Solution-Focused Groups in Schools

Regardless of the theoretical orientation used, solution-focused counseling interventions offer the school counselor options that fit into the demands of a hectic schedule that potentially limits the amount of time spent with students. In order to maximize the effectiveness of group time, school counselors may utilize solution-focused techniques with students, while teaching them steps so that they may potentially solve their own problems in the future. This approach supports strengths-based inquiry and does not look to explore past issues, but only the present and future orientation of the students (deShazer, 1988). While looking at students as agents for change in their own lives, school counselors cultivate power within students' perspectives and become advocates for individual change within the system. The more control the students believe they have to solve their own problems, the more likely they will be to do so. However, the school counselor must provide the appropriate level of information and guidance in order for students to fully integrate this approach into their daily lives.

Traditional group counseling models are based on students sharing their feelings, finding common ground with others who suffer a similar plight, and gaining the strength to overcome their issues. Through this process, students learn to communicate their feelings in a more effective way, and relate to others on a deeper level. Solution-focused group work emphasizes looking internally to discover strengths and resiliency toward solving problems in the past that may lead to healthy beliefs in their future-oriented problem-solving ability. Building on past successes and relating those behaviors to current situations helps the students gain power over their behavior and ultimately compile a mental list of coping skills they may draw from in the future.

Steps to utilizing solution-focused groups in schools. According to Cooley (2009), there are eight assumptions of solution-focused brief counseling. These assumptions guide the process of working from this perspective and help to form a template for change with groups:

1. All students have resources and strengths, even if they are not yet obvious to us or to the student.
2. If what you are doing is working, do more of it and if what you are doing isn't working, at least try something different.
3. Problems are not constant. There are times when the problem either does not exist or is less frequent.
4. Big problems do not necessarily require complex solutions.
5. Changes in one area will affect other areas.
6. Even if temporarily confused or uncertain, the student is the expert on the problem.
7. The solution may not necessarily be directly related to the problem. The solution can be found at the intersection of the future focus, the student's strengths and resourcefulness, and the counselor's respectful curiosity.
8. Change is inevitable.

(Cooley, 2009, p. 21)

When deciding who to invite to the group, the school counselor keeps the above assumptions in mind, and makes an educated decision as to who might be appropriate for the type of group they hope to create. Most referrals come from teachers, parents, or students themselves, but school counselors also create groups made up of students they believe would benefit.

Determining Necessity

The first step in creating a group is to determine if the group is really necessary, and how many students suffer from similar issues. The best way to make this determination is to create and distribute a needs assessment to all students, teachers, parents, and administrators. Oftentimes, parents and teachers believe a problem such as "bullying" is of high concern, only to find out that the real issue is low self-esteem among the students. By obtaining data related to students' needs, the school counselor will save precious time and energy determining what students believe is important to them and tailoring their group interventions to those specific needs. By making an effort to gain information from students, it will not only empower them to have a voice, but to feel they have an outlet to vent their concerns. The school counselor will already have begun to form relationships with students by merely asking them to share their feelings. Obtaining information from a formal needs assessment might also help the parents and teachers develop a better understanding of the students' needs and how to support them. Additionally, surveying administrators, teachers, and parents regarding their perceptions of students' needs increases the likelihood that they will support the school counselor in conducting groups. Final approval of the group topics should be sought from the administrator(s).

Laying the Groundwork

The next step is to educate students, parents, teachers, and administrators on what the group counseling process is, the purpose, details about time and space, and what they might expect if they participate. By making the process known to the stakeholders in the school, the school counselor will likely gain support and participation for this movement. Once the needs of students have been determined, and members of the school community have been briefed on why groups are effective within the school setting, the school counselor may begin to accept referrals for groups that have been created based on need. Referrals may come from sources within the school community, or from outside sources (i.e., family therapist, juvenile justice, social services). It is the school counselor's responsibility to determine a student's readiness for group participation, not the referring party. In order for groups to be successful, the school counselor facilitating the group needs to be knowledgeable of the needs of each member and have enough information to manage the interaction between members during the group sessions.

Timing is Everything

To increase the likelihood of obtaining the cooperation of the teachers and administrators, groups must be scheduled in a manner that is least disruptive to the academic mission and the school's schedule. School counselors often use a staggered schedule in which the group meets at different times in order to distribute students' missed time evenly among their classes (Greenberg, 2003). For example, at the middle/junior high and high school levels, the number of group sessions coincides with the number of school periods, and there is one group session per period. In elementary schools, which do not have specified class periods, a tiered schedule involves meeting one week at 9:30, the next week at 1:30, the third week at 10:30, and so on. The school counselor should first consult with teachers before scheduling groups to obtain their ideas regarding creating the least disruptive schedule. The school counselor can obtain the future testing/exam schedule of teachers to avoid scheduling groups during such times.

Another issue relating to the scheduling of groups concerns the number of group sessions. In middle/junior high and high schools, the number of group sessions often coincides with the number periods in the school. For example, if a school has eight periods, the group will be comprised of eight sessions, thus students only miss a class or a portion of a class once. The problem with staggering the schedule of groups is that the members may forget the group meeting times. School counselors can remind students of the meeting times by sending notes to both the teachers and the group members the day before the group meets and ask group members to remind each other of the meeting times.

Missed Work

The most disruptive aspect of group counseling in a school setting is the work missed by students. The school counselor should often remind students of their responsibility for making up missed work, and inform teachers of this group requirement (Greenberg, 2003). On days when the group meets, group members can obtain any homework assignments by meeting with their teacher, such as before school begins, lunchtime, in a free period, or even after school. The school counselor should often ask teachers whether group members are keeping up with their work, and failure to do so could result in having the student leave the group.

Location, Location, Location

Choosing a room that is appropriate for a confidential group session can be tricky in schools. There may not be a room that is available at the time you desire, and with limited access to conference rooms that offer privacy, facilitators may need to be creative in finding places to hold groups. One way to obtain group space is to work with a teacher or other professional within the building who may have space available during her/his planning period. Often, classrooms are free when students have recess or lunch. Utilizing a first grade classroom for a fourth grade group while the class is at recess just might be the ticket to successful time and space management. Other creative options include meeting in the band room while the band director has a planning period and other students (your group members) eat lunch. As long as the band director is okay with students eating lunch in the band room and you adhere to the set timeframe agreed upon, this option may also be feasible.

The Screening Process

As stated earlier in the chapter, when a referral is made the school counselor must interview each member to find out: (a) if they are committed to the process; (b) what issues they anticipate surfacing if they participate; (c) any other potential resistance issues the member has toward fully engaging in the group process; and (d) what the student hopes to gain from participating in the group. Finding out if the challenges they are facing match the referral, and determining if additional challenges to their success are present, may help the facilitator rule out certain members for a particular group, but also allow for group reassignment prior to the onset of any groups. For example, imagine a situation where Juan (a reserved fourth grader) approaches you to become part of a "Healthy Friendship" group, but tells you he refuses to be in a group with any of the boys in Mr. Thomas' class. You ask Juan to tell you about his interaction with the other boys, and he reveals that they have been bullying him about his family's financial situation since first grade. You express concern and let him know you will support him, no matter what group he finds himself in and that by being placed with those particular boys, he may discover common ground and actually build some new friendships. Juan refuses to hear anything about being with the other boys and asks to be removed from any possible group that semester. Do you accommodate Juan's request and place him in another group, away from the other boys, or let him sit this one out and hope he comes around next semester? In this case, it might be best to allow Juan to be in another group until he gains the confidence to work through his issues with the other boys. If he is convinced that this experience will be awful and he refuses to show up, the facilitator may be sabotaging the group's success before it even starts. Upon completion of the initial group process, it would then be appropriate to communicate with Juan your desire for him to join a group with the boys with whom he has issues (real or perceived), with the intention of successfully navigating that relationship.

As discussed earlier in the chapter, once a student expresses a commitment to the group counseling process, school counselors must obtain parental consent in order to include the student in the group (see Appendix A). An exception to this would include students who are over the age of consent (check your state's laws on the age of consent of minors) where parental permission is not required for participation. It would also be prudent to check your school district policy on consent for counseling participation. Many districts have a blanket consent policy that parents sign in the beginning of the school year in order to cover school-related events and participation in activities. There may also be an opt-out form that parents or guardians sign when they choose not to allow their children to participate in counseling or other mental health-related services. If a parent signed the opt-out form, but you believe the student may benefit from group participation, you may choose to contact the parent in an attempt to inform them of your program and what you offer to your students. In many cases, the parents will consent to group interventions offered to many students versus individual counseling, requested just for their child.

At this point in the process, students, parents, and teachers might notice something called "Pretreatment Change" happening with students. This phenomenon occurs when a student demonstrates some type of change as a result of being introduced to the group concept, but prior to the initial group meeting. The idea of change can be cultivated in individuals long before the actual changes in behavior occur. School counselors may nurture the pretreatment change process by discussing how students' behavior may have changed as a result of being included in the group formation. Student interaction may look different, but by recognizing this phenomenon within the first group meeting, participants may feel drawn to participate due to an already evident impact the process is having on their thoughts, feelings, or behavior.

At the onset of the first group meeting, the facilitator gains the support and buy-in of the members by creating a comfortable, inviting, and inclusive environment for the students. This may be accomplished by encouraging members to get to know one another through the use of an activity. Members who find something in common with others in the group will have a greater chance of returning, especially if they deem the group to be an effective use of their time. Membership of the group must be seen as something worthwhile and productive; whether or not the student has worked on any of their own issues or just helped support others, a sense of community must develop in order for the group experience to be deemed a success.

Once the members have become acquainted with one another and the facilitator, the next step is to develop a "Group Agreement" that will guide the behavior of group members, and help foster feelings of trust within the group. To reiterate, a conversation about confidentiality and how a breach might impact the group process is one way to instill the value of privacy and respecting self and others. Remember, this may be a relatively new concept for some students, and a very important factor for the potential participation of others. By talking openly about how the group might deal with confidential issues and offering suggestions when faced with tough situations (i.e., a friend asks you what was said in the group), members will have a better idea of how to respond to potential threats to confidentiality. The group will also be responsible for addressing breaches of confidentiality, and as part of the agreement, they agree to abide by the rules and support the goals of the group. The agreement should be unanimously supported by all members. If there is dissention regarding a particular group guideline, the members must work it out until a consensus is reached and all members are in agreement.

The facilitator is in charge of all group materials and the overall management and organization of the group process. Students must believe that the facilitator will be on time and show up prepared. For some students who have experienced abuse in their past, the facilitator's lack of preparedness, timeliness, and accountability may lead to feelings of fear, anger, or uncertainty. It is imperative that the facilitator notify the students as soon as they are able regarding any changes to the group schedule (i.e., room, time, day, topic) so they may mentally prepare for the change. By not doing this, the facilitator runs the risk of losing the members' trust, and potentially the group's support for the process.

Goal setting is an important part of solution-focused group work. Each student develops her/his own goals, which are fluid in nature and can evolve and change over the course of the group process. By setting goals, students take an increased role in the ownership of and emotional investment in the development of the group and their own growth. By demonstrating how to set a goal, students learn a lifelong lesson in how to work toward something positive in their lives and gain emotional muscle in the process. With each goal accomplished, students become more confident that they can achieve success. The more often they set goals, the more likely they will be to achieve what they want.

According to ASCA (2012), individual goals should be SMART: *Specific, Measureable, Attainable, Results-Oriented,* and *Time-Bound* (see Appendix C). These guidelines are meant to deter group members from setting goals that are too broad in scope, cannot be measured, have negative consequences (e.g., setting a goal to get expelled from school in order to have more time to play video games), or which seek the absence of something and not the addition of something that will help alleviate the problem symptoms. For instance, when a student states they are depressed, and sets a goal to not be depressed anymore, that student is not giving an indication as to what "not being depressed anymore" looks like. By encouraging the student to set a goal that outlines what they will be doing instead of being depressed (whatever that looks like for the individual), then there is a more clear picture of what to aim for. The group members may be able to assist the student in creating a picture of what a non-depressed day might look like, or activities the student might engage in when not depressed. This helps foster a sense of community among group members, with each invested in the others' well-being. When students feel connected to the group and responsible for the goals they set, it increases the likelihood that they will continue to work hard to achieve them.

Using the Miracle Question

In order to assist students with goal formation, it may be helpful to ask them to consider what life would be like if the problem no longer existed. For students that struggle to come up with a specific goal, the facilitator might ask:

"Let's suppose that when you went to sleep tonight a miracle happened in your life and the problem that you've been talking about no longer existed. When you woke up, how would you know that the problem was gone, what would be different? How would your parents or teachers know that the problem didn't exist anymore? Who else might notice and what would they say was different?"

This type of questioning often allows the student to "free think" about how their life might be without the existence of the problem. For some, this task allows them to ponder who might be impacted as a result of the problem not being an issue. For others, this might prove to be a way to name specific factors that have been eliminated and thus help them to outline goals rather quickly. The facilitator and group members may take note as the person is speaking and restate the information back to them in the form of possible goals to work toward. Some members may be grieving the loss of a person, pet, or relationship. In many cases, the member would state something like, "Yeah, I'd have my mom back," in response to the miracle question. When that happens, the facilitator needs to support the member as she/he grieves the loss and revisit the goal setting once the person has had a chance to get to a point where goal setting is appropriate. Pushing goals that suggest their grieving is being ignored is inappropriate and will most likely lead to the member leaving the group. By encouraging short-term goals (e.g., going to school each day, interacting with friends, completing homework), the school counselor is helping the student stay connected to the school community, while demonstrating compassion for the heartache and loss they are experiencing.

Once the group members have established goals, they may be ready to look for exceptions to their problems, or consider times when the problem was not a problem. For example, Channin came to the group with complaints about her father always yelling at her in the morning and as a result she was always upset and had a terrible time paying attention in her first period math class. When asked about a time when her father didn't yell at her, Channin thought about it and quickly retold the story from last week when she had a great morning. She said that when she woke up on Tuesday morning, she quickly got dressed, brushed her hair and teeth, fed the dog without being asked, and ate the breakfast her father had prepared for her. When she left for school, she remembers him telling her that he was proud of her and gave her the $3.00 she had asked for so she could get ice cream after school with her friends that day. When she recalled that moment, a big smile came across her face. She also recalled that she did well on a quiz in her math class that morning as well. Drawing from that particular experience, Channin was able to set a goal for getting up and ready in the morning without being asked. The absence of arguing with her father in the morning (the exception) set the tone for more great mornings and lowered the likelihood of being distracted and angry during her first period math class. By eliminating the cause of her distress in the morning, she may continue to excel.

In Channin's case, the facilitator did not have to search for the strengths that she possessed or the exceptions to her problem. In some cases, however, students are challenged by their situations and have little to offer when asked to recall times when the problem didn't exist. The facilitator's role is to help members see their strengths and promote a healthy self-image. When a member struggles to find an exception to a difficult situation, the facilitator may recall a time when they used good judgment when a conflict arose between group members, or when they returned a lost book to a classmate and showed compassion for someone else. There may be days when the facilitator is hard-pressed to find exceptions to a student's behavior, but by focusing on what the student has done well rather than their failures, the strengths-based approach will result in positive outcomes (Cooley, 2009). Being purposeful and persistent in helping find exceptions will result in a student's continued commitment to individual growth and the group process.

Group facilitation skills are developed over time. When using specific techniques, counselors must be aware of how the questions they ask may impact the flow or mood of the group. If a student begins to tell a story that has a negative outcome and the student engages in self-blame or doubt, the facilitator may use a technique from solution-focused theory called "reframing" to help the student see another side to the story. This technique, in which the counselor repeats the same information back to the student, but from a positive, empowering place instead of a negative, harmful one, can be very effective in helping students begin to see hope in their situation. The new meaning of the story may serve as a catalyst for future "glass half full" thinking instead of looking at the negative side to a situation. By demonstrating concern and compassion for finding strengths, this process may also help solidify the facilitator's role as a caring adult on whom students can rely.

Another technique used in solution-focused theory groups is to ask the members to rate their feelings on a scale from 0 to 10, with 0 being the very worst they could ever imagine, and 10 being the best they could ever image. This exercise, known as using "scaling questions," helps students truly determine how their current situation has impacted their life. In many cases, the worst possible situation is the death of a loved one, and the best is the achievement of a long-term goal such as graduation from college or winning the lottery. When students put their current problem into perspective, it helps diffuse irrational self-blame, doubt, or loathing. Oftentimes, students recognize when a problem has been given too much energy or how hard they've worked to remain stuck in a situation. By discussing the true highs and lows in a student's life, current problems become more manageable. Other useful ways to use a scaling question is to ask students to rate their current mood at the beginning and again at the end of each group session. Practicing this technique within the context of the group will allow each member the opportunity to express feelings and find common ground with others who might be experiencing similar situations. Gaining the knowledge that she/he is not alone can sometimes normalize a situation for the group member and in turn, the member may decide to discontinue asserting personal energy toward the problem.

Asking follow-up questions may help the members to discover the results of the work they've done toward identifying their strengths and "doing more of what works" throughout the week. For example, when Kenyon, a sixth grader who joined a group for children struggling with issues in blended families, was asked to identify how she was feeling at the onset of the weekly group, she stated she was "6" this week. The facilitator then asked a follow-up question, "Last week you said you were at 4 at the end of group, up from a 3. What happened this week to lead you to the 6 you're at today?" Another question might be, "Kenyon, how has your situation changed in order for you to be up to a 6 today?" By asking appropriate follow-up questions, the group members have the opportunity to express deeper feelings and share their accomplishments since the group met last. The facilitator may encourage other members to also ask follow-up questions as a means of helping them relate to one another. This encouraging process helps to bring the group closer through common understanding and empathic support for one another. Appropriate modeling of the process must take place over several meetings in order for the facilitator to reasonably expect members to engage in this type of questioning. While the members may feel comfortable with one another, they may look to the facilitator for guidance before asking another member to go deeper in their response.

Activities in Groups

Oftentimes, the school counselor will begin to plan a group with specific activities or a specific curriculum in mind. This process leads to the question, "How will I use this curriculum or activity to promote growth in my students?" Finding the right fit between your needs and the needs of your students can be challenging. With such an incredible amount of information available through professional organizations, recommendations from colleagues, and websites like *Pinterest* where school counselors "pin" their favorite guidance and group activities, knowing where to begin can be stressful. While looking for a curriculum to address a specific problem or issue, make sure you follow these simple steps: make sure the intervention you choose is age-appropriate, time-sensitive (can be completed within one group session), and engaging for students. Students will tune out after the first few minutes of the group if they believe the activity is boring, consumes too much energy to complete, or is irrelevant to their life (Cooley, 2009).

Cliques in Groups

One of the most challenging aspects of group counseling is addressing cliques that form between and among members in a group. As a group facilitator, it might be instinctual to avoid confronting members who show signs of resistance or choose to form their own alliances within the group (Cooley, 2009). This type of intrusion may pose a threat to the effectiveness of the group process. With that in mind, it is important for the facilitator to check her/his own biases toward the members of the group who appear to be aligning away from the other members. At times, counselors have difficulty dealing with members whose character traits mimic problematic behaviors within themselves or others in their lives. By checking biases at the door, and looking at the potential causes of the clique, the facilitator may then be able to understand how it occurred and how best to deal with those members' actions within the context of the group.

Recognizing the conflict among members and openly addressing the impact the clique has had on the group will allow the facilitator to demonstrate leadership skills and model how to effectively defuse disruption within the group process. Each member of the group should have a chance to discuss the specific ways in which the clique has impacted them, while allowing all participants a chance to respond. When a member uses sarcasm to avoid dealing with the situation, responding with humor is appropriate. However, responding in-kind with a sarcastic quip only attempts to equally degrade their character without solving the problem. Stick with a calm demeanor and focus on getting the issue out in the open. The intention of this process is to dissolve the clique and realign all the members with the original purpose of the group. Once all members have successfully recommitted to the group process, the facilitator may encourage continued processing of feelings related to other topics as they arise.

Group Behavior Management

When group facilitators are asked about the hardest part of leading a group, managing behaviors is the typical response (Williams et al., 2008). There is no "one-size-fits-all" response to group behavior management; however, the effective facilitator develops "tool kit" responses so the group can stay on target and be productive. Again, as a facilitator, you are a guide with a facilitating role, and rarely are you the sheriff lecturing or the teacher lecturing. As a facilitator, the role is about managing the interactions, not giving the answers or directing the group. This is not a hierarchy in which the facilitator has all the power and control, as opposed to the classroom where the teacher is the authority. An effective group facilitator gives the power back to the group and allows the group to practice the lifelong skills of problem-solving and risk-taking.

Power-Sharing Techniques

There are several ways in which an effective group facilitator can use power-sharing instead of overpowering. (Williams, Riedo & DeBard, 2007). Power-sharing attributes the bulk of power and decision-making to the participants in the group.

Circle Format

The simplest application of power-sharing is utilization of the circle format. The circle has no head or tail and all participants, including the facilitator, are part of the circle. A hierarchy does not exist in the circle. This inclusive format keeps the focus on the group as a whole. It also allows for the facilitator to monitor the body language of all of the participants. If a group member demonstrates inappropriate behaviors, the circle format makes the monitoring and intervention easier for the facilitator or co-facilitator. In a circle eye rolls and discounting body language can be immediately noticed and addressed by the facilitator (Williams et al., 2007).

Behavior Management Techniques

Another group facilitation tip utilizes the guidelines that were developed by the group members. To allow natural responses and interactions to occur, the facilitator must assist the group members to establish group norms, guidelines, or boundaries within which the members will operate. These norms create a safe space and help the group members hold each other accountable. If the group leader has facilitated the creation of the group norms or guidelines in an effective manner, the participants will "own" the guidelines as their own. Using these member-developed guidelines allows the facilitator to draw attention to the guidelines if inappropriate behavior is escalating. A simple reminder, asking all group members if they are following the group guidelines or if the group guidelines need to be changed, can re-focus groups or individual members into more appropriate behavior.

It is important, as a facilitator, to not direct negative behaviors toward a specific participant but to indirectly address behaviors. The group guidelines can be the initial behavior management technique; however, helping the group members learn to manage their own behaviors is a life skill. When something happens in the group, instead of directing attention toward the culprit, the facilitator can redirect the attention toward the group as a whole. Such questions as "How is the group working right now?" or "What helps this group be most successful?" may help the group work more effectively. Because the facilitator wants to focus on the behavior and not blame the person, it is important to avoid directing unnecessary attention to the individual. Discussing behaviors that work in the group and behaviors that will not work in the group also mitigates negative behaviors. However, there are always those participants that act out negative or distracting behaviors to the group. Sometimes those behaviors need specific interventions (Williams et al., 2007).

Naysayer. There will occasionally be participants who are negative. This behavior can be annoying to facilitators and participants alike. It can also be contagious if the person has power in the group. The impact of a toxic person can be debilitating to a group; however, to avoid directly responding to the individual as a negative person, one suggestion is for the leader to give the naysayer some type of leadership role to promote positive energy. Another suggestion would be to ask all participants what they liked about an activity and what they would change, so that the naysayer doesn't have all the power. The group can also create a guideline that says if a participant is going to say something negative they have to provide an idea about how to change it. As a last resort, the facilitator can remind group members that attendance is voluntary. The facilitator can remind members that if they are unhappy they can ask for permission to leave after they explain why they are making that choice to the rest of the group (Williams et al., 2007).

Over talker. The over talker can quickly drain the energy from everyone in the group. As a facilitator, you cannot roll your eyes when the individual talks or avoid calling on the over talker every time they want to talk. Ignoring the behavior may only make it more blatant. One suggested technique is the use of pipe cleaners. Each participant gets three pipe cleaners (or any other collection of objects). When one person wishes to talk, she/he has to put one pipe cleaner into the middle of the circle. When that person runs out of pipe cleaners they cannot share any more information. This strategy may also encourage the participant who doesn't talk very often. (It is important to not allow the participants to negotiate pipe cleaners or trade them.)

Quiet/Shy person. The pipe cleaner strategy is as helpful with the quiet participant as with the over talker. Directly asking each participant to share one thing about the activity gives the quiet person a chance to practice having a voice. The facilitator can gently encourage anyone who has not had the chance to speak to share first or give the quiet person a task where they can contribute to the group in some way.

Cliques. Factions of students can quickly overpower the rest of the group members and disempower group effectiveness. It is vital that the group facilitator continually divide group members in creative ways. As a facilitator, being unpredictable in how you divide up the groups for different activities will minimize the clique manipulations. The facilitator may have to speak directly about how it feels to be left out of group activities.

Additional Group Management Techniques

A Handbook for Leading Positive Youth Development Programs (Williams et al., 2007) offers a variety of additional group management techniques that may help participants have a more positive experience:

Rounds

Ask one question and go around the group so everyone contributes an answer. Although it might take longer, depending on the size of the group, it equalizes the energy and power in the group and gives all members a voice.

Passing

If there is a group member who doesn't want to talk at that moment, giving the person a pass for the time being is helpful. However, it is important to let the person know that the facilitator will come back to them after everyone else has spoken. This gives the person time to think about their answer while making them accountable for an answer. The accountability is important so that the "pass" does not become the norm for the group.

Talking Stick

This strategy is a tried-and-true method for effective group management. The only person who can talk is the person holding the talking stick. An addition to this strategy is to have the next speaker receiving the talking stick repeat what they just heard the previous speaker say. This reinforces active listening for the members of the group.

Freeze Frame

This is a minimally used strategy when the facilitator feels the physical or emotional safety of the group or a member is in jeopardy, and thus asks the group members to freeze and think about their thoughts or reactions to what is occurring in the group. Overuse of this strategy can cause members to dismiss it. However, used sparingly it is an effective message that there is an important reason why the facilitator needs to take control of the group.

While there will always be disruptive behaviors in group counseling, effective facilitation can mitigate the negative impact on the group process. The facilitator focuses on the behavior and not on blaming the person. One of the most powerful reasons to implement small group programs is to help the group members learn to manage their own behaviors through feedback and modeling in the group process. The power of the group process is that students can learn from each other.

Evaluation

School counselors should accumulate as much data as feasible to evaluate the impact of the group, and should seek to assess students' and teachers' perceptions, and changes in academic and behavioral data. Students should be asked about their perceptions of the effectiveness of individual sessions. Such questions could include "Did the sessions meet the objectives of the day?" (Greenberg, 2003, p. 105), and "Did you learn something new in group today?" Evaluation at the completion of the group should assess group member satisfaction, the degree to which members believed the group goals were achieved, and changes in group members' behavior or perceptions. Questions at the completion of the group could include "The thing I liked best about this group was ____," "The thing I did not like about this group was ____" (Greenberg, 2003, p. 73). Teachers should evaluate members at the conclusion of the group. The following Likert scale might be used: "5 = a lot of change/ improvement, 4 = much change/improvement, 3 = some change/improvement, 2 = little change/improvement, 1 = no change/improvement, 0 = cannot say/no opportunity to observe" (Greenberg, 2003, p. 174).

The perceptions of students often provide valuable information to school counselors regarding what activities to modify. However, such feedback is not likely to impress administrators and teachers who are increasingly being held accountable for demonstrating measurable gains in student achievement. Likewise, school counselors must seek to impact student achievement in a more objective, measurable manner. Depending upon the objectives of the group, behavioral data might be used to measure the rates of attendance or homework completion (ASCA, 2012), and on-task behavior. Forms of academic data that might be relevant to assess include standardized test data, grade point average, and number of classes passed.

Summary

There are considerable challenges to conducting group counseling in a school setting. Data must be collected to determine the necessity of group topics. School counselors must work hard to obtain the support of administrators, teachers, parents, and students. There is a considerable amount of coordination and paperwork as parents' written consent should be obtained, teachers and students must be consistently reminded of the group schedule, students must complete missed work, and evaluations must be conducted. Given the challenges in conducting group counseling, some school counselors opt not to conduct groups. However, we encourage school counselors to accept these challenges as the rewards may be worth the effort. Some studies have found that small group interventions can yield up to a moderate effect size on student achievement (Whiston, Tai, Rahardja, & Eder, 2011).

References

American School Counselor Association (2010). *Ethical standards for school counselors.* Available online at www.schoolcounselor.org/files/EthicalStandards2010.pdf (accessed December 10, 2014).

American School Counselor Association (2012). *The ASCA national model: A framework for school counseling programs* (3rd ed.). Alexandria, VA: Author.

American School Counselor Association (2014). *ASCA mindsets & behaviors for student success: K-12 college and career readiness standards for every student.* Alexandria, VA: Author.

Bailey, D. F., & Bradbury-Bailey, M. E. (2007). Promoting achievement for African American males through group work. *Journal of Specialists in Group Work, 32,* 83–96.

Bauer, S. R., Sapp, M., & Johnson, D. (2000). Group counseling strategies for at-risk rural high school students. *The High School Journal, 83,* 41–50.

Bemak, F., Chung, R. C., & Siroskey-Sabdo, L. A. (2005). Empowerment groups for academic success: An innovative approach to prevent high school failure for at-risk, urban African American girls. *Professional School Counselor, 8,* 377–389.

Brigman, G., & Campbell, C. (2003). Helping students improve academic achievement and school success behavior. *Professional School Counseling, 7,* 91–98.

Brown, N. W. (2009). *Becoming a group leader.* Upper Saddle River, NJ: Pearson Education.

Bruce, A. M., Getch, Y. Q., & Ziomek-Daigle, J. (2009). Closing the gap: A group counseling approach to improve test performance of African-American students. *Professional School Counseling, 12,* 450–457.

Conyne, R. K., Crowell, J. L., & Newmyer, M. D. (2008). *Group techniques.* Upper Saddle River, NJ: Pearson Education.

Cooley, L. (2009). *The power of groups: Solution-focused group counseling in schools.* Thousand Oaks, CA: Corwin/Sage.

Corey, G. (2015). *Theory and practice of group counseling* (9th ed.). Belmont, CA: Brooks Cole.

Corey, G., Corey, M. S., Callanan, P., & Russell, J. M. (2004). *Group techniques* (3rd ed.). Pacific Grove, CA: Thomson Brooks/Cole.

Corey, M. S., & Corey, G. (2006). *Groups: Process and practice* (6th ed.). Belmont, CA: Thomson Brooks/Cole.

deShazer, S. (1988). *Clues: Investigating solutions in brief therapy.* New York: W. W. Norton.

Erford, B. (2011). The ASCA national model: Developing a comprehensive, developmental school counseling program. In B. Erford (Ed.), *Transforming the school counseling profession* (pp. 44–57). Upper Saddle River, NJ: Pearson Education.

Gladding, S. T. (2008). *Groups: A counselling specialty* (6th ed.). Princeton, NC: Merrill.

Greenberg, K. R. (2003). *Group counseling in K-12 schools: A handbook for school counselors.* New York: Allyn and Bacon.

Hamayan, E., Marler, B., Sanchez-Lopez, C., & Damico, J. (2013) *Special education considerations for English language learners: Delivering a continuum of services* (2nd ed.). Philadelphia, PA: Caslon.

Hess, R. S., Magnuson, S., & Beeler, L. (2011). *Counseling children and adolescents in schools.* Thousand Oaks, CA: Sage.

Kaplan, L. S. (1995). Principals versus counselors: Resolving tensions from different practice models. *School Counselor, 42*(4), 261–267.

Koth, C. W., Bradshaw, C. P., & Leaf, P. J. (2008). A multilevel study of predictors of student perceptions of school climate: The effect of classroom-level factors. *Journal of Educational Psychology, 100*(1), 96–104.

Kozlowski, K., & Stone, C., (2013, January). *School Counselors and the Ethics of Advocacy Survey.* Unpublished raw data.

Lee, C. (2005). A reaction to EGAGS: An important new approach to African American youth empowerment. *Professional School Counseling, 8,* 393–394.

Lee, V. V., & Goodnough, G. E. (2007). Creating a systemic, data-driven school counseling program. In B. T. Erford (Ed.), *Transforming the school counseling profession* (2nd ed.; pp. 121–141). Upper Saddle River, NJ: Pearson Education.

Lieberman, M. A., Yalom, I., & Miles, M. (1973). *Encounter groups: First facts.* New York: Basic Books.

MacIver, D., & McCarroll, L., (1999). *Initiatives, games, and activities: An experiential guide.* Dubuque, IA: Kendall Hunt.

Malekoff, A. (Ed.) (2004). *Group work with adolescents: Principles and practice.* New York: The Guilford Press.

Nikels, H. J., Mims, G. A., & Mims, M. J. (2007). Allies against hate: A school-based diversity sensitivity training experience. *Journal for Specialists in Group Work, 32,* 126–138.

Paisley, P., & Milsom, A. (2007) Group work as an essential contribution to transforming school counseling. *The Journal for Specialist in Group Work, 32*(1), 9–17. doi: 10.1080/01933920600977465

Pérusse, R., Goodnough, G. E., & Lee, V. V. (2009). Group counseling in the schools. *Psychology in the Schools, 46,* 225–231.

Rolfe, G., Freshwater, D., & Jasper, M. (2001) *Critical reflection in nursing and the helping professions: A user's guide.* Basingstoke: Palgrave Macmillan.

Steen, S., & Bemak, F. (2008). Group work with high school students at risk of school failure: A pilot study. *Journal for Specialists in Group Work, 33,* 335–350.

Steen, S., & Kaffenberger, C. (2007). Integrating academic interventions into small group counseling in elementary school. *Professional School Counseling, 10,* 516–519.

Stone, C. (2013). *School counseling principles: Ethics and law* (3rd ed.). Alexandria, VA: American School Counselor Association.

Thomas, R.V., & Pender, D. A. (2008). Association for specialists in group work: Best practice guide 2007 revisions. *The Journal for Specialists in Group Work, 33,* 111–117.

Veach, L. J., & Gladding, S. T. (2007). Using creative group techniques in high schools. *The Journal for Specialists in Group Work, 32,* 71–81.

Whiston, S. C., Tai, W. L., Rahardja, D., & Eder, K. (2011). School counseling outcome: A meta-analytic examination of interventions. *Journal of Counseling & Development, 89,* 37–55.

Williams, R. L., Lantz, A., & Noorulamin, S. (2008). *Making smart choices: Social emotional intelligence for adolescent girls.* American School Counselor Association.

Williams, R. L., Riedo, S., & DeBard, S. (2007). *A handbook for leading positive youth development programs.* Denver, CO: Smart-Girl.

Yalom, I. (1995). *The theory and practice of group psychotherapy* (4th ed.). New York: Basic Books.

Chapter Eight
Consultation and Collaboration

Collaboration and consultation are vital components of a school counseling program. School counselors must partner with various stakeholders in order to support the school's academic mission, implement and maintain a comprehensive school counseling program, and effect systemic change. In *the ASCA National Model®* (2012), consultation and collaboration are defined as responsive services within the delivery component of the framework, and collaboration is one of the four model themes.

Within the literature, there are various definitions of consultation and collaboration. Among the various definitions of these terms, an element that is common to both collaboration and consultation is involvement with another to impact a third party. School counselors consult and collaborate with parents, teachers, administrators, and other important stakeholders in order to benefit students. Collaboration and consultation may be regarded as the primary behaviors through which schools contribute to systemic change. In this chapter, readers will learn about the models and theories of collaboration and consultation, and be provided with examples of collaboration and consultation conducted by school counselors. We also discuss the importance of involving low-income parents and parents of color.

Collaboration

Collaboration is included in the four model themes of *the ASCA National Model*® (2012), along with leadership, advocacy, and systemic change, all of which are contained within the edge of the frame of the model graphic. As the school counseling profession has moved away from primarily emphasizing providing direct services to at-risk students, it has instead focused on the implementation of a program and serving as an integral team player to advance the academic mission of the school, and thus the importance of collaboration has correspondingly increased. The school counselor's training in communication skills, group dynamics, and in working with systems puts him or her in a unique position to collaborate with others. School counselors seek to promote systemic change by providing leadership and advocacy, and collaboration is an essential part of all three of these model themes.

School counselors collaborate with colleagues in order to be a vital contributor to the school's academic mission. Traditional definitions of both collaboration and consultation emphasize the role of experts sharing their area of expertise. Historically, training for school counselors has emphasized understanding students' career development and labor trends, the college admissions process, children's social/emotional development, and mental health services available in the community. School counselors are often members of the various school committees addressing school improvement, such as teacher teams and/or data teams, and also participate on committees focusing on academically or behaviorally at-risk students, such as the Instructional Support Team/child study team, Individualized Education Plan (IEP) team, the Student Assistance Program (SAP), etc. School counselors also typically work as the school's liaison with community agencies, providing parents and students with referrals and coordinating the communication between the community agencies, while providing services to at-risk children and their families. Finally, school counselors are frequently involved in planning and presenting teacher-in-service sessions.

While school counselors are primarily responsible for creating and implementing the school counseling core curriculum, there are various collaborative components emphasized in *the ASCA National Model*® (2012). Several aspects of *the ASCA National Model*® reflect the importance of designing a program that meets the unique needs of the community. The vision and mission statements and the goals of the school counseling program are expected to support the school and district's mission, and school counselors are tasked with identifying and removing barriers to educational access for traditionally disadvantaged groups that are specific to the setting. In order to meet the unique needs of the school and community, school counselors conduct needs assessments and gather already-existing data to understand the perspectives of the various stakeholders.

Box 8.2

The Top Ten Ways School Counselors Can Support Teachers

1. **Call on counselors to help you understand the whole student.** When teachers notice red flags, such as behavioral issues or grades, school counselors are prepared to help teachers gain a more complete understanding of the issues behind the actions.
2. **Consult with counselors for professional advice.** When teachers find themselves stuck with strategies that aren't working with a particular student, a counselor who is trained to problem-solve can help them gain fresh ideas to age old problems.
3. **Tackle problems before they become insurmountable.** When teachers sense trouble brewing in class, language or behavior that causes them anxiety, they should talk with a school counselor who can help trouble-shoot and prevent a situation from escalating.

4. **Offer students an empathic listener.** When students are having problems that seem personal or sensitive or that have the potential to get them into trouble, send them to a school counselor who can provide a sounding board and help them find solutions.

5. **Guide students' decision-making.** When students act out repeatedly in class, teachers should inform a counselor who can work with them on decision-making. School counselors can also help the child reframe the situation and illustrate how different behaviors might be in their best interest.

6. **Collaborate with a counselor to integrate counseling and class lessons.** Work together to teach lessons in class about academics, careers, and personal/social issues. These lessons are preventive by design and developmental in nature to help students with their decision-making in school. For example, a lesson about bullying and harassment in a civics class could be paired with a project on laws about harassment.

7. **Work with counselors and teachers to design professional development that meets your needs.** In-service days provide great opportunities for counselors and teachers to explain their work and develop solutions to school-wide problems.

8. **Allow a counselor to make peace.** When students can't get along in class despite the teacher's attempts to separate them or diffuse tension, allow a counselor to mediate and work out a plan for how the two parties can peaceably coexist.

9. **Explore career options.** Educators may want to engage a school counselor in helping students understand how their academic work connects to specific careers.

10. **Ask a counselor to clarify the severity of a problem.** As students develop physically, rapid changes in their mood or behavior can leave teachers wondering whether certain behavior is normal or a cause for deeper concern. School counselors have been trained to ask the questions that get at the heart of what's really going on.

Reproduced with permission from I. Brodie (2013, April 29). *The top ten ways school counselors can support teachers*. Available online at www.ed.gov/blog/2012/06/the-top-10-ways-school-counselors-can-support-teachers/.

Ideally, school counseling programs have an advisory council, consisting of 8–20 members who reflect the diversity of the community, and which includes students, parents, school counselors, administrators, school board members, and business and community members. The advisory council is a key element of the democratic process essential for changing prevailing values and norms and developing support for implementation of the programs of the school counseling program. The advisory council assists with needs assessments, analyzing the collected data, disseminating the results to the various stakeholders, creating the foundation of the program, and managing and delivering the program. Action plans and closing-the-gap action plans typically specify other educators who may contribute in the delivery of components of the school counseling core curriculum.

School counselors also work with the school administration in completing an annual agreement regarding the expected duties of the school counselor, and the agreement is expected to be a process through which school counselors can educate administrators regarding the benefits of a comprehensive school counseling program. Lastly, school counselors collaborate with colleagues through their coordination of the various programs that may be closely associated with the school counseling program, which may include the bullying and violence prevention programs, mentoring and tutoring programs, etc.

Family-School Collaboration

Although most of the attention regarding the No Child Left Behind Act of 2001 (NCLB; 2002) has concerned the federal mandate requiring states to implement achievement tests and establish more stringent standards for teachers (Epstein, 2005), the Parent Involvement section and other sections of the NCLB Act include a variety of regulations, the aim of which is to promote family-school collaboration (NCLB, 2002). State departments of education and school districts must provide professional development opportunities that enhance educators' and parents' understanding of the importance of collaboration and the skills to achieve goal-oriented partnership programs. Schools must share with parents and the community information and decisions about students' placements and the performance of the school, including the aggregated and disaggregated results of state achievement tests, attendance and graduation rates, and information about teachers' qualifications. Finally, NCLB makes clear that schools are expected to increase equity in education by making more of an effort to include families, even those who are not currently involved, and by ensuring that communications with parents are clear, useful, and executed in languages that all parents understand.

Box 8.3

One group of students that is at risk for inequitable educational outcomes consists of students from families that are low income. School counselors can work to develop family-school partnerships by:

- challenging bias
- training school personnel to work with all families
- initiating outreach activities with families
- conducting research to establish effective practices
- highlighting the benefits of collaborative problem-solving
- accessing student and family strengths.

(Amatea, Daniels, Bringman, & Vandiver, 2004; Grothaus & Cole, 2010)

Epstein and her colleagues (2002) have developed the most comprehensive model for family-school collaboration and have conducted a rigorous program of evaluation that has demonstrated the effectiveness of the model in promoting family-school collaboration and enhancing students' academic achievement. In their model, the home, school, and community are referred to as "overlapping spheres," which influence both children and the conditions and relationships in the three contexts. The external model is comprised of the external contexts in which students live (e.g., home, school, and community), and the theory assumes that student achievement is enhanced when these external contexts collaborate. The internal model refers to the interactions and patterns of influence that occur between individuals at home, at school, and in the community.

Interactions between the three contexts occur both at the institutional level (e.g., the school creating a system by which parents can verify homework assignments) and at the individual level (e.g., parent-teacher conference). Epstein and her colleagues identified six main types of involvement interactions which are used to organize the school's activities in promoting parental and community involvement. She adapted a model indicating how school counselors can use the six types of family involvement in a prevention mode and in a treatment mode (Epstein & Van Voorhis, 2010).

Studies have found that schools that have implemented the overlapping spheres of influence theory using the six types of involvement have increased family-school collaboration (Epstein et al., 2002). Moreover, increases in family-school collaboration using Epstein et al.'s model was associated with increases in school climate, improved student behavior and school discipline, and increased reading achievement scores. Epstein and Sheldon's (2002) longitudinal study found that specific family-school collaboration activities were associated with increased attendance among elementary students, including providing workshops for parents regarding attendance matters, communicating with all families, and providing a school contact person for parents to call. Although the effectiveness of Epstein's adaptation of the parent involvement model for school counselors has not been evaluated, the widespread use of the parent involvement model among many state departments of education establishes its relevance for the role of school counselors in fostering family-school collaboration.

In support of this, Griffin and Steen (2010) studied school counselors' involvement in partnering with parents and community organizations, and used Epstein's "Six Types of School-Family-Community Involvement Interactions" to analyze the results. The findings revealed that although many of the school counselors perceived school-family-community partnerships to be useful and reported confidence in developing such partnerships, most school counselors indicated that they did not participate in such partnerships. The activities of school counselors who did report partnering with parents fit into the categories of collaborating with the community and parenting within Epstein's model, with low involvement reported in decision-making, volunteering, learning-at-home activities, and communicating with parents. The study also revealed that school counselors reported engaging in collaborative activities that did not fit into any of the categories in Epstein's theory, as they surpassed some of the basic partnership activities comprising Epstein's framework. Griffin and Steen (2010) categorized these advanced collaborative activities as forms of leadership and advocacy, and examples included establishing a leadership council, presenting to school boards, etc.

Griffin and Steen (2010) concluded that school counselors could increase their use of communication, volunteering, decision-making, and leadership and advocacy practices, and the authors provided recommendations based on a review of the school counselor literature regarding how such professionals tend to engage in these specific forms of collaboration. School counselors can communicate with parents regarding how they can support their child in establishing educational goals while also advertising their role and service as the school counselor. Moreover, they can establish a family resource center containing educational resources such as audiovisuals, brochures, and announcements concerning academic, career, and social/emotional issues. They have enhanced training in interpersonal communication skills and may be in the best position to initially establish a working alliance between family members and school personnel, using constructive communication skills and emphasizing the student's and families' strengths, establishing the trust essential for addressing more challenging and potentially conflictual issues.

School counselors may not only model such constructive communication and teaming skills during parent-teacher conferences, but may also collaborate with respected teachers in providing in-service training for the staff regarding effective strategies for relating to parents and collaborative decision-making, as many teachers do not feel prepared to interact with parents. School counselors can use parent volunteers to support the school counseling program, including designing and implementing workshops for other parents (Sheldon, 2003), identifying community resources, and tutoring (Griffin & Steen, 2010). The authors of this text have found that parents are often eager to hear the experiences of parents of children who have recently undergone important transitions, such as entering middle or high school, applying to college, etc., and that such parents can be included on such panel topics.

School counselors can collaborate with teachers in providing workshops for parents to increase their understanding of the academic curriculum, with school counselors contributing their expertise regarding how to structure such workshops to be informative for parents who have less formal education (Griffin & Steen, 2010). School counselors can involve parents in decision-making by surveying parents regarding their perceptions of needed services, and by including parents as part of the advisory council (ASCA, 2012).

Box 8.4

School counselors can help teachers' growth and development in the areas of:

- program development
- time management
- creative leadership
- accountability
- positive visibility.

(Kern, 1999)

Involving Low-Income Parents and Parents of Color

While parental involvement seems to be clearly associated with academic achievement for White students, the relationship between parental involvement and achievement for minority and low-income students is more mixed. Studies have found that low-income and minority students whose parents were involved in their school were more likely to gain admission to four-year colleges (Wadenya & Lopez, 2008), and have significantly higher standardized achievement test scores (Dietel, 2006), as compared to those students whose parents were not involved. However, while parent volunteering has been found to be associated with White students' academic achievement it has not been found to be related to the academic achievement of minority students and students in poverty (Desimone, 1999).

The literature has indicated a number of factors that explain lower rates of involvement of minority parents and parents of color (Holcomb-McCoy, 2010). These factors include language barriers, the fact that schools do not provide a welcoming environment, a cultural disconnection between schools and communities, and the lack of opportunities for parent involvement. Unfortunately, there is some evidence to suggest that school counselors in the past have contributed to the barriers to the involvement of low-income and minority families in discouraging such students from pursuing postsecondary education (e.g., Hart & Jacobi, 1992).

It has been suggested that parent involvement, which has been traditionally defined as volunteering, attending school conferences and events, and communicating with teachers, has been defined in ways that discount how other cultures promote achievement in their youth (Bower & Griffin, 2011). A broader definition of parent involvement can include providing nurturance and limit-setting, providing assistance with homework, establishing high expectations, and discussing with children their aspirations (e.g., Abdul-Adil & Farmer, 2006). Latino families tend to defer to school personnel and are less likely to contact them regarding potential problems, which may be interpreted by school personnel as a lack of involvement (Gaetano, 2007). Low-income families are more likely to have informal conversations and do unscheduled visits, which are often viewed as inappropriate by teachers (Fields-Smith, 2007).

Bower and Griffin (2011) evaluated the effectiveness of implementing the Epstein model of parental involvement in one urban elementary school with a high rate of poverty and minority student enrollment. While they found that the parents in the school were involved with their children, the implementation of Epstein's model did not result in increased parental involvement as parental involvement is defined in the model. They recommend that schools develop a broader definition of parental involvement, which may decrease the frustration that many teachers expressed regarding the low rate of parent participation in the parent-teacher organization meetings and informal open houses. To increase parental involvement, they recommend that schools seek a long-term approach to acquire the trust of parents, and that schools must conduct continued outreach efforts, even when initial attempts at connecting with parents appear to be unsuccessful. School counselors can coordinate cultural awareness workshops.

Schools must work hard at welcoming minority and low-income parents who are likely to be reluctant to participate with schools given past negative experiences and beliefs that their views will not be welcomed. School personnel should seek to understand the perspectives of minority and low-income parents, and thank parents for sharing their ideas and perspectives, and should avoid becoming defensive if parents' perspectives are seemingly critical. Schools need to be creative and flexible in how and when they provide opportunities for parental involvement. Schools should schedule some events in the evening, and may increase parental participation by providing food and daycare. Schools can provide opportunities within the community, providing informational sessions at churches, community agencies, etc. They should avoid excessive use of the technical language of education, including such acronyms as Individualized Education Plan (IEP), 504, percentile rank, etc., and should provide clear explanations of such language.

Teachers in the elementary school in Bower and Griffin (2011) which implemented Epstein's model of parental involvement developed home learning activities in which parents could participate. For example, in teaching measurement and capacity, teachers encouraged parents to ask their children to look in the refrigerator and kitchen to identify the capacity of objects (e.g., liters of milk, identifying the measurements used for ingredients, etc.).

Parental involvement and college access. Minority students are more dependent on school counselors for information about college than non-minority students (e.g., Bryan, Holcomb-McCoy, Moore-Thomas, & Day-Vines, 2009), and low-income students are more likely to rely upon school counselors for information about financial aid than are their high-income peers (Terenzini, Cabrera, & Bernal, 2001). Thankfully, research suggests that when school counselors actively support minority and low-income students and their families in middle school for college, versus simply providing information, such efforts increased students' likelihood of enrolling in a four-year college (e.g., Plank & Jordan, 2001). To increase the parental involvement of low-income and minority students in college readiness activities, Holcomb-McCoy (2010) recommends that school counselors develop innovative ways to disseminate information about colleges and financial aid. She suggests that school counselors train parent volunteers about the college admissions process and then arrange for the volunteers to conduct information sessions in the community with other parents. A comprehensive overview of financial aid is particularly important as minority and low-income parents tend to overestimate the costs of college attendance (e.g., Grodsky & Jones, 2004), and are less likely to be aware of the various forms of financial aid, such as scholarships (Sallie Mae Fund, 2003).

Collaboration with Various Stakeholders

Day-Vines and Terriquez (2008) provide an innovative and compelling example regarding the way in which school counselors can collaborate with various groups in order to achieve systemic change. Terriquez was a school counselor in an Oakland high school which was experiencing racial inequities in school discipline. The school was located in an affluent community, which through busing served a diverse student population of African American, Asian American, Latino, and White students. The school was described as racially segregated, in that high ability classes were predominately populated by White and the Asian American students, and the low ability classes were more likely to be composed of Latino and African American students. Analysis of the discipline referrals for one academic year indicated that African American and Latino males were eight times more likely than the White and Asian American male students to receive a referral.

A school-based, multi-racial youth leadership group called Youth Together was the first to express concern regarding the racial disparities in suspension rates, and organized student meetings during lunch and after school hours, at which many students shared the belief that teachers were fearful of African and Latino American males, and thus were more likely to remove such students from the classroom. With the support of teachers and the school counselor, Youth Together organized a meeting with the school administration, teachers, other school counselors, parents, and student groups to discuss the issue. Youth Together also surveyed the teachers and students regarding the strengths and potential areas for improvement in the school's discipline policies and procedures, with the results indicating support for achieving equitable treatment of students and training for teachers in improving their classroom management. These efforts resulted in the establishment of a school discipline committee composed of various stakeholders, including Youth Together students, parents, and other school personnel.

The school discipline committee analyzed the school discipline data, disaggregating the data by race and type of offense. One of the interesting results was that most of the discipline referrals made by teachers were for the category "defiance of authority," which was not clearly defined in the school's policies, supporting students' concerns that behavioral expectations varied considerably by classroom. The school counselor's role during this phase of the initiative was to validate students' concerns while also encouraging students to understand the perspectives of teachers.

The school discipline committee adopted a variety of interventions, including educating teachers and students about the school-wide rules and consequences for rule violations, by hosting several workshops for students during lunch, and the administration requiring the posting of the rules in the classrooms. The school discipline committee also coordinated an in-service workshop for all of the staff in which facilitators led small groups of teachers and youth leaders to identify the teaching strategies and discipline procedures that promoted positive student behavior. The small group discussion appeared to promote enhanced perspective-taking for both students and teachers.

One of the administrators on the school discipline committee initiated another intervention, observing and consulting with the teachers who had the highest discipline referrals to improve their classroom management strategies. The final intervention involved the administration of another survey of students to identify alternatives to out-of-school suspension. The number of suspensions decreased by over 75% for the following academic year, and the school discipline committee's recommendations eventually resulted in the development of a youth center which offered mental health services, tutoring, and youth development programs.

Day-Vines and Terriquez (2008) illustrate the power and importance of collaborating with various stakeholders to facilitate change. The multifaceted composition of the school discipline committee promoted perspective-taking and increased the likelihood that each of the represented groups would be more likely to support the changes to the policies and procedures concerning discipline. The considerable involvement of students enhanced their sense of empowerment and promoted their communication and self-management skills. The school counselor shared their expertise and training in conflict resolution, communication skills, and multicultural awareness and knowledge with students, teachers, and administrators. Finally, the school counselor's use of Galassi and Akos' (2007) strength-based approach helped the constituent groups perceive and use the resources each offered for collaborative problem-solving.

Box 8.5

One of the ways in which school counselors can support families is through a technique known to public service professions, called community asset mapping. It involves drawing a map of what is valuable in communities, and includes compiling a list of existing resources that can be used by all stakeholders. For additional information on this topic, consult the article, *School counselors and collaboration: Finding resources through community asset mapping,* by Griffin and Farris (2010).

Consultation

Consultation in schools is a service delivery model in which a clinician, serving as a consultant, uses problem-solving strategies (in order to alter an existing set of circumstances to become a desired set of circumstances) to address the needs of a consultee and a student (Kratochwill, 1990). Both a time- and cost-efficient way to provide a service to a large number of clients (e.g., children, families), consultants work with consultees, such as teachers and other educators, who then work with clients (children and their families) guided by consultative treatment plans. Consultants and consultees work collaboratively to share their knowledge bases to help solve academic, behavioral, and social/emotional problems in children. Thus, consultation is an indirect vehicle through which school-based educational and mental health professionals can combine their expertise to positively impact upon children's development and functioning. Although there are various models of school-based consultation, this chapter will focus upon solution-focused, systems, and behavioral consultation, as these consultation models may be considered to be the most frequently used by school counselors.

Solution-Focused Consultation (SFC)

The principles of solution-focused theory are compatible with the collaborative model of consultation. Notably, most of the models of consultation for schools use the collaborative, problem-solving model (Kahn, 2000), in contrast to the triadic-dependent consultation model. In the triadic-dependent approach to consultation, the consultant is regarded as an expert who is generally active and directive in prescribing an intervention for the consultee. Collaborative consultation deemphasizes the power differential between the consultant and consultee; rather, seeing each member of the consultation team as possessing potentially important insights and resources. The task of the consultant is to facilitate a constructive process that enables the consultee to develop more effective approaches in working with the student(s) in question. In the triadic-dependent model, the consultant offers his or her expertise, whether it be instructional strategies, behavior modification, and so forth to the consultee, whereas in the collaborative consultation model, the consultant's primary source of expertise is his or her ability to facilitate a constructive process.

A primary assumption of solution-focused theory is that individuals, whether they are students, teachers, or parents, have the resources to obtain their goals. However, such people may currently be experiencing difficulty because of their perspective of the problem. This is often referred to within solution-focused theory as having a problem-saturated perspective. The task of the solution-focused consultant is to help the consultee develop new perspectives of the students, himself or herself, and the situation, through the consultant's artful use of language. This implies another founding principle of solution-focused theory, which is that reality is partially a social construction and is maintained through the use of language.

Consultants' view of the student or the student's problem is influenced by their language. For example, a student's learning disability or behavioral disorder may become problematic for the teacher or parent because it is viewed from the most negative and pessimistic manner, and may be assumed by the parent or teacher to be objective reality. The solution-focused consultant attempts to access the consultee's "frame" of the situation, and help the consultee develop slightly modified or new frames which are more constructive. In illustration of this, a teacher may see a child's obsessive behaviors of checking to make sure his or her pencil is on his or her desk as interfering with the child's completion of academic tasks. A modified frame of this problem might be that the child's perseveration in making sure the pencil is on the desk is managing his or her anxiety and allowing him or her to focus on the academic work.

SFC emphasizes a positive frame by assisting consultees to identify and use their strengths, resources, and past successes to establish goals (Kahn, 2000). Rather than extensively focusing on the problem, the consultant encourages the consultee to focus upon past successes and exceptions to the problem, meaning when the problem did not exist or was less of a problem. The consultant does not provide direct suggestions, but rather engages the consultee in a constructive conversation that helps the consultee to develop a new perspective of the situation, resulting in the consultee devising his or her own solutions. Solutions that are generated by the consultee are considered preferable because the consultee is likely to use those solutions, since they stem from the consultee's resources and perspective. Another difference of SFC in comparison to traditional models of consultation is that there is less focus on the student or the object of the consultation, and more focus on those aspects of the situation that the consultee controls, such as his or her viewpoint of or interactions with the child.

SFC does not strictly adhere to distinct stages in comparison to traditional models of consultation, as the focus is primarily to help the consultee develop more constructive frames, but there is a general process that is followed. Kahn (2000) adapted the steps of Juhnke's (1996) solution-focused supervision model to the consultation process, which are as follows: (a) pre-session and initial structuring, (b) identifying consultation goals, (c) exploring exceptions, (d) helping the consultee decide upon a solution, and (e) summarizing and complimenting.

Pre-session and initial structuring. In the pre-session and initial structuring, the goals are to help the consultee to identify strengths and objectives. Kahn (2000) adapted Juhnke's (1996) pre-session supervision questionnaire to the consultation process. The questionnaire instructs teachers to identify the strengths and resources they can contribute to the consultation process, such as their teaching skills or interpersonal strengths. The questionnaire may also include goals for the student and consultee, including "How would you like the student to be? How would you like to be with your student? With your class? and How will you know such consultation is successful?" (p. 249). Such questions may create a shift in the consultee's thinking, as the consultee may be focused upon the negative aspects of the situation, such as the student's lack of progress or the consultee's inability to facilitate the student's progress, leading the consultee to think more about future possibilities, which often increases the consultee's hopefulness.

Establishing consultation goals. In examining the consultee's goals, there is little emphasis on discussing the problem, which is not considered productive, since the focus should be upon solutions. However, these authors recommend spending at least 5–10 minutes listening attentively to the consultee's perspective, even if it is quite negative, and reflecting the consultee's perspective back to the consultee using active listening skills. One reason why it may be helpful to first explore the consultee's perspective is that it helps the consultant understand the consultee's "frame of the problem," possibly indicating how the consultee's frame may be contributing to the problem. Also, it has been the authors' experience that some consultees are not ready to engage in problem-solving until they believe that their perspective of the problem has been understood and acknowledged. SFC shares similarities with behavioral consultation in that effective goals are considered to be concrete, behavioral, defined in measurable terms, and identified in the affirmative expectation (rather than identifying the absence of a behavior).

Exploring exceptions. A primary solution-focused technique used during this phase is exception seeking. This technique involves asking the consultee to identify times in which the problem did not occur, or occurred to a lesser degree, and then exploring with the consultee how he or she contributed to the success of that respective situation. In SFC, the consultant seeks to help the consultee identify the very specific thoughts and behaviors that may have contributed to the exception, and which consultees often overlook. For example, the consultee may be asked to provide specific details about how he or she asked the student to participate in a class discussion, what the consultee was thinking which contributed to his or her decision to invite the student's participation, how the student responded in terms of his or her behavior, and what these behaviors might indicate about the student's thoughts and feelings, etc. Scaling questions may be used during any of the consultation phases, and have particular relevancy for exploring exceptions as well.

Scaling questions. The consultee can be asked to assess on a 10-point scale the degree to which a student is demonstrating the respective goal. Typically, consultees and students provide a rating in the range of 3–8. The consultant then asks the consultee to identify how he or she thinks the student achieved whatever rating the consultee identified, and how the consultee contributed to the child's success. The consultant may use what is referred to as "not-knowing questions." Examples include the following: "What was it that you did that helped your son complete his homework on Thursday night?", "How did you help the child develop more interest in the reading assignment?" After exploring the things that have helped the child and consultee achieve at least a limited degree of success, the consultant asks the consultee what one additional point of success would look like on the scale; in other words, what is the next step the consultant could take? This question serves to counter the tendency of consultees to think in all or nothing terms, and instead think in terms of small, incremental steps toward change, which solution-focused theory would suggest is more consistent with the nature of lasting change.

Helping consultees decide on a solution. This phase is often brief, as the previous consultation phases should have helped the consultee develop new perspectives and solutions. The primary task of the consultant in this phase is to summarize and emphasize the new perspectives, solutions, and resources that the consultee has implied will likely contribute to progress, and asking the consultee to identify the concrete steps he or she plans to pursue.

Case Consultation: An Illustration of Solution-Focused Consultation (SFC)

Mrs. Dwyer is the mother of James, a seventh grade student in a suburban middle school. She has sought out the school counselor to discuss her concerns about James' inconsistency in completing homework.

Counselor: It is good see you, Mrs. Dwyer. I always appreciate it when parents contact me about their concerns, and I admire your interest in your son's education. Please tell me about your concerns.

Parent: Well, I'm just so frustrated with James. His teachers informed me that he hasn't been submitting his homework on a regular basis, and for this last marking period, his grades dropped from "B's" to "C's" in most of his academic subjects. His father and I accepted "B's", hoping James would pull them up to "A's", and now he seems to be going in the opposite direction.

Counselor: Let me see that I'm hearing you correctly. You and your husband were satisfied with the "B's" that James received for the previous marking period, but you are obviously unhappy with the "C's" he received this marking period, and his teachers have identified his inconsistency in completing homework as one reason for the decline in his grades in academic subjects.

Parent: Yes, I mean, I am just not sure what to do when it comes to his homework. I think my husband and I thought that we could back off a bit since he seemed to be doing well, and friends of ours who have children in high school had told us how at some point we have to allow James to be more responsible in doing in his work. Now we're wondering if we should go back to staying on top of him more.

Counselor: You're wondering about how to help James with his homework. You want James to assume more responsibility for doing his work, but are thinking about going back to what you did last marking period when it came to his homework.

Parent: Yeah, I know I feel sort of caught, and I think my husband feels similarly.

Counselor: So, if I understand it your goal right now is to help James increase his homework completion, is that accurate?

Parent: Yes, from what I understand from the teachers, they believe this is what brought James' grades down, as his test scores and quizzes were generally in the "B" range.

Counselor: Okay, on a ten-point scale, with 10 being James is handling his homework well, and 1 being James is not assuming any responsibility for his homework completion, where you would like him to be and what number would you currently give James?

Parent: I'd say he is at about a 3 since he is completing his homework sometimes.

Counselor: How about last marking period? What number would you give James when it came to completing his homework on that 10-point scale?

Parent: More like an 8. My husband and I believe he was completing and turning in his homework every time, but rather than a 10, I would give James an 8 because we often had to ask numerous times if he had homework before we would even look to see if he did, and we sometimes had to sit with him when he did it to make sure that he wouldn't go and do something else.

Counselor: And I heard that part of your goal is that you want him to complete his homework, but with less prodding from you and your husband. Could you tell me a time where you saw this happening, that James did his homework with less prodding from you and your husband?

Parent: Well, it hasn't happened a lot, but I can think of a time about a month ago. James did all of his homework right when he got from school without me even saying anything to him when he got off the bus.

Counselor: Wow, interesting. So what is your sense of how you helped James do that?

Parent: Well, the night before, both my husband and I sat down with James and explained to him that we want him to get his work done right after school as we thought he is more focused then. We also shared that once he gets his work done, that gives us more time to do something fun with him like play a video game.

Counselor: So you think sharing your perspective with James, that he is more focused right after school, and then explaining how this gives him more time to do fun things with you and your husband helped to motivate him?

Parent: Yeah, it seemed to work that night.

Counselor: Wow, it sounds like you have seen the success you are looking for.

Parent: I guess you're right. I guess we need to keep it going. It is hard because I don't think James did his homework the following night, and then we fell into what we do sometimes, which is to nag him, which just leads to an argument.

Counselor: So we know what an 8 looks like. What would a 9 look like, meaning what would James be doing if he were at a 9?

Parent: Well, obviously he would be doing his homework right away when he gets from school, and he would be more organized. Sometimes it takes me and James a while to figure out what homework he has to do, as he doesn't write it down in his agenda like he is supposed to.

Counselor: Okay, so a 9 would be James is getting his work after school, and he knows what he needs to do. What is your sense of how you help him to be a 9?

Parent: We've told him about the importance of using his agenda. I've been wondering if he has too much stuff in his backpack. I mean, he has to pull out tons of stuff just to get to his agenda.

Counselor: Ah, so you think you want to teach him to pare down to essential things?

Parent: Yes, and you know, I think it is something that my husband and I need to learn to better model for James. I mean, we tend to be a bit disorganized around the house, and I've been thinking I need to better show James how to organize things.

Counselor: It sounds to me like you have a number of ideas about what helps James to complete his work. You sense that reminding him the night before of your expectations seems to work, and helps you to avoid nagging him, and provides a reinforcer, something he can look forward to for completing his work. You see the next step as helping him to be organized in keeping track of what are his homework assignments, and you have several ideas regarding how you can help him to do that.

Case discussion and conclusions. Several aspects of solution-focused theory are displayed in this case example. First, the counselor focuses on positives throughout the session. The counselor initiates the session by praising the mother for being involved in her son's education, which helps to both establish the tone for the session and to develop rapport with the mother. Rather than focusing on what has not been working, the counselor focuses on the exceptions, meaning when things have gone well, and explores the details of what James did during the exception, and the mother's perceptions regarding her and her husband's contributions to James' exceptions.

The counselor uses a scaling question to identify what successes the mother perceives to already have happened. Furthermore, the counselor helps the mother to identify what will be the small steps that will yield future progress. Scaling questions help to combat people's tendency to think dualistically. When frustrated, people tend to minimize their strengths/resources, and exaggerate the degree of change needed to achieve a goal. Asking people to identify the progress they have already made, and what a point above the success they have already experienced will look like, helps people identify the small changes and details that will lead toward their goals. In other words, it encourages people to focus on the process of change rather than concentrate on whether they have or have not achieved the respective goal, which often is not particularly helpful in making progress toward that goal.

The counselor assisted the mother in generating her own ideas and solutions in assisting her son, which reflects another core principle of solution-focused theory – that people have the resources to resolve their own problems. The counselor could have readily offered direct suggestions, but refrained from doing so because of the fact that people tend not to follow the suggestions of others. Rather, the counselor helped the mother identify solutions that had already worked in her family and were generated by her, two conditions that are likely to increase the likelihood that the mother will use the ideas she generated. The authors' experience is that most people have done considerable thinking about their problem and have identified potential solutions for that problem, and rather than offering solutions that would work from the consultant's worldview, it is more effective to facilitate the consultee's exploration of the solutions he or she is considering.

The process and techniques used in SFC are extremely similar to the process of solution-focused counseling. The primary difference is that the consultant asks the consultee to identify his or her contributions to changes in the person of concern. The next model of consultation that will be explored in this chapter is systems theory consultation, which considers the multiple contexts of the consultee's and student's functioning in order to encourage long-lasting change.

Systems Consultation

Systems consultation is another model discussed in the school counseling literature. In the systemic approach, the problems and potential solutions are not seen as existing within the child, but rather within the nature of the interactions between the student and teacher and between the teacher and parents (White & Mullis, 1998). Indeed, Westwood (2002) found that some of the important components of successful inclusion plans for children with emotional and behavioral disorders included a positive teacher-child relationship, the support of the child's counselor in the inclusion process, and parental involvement.

Additionally, Weintraub (1998) found that regular education teachers considered some of the most effective interventions for students with problematic behavior to be consulting with parents to address problems perceived to be related to the student's home life and developing a relationship with the child to decrease alienation. The systemic approach to consultation is holistic in that it recognizes that the children's emotions and cognitions are interconnected, and that the thoughts, feelings, and behaviors of their parents and teachers are also interconnected. As in behavioral consultation, the child's behavior is seen as functional, and exploration of the various contexts of the child's life is necessary to determine the potential purpose of the behavior. In using systems consultation, the school counselor may first assist the teacher in examining the history of his or her relationship with the child, exploring the reciprocal nature of the interactions between the teacher and child.

The relationship between the teacher and child is investigated, and the teacher may be asked to consider how his or her behaviors, thoughts, and feelings impacted the child, and reciprocally, how the child's behaviors, thoughts, and feelings influenced the teacher. Through such questions, the consultant attempts to assist the teacher in developing new perspectives of the child and his or her relationship with the child that results in the teacher generating new solutions. According to the systems perspective, a consultant is often necessary when there is tension between a student and teacher because the teacher's perspective of the child and the situation has become restricted by his or her emotional intensity. In such cases, the consultant uses his or her objectivity and ability to see the relationship patterns to guide the teacher and/ or patterns to perceive the situation from a broader perspective.

In the systemic approach to school-based consultation, there is also considerable emphasis upon facilitating collaboration between the home and school (White & Mullis, 1998). The primary goals of involving the parents are to better understand the family context that may be contributing to the child's difficulties, obtain the parents' perspective and ideas to address the problem, and to increase family-school collaboration given the considerable empirical support demonstrating the relationship between academic achievement and family involvement (e.g., Epstein, 2005).

The consultant often acts as a facilitator of family-school collaboration. Often, the relationship between the teacher and parents has been soured by their mutual frustrations in addressing the challenging behaviors of the child. Frequently, the teacher and parents focus on each other as a source of the problem. In such situations, the consultant seeks to rebuild the relationship between the teacher and the parents through hosting parent-teacher conferences. In these meetings, the consultant uses a structured format of a problem-solving model to reestablish a more functional hierarchy and increased trust among the adults, thus facilitating more constructive communication between the parents and teachers and blocking unproductive communication. However, sometimes teachers are most concerned about remedying the academic difficulties that children are experiencing related to their emotional or behavioral problem(s). In such cases, instructional consultation, which is not discussed in this chapter, may be a valuable tool to help facilitate a change in a student's academic performance.

The authors have found that the solution-focused and systems consultation approaches can be readily integrated. Both approaches emphasize that the consultant collaborates with the consultee by facilitating a process in which the consultee explores the nature of his or her interactions with the person in question. The systemic approach to consultation may initially be used by the consultant to understand the history of the patterns between the consultee and the person of focus, and the consultant may use the solution-focused approach in the latter part of the consultation session to explore the positive contributions that the consultee is making toward the process and for exploring the implications for change.

Behavioral Consultation

Behavioral consultation (BC) involves a structured and systematic problem-solving method that enables the consultant (the school counselor) and teacher (the consultee) to collectively identify, define, and analyze the problem, and evaluate the effectiveness of the intervention. Akin-Little, Little, and Delligatti (2004) propose that the behavioral method of consultation can be preventative in nature when school counselors assist teachers in learning strategies to manage future behavioral problems. However, BC is principally used in order to help a teacher cope with the immediate behavioral problem of a child or adolescent.

Behavioral consultative processes. Similar to other consultation models, the four steps in the BC process include problem identification, problem analysis, plan implementation, and evaluation.

Box 8.6

Goals of Behavioral Consultation

- To produce behavioral change in the student.
- To produce behavioral change in the consultee.
- To produce behavioral change in the organization.

(Bergan & Kratochwill, 1990)

The consultant and consultee discuss the desired outcomes or changes resulting from the proposed interventions as well as when and where the intervention will occur and who implements the intervention. They will also set an expected date by which the behaviors will have changed as a result of the proposed intervention. What follows is a description of the steps unique to the BC process.

During the *problem identification step*, the consultant draws upon test data, observations, records, and interviews, for example, to glean information about the student and establish the objectives of the consultation. Thus, the problem identification step in the consultative process allows the consultant to better understand the needs of the consultee with respect to the student (Bergan & Kratochwill, 1990). During this stage, the consultant and consultee work together to clarify the presenting problem. Because the definition of the problem will lead to interventions, it is important that the definition of the problem behavior is succinct and presented in measurable, objective terms.

Consultees sometimes have difficulty describing the problem in clear and specific terms and often use vague or nonspecific terms to describe the behavior. Thus, during the initial problem identification stage, the consultant must assist the consultee in accurately describing the behavior in measurable terms (Gutkin & Curtis, 1999). Through the verbal communication process, the consultant can use elicitors, emitters, paraphrasing, and summarizing to improve problem identification. Furthermore, the consultant and consultee should agree upon the presenting problem behavior so that both are able to record the behavior as necessary. For example, the target behavior that is described as a classroom disruption may be redefined as "the number of times the student speaks without raising his or her hand during class or without being called upon by the teacher." In this way, the target behavior is specific and easily measured.

During the second step of the consultative process, *problem analysis*, the consultant seeks to identify the variables in the environment and in the student that are contributing to the maintenance of the problem. One of the first steps of this stage is to collect baseline data on the target behavior. When analyzing the problem behavior, the consultant looks at the antecedents and consequences of the behavior over time. Much of this information is gathered through observations of the student in his or her environment (Zins & Erchul, 2002).

Bergan and Kratochwill (1990) also discuss the importance of identifying the student's skill deficits during the problem-analysis stage. Skill deficits may be identified through observations, examination of work samples, and interviews. Identifying skill deficits allows the consultant to plan appropriate interventions later that assist in incrementally increasing the student's skills. For example, a child with poor social skills who has difficulty initiating conversations with peers may need to first learn common ways to introduce topics of conversation. As a part of the problem-analysis stage, consultants can also encourage the consultee to identify his or her strengths and other available supports that may be used as part of the intervention (Zins & Erchul, 2002).

After the target problem has been identified and analyzed, the consultant and consultee should brainstorm possible interventions in order to prepare for *plan implementation*. Zins and Erchul (2002) set forth principles to consider when consultants and consultees select interventions in the school setting, including the following: (1) Positive intervention approaches should be developed before the use of behavior reduction techniques unless the behavior is extreme; (2) Choose interventions that are the least intrusive and complex. Modifying variables in the child's environment may be easier and less intrusive than helping the student to learn a new skill or behavior; (3) When students must learn new skills, ensure that the strategies complement existing routines as much as possible; (4) Seek additional resources such as tutoring or community resources that may be used if the intervention is not effective in altering the student's behavior; (5) Consultants should provide ongoing support and reinforcement to consultees, since they are learning new ways to interact with the student; (6) Choose interventions that are time-efficient, non-intrusive and are perceived to be effective by consultees; and (7) Change should be targeted at the highest level of the organization as possible.

Regarding the *implementation stage* of the consultative process, Bergan and Kratochwill (1990) discuss several integral components. They assert that both the consultant and consultee should agree upon the nature of the problem, complete the skills analysis, design a plan, and arrange for a follow-up session with the consultee. When designing a plan, these researchers discuss the following steps: (1) establish objectives, (2) select interventions, (3) consider any barriers to the implementation of the intervention, and (4) select appropriate assessments. The consultee is expected to carry out the intervention plan during the implementation stage, although the consultant should remain available for monitoring and additional suggestions and/or revisions of the plan. Specifically, the consultant takes the lead in teaching the consultee behavioral skills of reinforcement or modeling, as well as teaching the consultee how to conduct observations. An important part of this stage is formative evaluation, in which the progress of the student is continually monitored to ensure that he or she is benefiting from the proposed intervention plan.

Finally, the *evaluation stage* is characterized by determining the effectiveness of the intervention, generalization, fading, and follow-up. The information shared between the consultant and consultee during this time include whether the goals of the intervention have been met by the student, the overall effectiveness of the plan, and a determination of whether the consultant-consultee relationship can be safely terminated (Kratochwill, 1990). In the case of unsuccessful interventions, a new plan may need to be made and implemented.

When evaluating intervention effectiveness, the same procedures used during the baseline data collection phase can be replicated. The evaluation plan should be devised prior to intervention implementation.

The effectiveness of the intervention should be evaluated in order to ensure treatment integrity and to identify potential side effects. When evaluating intervention effectiveness, there are two possible outcomes. One is that the intervention resulted in a successful attainment of treatment goals, and the process can then shift to follow-up monitoring, generalization, and fading. On the other hand, the intervention may have not resulted in a change or successful outcomes. In this case, the consultant and consultee may have to repeat the problem-solving process to reach alternative treatment intervention options (Zins & Erchul, 2002).

Once the effectiveness of the intervention has been evaluated, generalization of the intervention, follow-up, and fading of the reinforcement contingencies can be implemented. According to researchers, the factors that help to maintain positive behavior gains are not well understood (Zins & Erchul, 2002). However, researchers have identified ways to plan for generalization when developing the interventions, including identifying reinforcers in the naturally occurring environment that maintain the behavior, especially those that encourage independence in the student, such as self-monitoring or self-management (Meichenbaum & Turk, 1987).

Effectiveness of behavioral consultation. Empirical evidence, demonstrated primarily in single-case study designs, indicates that BC is effective in promoting positive behavioral changes (Guli, 2005; Wilkinson, 2005; Zins & Erchul, 2002). Although the use of BC may result in clinically significant treatment outcomes, there are several methodological issues to consider. As previously mentioned, intervention effectiveness is usually determined using case study designs in which one or two participants are studied. However, using a small sample size limits the generalizability of the research findings. Other methodological concerns identified in the consultation literature include problems related to replication, treatment integrity, and clearly identifiable procedures (Guli, 2005; Wilkinson, 2005). Suggestions to improve the rigor of consultation effectiveness studies include using between-subjects research designs, multiple baselines in single participant research, the reporting of effect sizes, reliability, and validity data in each study, and study replication (Guli, 2005).

In addition to single-subject research designs, there are barriers to the implementation of effective consultative strategies. Examples include lack of consultant training, difficulty identifying the target behavior(s), and lack of consultee training, among other factors (Kratochwill & Van Someren, 1995). Overall, while researchers suggest that BC is a useful indirect mode of service delivery, replicating studies that use more diverse populations and problems are needed in order to provide stronger evidence for its effectiveness. Another model of consultation, solution-focused theory, offers a number of advantages for school counselors when engaging in consultation.

Summary

It is likely that school counselors will be increasingly called upon to engage in collaboration and consultation for a variety of reasons. The NCLB Act (2002) requires that school personnel make concerted efforts to increase parent involvement, including hard-to-access parents, given that research demonstrates the positive relationship between parental involvement and academic achievement. Enhanced use of consultation and collaboration by school counselors is also consistent with the trend in the school counseling profession to maximize the impact of the school counselor through the utilization of comprehensive interventions that are more likely to impact the larger school environment in comparison to direct services, such as individual counseling.

It is possible that school counselors who positively influence teachers, administrators, and parents by imparting their training and expertise achieve a more significant impact than school counselors who rely upon solely providing a direct service to students. As a colleague of one of the authors stated, "If I help a teacher more effectively manage her class, teach a subject, or relate to students, it will likely help thousands of students over time." By using consultation and collaboration, school counselors thus adopt an expanded view regarding the way in which they can help students both at school and at home. School counselors are likely to be in a key position to promote the increased emphasis on facilitating school-family-community partnerships given their training and expertise in group dynamics, communication skills, and child and adolescent development. Moreover, enthusiastic adoption of this role may contribute to the further development of the identity of the school counseling profession.

References

Abdul-Adil, J. K., & Farmer, Jr., A. D. (2006). Inner-city African American parental involvement in elementary schools: Getting beyond urban legends of apathy. *School Psychology Quarterly, 21*, 1–12.

Akin-Little, K. A., Little, S. G., & Delligatti, N. (2004). A preventative model of school consultation: Incorporating perspectives from positive psychology. *Psychology in the Schools, 4*, 155–162.

Amatea, E. S., Daniels, H., Bringman, N., & Vandiver, F. M. (2004). Strengthening counselor-teacher-family connections: The family-school collaborative consultation project. *Professional School Counseling, 8*, 47–56.

American School Counselor Association (2012). *The ASCA national model: A framework for for school counseling programs* (3rd ed.). Alexandria, VA: Author.

Bergan, J. R., & Kratochwill, T. R. (1990). *Behavioral consultation and therapy: An individual guide.* New York: Springer.

Bower, H. A., & Griffin, D. (2011). Can the Epstein Model of parental involvement work in a high-minority, high-poverty school? A case study. *Professional School Counseling, 15*, 77–87.

Brodie, I. (2013, April 29). *The top ten ways school counselors can support teachers.* Available online at www.ed.gov/blog/2012/06/the-top-10-ways-school-counselors-can-support-teachers/ (accessed November 8, 2014).

Bryan, J., Holcomb-McCoy, C., Moore-Thomas, C., & Day-Vines, N. (2009). Who sees the school counselor for college information: A national study. *Professional School Counseling, 12*, 280–291.

Day-Vines, N. L., & Terriquez, V. (2008). A strengths-based approach to promoting prosocial behavior among African-American and Latino students. *Professional School Counseling, 12*, 170–175.

Desimone, L. (1999). Linking parent involvement with student achievement: Do race and income matter? *The Journal of Education Research, 93*, 11–30.

Dietel, R. (2006). *Get smart: Nine ways to help your child succeed in school.* San Francisco, CA: Jossey-Bass.

Epstein, J. L. (2005). Attainable goals? The spirit and letter of the No Child Left Behind Act on parental involvement. *Sociology of Education, 78*, 179–182.

Epstein, J. L., Sanders, M. G., Simon, B. S., Salinas, K. C., Jansorn, N. R., & Van Voorhis, F. L. (2002). *School, family, and community partnerships: Your handbook for action* (2nd ed.). Thousand Oaks, CA: Corwin Press.

Epstein, J. L., & Sheldon, S. B. (2002). Present and accounted for: Improving student attendance through family and community involvement. *The Journal of Educational Research, 95*, 308–318.

Epstein, J. L., & Van Voorhis, F. L. (2010). School counselors' roles in developing partnerships with families and communities for student success. *Professional School Counseling, 14*, 1–14.

Fields-Smith, C. (2007). Social class and African-American parental involvement. In J. A. VanGalen, & G. W. Noblit (Eds.), *Late to class: Social class and schooling in the new economy* (pp. 167–202). Albany, NY: State University of New York Press.

Gaetano, Y. D. (2007). The role of culture in engaging Latino parents' involvement in school. *Urban Education, 42*, 145–162.

Galassi, J. P., & Akos, P. (2007). *Strength-based school counseling: Promoting student development and achievement.* Mahwah, NJ: Lawrence Erlbaum.

Griffin, D., & Farris, A. (2010). School counselors and collaboration: Finding resources through community asset mapping. *Professional School Counseling, 13*, 248–256.

Griffin, D., & Steen, S. (2010). School-family-community partnerships: Applying Epstein's theory of the six types of involvement to school counselor practice. *Professional School Counseling, 13,* 218–226.

Grodsky, E., & Jones, M. (2004). *Real and imagined barriers to college entry: Perceptions of cost.* Paper presented at the annual meeting of the American Education Research Association, San Diego, CA.

Grothaus, T., & Cole, R. (2010). Meeting the challenges together: School counselors collaborating with students and families with low income. *Journal of School Counseling, 8,* 1–27. Available online at http://eric.ed.gov/?id=EJ895909 (accessed May 20, 2015).

Guli, L. A. (2005). Evidence-based parent consultation with school-related outcomes. *School Psychology Quarterly, 20,* 455–472.

Gutkin, T. B., & Curtis, M. J. (1999). School-based consultation theory and practice: The art and science of indirect service delivery. In C. R. Reynolds & T. B. Gutkin (Eds.), *The handbook of school psychology* (3rd ed.; pp. 598–637). New York: Wiley.

Hart, P., & Jacobi, M. (1992). *From gatekeeper to advocate: Transforming the role of the school counselor.* New York: College Entrance Examination Board.

Holcomb-McCoy, C. H. (2010). Involving low-income parents and parents of color in college readiness activities: An exploratory study. *Professional School Counseling, 14*(1), 115–124.

Juhnke, G. A. (1996). Solution-focused supervision: Promoting supervisee skills and Confidence through successful solutions. *Counselor Education and Supervision, 36,* 48–57.

Kahn, B. B. (2000). A model of solution-focused consultation for school counselors. *Professional School Counseling, 3,* 248–254.

Kern, C. W. (1999). Professional school counselors: Inservice providers who can change the school environment. *NASSP Bulletin, 83,* 10–18.

Kratochwill, T. R. (1990). *Behavioral consultation and therapy.* New York: Plenum.

Kratochwill, T. R., & Van Someren, K. R. (1995). Barriers to treatment success in behavioral consultation: Current limitations and future directions. *Journal of Educational and Psychological Consultation, 6,* 125–143.

Meichenbaum, D., & Turk, D. C. (1987). *Facilitating treatment adherence: A practitioner's guidebook.* New York: Plenum.

No Child Left Behind Act of 2001, Pub. L. No. 107–110 (2002).

Plank, S. B., & Jordan, W. J. (2001). Effects of information, guidance, and actions on post-secondary destinations: A study of talent loss. *American Educational Research Journal, 38,* 947–979.

Sallie Mae Fund (2003). *Financial aid: The information divide.* Available online at http://thesalliemaefund.org/smfnew/news/2003%5fnr184b.html (accessed September 30, 2015).

Sheldon, S. B. (2003). Linking school-family-partnerships in urban elementary schools to student achievement on state tests. *The Urban Review, 35,* 149–165.

Terenzini, P. T., Cabrera, A. F., & Bernal, E. M. (2001). *Swimming against the tide.* New York: College Board.

Wadenya, R. O., & Lopez, N. (2008). Parental involvement in recruitment of underrepresented minority students. *Journal of Dental Education, 72,* 680–687.

Weintraub, A. L. (1998). Tipping the balance: Perspectives of teachers in a regular elementary school on educating students with troubling behavior. *Dissertation Abstracts International: Section A. The Humanities and Social Sciences, 59*(10), 3741.

Westwood, C. A. (2002). The successful inclusion of children with emotional and behavioral disorders into general education settings. *Dissertation Abstracts International: Section A. The Humanities and Social Sciences, 64*(02), 401.

White, J., & Mullis, F. (1998). A systems approach to school counselor consultation. *Education, 119,* 242–252.

Wilkinson, L. A. (2005). Bridging the research-to-practice gap in school-based consultation: An example using case studies. *Journal of Educational and Psychological Consultation, 16,* 175–200.

Zins, J. E., & Erchul, W. P. (2002). Best practices in school consultation. In A. Thomas & J. Grimes (Eds.), *Best practices in school psychology vol. 1* (4th ed.; pp. 625–643). Bethesda, MD: The National Association of School Psychologists.

Chapter Nine
Academic Development

Box 9.1

2016 CACREP School Counseling Specialty Area Standards

2.a School counselor roles as leaders, advocates, and systems change agents in P-12 schools

2.b School counselor roles in consultation with families, P-12 and postsecondary school personnel, and community agencies

2.d School counselor roles in school leadership and multidisciplinary teams

3.d Interventions promote academic development

3.i Approaches to increase promotion and graduation rates

In this chapter, school counselors are exposed to information regarding the way in which they may work collaboratively with teachers and families in promoting students' academic development and success. A historic criticism of the role of school counselors is that by primarily focusing on the mental health needs of a comparatively small number of students rather than on the academic development of all students, school counselors have functionally reduced their potential positive impact. The aspects of school counseling services that have typically benefited all students, such as class scheduling and tracking students in academic/career paths, are increasingly viewed as administrative responsibilities instead of the developmental interventions that counselors are trained to provide (Galassi & Akos, 2012). Although school counselors, among their other responsibilities, can be critical educational team members in promoting students' academic development, they may lack confidence in their ability to effect change in children's scholastic performance. As an example of this, in one study, school counselors expressed doubt that they could impact student achievement on standardized tests with the interventions they typically use (Brigman & Campbell, 2003). Indeed, Stone and Clark (2001) report that school counselors have been "conspicuously absent" from educational reform reports and actually may be seen as incidental to students' educational progress as it is defined in terms of their academic achievement (p. 48). Consequently, the relationship between the school counselor and families in promoting children's academic progress will be a focus of this chapter. In *the ASCA National Model®* (2012), *the ASCA Mindsets & Behaviors* (ASCA, 2014) are depicted in three general areas to promote behaviors that enhance the learning process: academic, career, and personal/social development. In this chapter, the first broad domain, students' academic success, will be discussed.

The profession of school counseling is evolving in its definitions of the role of the school counselor in promoting students' academic achievement. Although perhaps not an intuitive competency, research has suggested that school counseling interventions may have a positive effect upon students' academic achievement and standardized achievement test scores (Wilkerson, Pérusse, & Hughes, 2013). In the past decade, one of the major reforms of the school counseling profession has been to increase school counselors' contributions to students' academic development (Galassi & Akos, 2012). However, the school counseling profession has not yet appeared to have achieved consensus regarding the way in which school counselors can increase their focus on children's academic development. In the research literature, there are any number of ways that school counselors are encouraged to support students' academic achievement, some of which appear to be more consistent with their fundamental role than others. Therefore, this chapter explores some of the ways in which school counselors can contribute to students' academic development, while respecting the unique contributions to children's overall school success that school counselors typically provide.

Research Supporting School Counselors' Work in Increasing Students' Academic Competence

Brown and Trusty (2005) contend that strategic interventions, in which there is a match among the needs of the students, the desired outcomes, and the intervention chosen, are more likely to increase students' academic achievement than comprehensive school counseling programs, since there is limited evidence for their effectiveness in improving students' academic skills. However, other research has suggested that evidence-based school counseling programs with measurable outcomes can indeed positively impact students' academic achievement. Schools that have been designated as a Recognized ASCA Model Program (RAMP; e.g., those with comprehensive, data-driven, accountable school counseling programs) demonstrated school-wide proficiency rates in English/language arts and Math that were significantly higher than compared to elementary controls, with four-year longitudinal results indicating a significant positive difference between RAMP-designated schools and their controls in math (Wilkerson et al., 2013). In an investigation of the effects of fully implemented comprehensive guidance and counseling programs on a number of student outcomes on a statewide basis in Missouri, researchers found that, among other beneficial effects, the comprehensive programming was significantly predictive of students earning higher grades (Lapan, Gysbers, & Petroski, 2001).

These results suggest that programs evidencing best practices in school counseling are able to demonstrate clinically significant gains in students' academic skills in comparison to programs not identified as using such practices. Thus, while school counselors' practices have traditionally been documented to have beneficial effects upon students' social, emotional, and behavioral health and functioning, these practices are also helpful in improving students' academic achievement.

The Education Trust, a nonprofit organization, established the Transforming School Counseling Initiative (TSCI), with one of its primary aims to modify the preparation of school counselors to enable them to promote the academic development of all students (Martin, 2002).

The TSCI argued that the profession of school counseling, through its responsibility for scheduling and educational placement, contributed to educational disparities between typically advantaged and disadvantaged students, encouraging minority and students from lower socioeconomic status levels to pursue vocational tracks of study as opposed to promoting college readiness (House & Sears, 2002). The TSCI appears to have influenced the design of *the ASCA National Model®* (2012), which while asserting that school counselors promote students' academic, career, and personal/social development, also explains that "the ultimate goal of a school counseling program is to support the school's academic mission" (ASCA, 2003, p. 52).

While TSCI and ASCA appear to be intending to move the school counseling profession in the direction of an enhanced commitment to academic development, other developments seem to be encouraging the movement of the profession in the opposite direction. Most states have eliminated the requirement for school counselors to have teaching experience, and with good cause, since research has suggested that teaching experience is not predictive of effectiveness for school counselors (e.g., Baker & Herr, 1976). The apparent challenge to the school counseling profession is the question of how do school counselors make a meaningful contribution to academic development when most do not have a background in teaching?

Research Supporting School Counselors' Work in Contributing to Students' Academic Development at the Systems Level

Galassi and Akos (2012) developed what is arguably the clearest framework of how *the ASCA National Model®* (2012) can be used by school counselors to focus upon students' academic development. *The ASCA National Model®* (2012) indicates that school counselors contribute to academic development at both the systems and student level. At the systems level, school counselors promote academic development through the functions of "leadership, collaboration with other educational professionals and community agencies, coordination of academic-related services, and advocacy to identify and remove systemic barriers to educational access and opportunity" (Galassi & Akos, 2012, p. 53). Galassi and Akos (2012) purport that school counselors must have an understanding of systemic change within the educational context. Also, school counselors should understand characteristics of schools that are high-performing and which have reduced the gap between typically advantaged and disadvantaged groups, and seek to facilitate such an environment in their collaborative efforts with school personnel.

As an example of the role of the school climate in promoting academic development, Galassi and Akos (2012) cite Brown, Benkovitz, Muttillo, and Urban's (2010) study comparing high-performing schools that had a minor achievement gap with high-performing schools that had a larger achievement gap. Brown and colleagues (2010) found that both types of schools evidenced the common beliefs that achievement occurs through collaboration, hiring practices are important, behavioral climate is essential, school personnel are committed to delivering the state curriculum, and that these characteristics were more pronounced in the high-performing schools, which had a smaller achievement gap. Also, these authors noted that administrators in the high-performing schools with small achievement gaps for students were more intentional in acknowledging and rewarding academic achievement, regularly monitoring teaching and learning by providing instructional feedback and support, and expecting a high level of achievement for all students. Other systems-level variables affecting academic achievement which Galassi and Akos (2012) encourage school counselors to be familiar with include the effectiveness of classroom instruction, emergence of career academies, smaller learning communities, and the importance of strength-based approaches.

Stone and Clark (2001) indicate that leadership is an increasingly valued and shared responsibility at the school level, and that school counselors should be foremost among school personnel who may partner with principals in assuming roles as educational leaders. However, these authors argue that school counselor leadership has not been adequately investigated or prioritized in school counselor training programs or in the practice of school counseling. Although school counselors may not perceive themselves as being school leaders, they do have unique opportunities to exert leadership. One of these roles is that of consultants who collaborate with others in the lives of students, such as teachers, administrators, family members, and community members. Another of these roles is that of advocates, particularly in reference to students' motivation, achievement, and planning for future goals. A third role is as trainers who provide in-service opportunities for teachers and parents in such topics as educational planning, motivation, student assessment and achievement, identification and interventions for students with special needs, and issues of student diversity (Stone & Clark, 2001).

Academic Development at the Student Level

In addition to their impact upon school systems, school counselors can promote academic development in their application of direct student services, which includes the school counseling core curriculum, individual student planning, and responsive services. Much of the research literature in the past decade concerning school counselors' use of direct services to promote students' academic development involves teaching students study skills through small group counseling and school counseling lessons. Galassi and Akos (2012) recommend that school counselors be familiar with the emerging research literature regarding how to effectively promote study skills, and in particular, Brigman and Webb's (2008) *Student Success Skills*.

Teaching students to use study skills. Accordingly, school counselors may wish to have a grouping of practical techniques to use to promote students' academic skills. Therefore, one of the ways that school counselors can support students' academic achievement is by instructing them in study skills. Information included in the following section comes from an excellent chapter regarding best practices in school psychologists' practice in teaching study skills, by Smith Harvey and Chickie-Wolfe (2007). Interested readers are encouraged to consult this resource for more information on this topic.

Students who are able to effectively organize their time and have good test-taking skills are able to achieve better grades as well as perform more proficiently on standardized tests.

Box 9.3

Did you know?

Some studies have found that test-taking skills training benefits students from low socioeconomic backgrounds more than twice as much as students who are not from low socioeconomic backgrounds (Scruggs, 1986).

Study skills involve self-regulation, in which students learn to use a variety of techniques to incorporate fundamental principles of effective learning into their studying and learning. Smith Harvey and Chickie-Wolfe (2007) explain that best practice in teaching study skills should include the techniques being embedded in the curriculum, since study skills taught in isolation are less likely to be maintained or used in multiple settings. A team of collaborative members that includes school counselors, teachers, parents, and students should be developed in order to teach the study skills, which first includes an ecological assessment of four steps (Smith Harvey & Chickie-Wolfe, 2007).

Ecological assessment – step one. First, team members analyze the problem together and define it using measurable and specific terms. This may include a classroom observation in which the students' academic skills and behaviors are identified and compared with peers.

Box 9.4

Did you know?

There are numerous study skills checklists and assessments available on the Internet.

This is followed by a student interview, in which students' motivation, emotions, and behaviors regarding study skills; environmental supports toward the use of study skills; and students' cognitive skills, reading skills, writing and reporting skills, math, science, and technology skills, test preparation and test-taking skills, and the use of metacognitive strategies are measured. A work session observation, in which the school counselor observes a student completing academic tasks, is conducted. During this first step, the student should describe his or her work methods, approaches to studying, textbooks, notebooks, assignment books, and completed work, along with the observer's analysis of classroom-completed work and homework samples from the student. A parent and teacher interview should occur, followed by the assembly of information to identify strengths and needs (Smith Harvey & Chickie-Wolfe, 2007).

Ecological assessment – step two. Following the assessment, the second step involves team members meeting to review gathered information, coming to an agreement about the desired or acceptable level of performance by the student(s), and identifying resources, including materials and supportive people. The potential interventions should be enumerated along with their positive and negative attributes. After interventions are selected, a timeframe to teach the study skills and implementation strategies are identified. The responsibilities for each team member are named, written, and reinforced through the writing of a signed contract (Smith Harvey & Chickie-Wolfe, 2007).

Ecological assessment – step three. In the third step, interventions are actualized, through interventions being implemented with guided instruction and modeling, with a transition to fading instruction as self-sufficiency is evidenced. Results should be tracked until the behavior reaches the acceptable levels of performance identified prior to the implementation of the intervention. Ideally, the student will monitor his or her own behavior, as self-monitoring is related to more independent and sustained learning (Smith Harvey & Chickie-Wolfe, 2007).

Ecological assessment – step four. After successful strategies have been ascertained, in the fourth step, the team should plan and initiate strategies in order for the student to generalize and maintain the study skills learned. In this level, goals should be set for successful generalization. Progress monitoring can be used to track progress in using the study skills effectively and consistently across settings. Smith Harvey and Chickie-Wolfe (2007) explain that goal setting and progress monitoring will likely need to be used in at least three settings to promote successful generalization of skills.

Consideration of students' motivation, emotions, and behavior. After an ecological analysis of the problem, team members should consider students' motivation, emotions, and behavior. Developing short- and long-term goals for each subject and including them in students' weekly planners can be a helpful intervention. School counselors should determine what the student attributes academic success and difficulty to, as pupils with an external locus of control need to experience the connection between the use of study skills and the result of academic success. Students also need to identify the purpose of learning materials, such as why the teacher gave the assignment or how the assignment will be useful in life (Smith Harvey & Chickie-Wolfe, 2007).

Another consideration for school counselors is to determine what kind of homework the student enjoys and dislikes, since many students assume that they generally dislike homework, when in fact they do enjoy some homework assignments. Less-preferred homework assignments may be completed first, sandwiched between preferred assignments, or completed after easier work has been accomplished. Finally, counselors should determine whether the student suffers from disabling academic anxiety. There is a curvilinear relationship between anxiety and performance; some anxiety is helpful in encouraging an optimal level of functioning, while too much anxiety can be crippling. Test anxiety affects between a third and a half of intermediate-level students, and can be identified by students during individual interviews or self-report measures. Direct interventions to diminish anxiety may range from relaxation techniques to medication, while indirect interventions include study-skill training, including test-taking strategies (Smith Harvey & Chickie-Wolfe, 2007).

Consideration of environmental supports. After considering students' motivation, emotions, and behaviors, attention should next be paid to the student's environmental supports. First, to what extent are the student's parents checking assignments and monitoring homework completion? Children typically require help from their parents with time management and organization of materials, and while students generally need less supervision as they age, those with learning difficulties will likely require more support for a longer period of time than typically developing adolescents. School counselors should check to see whether there is a regular, quiet time set aside for homework completion, and if there is enough support at home for the establishment of solid study strategies. This may require the identification of an alternative location to complete homework, such as an after-school program. Another consideration is what the student does when he or she gets stuck with homework completion at home. Is there a person from whom the student may seek help? Additionally, is there adequate communication between home and school to foster the student's homework completion? Please see the discussion of parent-school involvement later in the chapter. Teachers need to be able to talk with parents about problems with homework; likewise, parents need to be able to consult with teachers for assistance with children's homework and their organization (Smith Harvey & Chickie-Wolfe, 2007).

Consideration of students' cognitive skills. Next, the school counselor should analyze the student's cognitive skills that may promote or inhibit his or her learning. For example, does the student plan for learning, such as bringing home all necessary supplies for homework? Students should document short-term assignments in a homework book, and keep track of long-term assignments, such as projects or papers, in a calendar. School counselors will also want to establish whether the student uses estimation skills to gauge the amount of time necessary for assignments and schedules such assignments accordingly. When the student submits assignments, does he or she include his or her name, title of the assignment, and a date? School counselors should also determine whether or not the student corrects his or her papers before submission. Other necessary cognitive skills include the abilities to organize papers, keep work areas clean and organized, follow directions and information given, and take notes in class. Finally, the student should be able to pre-read reading materials before listening to a lecture, as such a practice tends to increase his or her understanding of the material presented (Smith Harvey & Chickie-Wolfe, 2007).

Test preparation and taking. Perhaps one of the most important sets of skills that students may possess is to be able to effectively prepare for assessments of their learning. This includes spacing learning across several study sessions, conducting weekly reviews, and using effective memory-enhancing strategies, such as rehearsing, making organizational charts, using associative strategies (e.g., peg words), and using graphic organizers. School counselors should also determine whether the student uses study guides while studying. It is typically helpful to assemble information into meaningful groupings, although teacher-provided study guides that require students to add their own elaborative information can also be valuable. School counselors should also ask whether or not the student is able to predict test questions, and use corrected assignments and tests as a learning tool. Finally, it is important to recognize if the student knows and can use good test-taking strategies. For example, he or she should come to an exam with all necessary materials, skim through a test to determine its layout prior to allocating time to each section, record memorized material as soon as possible, try to answer every question, immediately eliminate incorrect multiple-choice responses, and so forth (Smith Harvey & Chickie-Wolfe, 2007).

Solution Shop: A solution-focused counseling and study skills program for middle school students. One example of the use of study skills instruction embedded in a counseling curriculum is *Solution Shop*, a data-driven counseling and study skills program. Cook and Kaffenberger (2003) explain that in using the program, school counselors invite middle school students with two or more failing grades to participate, in groups of ten. Each student then develops both individual academic and personal goals, after which the student participates in solution-focused group counseling and study-skill instruction for part of one class period. During the other part of the period, students receive individualized tutoring. At the end of the first year of the program, 57% of the students who participated in *Solution Shop* had improved GPAs (Cook & Kaffenberger, 2003).

Implementing interventions to improve students' success skills. Students' academic achievement may also be positively impacted upon by counselor-led interventions designed to improve student success behavior. Brigman and Campbell (2003) conducted a study in which they encouraged school counselors to use a research-based group and school counseling lessons curriculum, *Student Success Skills* (SSS; Brigman & Goodman, 2001). This curriculum was developed in response to studies that found a set of skills to be fundamental to students' school success: cognitive and metacognitive skills, including goal setting, progress monitoring, and memory skills; social skills, including interpersonal skills, problem-solving, listening and teamwork skills; and self-management skills, including the ability to manage attention, motivation, and anger.

The process of teaching skills used in this curriculum followed the instruction model identified by Wang, Haertel, and Walberg (1994) as being effective, an Ask, Tell, Show, Do, Feedback method. Brigman and Campbell (2003) found that the combined school counselor interventions of group counseling and school counseling lessons were associated with a positive effect upon students' academic achievement and behavior. In a later study conducted by Campbell and Brigman (2005), use of the SSS curriculum was associated with improvement in math and reading on the Florida Comprehensive Achievement Test. In an additional investigation authored by Brigman, Webb, and Campbell (2007), the authors found improvements in math achievement, but the increase in reading scores was not as strong as it had been in previous studies. Additionally, a statistically significant difference was not found between the treatment and comparison groups in the area of reading achievement (Brigman et al., 2007). The SSS intervention seems to be similarly effective among students from different racial and ethnic groups; research has suggested that White, Latino, and African American students showed comparable gains in their academic achievement after SSS participation (Miranda, Webb, Brigman, & Peluso, 2007).

Format for group sessions. This group counseling intervention entails eight weekly sessions of forty-five minutes each, after which four booster sessions occur. Brigman and Campbell (2003) explain that the group format is comprised of three sections: the beginning, middle, and end. The beginning phase of the session had four tasks, including a temperature check on feelings/energy, a review of the past session, a focus upon goals and progress associated with academic achievement and school success behavior, a preview of the day's meeting, and a rationale or benefits statement that related to engagement in the activity (Brigman & Campbell, 2003).

The middle phase of each session included the introduction of the main activity, in which the leader used the "Ask, Tell, Show, Do" method of skill and knowledge building. Before the presentation of a new topic, counselors "Ask" students to define and relate their existing knowledge and how they currently use this skill or concept. Second, the students "Tell" or offer new information related to the skill/information being discussed and third, "Show" the use of this skill or information. Finally, the "Do," or guided practice, provides the students with the chance to apply the new ideas/skills; this typically involves role-play and feedback but may include art, music, games, or story-telling or reading with different endings suggested by the students (Brigman & Campbell, 2003).

The ending of the group session also includes four tasks. The first is a review of the content that was covered in the session, while the second is to process or discuss the thoughts and feelings of participants during their participation in the activities of the session. The third task is for students to set a goal, consider what was most meaningful in the session, and choose how they will use a particular technique the next week to reach their goal. The final task of the session is a preview of the next session conducted by the leader (Brigman & Campbell, 2003).

Format for school counseling lessons. Brigman and Campbell (2003) describe the format for school counseling lessons as including three main topics: (1) cognitive skills, including memory strategies, setting of goals, and progress monitoring; (2) social skills, including conflict resolution, social problem-solving, and teamwork skills; and (3) self-management skills, including anger management, motivation, and career awareness. The school counseling lessons are taught in a four-part format in accordance with the small group sessions. Activity one includes the use of an introduction, something that stimulates the children's attention, and a rationale that encourages children to value the topic being taught. Children share what they already know, provide a definition of the topic being discussed, and may think about ways to handle a proposed problem though the use of quotations, puppets, visual aids, and so forth. School counselors may also use pair sharing and group discussion skills to respond to student comments and interweave students' ideas with one another. Once the activity is completed, small groups present their information to the entire class, after which students summarize the content of the lesson and engage in setting a goal. Students consider the activity, what they learned, and how they can use the information learned. Children are encouraged to think of something they had learned from the lesson that they could use, and to share this with their partners, while volunteers report on how they would apply the lesson with the entire class.

Differentiation for School Counseling Lessons

When teaching lessons such as those in the SSS program, it is important for school counselors to consider the need for differentiation based upon students' ages and ability levels (Galassi & Akos, 2012). For example, instruction for younger students is likely to be comprised of more concrete terminology, a shorter duration of lesson, and visual aids, such as puppets. Correspondingly, older students will likely be able to comprehend a more abstract presentation of information (e.g., imagine how a peer might feel if…), and activities such as role-playing examples of social situations. Similarly, when planning lessons for students with disabilities, school counselors will also want to pay attention to differences in reasoning skills, adjusting the language and activities for the needs of the students receiving the instruction. Students with cognitive disabilities will likely require short bursts of instruction, with activities in multiple modalities, overlapping concepts, and repetition. Manualized treatment programs may be particularly helpful for students who have difficulty with information processing, as the scripted lessons are likely to adhere to a developmental sequence with information building upon skills that have already been acquired. Other methods for differentiation include addressing content, such as using student questions and interests to help guide instruction; addressing the process, or how students arrive at the content, for example, through using learning centers and contracts; and addressing products, the ways that students demonstrate a culminating understanding of the content, including computer-based presentations (Akos, Cockman, & Strickland, 2007).

Curriculum Mapping

Another issue that Galassi and Akos (2012) address is the need to be able to integrate counseling topics into traditional curricular mapping. Typically, there is an academic scope and sequence that is identified in school district curricula in which certain topics are covered in different grades and subject areas so that educators can ensure that information is not missing when academic skills are taught. In the era of high-stakes testing, schools must demonstrate that there is a systematic coverage of content.

Curricular mapping facilitates the breadth and depth of a specific curriculum, with the scope of the curriculum reflecting what is going to be taught of a subject during each grade level, and the sequence signifying the order in which the lessons are to be taught. Upon examining the curriculum, school counselors can identify where counseling topics naturally fit, and use the curriculum to develop a thematic unit, in which lessons are constructed around a common theme. For example, when students are reading a classic novel, such as the Lord of the Flies, it may be an ideal time to discuss the negative effects of bullying upon both perpetrators and victims.

Individual Student Planning

Intuitively, selecting the right courses for each student is critical for his or her success. Galassi and Akos (2012) state that the impact of course selection upon academic success is an important mechanism by which school counselors can promote students' academic development. School counselors can work to assign students to rigorous academic programs as well as to change schools' practices that deter equity and diminish students' opportunities (Stone & Clark, 2001). Typically, students from low-income families appear to be less likely to have access to guidance about their coursework both at home and at school, while more economically advantaged students tend to enjoy more time in interviews about interests and abilities with school counselors (Stone & Clark, 2001).

In one study, researchers investigated how credits in intensive mathematics courses affected students' completion versus non-completion of the bachelor's degree in college. Of all variables studied, the completion of intensive math courses, including Algebra 2, trigonometry, pre-calculus, and calculus, had the strongest effects of all curricular areas upon degree completion. The authors of this study, Trusty and Niles (2003), argue that it is of utmost importance that school counselors inform and advise students and parents effectively. Counselors should use student data from multiple sources, including achievement test scores, aptitude test scores, performance samples, teacher observation, and outcomes from guidance activities, in order to help students in making scheduling decisions and assisting them in postsecondary education and career planning (Trusty & Niles, 2003).

Promoting the Relationship Between Academic and Career Development

Galassi and Akos (2012) also indicate that school counselors can be helpful to students in connecting academic development and planning to traditional career counseling. First, school counselors can work to influence the beliefs and attitudes of teachers and administrators to promote the concept that all students should be encouraged to achieve high standards (Stone & Clark, 2001). While conducting career counseling activities, the competency of which is discussed in Chapter 10: College and Career Readiness, school counselors can connect the skills necessary to succeed in various professions with the competencies that can be developed through coursework in various academic subjects. As mentioned, the selection of particular courses can be critically important not only for students to gain admission to college, but also to graduate from college.

One of the ways in which school counselors can link high school classes to postsecondary educational and vocational opportunities is through implementing the Common Core State Standards (CCSS). The CCSS were developed using a backward design that used college- and career-ready standards as a point of departure, and working back through each grade. This method was successful in accomplishing grade-level shifts in content down through each grade. The CCSS reflects a shift in the instructional goals from high school completion to college and career readiness, which permits each student to work toward college and career readiness (Achieve, College Summit, NASSP, & NAESP, 2013).

School counselors may work with students who do not typically enroll in STEM courses, for example, in order to encourage them to take the classes that will prepare them for college and professions in which women and students of color are historically underrepresented. House and Hayes (2002) explain that opportunities for students, particularly those who are poor and those of color, are almost always highly related to their course of study. Students who do not benefit from the receipt of a rigorous curriculum, with support to keep them in such classes, may face insurmountable barriers to gaining employment in increasingly sophisticated workplaces (Schneider & Stevenson, 1999). School counselors have access to vital data about student placements, academic success and failure of all students, and course-taking patterns. They also know which teachers are known to hold high standards for all of their students, and who are skilled in helping all students attain these standards (House & Hayes, 2002).

Encouraging School Attendance and Preventing Student Dropout

Of course, in order for students to be academically successful, they need to stay in school. White and Kelly (2010) argue that there are significant social, psychological, and financial consequences associated with school dropout. In 2003, the median income of individuals aged 18 years and older who completed a high school credential was $20,431 in comparison to $12,184 for those who had dropped out (Laird, DeBell, & Chapman, 2006). Students who are truant from school appear to be more likely to experience adult criminality, violence, marital discord, and problems with their place of employment than their peers who graduate from high school (Gonzales, Richards, & Seeley, 2002).

Of particular worry, students of color are more likely to drop out of high school than their White peers (Darling-Hammond, 1998). Wirt et al. (2002) report that in 2003, 91% of White students, 89% of African American students, and 62% of Latino students completed high school or its equivalent. A more recent estimate suggested that in 2008, 17% of Hispanics dropped out of high school in comparison to 5% of non-Hispanic White students, 4% of Asian students, and 9% of Black students (US Census Bureau, 2011).

While the high school completion gap has closed to some extent between White and African American students, Latino students, particularly those who are immigrants, are much less likely to complete school than their White peers (Trusty, Mellin, & Herbert, 2008).

Galassi and Akos (2012) suggest that school counselors become knowledgeable about some of the major national resources and reports in this area, such as the National Dropout Prevention Network (www.dropoutprevention.org), of which the mission is to increase students' graduation rates through research and the development and dissemination of evidence-based solutions. Of critical importance is not only for school counselors to become aware of the problem of students dropping out and evidence-based solutions to the problem, but also being able to access dropout data in one's own district (to identify particular subgroups of students that are at risk of dropping out), identify initiatives to discourage dropout in one's own district, and developing, proposing, and advocating for individual and systems-level interventions to combat the problem of student dropout in one's own school system (Galassi & Akos, 2012).

In a review of intervention approaches on the probability of school dropout, White and Kelly (2010) found only one study that actually included dropout as a dependent variable (Wirth-Bond, Coyne, & Adams, 1991). The complexity of conducting research on such a systemic and multifaceted problem and the recent focus in the school counseling literature upon remedial or crisis topics are likely contributing factors to this issue. Nevertheless, White and Kelly (2010) summarize the best practices for school counselors in preventing school dropout, including strategies addressing protective factors such as social support (e.g., instituting a peer mentoring system or buddy system), monitoring and mentoring (e.g., assigning adult mentors or advocates to identified at-risk students to track progress and collaborate with parents), personal and social skill development (e.g., providing explicit social skills instruction), and parental involvement (e.g., offering parent training), and addressing risk factors such as academic instruction (e.g., assisting teachers in providing more academic instruction and less time on behavior management), and academic support (e.g., offering after-school study skills and time management classes).

Tutoring and Peer Tutoring

One approach for improving students' academic achievement that enjoys broad empirical support is tutoring, including peer tutoring. Indeed, Trusty and colleagues (2008) explain that the strategic intervention (discussed earlier – a technique that is designed to closely match students' needs and proximal outcomes, which is supported and refined by research) that appears to have the strongest empirical evidence is peer and cross-age tutoring and peer facilitation. Robinson, Schofield, and Steers-Wentzell (2005) indicate that tutoring has academic benefits for tutors and tutees and that average- and low-achieving students appear to be effective tutors. Moreover, programs that are designed to allow students to work both as tutors and tutees seem to be effective in promoting students' academic achievement (Trusty et al., 2008).

Peer tutoring can be described as students using direct instruction to target peers, and is characterized by peer pairing techniques and the instructional repertoire of the tutor. Potential problems and concerns of peer tutoring include the competence of the tutor, the issue of informed consent, negative side effects, such as bullying between tutor and tutee, and accountability. Greenwood, Carta, and Hall (1988) report that peer tutoring has been applied to a wide range of academic subjects, from learning how to roll a ball to social studies units for secondary students. While the goal of peer tutoring has historically been to teach the subject matter independent of the teacher, the movement of class-wide peer tutoring has permitted the use of the best available matches or the use of materials or teacher monitoring to negate the potential negative outcomes of the differential ability levels of tutors and tutees. Typically, peer tutoring arrangements allow the tutee repeated opportunities to respond, immediate feedback and consequences, remediation for incorrect answers, and tutor-collected outcomes data. Additionally, tutors who are given specific training are more likely to use the desired tutoring behavior than untrained tutors (Greenwood et al., 1988).

Systematic tutoring procedures are those in which students learn highly specific instructional behaviors, and have facilitated tutoring over a long period of time with a large number of students. Units of academic content can be sequenced so that once the tutee learns a skill, the next can be immediately taught, with the systematic coverage of content ensured. Furthermore, peer tutoring may be used with students of all ability levels, including those with disabilities assuming both roles as tutors and tutees. Maher, Maher, and Thurston (1998) propose a model in which students with disruptive behavior disorders work as tutors, in which the purpose and goals for the disruptive student (the tutor) and the tutee are described, an explicit tutoring process is provided, training in the particular tutoring program is offered, the disruptive student is given techniques to monitor his or her involvement in and performance as a tutor, and a program evaluation plan is instituted to gauge the benefits for the tutor and tutee. Peer tutoring actually may allow for students to be educated in a less restrictive setting rather than the one-to-one teaching context that may be otherwise necessary. School counselors may wish to be particularly cognizant of the need for fidelity in peer tutoring programs, such as the use of a procedure checklist for tutoring techniques and reinforcement contingencies (Greenwood et al., 1988).

Parental Involvement

Another variable that appears to influence students' academic achievement is parental involvement. A body of research has established that parental involvement is positively associated with students' academic achievement, and attendance, among other outcomes (Van Velsor & Orozco, 2007). In the school counseling literature, parent involvement is often conceptualized as school-family-community partnerships, which are collaborative relationships between school personnel, families, and community members in which all are considered to be equal in the planning, coordinating, and implementing of programs and activities at home, at school, and in the community to help to increase the social, academic, and emotional success of students (Bryan & Holcomb-McCoy, 2004).

The nine school-family-community partnership programs that are most frequently found in schools include mentoring programs, parent centers, family/community members serving as teachers' aides, parent and community volunteer programs, home visit programs, parent education programs, school-business partnerships, parent/community members participating in site-based management, and tutoring programs (Bryan & Holcomb-McCoy, 2004). Cox (2005) integrated the results of 18 empirical studies that involved parent education collaborations and children's success behaviors at school, including grades and quality of work, and found these interventions were the most successful when characterized by two-way communication and equal participation among parents and educators in the intervention (Trusty et al., 2008).

Regardless of school level, school counselors in one study found it important to be involved and to play major roles in school-family-community partnerships (Bryan & Holcomb-McCoy, 2004). In this investigation, elementary counselors perceived partnership programs and their personal role in these partnerships to be more important in their schools than secondary-level counselors. Furthermore, irrespective of the counselor's work setting, more importance for the role of the school counselor was reported for mentoring and parent education programs in comparison to other school-family-community partnerships (Bryan & Holcomb-McCoy, 2004).

As an example of an intervention to increase family-school connections, Epstein and Van Voorhis' (2001) interactive homework approach is designed to increase families' involvement in their children's education as well as to improve communication between parents and teachers. Teachers Involve Parents in Schoolwork (TIPS) is a way for students to include their families, friends, and community members in their education by sharing interesting things they are learning in school, such as gathering parents' memories or experiences about a historical event. The TIPS intervention was found to significantly improve student achievement and family support of children at school, and school counselors can support such an approach by providing leadership and advocacy in supporting TIPS (Galassi & Akos, 2012).

Obstacles to school-family-community relationships include cultural barriers and accessibility, lack of connectivity (i.e., a lack of trust among schools, families, and communities), and a lack of resources (i.e., poor funding for collaboration; Trusty et al., 2008). Trusty and colleagues (2008) recommend that school counselors work to promote safe school environments, positive communication, and reduction or elimination of barriers for students and families. Nationally recognized school-family-community partnership models, including the school and family integration model (Bemak & Cornely, 2002), can help to guide school counselors in their roles and tasks in creating successful school-family-community partnerships. School counselors can use data collected from systematic needs assessments, develop a plan of action, including measurable proximal and distal outcomes, and evaluate these outcomes in order to create a structure to guide school-family-community partnerships (Trusty et al., 2008).

Closing-the-Gap Action Plans

One of the persistent problems in the US educational system is inequity in academic achievement and attainment, with students of color and those from economically disadvantaged families underachieving in comparison to White and economically advantaged peers (Bruce, Getch, & Ziomek-Daigle, 2009). Contextual forces such as racism, poverty, family involvement, exposure to quality education, ethical and equitable educational practice, and personal and cultural identity development are considered to be those variables that may potentially contribute to achievement differences among students. Regardless of the etiology of the disparity in achievement between students, for ethical and pragmatic reasons, it is important that school counselors take the responsibility to remedy the underachievement of students among specific demographic subgroups (Bruce et al., 2009).

In *the ASCA National Model®*, "closing-the-gap activities address important issues of equity and student achievement" (2012, p. 104). Closing-the-gap action plans can be perceived as a social advocacy role for school counselors. Such a role involves helping all students to gain access to vigorous academic preparation and support for success in these programs. House and Martin (1998) describe this role as being based upon the belief that individual or collective action must be taken to remedy injustices or to change the status quo to benefit an individual or group. In a democracy, educational equity is built upon the foundational principle that all children, particularly those who are at risk for being underserved – youth of color or who are socioeconomically disadvantaged – are more aptly prepared for future success than the prior generation.

Trusty and colleagues (2008) advocate for the use of the proximal-distal framework to help counselors to develop logical causal sequences and develop helpful perspectives on developmental contexts that will assist their work in closing achievement gaps. Nevertheless, school counselors should recognize that principally, students' academic and social engagement in school is critically important to closing achievement gaps. Human relationships within schools and among schools, students, families, and communities comprise the foundation of student engagement.

Closing-the-gap action plans may vary depending upon the age of the students, the context of the school system, and specific student needs. Regardless of the specifics of the plan, however, the ability to aggregate and disaggregate student information is essential to help school counselors to identify and eliminate school practices that may be impeding equitable access and opportunities for success in rigorous coursework (Stone & Clark, 2001). Examples of successful plans include the impact of a group counseling intervention, which consisted of eight weekly group counseling sessions, upon African American students' achievement levels during high-stakes standardized proficiency testing in Georgia, in which all participants received passing scores on the English language arts and math sections of the assessment. The achievement gap between African American and White students was also narrowed, in that 63.2% of African American students achieved a pass rate (up from the 38.7% pass rate from the previous school year) in comparison to 70.5% of White students (Bruce et al., 2009). Essentially, closing-the-gap action plans may be a powerful means to ensure access to high-quality education and its employment correlates for all students.

Motivational Interviewing and the Transtheoretical Model of Change

Motivational interviewing (MI) and the transtheoretical model (TTM) of change are two psychological frameworks, which are often used in conjunction, that currently are not widely used among school counselors but may have considerable relevancy in promoting students' academic development. Simply defined by Miller and Rollnick (2012, p. 29), "Motivational interviewing is a collaborative conversation style for strengthening a person's own motivation and commitment to change." The helpee is encouraged to be an active member in achieving lifestyle change as the helper assumes a collaborative approach, working "with" and "for" the helpee, enabling him or her to activate their own motivation and resources for change.

MI embodies elements of person-centered counseling theory (Miller & Rollnick, 2012). Person-centered theory focuses on the idea that a person is trustworthy and can solve their own problems, and that people truly want to self-actualize and be the best version of themselves. Carl Rogers (1954) theorized that a counseling relationship that is rooted in acceptance but not approval of actions and empathy for a person's experience promote self-change. Much like person-centered theory, MI allows this process to happen because the purpose is to see the world through another person's eyes and allow the person to set an agenda for change (Miller & Rollnick, 2012). MI allows a person to see their options for reaching a goal through the use of conversation to elicit their personal thoughts and attitudes toward change. MI assumes that a person has the strengths and resources to achieve his or her goal, and they must overcome their ambivalence about changing. Another person cannot force someone else to change; they must want it for themselves (Miller & Rollnick, 2012). MI provides the environment of support and understanding that a person needs in order to make a commitment to change.

In MI, counselors create an environment that promotes the person's autonomy and decision-making skills. Counselors must realize that a person may desire to change a behavior, or they may be seeking counseling to accept a behavior or condition (Miller & Rollnick, 2012). MI is often used in conjunction with Prochaska, Norcross, and DiClemente's (1994) theory of change. The TTM of Change is effective in eliciting change of behaviors and acknowledges that change can happen on a continuum. This theory hypothesizes that people who make significant behavioral changes, such as quitting smoking or modifying their diet, undergo a series of changes or stages in which they display changes in thoughts, feelings, and behaviors. Prochaska et al. (1994) found that there are six stages of change people pass through while

Table 9.1 Transtheoretical (Stages of Change) Model for Academic Behaviors

Stage of Change	Characteristic	Student Statement	Appropriate Intervention	Sample Dialogue
Precontemplation	– No intention of changing, and avoids discussion of the issue. Either sees situation as hopeless, or denies existence of the issue.	– "I will be okay, I'm fine." – "Grades do not count until I get to high school." – "Why do people keep annoying me about this." – "I just have to be here so they stop bugging me."	– In a respectful manner discuss the possible consequences of continued academic underachievement.	– "What do you think will likely happen if your grades stay the same as they are now?"
Contemplation	– Aware of problem and considering making changes but lacks commitment. May remain in this stage for considerable time.	– "I want better grades but it is hard to do my homework every night." – "I can't study every night for an hour, and my teacher is too busy to help. I will try something else next time."	– Discuss advantages and disadvantages of making changes.	– "Would you like to explore what you see as the advantages and disadvantages of getting better grades?"
Preparation	– Recognizes advantages of making changes and thinking about how to change. May have made small behavioral changes.	– "I really want to get better grades and I have ideas on how to to do so." – "Last week in math when I was frustrated I was able to take a break and come back to the problem in a little while." – "I know I could improve my math grade if I organized my binder, studied every night for an hour, asked my teacher to explain what I don't understand, or asked a friend to help me."	– Explore the student's perspectives regarding his or her small steps, asking what the student thinks are effective, and what are additional steps the student plans to take. – Ask the student if he or she is interested in learning about evidence-based strategies, such as strategies for note-taking, test-taking, etc.	– "It sounds like you feel proud about the changes you have started to take."
Action	– Actively engaging in steps to change.	– "I'm working hard to get better grades." – "For the last week I've been completing my homework each night as soon as I get home from school for one week."	– Explore the student's self-generated strategies for improvement, including what he or she has found to be effective, why the student thinks it is effective, what the student plans to increase. – Explore the student's thoughts and feelings regarding the progress he or she is making in an attempt to instill in the student a sense of pride.	– "What have you learned about what works?" – "What do you plan to do more or less of?"

Continued

Table 9.1 (cont.)

Stage of Change	Characteristic	Student Statement	Appropriate Intervention	Sample Dialogue
Maintenance	– Achieved goals. Student adjusts his or her behaviors to maintain commitment to changes/goals. The student may be aware of obstacles to maintaining progress, such as tendency to not follow through on plans when around peers.	– "I do not want anything to get in the way of the changes I've made, as I really want to get into that college." – "It is really hard to keep things up when I am around some of my friends." – "My friends don't have to do their homework right after school, but I know if I don't I will not complete it. I will try to finish it right after school or in a study hall if I know I want to do something with friends after school."	– Help student identify potential obstacles to maintaining changes, and solutions to address identified obstacles.	– "You are really committed to this, it is really important to you."
Termination	– Behavioral changes have been achieved and are thoroughly integrated into the student's daily functioning. There is little chance of relapse.	– "I'm really into what I'm doing. It is hard to believe that I used to struggle with school." – "I've organized all my binders and folders so that I can easily find my work and classroom materials; I know that this takes me only a few minutes after class and has enabled me to complete my work on time and not become frustrated."	– Help student reflect upon the various changes that he or she has made. – Explore how the behavioral changes the student has made has resulted in changes regarding the student's self-efficacy/confidence.	– "You have worked really hard. What does this say to you about your ability to achieve your goals?"

Modified from: Prochaska, J. O., Norcross, J. C., & DiClemente, C. C. (1994). *Changing for good: The revolutionary program that explains the six stages of change and teaches you how to free yourself from bad habits.* New York: William Morrow.

trying to adjust their habits. The six stages of change include: precontemplation, contemplation, preparation, action, maintenance, and termination (Prochaska et al., 1994). Within TTM, the counselor meets the person at his or her stage of change. A person must be cognizant of his/her stage of change in order to make progress. TTM allows a person to overcome their ambivalence about change, see their reasons for certain behaviors, and acknowledge feelings associated with the desire to change. It is essential to recognize and understand these stages of changes since a person can rotate and cycle through these stages numerous times before the termination of the behavior occurs. Table 9.1 provides a brief summary of the six stages of change proposed by Prochaska et al. (1994) and describes how these stages can be seen in an academic setting.

Many educators assume that students should be fully motivated to learn, and experience frustration with academically at-risk students. MI and TTM imply that educators must first understand the student's desire to change, and not ignore the fact that students may be ambivalent about academic underachievement and may not regard it as a significant problem. MI provides teachers with a framework to help students to overcome their ambivalence and find the motivation to change without demoralizing or forcing a change to happen.

Strait et al. (2012) found that middle school students who participated in an MI process were more likely to exhibit increased class participation and positive academic behavior over time than students who did not participate in the MI process. The study required students to engage in an MI session with a school or clinical psychology graduate student in which they completed a self-assessment, received support and feedback, and developed a plan for change. The researchers believed that the intervention appeared to be successful because it helped students realize that they possessed the resources for progressing toward their goals.

Use of MI and TTM in Individual Planning and Individual Counseling

School counselors can infuse MI and TTM in individual counseling to promote academic development. When conducting individual planning or individual counseling, school counselors must first identify where students are in the stages of change in order to see where to initiate the MI conversation. Since school counselors often have limited time to work with students, MI can be applied in one to three quick individual sessions. The collaborative and conversational nature behind MI can be used to strengthen and develop a student's commitment to change (Miller & Rollnick, 2012). Students will be more likely to invest in this process because they are leading the conversation and their ideas are being used to solve their own problems, which is likely to increase students' academic efficacy.

School counselors should follow the four processes of motivational interview engaging, focusing, evoking, and planning with each student (Miller & Rollnick, 2012). Engagement establishes the connection between the student and the counselor and enables the student to begin to connect with someone who supports their ideas about changing. During the focusing piece of MI, a school counselor focuses on what the student wants to discuss as a problem. Areas of concern for counselors and students may or may not be the same so a counselor must maintain a specific direction that will lead to a positive and necessary change for the student to become successful. Once the counselor and student have identified a problem, the MI process continues with evoking, and the student actively finds ideas and reasons for wanting to change their behaviors. Here the counselor is able to assist the student in finding realistic ways to solve a problem and narrow down their options while helping them to realize they can change and can do it independently. Finally, a student can develop a plan about how and when to change. Developing a commitment to change, and creating a specific plan of action to change can be done with the school counselor's assistance. The student's plan can be changed and revisited as new challenges arise in order to maintain continuous commitment to the plan.

MI suggests that students will be more likely to be academically engaged because they have selected the goals and are a more active participant in the process of change. An example of using MI in schools would be for school counselors to enable students to create their own self-designed behavior contracts. These contracts could be for behaviors that occur (or do not occur) at school or home to increase appropriate behavior and academic success. To develop the contract, counselors can start with identifying the behavior that needs changing and use Miller and Rollnick's (2012) five beginning questions listed below to foster the student's ideas for change (See Box 9.5).

Box 9.5

Miller and Rollnick's (2012) Five Beginning Questions in Motivational Interviewing (p. 11)

1. "Why would you want to make this change?"
2. "How might you go about it in order to succeed?"
3. "What are the three best reasons for you to do it?"
4. "How important is it for you to make this change, and why?"
5. "So what do you think you will do?"

Source: Miller, W. R., & Rollnick, S. (2012). *Motivational interviewing: Helping people change* (3rd ed.). New York: Guilford Press.

From here, a counselor and the student would begin to develop a contract and plan that the student could follow. The counselor would be able to use MI in a few brief sessions to review the student's plan and progress.

Use of MI and TTM in Consultation with Parents and Teachers

It is important to realize that MI in an academic setting requires the support of teachers and parents. School counselors are in the unique position to advocate for the student's ability for self-directed change and assist parents and teachers in understanding how they can support students' continued commitment for academic improvement. School counselors can encourage parents and teachers to be on the lookout for a student's strengths, good steps, and intentions. They should be "accentuating the positives," meaning that even small progress should be acknowledged (Miller & Rollnick, 2012). Parents and teachers need to be aware of the fact that students may be resistant to change, and constantly focusing on the problem "behaviour" or the student's "negative attributes" until the student is ready to change his or her behavior will only be detrimental to the process of change. Change takes time and the process can be frustrating for parents and teachers. School counselors can help parents and teachers explore how they manage their frustration when relating to a student regarding academic difficulties.

School counselors can explain the benefits and process of MI with parents and teachers. They can share with parents and teachers that students may feel angry, defensive, uncomfortable, and powerless when they are being "told" to change or have realized there is something they would like to change about themselves (Miller & Rollnick, 2012). Students can be allowed to experience the natural consequences of what happens if they choose to continue a behavior that is self-defeating and need to see the benefits of self-directed change. This is especially true for students in the precontemplative stage as they may not see their behaviors as a problem and will rarely take responsibility for their actions even if there is a negative consequence (Prochaska et al., 1994).

School counselors can educate teachers and parents about the stages of change and how to respond to students at the various stages. They can assist parents with ways to stay engaged with the student, empower him/her to change, be open to their ideas, and make sure the student feels understood (Miller & Rollnick, 2012). Again, this can be a challenging process because many students feel as though they have tried everything possible or are in denial that the problem exists (Prochaska et al., 1994). For example, if a student is getting failing grades in math for two straight grading quarters and says he does not study or try, the school counselor may suggest that parents and teachers use MI techniques to help the student acknowledge his problem and develop a plan to be more successful. School counselors can remind parents and teachers to avoid demanding change, telling the student what he "should" do, or demeaning the student's efforts to change by saying they can do "better." It is important to remember that during the change cycle a person is doing the best they know how to in order to maintain a behavior or try to change it (Prochaska et al., 1994). School counselors can train parents and teachers to ask the student what his process would be to earn higher grades in math, identify what would be "good grades" from the student's perspective, and explore with the student how improved grades might benefit them.

Summary

Although school counselors have not always been perceived as school personnel who can help to promote students' academic development, their roles in contributing to students' academic success at the systems level, such as engaging in school reform activities, and at the student level, such as teaching study skills and success skills, are both intuitive to their professional responsibilities and supported by research. School counselors can work to support students' academic development through such specific methods as curriculum mapping, individual student planning, career development activities, encouragement of school attendance and helping students to avoid dropping out, planning for students to be tutored or to work as peer tutors, encouraging parent involvement, and constructing close-the-gap action plans. In these ways, school counselors can be as important to students' academic success as they are to students' social, emotional, and behavioral development.

References

Achieve, College Summit, NASSP, & NAESP (2013). *Implementing the common core state standards: The role of the school counselor.* Available online at www.achieve.org/publications/implementing-common-core-state-standards-role-school-counselor-action-brief (accessed January 3, 2015).

Akos, P., Cockman, C. R., & Strickland, C. A. (2007). Differentiating school counseling lessons. *Professional School Counseling, 10,* 455–463.

American School Counselor Association (2003). *The ASCA national model: A framework for school counseling programs.* Alexandria, VA: Author.

American School Counselor Association (2012). *The ASCA national model: A framework for for school counseling programs* (3rd ed.). Alexandria, VA: Author.

American School Counselor Association (2014). *Mindsets & behaviors for student success: K-12 college- and career-readiness standards for every student.* Alexandria, VA: Author.

Baker, S. B., & Herr, E. L. (1976). Can we bury the myth? Teaching experience for school counselors. *Bulletin of the National Association of Secondary School Principals, 60,* 114–118.

Bemak, F., & Cornely, L. (2002). The SAFI model as a critical link between marginalized families and schools: A literature review and strategies for school counselors. *Journal of Counseling & Development, 80*, 322–331.

Brigman, G., & Campbell, C. (2003). Helping students improve academic achievement and school success behavior. *Professional School Counseling, 7*, 91–98.

Brigman, G., & Goodman, B. E. (2001). Academic and social support: Student success skills. In G. Brigman & B. E. Goodman, *Group counseling for school counselors: A practical guide* (pp. 106–121). Portland, MA: J. Weston Walch.

Brigman, G., & Webb, L. (2008). *Student Success Skills: Helping students develop the academic, social, and self-management skills they need to succeed (Classroom Manual)*. Boca Raton, FL: Atlantic Educational Consultants.

Brigman, G. A., Webb, L. D., & Campbell, C. (2007). Building skills for school success: Improving the academic and social competence of students. *Professional School Counseling, 10*, 279–288.

Brown, D., & Trusty, J. (2005). School counselors, comprehensive school counseling programs, and academic achievement: Are school counselors promising more than they can deliver? *Professional School Counseling, 9*, 1–8.

Brown, K. M., Benkovitz, J., Muttillo, A. J., & Urban, T. (2010). *Leading schools of excellence and equity: Closing achievement gaps via academic optimism*. Charlotte, NC: Information Age Publishing.

Bruce, A. M., Getch, Y. Q., & Ziomek-Daigle, J. (2009). Closing the gap: A group counseling approach to improve test performance of African American students. *Professional School Counseling, 12*, 450–457.

Bryan, J., & Holcomb-McCoy, C. (2004). School counselors' perceptions of their involvement in school-family-community partnerships. *Professional School Counseling, 7*, 162–171.

Campbell, C. A., & Brigman, G. (2005). Closing the achievement gap: A structured approach to group counseling. *The Journal for Specialists in Group Work, 30*, 67–82.

Cook, J. B., & Kaffenberger, C. J. (2003). Solution Shop: A solution-focused counseling and study skills program for middle school. *Professional School Counseling, 7*, 116–123.

Cox, D. D. (2005). Evidence-based interventions using home-school collaboration. *School Psychology Quarterly, 20*, 473–497.

Darling-Hammond, L. (1998). Unequal opportunity: Race and education. *The Brookings Review, 16*, 28–32.

Epstein, J. L., & Van Voorhis, F. L. (2001). More than minutes: Teachers' roles in designing homework. *Educational Psychologist, 36*, 181–193.

Galassi, J. P., & Akos, P. (2012). Preparing school counselors to promote academic development. *Counselor Education & Supervision, 51*, 50–63.

Gonzales, R., Richards, K., & Seeley, K. (2002). *Youth out of school: Linking absence to delinquency*. Denver, CO: Colorado Foundation for Children and Families.

Greenwood, C. R., Carta, J. J., & Hall, R. V. (1988). The use of peer tutoring strategies in classroom management and educational instruction. *School Psychology Review, 17*, 258–275.

House, R. M., & Hayes, R. L. (2002). School counselors: Becoming key players in school reform. *Professional School Counseling, 5*, 249–256.

House, R. M., & Martin, P. J. (1998). Advocating for better futures for all students: A new vision for school counselors. *Education, 119*, 284–291.

House, R. M., & Sears, S. J. (2002). Preparing school counselors to be leaders and advocates: A critical need in the new millennium. *Theory into Practice, 41*, 154–162.

Laird, J., DeBell, M., & Chapman, C. (2006). *Dropout rates in the United States: 2004* (NCES 2007–024). US Department of Education. Washington, DC: National Center for Education Statistics. Available online at http://nces.ed.gov/pubsearch (accessed February 22, 2015).

Lapan, R. T., Gysbers, N. C., & Petroski, G. F. (2001). Helping seventh graders be safe and successful: A statewide study of the impact of comprehensive guidance and counseling programs. *Journal of Counseling & Development, 79*, 320–330.

Maher, C. A., Maher, B. C., & Thurston, C. J. (1998). Disruptive students as tutors: A systems approach to planning and evaluation of programs. In K. J. Topping & S. Ehly (Eds.), *Peer-assisted learning* (pp. 145–163). Mahwah, NJ: Lawrence Erlbaum Associates.

Martin, P. J. (2002). Transforming school counseling: A national perspective. *Theory into Practice, 41*, 148–153.

Miller, W. R., & Rollnick, S. (2012). *Motivational interviewing: Helping people change* (3rd ed.). New York: Guilford Press.

Miranda, A., Webb, L., Brigman, G., & Peluso, P. (2007). Student success skills: A promising program to close the academic achievement gap for African American and Latino students. *Professional School Counseling, 10*, 490–497.

Prochaska, J. O., Norcross, J. C., & DiClemente, C. C. (1994). *Changing for good: The revolutionary program that explains the six stages of change and teaches you how to free yourself from bad habits.* New York: William Morrow.

Robinson, D. R., Schofield, J. W., & Steers-Wentzell, K. L. (2005). Peer and cross-age tutoring in math: Outcomes and their design implications. *Educational Psychology Review, 17*, 327–362.

Rogers, C. (1954). *Psychotherapy and personality change.* Chicago: University of Chicago Press.

Schneider, B., & Stevenson, D. (1999). *The ambitious generation: America's teenagers motivated but directionless.* New Haven, CT: Yale University.

Scruggs, T. E. (1986). Teaching test-taking skills to elementary-grade students: A meta-analysis. *Elementary School Journal, 7*(1), 69–82.

Smith Harvey, V., & Chickie-Wolfe, L. A. (2007). Best practices in teaching study skills. In A. Thomas & J. Grimes (Eds.), *Best practices in school psychology* (5th ed.; pp. 1121–1136). Bethesda, MD: NASP.

Stone, C. B., & Clark, M. A. (2001). School counselors and principals: Partners in support of academic achievement. *NASSP Bulletin, 85*, 46–53.

Strait, G. G., Smith, B. H., McQuillin, S., Terry, J., Swan, S., & Malone, P. S. (2012). A randomized trial of motivational interviewing to improve middle school students' academic performance. *Journal of Community Psychology, 40*, 1032–1039.

Trusty, J., Mellin, E. A., & Herbert, J. T. (2008). Closing achievement gaps: Roles and tasks of elementary school counselors. *The Elementary School Journal, 108*, 407–421.

Trusty, J., & Niles, S. G. (2003). High-school math courses and completion of the bachelor's degree. *Professional School Counseling, 7*, 99–107.

United States Census Bureau (2011). *School enrollment in the United States: 2008. Population characteristics* (P20–64). Washington, DC: US Department of Commerce. Available online at: www.census.gov/prod/2011pubs/p20-564.pdf (accessed February 13, 2015).

Van Velsor, P., & Orozco, G. L. (2007). Involving low-income parents in the schools: Communitycentric strategies for school counselors. *Professional School Counseling, 11*, 17–24.

Wang, M. C., Haertel, G. D., & Walberg, H. J. (1994). Educational resilience in inner cities. In M. C. Wang & E. W. Gordon (Eds.), *Educational resilience in inner-city America: Challenges and prospects* (pp. 45–72). Hillsdale, NJ: Lawrence Erlbaum.

White, S. W., & Kelly, F. D. (2010). The school counselor's role in school dropout prevention. *Journal of Counseling & Development, 88*, 227–235.

Wilkerson, K., Pérusse, R., & Hughes, A. (2013). Comprehensive school counseling programs and student academic outcomes: A comparative analysis of ramp versus non-ramp schools. *Professional School Counseling, 16*, 172–184.

Wirt, J., Choy, S., Gerlad, D., Provasnik, S., Rooney, P., Watanbe, S., & Tobin, R. (2002). *The condition of education 2002* (NCES 2002–025). US Department of Education, Washington, DC: US Government Printing Office.

Wirth-Bond, S., Coyne, A., & Adams, M. (1991). A school counseling program that reduces dropout rate. *The School Counselor, 39*, 131–137.

Chapter Ten
College and Career Readiness

Box 10.1

2016 CACREP School Counseling Specialty Area Standards

1.c Models of P-12 comprehensive career development
2.c School counselor roles in relation to college and career readiness
3.e Use of developmentally appropriate career counseling interventions and assessments
3.j Interventions to promote college and career readiness
3.k Strategies to promote equity in student achievement and college access

---

The ASCA National Model® (2012) provides school counselors with a framework intended to guide comprehensive, inclusive, equitable school counseling programs that address the needs of all students. A robust career and college readiness program is an integral part of a school counseling program, and can help to engage students in academic courses if they are aware of the connection the coursework has to their future careers. Students must be provided with the tools and knowledge to make informed decisions regarding their current academic plans and future options. In this chapter, multiple resources and a theoretical framework for engaging students in their own career exploration journey will be presented. Relevant national organizations that support school counselors' efforts to promote a career and college-ready workforce will also be discussed. We provide practical strategies for individual student planning and for supporting students in applying to college and for financial aid. Finally, we will discuss specific considerations in promoting the college and career readiness of students with disabilities.

While ASCA provides a framework for school counselors to utilize in the creation of school counseling programs and curricula, also provided is a definition of the school counselor's role in academic and college/career planning (ASCA, 2013a). That definition includes the following statement:

School counselors understand national, state, and local requirements and programs that may affect future opportunities for career and college readiness and therefore play a critical role in academic and career planning. The professional school counselor takes a proactive role in assisting students, families, and staff as they assess student strengths and interests and encourage the selection of a rigorous and relevant educational program supporting all students' career and college goals. Professional school counselors provide all students the opportunity to:

- Demonstrate skills needed for school success
- Demonstrate the connection between coursework and life experiences
- Make course selections that allow them the opportunity to choose from a wide range of postsecondary options
- Explore interests and abilities in relation to knowledge of self and the world of work
- Identify and apply strategies to achieve future academic and career success
- Demonstrate the skills for successful goal setting and attainment
- Develop a portfolio to highlight strengths and interests

(ASCA, 2013a, para 3)

School counselors are better situated than any other school professional to offer career and college information to students and parents in the school community (McDonough, 2005), and to facilitate career and college readiness by fostering a climate of support that encourages postsecondary exploration for all students (Holcomb-McCoy, 2010).

Box 10.2

Did you know?

Although school counselors receive more training in career development than teachers, a survey of high school graduates revealed that students viewed teachers as offering more help in exploring college and career options than school counselors (Johnson, Rochkind, Ott, & DuPont 2010). This finding is likely due to a number of factors, including the large caseloads of school counselors. One implication of this finding is that school counselors can train teachers in promoting students' career development.

Recently, school counselors have been provided with the challenge of better preparing tomorrow's workforce before students leave high school to pursue various postsecondary options. *The ASCA Mindsets & Behaviors for Student Success* (ASCA, 2014) provide school counselors with a framework in which to promote the engagement of students in their own career exploration journey. These "mindsets" and "behaviors" directly correlate with the domains of *the ASCA National Model®* (2012) and support professional school counselors' roles statement regarding academic and college/career planning mentioned earlier in this chapter. The mindsets and behaviors were designed to help school counselors connect the school counseling core curriculum to the concrete thoughts and feelings students have about themselves and their postsecondary options (ASCA, 2014). The direction ASCA has taken with specific regard to the promotion of career and college planning speaks volumes as to the importance of developing and delivering a comprehensive career development program in schools.

ASCA's call for change supports the movement at the national and state levels. In 2010, President Obama called upon educators to encourage graduates of high school to be career and college-ready, regardless of socioeconomic status, race, gender, ethnicity, language background, or ability/disability status (US Department of Education, 2010). First Lady, Michelle Obama, spearheaded the creation of the Reach Higher Initiative in 2014 to provide support for school counselors and other educators in helping students obtain postsecondary education and employment. In her speech to honor the School Counselor of the Year, she stated that counselors are the people who "track students down who don't think they're college material, or who don't think they can afford it, and they shake them up and they tell them, 'You have what it takes, I believe in you, now fill out those FAFSA forms and sign up for those AP classes, get started on those college essays'" (Waldo, 2015). Ostensibly, by helping students find their paths while taking courses in high school, they will be more likely to graduate from college in fewer years, and with more focus on preparing for the job market they will enter. Governor John Hickenlooper (D-CO) stated in a speech to educators that he believed in the valuable work of school counselors to engage students in the process of finding careers, not just graduating high school, in order to make an impact on the workforce and expand the postsecondary options for students (J. Hickenlooper, personal communication, May 16, 2014). The governor believed in this statement so much so that he signed a bill granting $8 million to Colorado School Counselor Corps to fund additional school counseling positions in Colorado public schools.

Other states have answered ASCA's call by mandating, through legislation, that students have a career plan in place prior to high school graduation. In the State of Texas, House Bill 5: The Foundation High School Program was passed in early 2014 and mandated that all students declare a career pathway, and take specific courses within their designated pathway, in order to meet the requirements for graduation (Texas Education Association, 2014). This bill required all school counselors to provide information to students and parents during the middle school years and prior to the start of ninth grade, when the official declaration of pathways needed to take place. This increased responsibility upon school counselors to perform career development tasks requires more training and curriculum revision in order to meet the needs of the students and fulfill the state requirements. Indeed, the task of increasing the focus of school counseling programs on career and college readiness may prove challenging, due to the increase in testing responsibility some school counselors face as a result of the current state of the No Child Left Behind legislation (Schenck, Anctil, Smith, & Dahir, 2012), and also the challenge of teachers unwilling to relinquish instructional time in order for school counselors to provide career guidance (Zunker, 2012).

Despite these obstacles, another important piece of legislation came in the passing of HR 10, an amendment to the Success and Opportunity through Quality Charter Schools Act, "which gives priority to charter school grant applicants that offer comprehensive career counseling" (Langevin, 2014, "Langevin and Thompson Continue Push," para 1). A movement toward school counselor competency in career counseling may be apparent as charter schools feel pressured to create and/or expand their career development programs in order to meet this new grant priority status (Morgan, Greenwaldt, & Gosselin, 2014). It is not yet certain whether this action will eventually impact all public schools applying for federal funding, but it does add to the discussion of the importance of school counselors to be knowledgeable and comfortable managing career development programs in schools.

Now, more than ever, there is research supporting the need to prepare students at an earlier age for career and college readiness (ACT, 2013; Arrington, 2000). As stated previously, Secretary of Education Duncan challenged school counselors with the task of helping students plan for college, assisting them with creating a path to graduation, and serving as the bridge for students enrolling in college. According to McDonough (2005), there is not a school professional more important to a student's career and college readiness than the school counselor. In an effort to help guide all school counselors toward preparedness for this journey, it is necessary to clearly define the meaning of career and college readiness.

Based on recent reports from American College Testing (ACT) (2008), college and career readiness means, students will have the knowledge, skills and academic preparation needed to enroll and succeed in introductory college credit-bearing courses within an associate- or bachelor-level degree program without the need for remedial courses. Students need these same attributes and levels of achievement to enter and succeed in postsecondary workforce education programs or to obtain a job that offers a living wage and the chance for career advancement.

(ACT, 2008, p. 1)

Utilizing this definition, there is a critical point at which students' academic skills and coursework must be on target: the eighth grade (ACT, 2008; Arrington, 2000; College Board, 2010). If students are not on target in core academic areas by this grade level, they run the risk of being left behind with limited postsecondary options. Notably, this predictive power is especially significant for underrepresented youth (ACT, 2013). From what we know from the research, students of poverty are less likely to have fulfilled the academic prerequisites for optimal postsecondary options than their counterparts in more affluent households (Grodsky & Jones, 2007). Encouraging middle school students to take rigorous coursework is a key component in promoting career and college readiness for these grade levels.

Professional School Counselors: Advocates for Postsecondary Readiness

At the high school level, rigorous coursework leads to career and college readiness (ACT, 2013, 2008); however, it will not have the desired impact unless there is an increase in students coming from middle school who have been prepared for such rigor. Current research supports the fact that only two in ten eighth graders are on track to be able to take college-level courses by the time they graduate from high school (ACT, 2008). The College Board (2010) estimates that as many as 86% of high school students want to go to college. If, however, these aspiring students are not on the appropriate course trajectory by the time they are in the eighth grade, they will be destined to fall short of their aspirations and the effects may be irreversible (ACT, 2008). Middle school counselors are instrumental in designing and implementing effective education-career planning systems in middle schools to help students become intentional in their educational and career development. With the proper support and resources, school counselors may be the best advocates students have for reaching postsecondary success. Knowing the right resources to provide and incorporating a structured career guidance delivery system into a systemic counseling program is the most effective way to reach the most students.

As Arrington (2000) indicated, the lack of planning for high school can limit postsecondary options for students when they transition out of high school. The consequences of failing to develop a four-year academic course plan prior to entry into high school can ultimately limit or eliminate career choices, and result in lower pay and fewer career opportunities. While the majority of students indicate a desire to go to college, less than 32% of students can even identify the classes required to attend college (Hughes, Karp, Fermin, & Bailey, 2005). Thus, making one of the "key components in a career guidance system a four or six-year plan of study" is of critical importance (Arrington, 2000, p. 106). The US Department of Education (2005) suggests that career guidance efforts have the biggest impact on students in middle school. ACT supports this by stating, "without sufficient preparation before high school, students cannot maximize the benefits of high school-level academic enhancements…all students must be prepared to profit from high school" (ACT, 2008, p. 35). Through proper preparation and a systemic guidance curriculum, school counselors provide students with what they need to be academically, socially, emotionally, and career/postsecondary ready. This type of purposeful intervention strategy requires school counselors to not only advocate for students, but become systemic leaders within schools.

According to ASCA, school counselors are an important part of the leadership team within schools (ASCA, 2012). They also have a responsibility to be involved in the development and implementation of

Figure 10.1 School Counselor Assisting Students. Copyright: www.istockphoto.com.

models that impact students' education process. The College Board (2011) discovered that school counselors do not believe they are given adequate training to implement career and college readiness practices into their counseling programs. Furthermore, if the Common Core Standards, which are based upon career and college readiness markers for all students, are mandated to be put into practice, school counselors should be brought into the discussion regarding how the standards will be addressed and implemented. According to the National Office of School Counselor Advocacy (Bridgeland & Bruce, 2014, p. 8), "Common Core State Standards aim to raise standards for all students, regardless of their race, ethnicity or socioeconomic background...As new training materials are created for teachers, they should be created for counselors as well."

In order to empower school counselors to be leaders within schools, they must be provided the guidelines by which they will work. Through the implementation and use of the *Middle School Career and College Readiness Standards* (MS-CCRS; see Appendix D), school counselors who serve the middle grades will have the necessary structure and accountability tool to effectively perform their roles within the schools. Students will be provided with information that will prepare them for their transition into high school, and will be helped to develop a vision of themselves beyond secondary school. While these standards were developed with middle school students in mind, they may certainly be modified to meet the developmental needs of elementary as well as early high school students.

Factors that influence postsecondary readiness

The academic skills necessary for career and college readiness are not only attributed to earlier course selection, but also to social-emotional learning (Holcomb-McCoy, 2010). Behaviors and academic discipline constitute a large portion of the necessary markers for career and college readiness, with these behaviors and discipline patterns developing long before the high school years (ACT, 2008). As early as the sixth grade, students who have earned an unsatisfactory grade in a core class due to behavior have only a 10 to 20% chance of graduating from high school on time (ACT, 2008).

Additional predictors of career and college readiness and high school completion include demographics such as race/ethnicity, language, and socioeconomic status (Deil-Amen & Tevis, 2010). The research literature reveals that students from lower social economic families are more likely to overestimate the cost of attending college, underestimate the availability of financial aid, and exhibit poor knowledge of the academic prerequisites for college admission, thus making the family as a whole a factor in determining a student's readiness for college (Deil-Amen & Tevis, 2010; Grodsky & Jones, 2007). However, Belasco (2013) stated that seeing a school counselor for career and college information resulted in a positive move toward readiness for students from low-SES homes. For this reason, financial literacy was an area representing a need for particular attention, and will be further discussed in this chapter. If students are aware of the cost of postsecondary education, their self-efficacy toward attaining their aspirations may become more concrete. School counselors are in a unique position to educate students, parents, and community members as to the financial incentives for attending postsecondary institutions and the long-term reward of pursuing career goals. It is the role of the school counselor to bring the community together to support students and rally for a successful future (ASCA, 2012).

Results of research studies have demonstrated that parental values and attitudes toward education, neighborhood norms, and community resources (also known as environmental expectations) were additional predictors of high school success or potential dropout (Bryan, Moore-Thomas, Day-Vines, & Holcomb-McCoy, 2011). In Arrington's (2000) research, 54% of parents began talking to their children about postsecondary options as early as fifth grade, and 19% began earlier in elementary school. Waiting until a child reaches high school age to discuss postsecondary options is far too late. While school counselors cannot change these values and demographics of a student's life, there are many interventions that can impact middle school students' career and college readiness. Some of these include helping students connect with teachers and counselors within the school in order to create a career and college-ready school climate.

School counselors play many roles in the lives of students, but the one that might be the most influential is the one that helps them see themselves within the context of their future. By offering a variety of postsecondary planning options, students gain the tools and support they need to overcome the barriers, real or perceived, to reaching career success. School counselors and other school professionals engage in helping behaviors designed to foster student academic, social/emotional, and career success, but often their efforts are not cohesively organized or regularly evaluated. One of the ways in which the career and postsecondary planning curriculum may be structured is by using a set of standards, competencies, and indicators to plan the curriculum, implement activity-based interventions, evaluate student outcomes, and be able to report the necessary data to stakeholders.

Middle School Career and College Readiness Standards (MS-CCRS)

As stated previously, the literature supports the idea of increasing exposure to career planning at the middle grade level, and with that, a call to school counselors to be the specific change agents in that process. Given the movement at the national level (Bridgeland & Bruce, 2014) and the need for further support for middle school counselors providing postsecondary programming, the *Middle School Career and College Readiness Standards* (MS-CCRS) were created (see Appendix D). The specific career and college areas identified in the standards include: *personal awareness, career awareness, postsecondary aspirations, postsecondary options, environmental expectations, academic planning, employability skills,* and *financial literacy.* The MS-CCRS were developed to inform school counselors, administrators, teachers, parents, students, and community stakeholders of the relevant knowledge, skills, and attitudes that middle level students need to attain before they transition into high school. Each standard, by definition, is outlined below with specific competency markers and indicators. The competency markers are to serve as a guide for middle school counselors, or a metaphoric umbrella under which related indicators further define the ways in which students might meet the standard. The indicators are not meant to be so specific that school counselors lose their autonomy in the process, but provide a means by which they might expand their services to provide activities and learning opportunities for their students.

The development of these standards is a result of information provided by the National Office for School Counselor Advocacy (NOSCA), the National Occupational Information Coordinating Committee (NOICC), the American School Counselor Association (ASCA), and information from other relevant research found in the career counseling and education literature already mentioned in this chapter. The developmental nature of these standards will help to guide school counselors and other educators in helping to transition middle school students to become career and college-ready as they enter high school. These standards (see Appendix D) serve as a "jumping off point" for school districts to engage in reform that is proactive and on track with the Department of Education's vision for the future (Bridgeland & Bruce, 2014). Career and college readiness is a driving force in P-20 education systems, and school counselors will be the leaders in this movement.

These standards represent a set of markers by which school counselors, students, parents, and community members may measure the progress of students toward career and postsecondary planning. It is not an all-encompassing list of needs, but provides a framework from which school counselors may develop their own programs that address the needs of their particular school community. Many school counseling programs require a differentiated curriculum in order to meet the needs of all students. Career development programs are no exception. School counselors' roles have evolved over the years, from helping students find "*jobs* to *occupations* to *careers*" (Schenck, Anctil, Smith, & Dahir, 2012, p. 222). While there seemed to be a push for all students to attend college back in the 1990s and 2000s, a reinvented wave of possibilities is being presented through career and technical education (CTE) programs that is focusing the attention of law-makers and school administrators alike.

Career and Technical Education as a Resource for Student Success

Throughout our nation's history, there have been differing views on what the outcomes of public education should be. According to Schenck et al. (2012), three major themes can be found in the most recent history of career guidance in schools. The first is the minimal attention that career counseling has been paid within school counseling programs, the second is "the role equity, educational access, and social justice played in career guidance" (p. 223), and the third is the recognition that career decision-making must be an integral and interrelated component of a comprehensive, equitable school counseling program. *The ASCA Mindsets & Behaviors for Student Success* (2014) provide additional support for career education and guidance within a comprehensive school counseling program. However, more resources are needed to provide support for the needs of *all* students. Career guidance is comprehensive in nature and enhances the opportunities for students and parents to gain an understanding of what academic and career options are available, but a one-size-fits-all approach is something of the past, not the future of postsecondary readiness. Alternative models of career exploration and coursework are necessary to truly provide access and equal opportunity to a wide range of diverse students. Through career and technical education coursework, all students have a chance for academic, social/emotional, and career success.

The historical misunderstanding has been that CTE programs have been seen as inferior in educational arenas and by parents, due to the implications that CTE would lead to jobs in the workforce before formal college education would occur (Niles & Harris-Bowlsby, 2002). With the advancement in opportunity for students to complete college coursework while still in high school, the idea of bridging the gap for students to attend college increased in popularity. In reality, students are gaining the knowledge and skills needed to be successful in college and in the workplace through the career and technical education curriculum presented at the middle and high school levels (Association for Career and Technical Education [ACTE], 2014).

Students who participate in CTE coursework and related student organizations are more likely to experience academic achievement, career self-efficacy, employability skills, commitment to education, and postsecondary success. Conversely, students who do not participate in some form of CTE in high school face lower academic performance, increased engagement in at-risk behaviors, and higher dropout rates than their CTE counterparts (Southern Regional Education Board, 2012). In order for school counselors to engage students in traditional academic offerings and CTE opportunities, it is important to learn about the various two-year, four-year, and technical college curriculum, and state/national organizations that support CTE. Through the Association for Career and Technical Education (www.acteonline.org; ACTE), and the various state divisions, school counselors can access a plethora of information to better assist their students in pursuing CTE courses and student organizations as part of their career and college readiness programs. There are currently 11 Career and Technical Student Organizations (CTSOs) recognized by the US Department of Education, with state divisions that support various career pathways in order to provide students with the opportunity to engage in their desired profession while still in high school (see Table 10.1).

With more than 2 million members among the national student career-focused organizations, CTE students are making an impact upon the way that education is perceived by this generation of students. According to ACTE (2014), those who participated in student organizations during tenth grade had higher grade point averages, and were more likely to be enrolled in college at age 21 than non-participants. School counselors are in a prime position to educate, inform, and encourage students to become involved in career-related organizations as a means of fostering a career-ready and college-attending culture within their school and community.

Other ways in which school counselors are promoting career and college cultures in their schools are by providing students with alternatives to the traditional "career fair," in which students file into the gymnasium or other campus gathering spot and gravitate toward the table that offers the most enticing "freebies" and not necessarily the information that interested them.

Box 10.3

Did you know?

Career fairs may also have implications for promoting social justice. Kolodinsky et al. (2006) found that a career fair involving mostly female professionals demonstrating their professions increased the occupational self-efficacy of 139 predominantly high school-aged female adolescents, of which more than half identified as a minority.

Table 10.1 Career and Technical Student Organizations

Business Professionals of America	BPA is the leading CTSO (Career and Technical Student Organization) for students pursuing careers in business management, office administration, information technology, and other related career fields. BPA has 43,000 members in over 2,300 chapters in 23 states. BPA is a co-curricular organization that supports business and information technology educators by offering co-curricular exercises based on national standards.	www.ctsos.org/ ctsos/business-professionals-of-america/
Distributive Education Clubs of America (DECA)	DECA prepares emerging leaders and entrepreneurs in marketing, finance, hospitality, and management in high schools and colleges around the globe. With over a 60-year history, DECA has impacted the lives of more than ten million students, educators, school administrators, and business professionals since it was founded in 1946. Their strong connection with our organization has resonated into a brand that people identify as a remarkable experience in the preparation of emerging leaders and entrepreneurs.	www.ctsos.org/ ctsos/deca/
Future Business Leaders of America – Phi Beta Lambda	Future Business Leaders of America – Phi Beta Lambda is a nonprofit 501(c)(3) education association with a quarter of a million students preparing for careers in business and business-related fields. The association has four divisions: Future Business Leaders of America (FBLA) for high school students; FBLA-Middle Level for junior high, middle, and intermediate school students; Phi Beta Lambda (PBL) for postsecondary students; and Professional Division for businesspeople, FBLA-PBL alumni, educators, and parents who support the goals of the association.	www.bpa.org/
Family, Career and Community Leaders of America (FCCLA)	FCCLA is the only national career and technical student organization with the family as its central focus. Since 1945, FCCLA members have been making a difference in their families, careers, and communities by addressing important personal, work, and societal issues through family and consumer sciences education, and through the opportunity to expand their leadership potential and develop skills for life.	www.fcclainc.org/
Future Educators Association	FEA is an international student organization dedicated to supporting young people interested in education-related careers. By staying true to its mission while incorporating the latest in technology and education research, FEA continues to help: • Attract exemplary future educators and begin averting teacher shortages at a local level, particularly within the areas of math, science, and special education; • Encourage students from diverse cultural and ethnic backgrounds to enter the education profession; and • Elevate the image of teaching and promote it as a challenging and rewarding career.	www. futureeducators. org/
HOSA – Future Health Professionals	HOSA – Future Health Professionals is a national student organization recognized by the US Department of Education and the Health Science Education Division of ACTE. HOSA's two-fold mission is to promote career opportunities in the health care industry and to enhance the delivery of quality health care to all people. HOSA's goal is to encourage all health occupations instructors and students to join and be actively involved in the HSE-HOSA Partnership.	www.ctsos.org/ ctsos/hosa/
National FFA Organization (Formerly known as the Future Farmers of America)	FFA envisions a future in which all agricultural education students will discover their passions and build on that insight to chart a course for their education, careers, and personal futures. FFA makes a positive difference in the lives of students by developing their potential for premier leadership, personal growth, and career success through agricultural education. FFA is one part of the three-component model for school-based agricultural education. The other two parts of the model include the agricultural education classroom/laboratory and supervised agricultural experience, with hands-on agricultural programs in every state in the nation, Puerto Rico, and the Virgin Islands.	www.ffa.org/Pages/ default.aspx
National Postsecondary Agricultural Student (PAS) Organization	The National Postsecondary Agricultural Student Organization (PAS) is an organization associated with agriculture/agribusiness and natural resources in approved postsecondary institutions offering baccalaureate degrees, associate degrees, diplomas, and/or certificates.	www.nationalpas. org/

Continued

Table 10.1 (*cont.*)

National Young Farmer Educational Association (NYFEA)	NYFEA's purpose is to develop leaders, inspire service, strengthen communities, and enhance the success potential for American agriculture, especially the young and beginning producers and young agribusiness professionals.	www.nyfea.org/
SkillsUSA	SkillsUSA is a partnership of students, teachers, and industry working together to ensure America has a skilled workforce. SkillsUSA is an applied method of instruction for preparing America's high performance workers in public career and technical programs. SkillsUSA also promotes understanding of the free-enterprise system and involvement in community service. 130 trade, technical, and skilled service occupational titles are represented in the curricula of SkillsUSA member students, covering the construction, manufacturing, transportation, health sciences, information technology, communications, personal services, hospitality, public safety, and engineering technology industries. The organization has 13,000 school chapters in 54 state and territorial associations. More than 14,500 instructors and administrators are professional members of SkillsUSA.	www.skillsusa.org/
The Technology Student Association (TSA)	TSA is a national organization devoted exclusively to the needs of students interested in science, technology, engineering, and mathematics (STEM). Open to young people enrolled in – or who have completed – technology education courses, TSA's membership includes more than 200,000 middle and high school students in 2,000 schools spanning 48 states. TSA partners with universities and other organizations to promote a variety of STEM competitions and opportunities for students and teachers. Members learn through exciting competitive events, leadership opportunities, and much more.	www.tsaweb.org/

In Wilmot, WI, professional school counselor, Allen Reynolds offered his students an alternative to this type of general information session, and instead provided students with the opportunity to attend targeted panel discussions with local leaders in each profession. Students were encouraged to attend as many 45-minute panel discussions as they liked, which were offered at various times throughout the year. Each panel represented a specific set of career options within each of the 16 clusters outlined in the National Career Clusters® Framework. Panelists offered information for students interested in entry-level, mid-level, and professional-level positions and added personal anecdotes to engage students in the development of their own professional plan. According to Reynolds (2013), 90% of students reported that the panels had a positive impact on their college and postsecondary planning, which was a stark improvement over the feedback from previous years' career fairs. This innovative approach to addressing the psychoeducational delivery of career-related information to students would likely drastically diminish students being exposed to information they deemed as irrelevant.

21st-Century Students in the Global Workforce

The nonprofit think tank, The Partnership for 21st Century Skills (P21), was created to promote and enhance student outcomes in education leading to a workforce capable of meeting the needs of our ever-changing global economy (Young, 2014). In order to support student growth toward "global competence," P21 developed a definition by which school counselors and other educators might guide students. According to Young (2014, para 1):

> Global competence means being able to work on problems that cut across the world's geographical, cultural, and political boundaries; it means being prepared for life in our increasingly interconnected world. You cannot be considered a true 21st Century Citizen if you are not globally competent.

School counselors have the opportunity to promote globally competent citizens and future workers by infusing cultural aspects into their career counseling curriculum and academic planning efforts. Students with a broad knowledge of jobs and careers that transcend the boundaries of their country will be better prepared to explore career paths that take them from their families of origin. Creating a dialogue about careers in other areas of the world is another way to engage students who show an interest in cultural differences or world travel. Breaking down the barriers of race, ethnicity, and gender through cultural career exploration within and outside of certain career clusters will only serve to enhance the school counselors' "tool box" of intervention strategies to effectively engage more students into their own career exploration process.

According to ACTE (2014), The National Career Cluster® Framework consists of 16 separate clusters that are grouped by industry to enable educators to enhance student learning through systemic, purposeful, engagement in career preparation. The 16 clusters include:

1. Agriculture, Food & Natural Resources
2. Architecture & Construction
3. Arts, A/V Technology & Communications
4. Business, Management & Administration
5. Education & Training
6. Finance
7. Government & Public Administration
8. Health Science
9. Hospitality & Tourism
10. Human Services
11. Information Technology
12. Law, Public Safety & Security
13. Manufacturing
14. Marketing, Sales & Service
15. Science, Technology, Engineering & Mathematics
16. Transportation, Distribution & Logistics

Within each designated industry, there are clusters representing career pathways that are driven by a student's plan of study. By breaking down the individual courses a student may take within the school community into cluster areas, school counselors will be able to engage students in relevant conversations regarding the workforce jobs or college majors that may lead to employment within each industry. While this model is not new, many school counselors are not familiar with the way in which they may use the clusters to foster student engagement and ultimately impact the sequence of courses students complete that lead to focused college or career preparedness. The State of Colorado offers a comprehensive model for identifying career clusters and pathways, in addition to "Postsecondary & Workforce Readiness" indicators (Colorado Community College System, 2010). This model also represents the addition of a 17th cluster known as *energy* that has become one of the fastest growing industries in the state. Florida and Georgia have also added "energy" to their career cluster models, and many other states may follow suit, given the impact this valuable resource has on a state's economy and workforce. School counselors provide guidance and information regarding what opportunities are available to students, but in many ways, the economic impacts of industry on the state in which they live dictates the needs and salary ranges for given occupations. Looking at global options that may be available in a particular career field may provide students with increased power in career decision-making after high school. This is just one of the ways in which school counselors assist students in overcoming real or perceived barriers to career success.

Finding creative ways to provide career and college-ready support for students and families is a joint effort, with input from multiple entities within every state and community. The school counselor, however, is the point of contact for programming and coordination of the information and materials that are made available for student consumption. Without adequate programming to support the flow of career and college information, students may lack the knowledge to plan for postsecondary life. In addition to *the ASCA Mindsets & Behaviors for Student Success* (2014), student standards, and state and national organizations, school counselors may utilize an array of career assessments and other tools for assisting students in their journey toward postsecondary readiness. In Box 10.4–10.6 below, several web-based resources are listed that may be utilized by school counselors in order to help students explore options, learn to calculate the costs of school or training, or learn about their likes and dislikes in life. These resources are merely a suggestion and do not represent the entirety of what is currently available for use on free or for-profit sites.

Box 10.4

Web-based Resources to Support Career and College Readiness

Utah State Office of Education:

www.schools.utah.gov/cte/ccgp

Washington State Career and College Handbook:

www.k12.wa.us/SecondaryEducation/CareerCollegeReadiness/pubdocs/Handbook.pdf

Washington State, Lesson Plans for Career Readiness:

www.k12.wa.us/SecondaryEducation/CareerCollegeReadiness/CareerReady.aspx

Colorado Department of Education, Career and College Readiness:

www.collegeincolorado.org

Individual Career and Academic Plan Resources: Colorado Community College System:

www.coloradostateplan.com/ICAP.htm

Maryland State Department of Education, Career and College Readiness:

www.marylandpublicschools.org/MSDE/divisions/careertech/career_technology/index.html

Maryland State College and Career Readiness Standards:

www.mdk12.org/instruction/commoncore/index.html

College and Career Readiness Success Center:

www.ccrscenter.org/about-us

Career Development for Career Guidance Professionals:

http://knowitall.scetv.org/careeraisle/guidance/index.cfm

National Career Development Association – Internet Sites for Career Planning:

www.ncda.org/aws/NCDA/pt/sp/resources#list_resources_all-R102-NCDA

National Career Development Association – FREE Resources for School Counselors:

www.ncda.org/aws/NCDA/pt/sd/news_article/6237/_self/layout_details/true

US Department of Education, National Initiatives in Career and Technical Education:

http://cte.ed.gov/nationalinitiatives/gandctools.cfm?&pass_dis=1

Career Isle:

http://knowitall.scetv.org/careeraisle/students/index.cfm

SPARC National has report cards that include Career Development Outcomes:

http://sparc.schoolcounselorcentral.com

Box 10.5

Career Guidance Resources for Students with Disabilities, Colorado Community College System:

Dual Enrollment Learning Opportunities for Students with Disabilities:
www.coloradostateplan.com/Counseling/SpEdCE_IEPmatrix.docx

Dual Enrollment Options and Students with Disabilities:
www.coloradostateplan.com/Counseling/ConcurrentEd2.docx

Find Your Career Path Abroad:
www.miusa.org/ncde

"How to" Guide for Making College Affordable:
www.affordablecollegesonline.org/college-resource-center/affordable-colleges-for-students-with-disabilities

Navigating the Path to College:
http://ies.ed.gov/ncee/wwc/PracticeGuide.aspx?sid=11

Online Learning for College Students with Disabilities:
www.accreditedschoolsonline.org/resources/best-accredited-colleges-schools-for-students-with-disabilities

Students with Disabilities College & Career Website:
www.thinkcollege.net

Box 10.6

Video Resources:

JobsMadeReal: www.jobsmadereal.com
Success in the New Economy: http://vimeo.com/67277269
Gigniks: Invent Yourself: www.youtube.com/user/GigniksCareerVideos
EEOC Youth@Work: Harassment and Discrimination:
www.youtube.com/watch?v=LkhvV3g1zA8&feature=youtu.be
Is Your Daughter Safe at Work?: www.pbs.org/now/shows/508
FAFSA Hooray: www.youtube.com/watch?v=e2d7IfFgxTs
Next Vista for Learning Careers Videos: www.nextvista.org/collection/light-bulbs/careers
ESL Students Work Voices:
http://blogs.kqed.org/education/category/post-secondary-esl/work-voices/page/2
RoadTrip Nation: www.roadtripnation.com
Skills to Pay the Bills: www.dol.gov/dol/media/webcast/20121015-softskills
Your Life, Your Money: www.youtube.com/embed/lpLBvrATSl4

Individual Student Planning

One of the primary activities school counselors use to promote career development is the use of individual student planning, which is categorized as a direct student service within *the ASCA National*

Model® (2012). In *the ASCA National Model*® (2012) individual student planning is defined as "ongoing systemic activities designed to help students establish personal goals and develop future plans, such as individual learning plans and graduation plans" (p. 85). As of 2011, 23 states require districts to develop individualized student learning plans (Rennie Center for Education Research and Policy, 2011).

School counselors typically use classroom lessons and small group activities to present developmentally relevant career information. They promote students' awareness of their abilities through career interest inventories, such as Holland's (1994) *Self-Directed Search* (SDS), career aptitude tests, such as the *Differential Aptitude Test* (DAT: Bennett, Seashore, & Wesman, 1975), and Dunn, Dunn, and Price's (1989) *Learning Style Inventory*. Lessons and group activities are used to administer the instruments, or to demonstrate to students how to complete such instruments that are typically incorporated into the school's online career exploration programs. Popular online career exploration programs include Career Cruising® (http://public.careercruising.com/en), Bridges® (https://access.bridges.com/auth/login.do), and Naviance® (www.naviance.com). For school districts that do not purchase online career exploration programs, free online career exploration programs are available through the College Board® (www.collegeboard.org), and some state departments of education offer such programs. Lessons and group activities are used to help students interpret the results of these assessments. School counselors also use classroom lessons for a variety of career-related information, including promotion standards, elective options, graduation, college and workforce requirements, workforce trends, career pathways, financial aid options for postsecondary education and training, etc.

Many schools, particularly at the middle/junior high and high school levels, require school counselors to meet individually with each student on their caseload every year to complete the student's individual student plan. Typically, classroom lessons and group activities are conducted in the first half of the year to provide career and educational information to students, and in the second half of the school year the school counselor and student meet individually, processing the results of the student's career exploration activities, in order to select classes that support the student's career and postsecondary goals. In such individual meetings, the school counselor has the best opportunity to assess the student's career maturity, which may be defined as the degree to which the student's selected career path is based upon a thoughtful reflection of the student's career interests and abilities and life goals. There are a number of career development theories that may be used to assess career maturity. We recommend Marcia's identity phases to assess career maturity because it more broadly incorporates the entire student, assessing the student's psychosocial maturity, and thus has clearer implications for both career and personal/social development.

Use of Marcia's Identity Statuses in Individual Student Planning

Marcia (1966) constructed an expanded framework of Erik Erikson's (1956) identity vs. role confusion stage, in which adolescents are tasked with the challenge of developing a consistent identity. Marcia proposed that individuals in the identity vs. identity confusion stage may exist within one of four identity statuses: (1) identity diffusion, (2) identity foreclosure, (3) identity moratorium, and (4) identity achieved. The statuses differ in terms of whether the person has undergone an exploration of one's values, worldview, abilities, interests, etc., which is referred to as a crisis in Marcia's framework, and whether a person is committed to a worldview/values. Most early adolescents are either in the identity diffusion or identity foreclosure status. In the identity diffusion status, the individual is not exploring his or her worldview/values, nor is the individual committed to a particular worldview/values. The student in identity diffusion often cannot name a career or educational pathway beyond high school, and is likely to exhibit anxiety when thinking about the issue, as the student wishes to avoid thinking about the future. In contrast, in the identity diffusion status, the individual is committed to a particular worldview/set of values, which the student has typically simply acquired from his or her parents without a period of reflection/exploration.

In terms of career development, the student in the identity foreclosed status often can readily identify a career he or she wishes to pursue, and typically the career the student identifies is of high status (e.g., doctor, lawyer, engineer), but the student has difficulty explaining what he or she finds appealing about the profession. In the identity moratorium status, the student is in the process of exploring his or her worldview; in other words, the student is within the midst of the identity crisis and is not firmly committed to a worldview. The student in the identity moratorium status may have a variety of career interests and have difficulty differentiating among these interests. The identity achieved student has undergone an exploration of self and has a mostly consistent worldview/set of values. The student in identity achievement has moved beyond career exploration and has entered the phase of career decision-making, in which he or she is pursuing a career path that the student sees as compatible with his or her worldview.

Marcia's identity statuses have clear implications for individual student planning. For the student in identity diffusion, the objective is to support the student's initiation of career- and self-exploration. The school counselor can promote such self-awareness through processing the results of career interest inventories, asking the student to describe his or her ideal picture of him/herself within ten years, what strengths the student thinks others see in him or her, what school subjects or elective school activities tend to interest the student, exploring the student's ideas for how to obtain additional experiences and information, etc. The school counselor can manage the student's anxiety by acknowledging that such an exploration can be kind of scary, but also exciting, by normalizing the fact that other students are in a similar position of not being sure of what they want to do, etc. The school counselor wants students in the identity foreclosed status to think more critically about his or her career choices, asking such questions as "What do you think of your dad's encouragement to become a lawyer. Does that fit with how you see yourself?", "What do you think you would like about that career?", "What do you know about the activities of lawyers?"

The hope for middle/junior high, and high school students is that they are in the identity moratorium status, exploring various career options as they learn more about themselves and are in the process of developing a worldview that is differentiated from their parents and peers, while being able to also maintain connection with parents and peers. The school counselor can support students' self- and career-exploration by helping them make sense of contrasting thoughts and values. The exploration process involves uncertainty and anxiety, which may manifest in the student wanting to avoid assuming responsibility for such large life choices by seeking others who will make decisions for them. The school counselor should avoid pushing students to make large life decisions without a student having undergone a considerable process of reflection. The school counselor can normalize the student's anxiety, and explore with the student how he or she effectively balances self-exploration and managing the anxiety associated with such self-exploration. Self- and career-exploration involve a focus on the future, as the student thinks about the self he or she wishes to become. However, the student can also be encouraged to think about how he or she can alternate between thinking about the future and maintaining a present focus through leisure activities, exercise, relaxation exercises, mindfulness, etc. Often the primary assistance the student in the achievement status wants from the school counselor is specific information regarding careers and postsecondary options. The identity achieved student has resolved important questions about his or her future, and wants specific information to pursue his or her career vision.

College Applications

A significant portion of time for high school counselors is devoted to assisting students in the college application process, particularly for districts with a large college-going culture. In assisting students who are applying to college and other postsecondary options, the school counselor should seek to maintain a focus on promoting students' development and avoid simply serving as a person who processes college applications, as much of such work can be considered clerical and schools may ultimately decide that a Master's-level professional position is not necessary for such work. High school counselors should seek to manage their time wisely in regards to college applications. Rather than frequent meetings with individual students to complete college applications, the high school counselor can conduct school counseling lessons in which they teach students the process for applying for college, variables to consider in selecting a college, how to use search engines, such as The College Board® and Naviance®, to research colleges and scholarships, tips for writing college admissions essays, etc.; school counselors should provide such information to parents through informational sessions. Providing such information through classroom lessons and the school counseling program's website reduces the amount of time spent responding to individual students and parents. However, responding individually to students and parents can never be entirely eliminated given that many parents and students have considerable anxiety about the next potential chapter of their lives, and thus have difficulty processing such information in large-group settings. High school counselors can arrange to have recent high school graduates speak to students about the personal/social process they underwent in pursuing postsecondary options, and have parents of recent high school graduates speak to parents whose children are currently undergoing the process. There are a number of new technological resources that can assist school counselors in effectively managing the time involved with college applications.

Naviance®

Naviance® (2009) is a college and career readiness program that can interface with the school's student information system to allow for ready access to grades and college entrance examination scores (e.g., SAT, ACT). Students are able to access Naviance® online to research colleges and careers, manage college applications, construct individualized learning plans, take a career interest inventory, build a resume, request recommendations from school personnel, request transcripts, research scholarships, etc. Naviance® provides school counselors with the annual results of the student bodies' college acceptance rates, allowing the school counselor and student to predict the likelihood of acceptance to a particular college/university based upon previous students' applications. Many high schools report that the implementation of Naviance® resulted in an increase in the number of colleges to which students apply, and an increase in college enrollment. Naviance® also interfaces with the Common Application (www.commonapp.org), which is a free, electronic admissions process that is accepted by many colleges and universities.

Financial Aid

Part of creating a college-going culture involves helping students and families understand the associated costs of postsecondary education and training. To educate students and parents about financial aid, school counselors should conduct lessons and parent information sessions and include this information on the school counseling program's website. Families must be informed that colleges typically assume that students will have some responsibility for financing their education, typically through borrowing loans (Martin, 2013). The student and his or her family should be encouraged to project the potential costs of the education over the students' potential to repay the debt depending upon his or her career aspirations, as student loan debt may impact the student's ability to attend graduate school, purchase a home, or start a family. If the student is determined to enroll in his or her dream school, but the financial aid package the school is offering and the family's resources are limited, the family may consider the option of the student attending a lower-cost school, such as a community college, for two years and then transferring to the student's ideal school. The family should be encouraged to review The College Board's Net Price Calculator (http://netpricecalculator.collegeboard.org) and the federal government's College Navigator (https://nces.ed.gov/collegenavigator) to obtain a sense of the costs of higher education. In the following section we provide an overview of financial aid so that persons entering the profession have a basic understanding which they can expand upon with professional experience.

Financial aid may be divided into two categories: need-based and non-need-based (Martin, 2013). Need-based and non-need-based funds may be further subdivided into four types: scholarships, grants, loans, and employment. Most forms of financial aid require the student to complete a Free Application for Federal Student Aid (FAFSA).

There are several components which are calculated to determine a student's eligibility for financial aid (Martin, 2013). First, the college constructs an estimate of a student's costs for an academic year, and this estimated cost includes tuition and fees, room and board, books, computer, and transportation. Second, the student's expected family contribution (EFC) is calculated from the demographic and financial information provided by the student in the FAFSA. The student's financial aid is calculated by subtracting the estimated cost of attendance from the EFC. See Box 10.7 for types of federal grants and Box 10.8 for types of federal loans.

Box 10.7

Types of Federal Grants

Pell: Awarded to the neediest students based on EFC. The maximum amount per year is $5,755 as of 2015–16.
Federal Supplemental Educational Opportunity Grant (FSEOG): Awarded to the neediest students based on EFC. The maximum amount per year is $4,000 as of 2015–16.
Teacher Education Assistance for College & Higher Education (TEACH): Available for students who are willing to teach in a high-need field (e.g., math, science) at a Title I school after graduation. The maximum amount per year is $4,000 as of 2015–16.

(https://studentaid.ed.gov/sa/types/grants-scholarships)

Box 10.8

Types of Federal Loans

Direct Subsidized: The federal government pays accruing interest (4.29% as of July, 2015) while borrowers are enrolled at least half-time.
Direct Unsubsidized: A non-need-based loan. Interest (4.29% as of July, 2015) accrues while borrower is enrolled.
PLUS: Borrowed by parents of dependent students to help meet costs not covered by other forms of financial aid. The maximum amount that may be borrowed per year is the difference between the student's cost of attendance and other aid received.
Federal Perkins: A need-based, subsidized loan. The maximum annual amount for bachelor's students is $5,550 as of July, 2015. The interest rate is 5% as of July, 2015.

(https://studentaid.ed.gov/sa/types/grants-scholarships)

College and Career Readiness for Students with Disabilities

School counselors seek to promote the college and career readiness of all students, including students with disabilities whose career development has traditionally received less focus within schools. The

Individuals with Disabilities Education Act (IDEA) of 2004 mandates that students in special education be provided transition services, which includes the construction of a transition plan by age 14. While special education teachers typically coordinate Individualized Education Plans (IEPs), IDEA requires the involvement of related professionals when appropriate. ASCA recommends school counselor participation in transition planning, as indicated in ASCA's (2013b) professional position statement on Students with Disabilities. However, some studies (e.g., Milsom, 2002) have found that many school counselors report not participating in the development of transition plans for students with disabilities. In the following section, we explore how school counselors can promote both the college and career readiness of students with disabilities, focusing on how to assist students with disabilities who may be seeking vocational options following high school, and students who may pursue college.

School counselors can assist the IEP team in developing the transition plan by providing up-to-date information about the world of work, matching the students' abilities and interests to career options, encouraging students to broaden their perspectives as a caution against changes in the labor market (Wadsworth, Milsom, & Cocco, 2004). They can help students with disabilities increase their awareness of their interests and abilities through short-term job tryout experiences and job shadowing, and by examining students' volunteer, leisure, and daily living activities. School counselors can help the student and the IEP team identify the students' career values and pursue exploration activities consistent with those values. For example, for a student with a moderate intellectual disability (ID), his or her interest in being a firefighter may be related to having respect by wearing a uniform and the perceived opportunities to connect with others. Career exploration activities can be designed to incorporate the student's values, having the student training as a fire safety officer, wearing a uniform, and conducting fire safety and fire extinguisher checks with school staff. For students with ID, the preferred method to assess career interests and abilities involves an assessment of work behavior; however, there are inventories that are often used, including the *What I Like to Do Inventory* (Meyers, Dringard, & Zinner, 1978) and the *Audio-Visual Vocational Preferences Test* (Wilgosh, 1994). When conducting career exploration activities with adolescents with ID, school counselors should first teach the steps of decision-making. Instructional activities can also be designed to promote the vocational skills of students with ID (Wadsworth et al., 2004). For example, vocational skills that can transfer to various employment opportunities in clerical and reception jobs may include mechanical skills (e.g., use of office equipment), social skills (e.g., active listening skills), and hygiene (e.g., expected dress and appearance).

Career exploration activities for the elementary- and middle-school levels can prepare students with disabilities to make career choices in young adulthood (Wadsworth et al., 2004). School counselors can assist the IEP team in relating classroom activities such as decision-making and social skill development with vital aspects of career development. School counselors may collaborate with teachers to help students with ID to develop career interests and choose from vocational activities. For example, instructional activities may be designed to expose students to various job-related skills (e.g., following directions) and habits (e.g., timeliness). School counseling lessons can expose students with ID to different job-related environments (e.g., working alone vs. in a group) and patterns (e.g., sporadic activity vs. repetitive consistency).

College Readiness of Students with Disabilities

There has been an increase in the number of students with disabilities in the US who attend postsecondary education (US Census Bureau, 2009). For example, whereas in 1990 only 26% students with disabilities enrolled in college within four years of high school graduation, by 2005 nearly 46% of students with disabilities enrolled in postsecondary education (Newman, Wagner, Cameto, Knokey, & Shaver, 2010). Federal legislation provisions, such as the transition planning requirement of IDEA (2004) and Section 504 of the Rehabilitation Act, which requires that postsecondary institutions which receive federal funding provide reasonable accommodations for students with a disability, have increased the postsecondary participation of students with disabilities. Despite the increase in college attendance among students with disabilities they are still less likely to enroll in college (Newman et al., 2010), and graduate from college (e.g., Wagner, Newman, Cameto, Garza, & Levine, 2005). The National Joint Committee on Learning Disabilities (NJCLD) asserted "that many students with learning disabilities do not consider postsecondary education options (2- and 4-year colleges and vocational schools) because they are not encouraged, assisted, or prepared to do so" (1994, p. 1).

As advocates for all students, school counselors can fulfill vital roles in assisting students with learning disabilities to transition to college (Milsom & Hartley, 2005). Milsom and Hartley (2005) recommend that for students with disabilities who are transitioning to postsecondary institutions, school counselors can promote development in four areas: (1) Knowledge of Disability; (2) Knowledge of Postsecondary Support Services; (3) Knowledge of Disability Legislation; and (4) Ability to Self-advocate.

(1) Knowledge of Disability: School counselors can collaborate with special education teachers in helping students obtain knowledge of their disability, providing small group or individual sessions to help students understand how their skills and abilities relate to potential future careers and college majors.

(2) Knowledge of Postsecondary Support Services: When choosing a college, students with learning disabilities should obtain information about the specific admission requirements for students with disabilities and the availability and process for obtaining support services. Support services that must be provided by postsecondary institutions under Section 504 include the use of auxiliary aids such as taped texts, exam readers, and note takers.

(3) Knowledge of Disability Legislation: Many students are not closely familiar with the federal legislation concerning students with disabilities and may not realize that the provisions of IDEA do not apply to postsecondary institutions. Rather, students with disabilities are eligible for reasonable accommodations under Section 504 of the Rehabilitation Act. Section 504 only requires postsecondary institutions to provide services for students who request them and who provide appropriate documentation; it is vital that students with disabilities and their families are aware of their legislative rights.

(4) Ability to Self-Advocate: School counselors can work with special educators to help students with disabilities practice self-advocacy skills. Students with disabilities can be instructed in the components of assertive communication, which can then be periodically role-played under the supervision of special educators.

Individual Planning with Students with Disabilities

Wren and Einhorn (2000) provide suggestions for school counselors when conducting individual planning with students with disabilities. For students with disabilities that have short attention spans, school counselors may schedule shorter sessions, allow frequent breaks, remove distracting objects, provide noiseless objects to hold, or allow students to stand or pace. To increase students' retention of information, school counselors can use the beginning and end of sessions to review information, ask a student to clarify his or her understanding of the information provided, decrease sentence complexity and length, and slow the pace of sessions. Students with disabilities often lack self-esteem and efficacy, and school counselors can provide students with skills to manage their anxiety and fear related to taking on new risks, such as enrolling in more challenging classes and postsecondary institutions.

Summary

The need exists for school counselors to take an active role in students' career and postsecondary planning. By utilizing existing resources and engaging students, parents, teachers, administrators, and community members in the process of planning for a future after high school, students will be more readily equipped to navigate the complex world of work, training, or college life. This chapter contains pertinent information that school counselors need to know in order to be in the position to provide appropriate services to students and create a climate of postsecondary readiness in their building. Cultivating a system of resources for students and parents to use as they navigate the plethora of options available will increase the likelihood for career and life success for every student. The resources in this chapter are just a sample of what is continually being offered online for free or at low cost. By creating a school-specific resource portal for students, with information that is most useful to them, school counselors may have a better chance of truly supporting all students toward their goals for postsecondary success.

References

ACT, Inc. (2008). *The forgotten middle ensuring that all students are on target for college and career readiness before high school.* Available online at www.act.org/research/policymakers/pdf/CollegeReadiness.pdf (accessed May 1, 2015).

ACT, Inc. (2013). *The condition of college and career readiness.* Available online at www.act.org/research/policymakers/cccr13/index.html (accessed December 20, 2014).

American School Counselor Association (2012). *The ASCA national model: A framework for school counseling programs* (3rd ed.). Alexandria, VA: Author.

American School Counselor Association (2013a). *The professional school counselor and academic and college/career planning.* Alexandria, VA: Author. Available online at http://asca.dev.networkats.com/asca/media/asca/home/position%20statements/PS_AcademicPlanning.pdf (accessed January 21, 2015).

American School Counselor Association (2013b). *Position statement: The school counselor and students with disabilities.* Available online at www.schoolcounselor.org/asca/media/asca/PositionStatements/PS_Equity.pdf (accessed September 14, 2015).

American School Counselor Association (2014). *The ASCA mindsets & behaviors for student success: K-12 college- and career-readiness standards for every student.* Alexandria, VA: Author. Available online at https://schoolcounselor.org/asca/media/asca/home/MindsetsBehaviors.pdf (accessed August 21, 2015).

Arrington, K. (2000). Middle grades career planning programs. *Journal of Career Development, 27,* 103–109.

Association for Career and Technical Education (2014). *What is CTE?* Alexandria, VA: Author. Available online at www.acteonline.org/cte/#.VNAWD2jF-N0 (accessed December 7, 2014).

Belasco, A. S. (2013). Creating college opportunity: School counselors and their influence on postsecondary enrollment. *Research in Higher Education, 54,* 781–804.

Bennett, G. K., Seashore, H. G., & Wesman, A. G. (1975). *Differential aptitude tests.* New York: Psychological Corporation.

Bridgeland, J., & Bruce, M. (2014). *2011 national survey of school counselors.* College Board National Office for School Counselor Advocacy. Available online at www.civicenterprises.net/MediaLibrary/Docs/counseling_at_a_crossroads.pdf (accessed March 3, 2016).

Bryan, J., Moore-Thomas, C., Day-Vines, N. L., & Holcomb-McCoy, C. (2011). School counselors as social capital: The effects of high school college counseling on college application rates. *Journal of Counseling & Development, 89,* 190–199. doi:10.1002/j.1556-6678.2011.tb00077.x

College Board (2010). *Eight components of college and career readiness counseling.* National Office for School Counseling Advocacy. New York: College Board Advocacy and Policy Center. Available online at https://secure-media.collegeboard.org/digitalServices/pdf/nosca/11b_4416_8_Components_WEB_111107.pdf (accessed March 3, 2016).

College Board National Office for School Counselor Advocacy (NOSCA) (2011). *School counselors literature and landscape review: The state of school counseling in America.* Available online at http://media.collegeboard.com/digitalServices/pdf/advocacy/nosca/counselors-literature-landscape-review.pdf (accessed November 11, 2015).

Colorado Community College System (2010). *Colorado career cluster model*. Available online at www.colora-dostateplan.com/counselors.htm (accessed November 13, 2014).

Deil-Amen, R., & Tevis, T. L. (2010). Circumscribed agency: The relevance of standardized college entrance exams for low-SES high school students. *The Review of Higher Education, 33*, 141–175.

Dunn, R., Dunn, K., & Price, G. E. (1989). *Learning style inventory (LSI)*. Lawrence, KS: Price Systems.

Erikson, E. H. (1956). The problem of ego identity. *Journal of the American Psychoanalytic Association, 4*, 56–121. doi:10.1177/000306515600400104

Grodsky, E., & Jones, M. T. (2007). Real and imagined barriers to college entry: Perceptions of cost. *Social Science Research, 36*(2), 745–766.

Holcomb-McCoy, C. (2010). Involving low-income parents of color in college-readiness activities: An exploratory study. *Professional School Counseling, 14*, 115–124.

Holland, J. L. (1994). *Self-directed search*. Odessa, FL: Psychological Assessment Resources.

Hughes, K. L., Karp, M. M., Fermin, B. J., & Bailey, T. R. (2005). Pathways to college access and success. Washington, DC: US Department of Education, Office of Vocational and Adult Education. Available online at www2.ed.gov/about/offices/list/ovae/pi/cclo/cbtrans/finalreport.pdf (accessed July 21, 2014).

Individuals with Disabilities Education Improvement Act of 2004 [IDEA], 20 U.S.C. 1400 et seq. (2004).

Johnson, J., Rochkind, J., Ott, A. N., & DuPont, S. (2010). *Can I get a little advice here? How an overstretched high school guidance system is undermining students' college aspirations*. Bill and Melinda Gates Foundation. Available online at www.publicagenda.org/files/can-i-get-a-little-advice-here.pdf (accessed April 29, 2016).

Kolodinsky, P., Schroder, V., Montopoli, G., McLean, S., Mangan, P. A., & Pederson, W. (2006). The career fair as a vehicle for enhancing occupational self-efficacy. *Professional School Counseling, 10*, 161–167.

Langevin, J. (2014). Langevin and Thompson continue push for career counseling programs. Press release (May 9, 2014). *Issues: Economy and jobs, education, vote*. Available online at https://langevin.house.gov/press-release/langevin-and-thompson-continue-push-career-counseling-programs (accessed March 3, 2016).

Marcia, J. E. (1966). Development and validation of ego-identity status. *Journal of Personality and Social Psychology, 3*, 551–558.

Martin, J. (2013). Applying the essentials of financial aid to an understanding of financial aid Packaging models. In *Fundamentals of college admission counseling* (3rd ed.; pp. 80–91). National Association for College Admission Counseling.

McDonough, P. M. (2005). Counseling matters: Knowledge, assistance, and organizational commitment in college preparation. In W. G. Tierney, Z. B. Corwin, & J. E. Colyar (Eds.), *Preparing for college: Nine elements of effective outreach* (pp. 69–87). Albany, NY: State University of New York Press.

Meyers, C., Dringard, K., & Zinner, E. (1978). *What I like to do*. Chicago: Science Research Associates.

Milsom, A. (2002). Students with disabilities: School counselor involvement and preparation. *Professional School Counseling, 5*, 331–338.

Milsom, A., & Hartley, M. T. (2005). Assisting students with learning disabilities transition to college: What school counselors should know. *Professional School Counseling, 8*, 436–441.

Morgan, L. W., Greenwaldt, M. E., & Gosselin, K. P. (2014). School counselors' perceptions of competency in career counseling. *The Professional Counselor, 4*(5), 481–496. doi:10.15241/lwm.4.5.481

National Joint Committee on Learning Disabilities (1994). *Secondary to postsecondary education transition planning for students with learning disabilities. College perspectives on issues affecting learning disabilities: Position papers and statements*. Austin, TX: Pro-Ed.

Naviance (2009). *Individual student learning plans: Improving student performance*. Arlington, VA: Author.

Newman, L., Wagner, R., Cameto, R., Knokey, A. M., & Shaver, D. (2010). *Comparisons across time of the outcomes of youth with disabilities up to 4 years after high school. A report of findings from the National Longitudinal Transition Study-2 (NLTS2)*. Menlo Park, CA: SRI International.

Niles, S. G., & Harris-Bowlsbey, J. (2002) *Career Development Interventions in the 21st Century*. Columbus, OH: Merrill Prentice Hall.

Rehabilitation Act of 1973, Section 504, 29 U.S.C. 794.

Rennie Center for Educational Research and Policy (2011). *Student learning plans: Supporting every student's transition to college and career.* Cambridge, MA: Author.

Reynolds, A. (2013, August). Targeted career panels. *Career Convergence Magazine.* National Career Development Association. Available online at http://ncda.org/aws/NCDA/pt/sd/news_article/78854/_PARENT/CC_layout_details/false (accessed March 3, 2016).

Schenck, P. M., Anctil, T. M., Smith, C. K., & Dahir, C. (2012). Coming full circle: Reoccurring career development trends in schools. *The Career Development Quarterly, 60*(3), 221–230.

Southern Regional Education Board (2012). *High schools that work: 2012 assessment.* Available online at www.sreb.org/page/1078/high_schools_that_work.html (accessed July 27, 2013).

Texas Education Association (2014). *House bill 5: Foundation high school program.* House Bill 5, 83rd Texas Legislature, Regular Session, 2013. Austin, TX: Author. Available online at http://tea.texas.gov/Curriculum_and_Instructional_Programs/Graduation_Information/House_Bill_5__Foundation_High_School_Program/ (accessed March 3, 2016).

US Census Bureau (2009). *American community survey.* Suitland, MD: Author.

US Department of Education, Office of the Deputy Secretary (2010). *Race to the top.* Washington, DC: Government Printing Office. Available online at www2.ed.gov/programs/racetothetop/index.html (accessed November 3, 2014).

US Department of Education, Office of Vocational and Adult Education (2005). *Getting ready for college early: A handbook.* Washington, DC: Government Printing Office. Available online at www2.ed.gov/pubs/GettingReadyCollegeEarly/index.html (accessed October 2, 2015).

Wadsworth, J., Milsom, A., & Cocco, K. (2004). Career development for adolescents and young adults with mental retardation. *Professional School Counseling, 8,* 141–147.

Wagner, M., Newman, L., Cameto, R., Garza, N., & Levine, P. (2005). *After high school: A first look at the postschool experiences of youth with disabilities. A report from the National Longitudinal Transition Study-2 (NLTS2).* Menlo Park, CA: SRI International.

Waldo, E. (January 30, 2015). *The White House honors the 2015 school counselor of the year.* The White House Blog. Available online at www.whitehouse.gov/blog/2015/01/30/white-house-honors-2015-school-counselor-year (accessed February 4, 2015).

Wilgosh, L. (1994). Assessment of vocational preferences for young people with intellectual impairment. *Developmental Disabilities Bulletin, 22,* 63–71.

Wren, C., & Einhorn, J. (2000). *Hanging by a twig: Understanding and counseling adults with learning disabilities and ADD.* New York: Norton & Company.

Young, D. (2014). Driving question: How can we build a framework for global competency for college & career ready students for this century? *Partnership for 21st Century Skills, 1,* 6–10. Available online at www.p21.org/news-events/p21blog/1460-young-global-competency-p21s-call-to-action (accessed February 2, 2015).

Zunker, V. G. (2012). *Career counseling: A holistic approach* (8th ed.). Pacific Grove, CA: Brooks/Cole.

Chapter Eleven
Prevention/Auxiliary Programming

Traditionally, some of the ways in which school counselors have sought to impact the entire student population has been through their implementation and coordination of prevention and peer programs. School counselors have long been involved in both prevention and peer programming, as indicated by the ASCA position statements on conflict resolution and bullying/harassment prevention (ASCA, 2011), which were adopted in 1994 and revised in 2011, and peer helping, which was adopted in 1978 and most recently revised in 2015 (ASCA, 2015). In *the ASCA National Model®* (2012), devising clear guidelines for bullying and harassment is listed as an example of the type of systemic change that is relevant for school counselors. In this chapter, we review the research regarding the effectiveness of peer mediation and peer support programs, and violence and bullying prevention programs, and the school counselor's role in implementing and coordinating such programs. In addition, we provide an example of a school counselor's use of consultation and individual counseling to assist a student victim of bullying.

School Violence

School counselors have been historically associated with prevention programs that are aimed at reducing school violence. Some have argued that school counselors contribute to the academic mission of the school by addressing the social/emotional needs of students, citing Abraham Maslow's hierarchy of needs theory that posits that physical and psychological safety needs must be satisfied in order for students to attend to the higher order need of academic learning. Indeed, research studies consistently reveal that school violence is one of the strongest predictors of academic achievement (e.g., Chen & Weikart, 2008). There is evidence to suggest that school violence has declined in recent years, but aggression occurring within schools is still of concern. The percentage of students between the ages of 12 and 18 who reported being the victim of verbal abuse decreased from 12% in 2001 to 9% in 2011 (US Department of Education, 2014). Between 2007 and 2011, the percentage of students between the ages of 12 and 18 who reported being bullied decreased from 32% to 27%. The percentage of students between the ages of 12 and 18 who reported being afraid of attack or harm at school decreased from 12% in 1995 to 4% in 2011.

Box 11.2

What is School Violence?

School violence is a subset of youth violence, a broader public health problem. Violence is the intentional use of physical force or power against another person, group, or community, with the behavior likely to cause physical or psychological harm. Youth violence typically includes persons between the ages of 10 and 24, although pathways to youth violence can begin in early childhood.

Examples of violent behavior include:

- bullying
- fighting (e.g., punching, slapping, kicking)
- weapon use
- electronic aggression
- gang violence.

School violence occurs:

- on school property
- on the way to or from school
- during a school-sponsored event
- on the way to or from a school-sponsored event.

(Centers for Disease Control and Prevention, 2013)

Policymakers' recognition of the substantial role that school violence and school climate have on academic achievement is reflected in the No Child Left Behind (NCLB; 2002) Act. The "Safe and Drug-Free Schools" provision of NCLB requires that state departments of education identify schools that are unsafe. Schools that have consistently high levels of violent behavior for two years are designated as "persistently dangerous" and suffer penalties, such as voluntary student transfers. The fact that school violence is a focus of NCLB can be used by school counselors in advocating to administrators and parents for the need for prevention programs.

Risk Factors for School Violence

Risk factors for youth violence include socialization with delinquent peers, lack of parental supervision, physical and inconsistent parental discipline, and low socioeconomic status (Snyder & Sickmund, 1999).

Poor study skills, attention problems, negative attitudes toward school, and alcohol and drugs are also associated with youth violence (Henry, Tolan, Gorman-Smith, & Schoeny, 2012).

Violence Prevention Programs

There is considerable variation in the assumptions and nature of violence prevention programs. Some programs focus on tailoring individualized approaches to students who have been identified as being at risk for aggression. Violence prevention programs that are labeled as "universal" involve a curriculum that is provided to all students within a school or grade level. Finally, multiple approach programs seek to involve parents, peers, and/or the community in addition to the school's curriculum (Park-Higgerson, Perumean-Chaney, Bartolucci, Grimley, & Singh, 2008). Some violence prevention programs provide instruction regarding the causes of violence and strategies for avoiding violence (Hahn et al., 2007). Such programs assume that students often lack the skills to manage interpersonal conflict without using aggression, and provide students with conflict resolution skills, including anger management, active listening, and problem-solving. Other programs assume that aggressive students lack positive self-esteem, and teach students pro-social skills and encourage parents and teachers to reinforce students' exhibition of pro-social behaviors. For example, in the elementary level PeaceBuilders program, students are rewarded for demonstrating behaviors consistent with simple behavioral rules, such as "praise people" and "right wrongs." Many violence prevention programs are available commercially and have manuals to increase treatment fidelity.

Effectiveness of Violence Prevention Programs

The research regarding violence prevention is decidedly mixed. Hahn et al.'s (2007) meta-analysis of 53 studies of universal violence prevention programs revealed that such programs reduced violence among children at all grade levels, yielding on average a 15% decrease in the frequency of violence. Interestingly, whereas programs administered by teachers were found to be effective, programs administered by administrators and school counselors were not found to be effective. The authors did not speculate about why teacher-led violence prevention programs were found to be more effective than those led by school counselors. Perhaps this finding indicates that school counselors must receive better preparation for conducting instruction? The results of Park-Higgerson et al.'s (2008) meta-analysis of 26 randomized controlled studies of violence prevention programs differs from that of Hahn et al. (2007) in some important respects. Park-Higgerson et al. (2008) found that programs that focused on at-risk children, in comparison to universal programs, involved students in the fourth grade or higher, and were administered by education specialists, in comparison to teachers, yielded slightly stronger effects in reducing aggression.

School Bullying

Bullying is another form of aggression that is common within schools, and this form of aggression has received considerable attention from school personnel and researchers in the past decade. While school personnel may use the terms violence and bullying interchangeably, bullying is defined as a distinct form of aggression that involves the following three conditions that distinguish it from violence: (1) a person of greater power seeks to harm another; (2) the power imbalance can take a variety of forms which may include physicality, social popularity, intelligence, socioeconomic status, and race/ethnic status; and (3) the negative actions are repeated (Olweus & Limber, 2010). In summary, bullying typically differs from other forms of violence between students in that the perpetrator has greater power than the victim, and the aggressive acts are committed by the perpetrator over a period of time.

In 2011, approximately 28% of students between the ages of 12–18 reported being bullied at school during the academic year, and 9% reported experiencing cyberbullying (US Department of Education, 2014). Bullying behaviors are often categorized by type, including verbal bullying, which includes being made fun of and called names; physical bullying, which includes being pushed, shoved, tripped, or the destruction of property; and relational bullying, which includes being the subject of rumors, manipulation of a child's friendships, and social exclusion.

Risk Factors for Bullying Perpetration and Victimization

Cook, Williams, Guerra, Kim, and Sadek (2010) conducted a meta-analysis of the predictors of bullying perpetrators, those who are victims, and bully-victims. The study revealed that in comparison to non-violent peers, perpetrators of bullying are more likely to exhibit externalizing (i.e., defiance, aggression, disruption, and noncompliant responses) and internalizing behaviors (i.e., withdrawn, depressive, anxious, and avoidant responses), a lack of social competence, academic difficulties, negative attitudes and beliefs about self and others, difficulty in resolving problems with others; and experience a family environment high in conflict, a lack of parental monitoring, and negative influence by peers.

Victims of bullying exhibit internalizing and externalizing behaviors, a lack of social skills, negative cognitions about self, difficulties in resolving interpersonal conflicts, come from negative community, family, and school environments, and are rejected and isolated by peers. Bully-victims share many characteristics with victims and perpetrators. Bully-victims are more likely than their peers to demonstrate both externalizing and internalizing behaviors, have negative beliefs about themselves and others, have academic problems, lack social problem-solving skills, and are negatively influenced by and rejected by peers. Cook et al. (2010) conclude that the high level of shared predictors support the theory that the three bully status groups have a common etiology.

Social Information Processing Models and Aggression

Social information processing (SIP) models are probably the most commonly used theory to explain youth aggression, including for overt violence and bullying. Crick and Dodge (1996) assert that SIP involves five mental steps resulting in a behavioral action. Research generally supports the contention of SIP models that aggressive children exhibit deficits in social informational processing theory. Aggressive children register fewer and less benign social cues, either due to deficits in memory or selective attention (step 1), are more likely to attribute hostile intentions to the actions of others (step 2), are more likely to choose goals that damage relationships with peers (step 3), generate less pro-social responses (step 4), regard aggressive responses more favorably, expect positive outcomes from aggressive behavior, and feel confident in engaging in aggression (step 5; Camodeca & Goossens, 2005).

Proactive vs. Reactive Aggression

Another common distinction used to understand aggression in youth is reactive and proactive aggression (Camodeca & Goossens, 2005). Reactive aggression is a defensive response to perceived aggression in others and is accompanied by anger. In contrast, proactive aggression is planned, intentional use of aggression to achieve a goal, and may invoke pleasure or satisfaction. Camodeca and Goossens' (2005) review of the research indicates that perpetrators of bullying exhibit both reactive and proactive aggression, while bully-victims only show reactive aggression. Crick and Dodge (1996) found that reactively aggressive children exhibit hostile attribution bias, meaning that they tend to misperceive others to have aggressive intent, and thus respond with aggression. Proactively aggressive children regard the use of aggression more positively, viewing it as an effective way to achieve goals.

Implications of the SIP Model and Proactive and Reactive Aggression for Counseling

Both SIP models and the distinction between proactive and reactive aggression have implications for working with such students in individual and group counseling. Reactive and proactive aggressors can be assisted in learning to intentionally examine how they process social events. They can be taught the foundational principle of cognitive-behavioral theory, which is that thoughts have a strong influence upon emotions, sensations, and behaviors. They can be taught to delay their response in order to examine the accuracy of their thoughts. They can be taught to examine their goals in social situations, pro-social ways to obtain status, and to "think through" the likely consequences of their actions. For example, while bullying appears to be a fairly effective way for perpetrators to obtain status in elementary and middle school, the popularity of bullying perpetrators tends to decline in high school.

Effectiveness of Bullying Prevention

During the past several decades, many states have enacted legislation requiring schools to incorporate anti-bullying policies within their student codes of conduct and implement evidence-based bullying prevention programs. However, until recently, systematic reviews suggested that bullying prevention programs were not effective or produced only modest results. Thankfully, however, a recent meta-analysis by Ttofi and Farrington (2011) found that bullying prevention programs on average reduced the frequency of bullying by 20–23% and the number of students identifying as victims by 17–20%. Specifically, these researchers found that characteristics of bullying prevention programs that are associated with effectiveness include the intensity and duration of the program, the use of meetings to educate parents about bullying and parent-teacher conferences, and enhanced playground supervision.

Additionally, the use of firm disciplinary methods, such as employing a range of sanctions, including having teachers and administrators engage in serious talks with perpetrators, being observed by teachers during recess time, and loss of privileges, are also associated with effective bullying prevention. Working with peers, in the form of peer mediation, peer mentoring, and encouraging bystander involvement, was actually associated with increases in victimization.

Box 11.3

Essential Bullying Intervention Elements (Ttofi & Farrington, 2011)

School-based bullying prevention programs are widely implemented but not always evaluated. However, research suggests promising program elements include:

- comprehensive programs that are implemented over a long duration
- use of meetings to educate parents about bullying and parent-teacher conferences
- enhanced playground supervision
- use of firm disciplinary methods, including having serious talks with perpetrators, increased observation during recess, and loss of privileges.

The use of components of the *Olweus Bullying Prevention Program* (Olweus & Limber, 2010), which is the most commonly used program both in the United States and other countries, was also found to be a positive predictor of effectiveness.

Olweus Bullying Prevention Program (OBPP: Olweus & Limber, 2010)

The OBPP is a comprehensive, school-wide program that seeks to reduce bullying and enhance the school climate through the restructuring of the school environment. The program is based on social learning theory in its encouragement of school personnel to assume leadership in fostering a sense of community by modeling and showing interest in students. Other social learning theory tenants include the promotion of adults and, to a more limited degree, students, reducing opportunities and reinforcement for bullying. The OBPP principles suggest that school personnel, and ideally parents, (1) demonstrate warmth and interest in students; (2) establish firm expectations regarding acceptable behavior; (3) use consistent non-corporal consequences for violation of rules; and (4) serve as positive role models for students. These goals and principles are incorporated into school-level (e.g., coordination committees, training for staff, conducting a survey to determine frequency and location of bullying), classroom-level (e.g., weekly classroom lessons on bullying), Individual-level (e.g., increase supervision particularly of problem areas, individual sessions with victims and perpetrators), and community-level components (e.g., increase understanding of the issue and program within the community).

School counselors can assume a leadership role in coordinating and implementing such prevention programs as OBPP. They should be an essential member of the various planning committees of OBPP, whose responsibilities typically include data coordination, training of staff and parents, implementation of the curriculum for students, enhancing supervision for areas of the school where bullying is found to more likely occur, as indicated by surveying students, educating the larger community, etc. School counselors can coordinate the data collection for various aspects of implementing such a program. They can assess students', teachers', and parents' perceptions regarding the frequency of bullying, and their perceptions of the need for such a program. School counselors also can evaluate the effectiveness of the specific components of the program, assessing the impact of classroom lessons on helping students report bullying, more effectively managing their emotional responses to victimization, including typically rejected/isolated students in socialization, engaging in safe Internet behaviors, etc. Furthermore, school counselors can work individually with students who continue to bully even after the implementation of the program. Young et al. (2009) provide a description of how the school counselors of a middle school assumed leadership in implementing and evaluating a bullying prevention program, which eventually resulted in their principal removing their responsibility for test coordination.

School-wide Positive Behavioral Intervention and Supports (SWPBIS)

A recent trend in school-based efforts to reduce aggression has been the use of School-wide Positive Behavioral Intervention and Supports (SWPBIS). SWPBIS is a prevention-oriented multi-tiered framework for the implementation of evidence-based practices with high fidelity to promote academic and social behavioral outcomes for all students (Sugai, Horner, & Algozzine, 2011). SWPBIS is based on a behavioral model, which assumes that problematic behaviors are the result of students not understanding the behavioral expectations, lacking the behavioral skill set, and/or receiving environmental reinforcement. Whereas OBPP recommends assigning negative consequences to students who bully (Olweus &

Limber, 2010), SWPBIS emphasizes the use of reinforcement to promote pro-social or desirable behaviors and does not recommend the use of punishment to eliminate bullying behaviors (Sugai et al., 2011). However, it should be noted that the nature of consequences used in OBPP, which include firm talks with students who bully, increased supervision, etc., cannot be overly punitive.

The Tier 1 level of intervention involves teachers instructing students in how to behave in a respectful, pro-social manner through the acquisition of social skills and character traits, with the expectation that approximately 85–90% of students will respond to the universal level of intervention. At Tier 2, students who continue to display problematic behaviors are provided with additional support in the form of more intensive skills instruction, enhanced adult monitoring and positive attention, more specific and consistent feedback regarding students' behavioral progress, and additional academic supports if indicated.

Two types of Tier 3 interventions that have received empirical support, and which school counselors are often involved in implementing, are the *Behavior Education Program* (BEP) and the *Strong Kids Curriculum Program* (SKCP; Mitchell, Stormont, & Gage, 2011). In the BEP, also known as Check-In/Check-Out (CICO), the student is issued a daily behavior report card (DBRC) to document behavior aligned with school-wide expectations at Tier 1. Each morning, the student meets with an adult facilitator, then carries the DBRC to each class and receives feedback and reinforcement from the teacher using a point system. At the end of the school day, the student checks-out with the BEP facilitator and takes the form home for a parent's signature. The *Strong Kids Curriculum* seeks to promote socio-emotional competence. The 12-lesson curriculum includes the topics of identifying feelings in self and others, managing stress and anger, rational thinking, conflict resolution, and goal setting.

At Tier 3, students who did not respond to Tier 1 and 2 interventions receive even more intensive support in the way of individually tailored behavioral modification plans, and the use of mental health services, typically in the form of wraparound services. The assumption is that through the support of school and mental health personnel, the student's caregivers can modify the home environment to remove reinforcers associated with the child's aggression.

Students are often identified as in need of Tier 2 and Tier 3 interventions through the use of standardized measurements and assessment procedures. Common assessment screens include office discipline referrals (ODRs), teacher rating scales, and multiple-gate screening systems. The *Systematic Screening for Behavior Disorders* (SSBD) is a highly supported measure for identifying students at risk for internalizing and externalizing behaviors (Lane et al., 2009). The SSBD is a multiple-gated system, where students' progress into advanced gates is based upon specific criteria. At gate one, teachers rank students according to internalizing and externalizing characteristics. The top three students identified with the most concern receive further assessment. At gate two, the classroom teacher completes teacher rating scales for the six identified students. Students who receive scores exceeding normal expectations move to gate three, which involves behavioral observation in academic and social settings.

School counselors often have multiple roles to play in the SWPBIS model. They may assist teachers in implementing the universal social skills and character trait curricula at the Tier 1 level, or may coordinate the assessment procedures for identifying the necessity of moving students into Tier 2 and 3 interventions. School counselors also may be the primary implementer of social skills training at the Tier 2 and 3 levels, or may coordinate the CICO program. At the Tier 3 level, they may serve as the school liaison who seeks to increase parent involvement and provides the family with referrals for mental health services. The PBIS Center's website (www.pbis.org) has free and downloadable materials, including materials related to bullying prevention.

Peer Helping

Peer helping programs are another type of programming used by schools to improve the school's climate and promote students' socio-emotional development. Peer helping can take a variety of forms. For example, a survey conducted in 2006 found that among public schools in western New York, 34% offered peer mediation, 34% offered peer tutoring, 19% had a peer leadership program, 15% had a peer mentoring program, and 11% offered peer counseling (Bogner & Wagner, 2006). We will focus on peer mediation, as school counselors often coordinate peer mediation programs, and briefly discuss some of the other types of peer helping programs.

Box 11.4

The Professional School Counselor's Role in Peer Helping

Did you know?

The school counselor is responsible for determining the needs of the school population and for implementing a peer support program designed to meet those needs (ASCA, 2015, p. 42).

Training students to assist their peers can be advantageous for the school counseling program. Many students would prefer to obtain help from a peer rather than an adult. Peer programs can also extend the outreach of the school counseling program and increase student awareness of the services offered (ASCA, 2015). Box 11.5 identifies the responsibilities of professional school counselors in regards to peer helping programs as indicated in ASCA's (2015) position statement on peer support programs.

Box 11.5

ASCA's (2015) Position Statement Regarding the School Counselor's Role in Implementing Peer Support Programs

School counselors:

- have unique responsibilities when working with peer helping or student assistance programs and safeguard the welfare of students participating in peer-to-peer programs under their direction
- are ultimately responsible for appropriate training and supervision for students serving as peer support individuals in their school counseling programs (ASCA, 2010; Latham, 1997)
- create a selection plan for peer helpers reflecting the diversity of the population to be served
- develop a support system for the program that communicates the program's goals and purpose through positive public relations
- monitor, evaluate and adjust the program and training on a continual basis to meet the assessed needs of the school population the program services
- report results to all school stakeholders (e.g., students, teachers, administrators, parents, community).

Reproduced with permission from the American School Counselor Association (2015). *Position statement: The school counselor and peer support programs*. Available online at www.schoolcounselor.org/asca/media/asca/PositionStatements/PS_PeerHelping.pdf (accessed September 18, 2015).

Peer Mediation

Peer mediation programs involve training students to conduct mediation with students engaged in conflict. In many peer mediation programs, the trained students conduct formal mediation sessions with peers who either requested the assistance of a mediator, or were referred to mediation by a teacher or administrator. Typically, formal mediation sessions involve two trained mediators and the disputants, and there is a school personnel member who has also received peer mediation training who oversees the session. However, peer mediation programs are also used with the presumption that there is a spillover effect whereby students who are trained in mediation and conflict resolution will utilize these skills with their peers and family members outside of formal mediation sessions. Therefore, school counselors hope that the students who participate in the mediation process will obtain conflict resolution skills that they apply in subsequent conflicts.

Box 11.6

Factors Essential to Making Peer Mediation Work

- Planning: Effective peer mediation programs require advance planning, considering such issues as how mediators will be chosen, where and when the mediation will occur, and what types of conflicts peer mediators can address, among others.
- Training: The initial training of peer mediators requires 12–15 hours, in which students will learn the basic principles of peer mediation, why conflict occurs, etc. Students will also be taught communication and problem-solving strategies to defuse conflict. Role-playing and active learning help students to move toward solutions for all students involved in conflict.
- Ongoing Implementation: Ongoing monitoring of the program is important for its success, including the extent to which mediators are used, the success of the mediators, and how the mediators and their peers view the success of the program. Weekly or bi-weekly training should be planned for mediators, and peer mediation should be part of a whole-school effort (Skiba & Peterson, 2000).

Empirical support for peer mediation. Research suggests that peer mediation benefits both students trained to be peer mediators, and the study body as a whole. Peterson and Skiba (2001) concluded from a review of the research literature that peer mediation training increased the self-esteem and academic achievement of peer mediators. Other studies have found that students trained to be peer mediators successfully learned and retained the steps of conflict resolution for up to at least six months (Johnson & Johnson, 1996). From a review of the research literature, Carruthers and Sweeney (1996) concluded that peer mediators experience an improvement in their attitudes toward school, and the parents of mediators reported observing an improvement in their child's grades and attitudes toward school.

Johnson and Johnson's (2004) meta-analytic study of the efficacy of the *Teaching Students to be Peacemakers program* (TSP), which includes both conflict resolution and peer mediation, revealed increased academic achievement and long-term retention of academic material, and a marked decrease in discipline referrals. Peer mediation also appears to benefit the students who receive peer mediation. Generally, studies indicate that disputants reach agreement 80 to 95% of the time (Carruthers & Sweeney, 1996). However, the most frequent agreement achieved by disputants is to avoid or ignore each other (Johnson & Johnson, 1996).

Cantrell, Parks-Savage, and Rehfuss (2007) conducted one of the few longitudinal studies on the effectiveness of a peer mediation program. They found the *Peace Pal program* had a number of positive benefits for an elementary school. The program yielded a decrease in total out-of-school suspensions for each of the three post-program years for both White and African American students. Nearly all of the disputants reported being satisfied with the results of the peer mediation sessions. Furthermore, the students who were trained as peer mediators demonstrated an increase in knowledge concerning conflict resolution and mediation, and they viewed the program as valuable.

Training/program implementation for peer mediation. While peer mediation training programs vary, most programs focus on helping students understand the nature of conflict and its causes, and teaching peer mediators communication, problem-solving, and negotiation skills (Smith & Daunic, 2002). In addition, much of the training in peer mediation programs involves teaching students the mediation process. An example of the steps of mediation can found in Box 11.7.

Implementing a peer mediation program requires considerable planning and resources (Smith & Daunic, 2002). Some studies have found that it takes two to five years before a peer mediation program demonstrates positive results, as both students and teachers gradually accept peer mediation as a legitimate conflict resolution process (e.g., Cameron & Dupuis, 1991). The school must determine which students and staff will receive training, when and where mediation will occur, what the referral process will be, and which types of conflicts mediators will address. School counselors often coordinate the peer mediation program and train the peer mediators, given their training in communication skills and focus on social/emotional development. However, it is recommended that school counselors collaborate with other school personnel in coordinating the peer mediation program for a variety of reasons. Training teachers to serve as observers of mediations serves to extend the reach of the program, and hopefully increases teachers' investment in the program, which is essential for the success of the peer mediation program. Furthermore, involving other, hopefully influential, school personnel increases the likelihood that the program will transform the school culture, by not only impacting how students resolve interpersonal conflict, but also by modifying the relationships between students and teachers.

Box 11.7

Steps of Mediation

- Laying the Ground Rules

  "How this works is that both of you will have a chance to explain your concerns, meaning what is bothering you. While the one person is speaking, the other person is listening, trying to understand how the other person sees the problem. When the person is done talking, the listener will explain what he or she heard the other person saying. Then the listener will have a chance to say how he or she sees things. Once we think we really understand how the other person sees the problem, then we will talk about what it is that we want from each other. Finally, we will talk about ideas about how we can get what we want from each other. Are you each willing to take turns in talking with each other? Another important rule in here is that you must be respectful, meaning that you will not make nasty comments or put the other person down. Are you willing to be respectful toward each other?"

- Understanding Each Other

  It is usually best to have the original complainant start speaking first since he or she has a more clear idea of what is bothering him or her. The mediators should keep notes to help them identify the students' issues. Once the complainant is finished, a mediator can ask the listener, "Tell Jennifer what you heard her saying just now." Obviously a potential problem is that the listener interrupts the speaker in an attempt to defend him or herself. The mediator may remind the listener that he or she will have a turn soon. Or, the listener may take the offensive and say something nasty, at which point the mediator can remind him

---

or her about the agreement to be respectful. Once the listener has stated back to the speaker what he or she heard him or her saying, the mediator should ask the speaker, "Do you think the listener heard what you had to say?" If the speaker thinks the listener has not heard him or her, the mediator should ask the speaker to help the listener to better understand him or her by pointing out what the listener left out or where he or she is confused. Only once the speaker feels that he or she has been "heard" should the mediators move on to having the listener talk about how he or she sees it, repeating the process.

- Identifying Wants

  An indication that the disputants understand each other is that there is a noticeable reduction in tension and they have little left to share. Next, the mediator should ask the students to talk to each other about what it is that they want. The mediators may have to help the students with identifying their wants, and the mediator can refer to their notes for comments made earlier by the disputants that imply a want. The mediator can summarize the disputants' wants. For example, "Jennifer, what I hear that you want from Amy is that you want Amy to come to you and tell you if she is angry with you, rather than saying things to other people. Is that right?" Then you repeat the process for Jennifer. What would she want the other person to do if she was angry? Where? When? How?

- Exploring Solutions

  Next, the mediators should identify areas of agreement between the students. For example, "Jennifer and Amy, I hear that both of you want the other to be upfront about disagreements, meaning if you're angry with each other, you will share it with each other. Is that correct?" The mediators may further explore with the disputants how they plan on carrying out the agreed-upon solution. For example, the mediators may ask them how they want to interact the next time they see each other. For younger (below the age of 14) and concrete operational students, you may wish to do a more formal brainstorming session in which you write down each suggested solution without evaluation. Once each of the students has identified at least a couple of solutions, you want to have them evaluate each one and ask if they are willing to do that suggested solution. Once they've identified agreed solutions, you have them sign the solution page, as if it were a contract.

  Source: Adapted from Kolbert, J. B., & Field, J. E. (2004, June). The steps of mediation for school counselors. *The Pennsylvania Counselor, LI*(5), 14–16.

Sellman (2011) concluded from his qualitative examination of nine schools that implemented peer mediation programs in England that successful peer mediation programs resulted in more egalitarian relationships between students and teachers. He also concluded that for programs to be effective, the staff needed to concede ownership of the program to students, and permit students to resolve interpersonal conflict through peer mediation in contrast to the traditional response of teachers addressing student conflict through their application of punitive measures.

The training and selection of peer mediators is an ongoing process, as new mediators must be continually identified as the former peer mediators graduate. Day-Vines, Day-Hairston, Carruthers, Wall, and Lupton-Smith (1996) recommend that the peer mediators vary in terms of academic abilities, gender, and cultural background. Such diversity can increase the perspective-taking of the mediators, and possibly increase the students' use of the peer mediation program if they see peer mediators who are similar to themselves. Students should also be selected for their communication and problem-solving skills. The initial training of peer mediators is often a one- to two-day affair, and it is recommended that this training occur after school or on a weekend to avoid interfering with academic time. In this initial training, peer mediators gain an understanding of conflict, practice active listening skills, learn the steps of mediation, and role-play mediation sessions. Typically, new peer mediators undergo an apprenticeship period in which they observe real mediation sessions conducted by more experienced peer mediators. Teachers who observe the mediations should provide immediate feedback to the peer mediators following sessions, and booster training for both the peer mediators and involved teachers are required to increase treatment fidelity.

Peer Helping/Support

In peer helping/support, selected students are trained by the school counselor to assist their peers with slight to moderate problems. McGannon, Carey, and Dimmitt (2005) concluded from the quite limited literature that peer helpers benefited to a larger degree in comparison to the students to whom they were providing services. There are also a number of other concerns with peer helping programs, including how to ensure that the peer helpers maintain the confidentiality of their peers' concerns and do not address issues that are beyond their level of training. School counselors are ethically responsible for the welfare of both the helper and student receiving help, and thus there must be considerable investment in the oversight of the peer helping program, and the training of the peer helpers. The training for peer helpers must include an understanding of the role of the helper, active listening skills, helping a peer in the process of problem-solving, and confidentiality and its limitations. Additionally, peer helping programs may consider providing training in understanding aggression and its various forms, including sexual harassment, bullying, dating violence, etc. There are many tasks that can be included in a peer helper program but a word of caution is to not overwhelm the students with too much information or duties that are developmentally inappropriate. Most peer helpers are dedicated to assisting others and can become easily overwhelmed themselves with other students' life difficulties. Helpers must also be taught how to disengage from others' pain.

Peer Tutoring

Typically, school counselors do not coordinate programs involving peer tutoring, which is sometimes also referred to as peer assisted learning. However, school counselors may be involved in peer tutoring programs in the way of instructing peer tutors in active listening skills and referring students to the school counselor.

Evaluation of Peer Programs

The National Association of Peer Programs (NAPP) has developed a rubric for evaluation and program implementation (Black, Routson, Spight, Tindall, & Wegner, 2007). Utilizing formative or process data, such as the number of peer helpers, number of interventions, selection process, types of services, and program activities is helpful in the evaluation of provided services. However, more importantly, coordinators of the peer programs must evaluate the impact of the program in terms of behavioral and/or academic outcomes. Results data will include whether the activities and/or program achieved the established goals. Assessments can include perception data with surveys, pre-post assessments, and opinion data. Utilization of achievement-related data such as school-wide trends in discipline reports or attendance rates may be helpful for demonstrating outcomes. Another method of results data may include achievement data that is specific to topics covered within the program, such as the impact of the program on peer helpers' grade point average or state achievement test scores.

Social and Emotional Learning Programs (SEL)

A common criticism of some violence and bullying prevention programs is that they emphasize the elimination of problematic behaviors. In other words, the criticism is that these programs focus on what students should not be doing rather than instructing students in pro-social behaviors, meaning what students should be doing. Some educators have even argued that by focusing on aggression and defining its various forms, etc., such programs actually have the potential for increasing aggression by teaching children who are prone to aggression more sophisticated ways of harming others. Certainly, SWPBIS (Sugai et al., 2011) and violence prevention programs that provide instruction in non-violent conflict resolution strategies emphasize the acquisition of pro-social behaviors. However, other types of programs aimed at promoting pro-social behavior are programs that involve social and emotional learning (SEL).

SEL has been defined as the "process of acquiring core competencies to recognize and manage emotions, set and achieve positive goals, appreciate the perspectives of others, establish and maintain positive relationships, make responsible decisions, and handle interpersonal situations constructively" (Elias et al., 1997, p. 5). SEL programs seek to promote the development of self-awareness, self-regulation/management, social awareness, relationship skills, and responsible decision-making (Collaborative for Academic, Social, and Emotional Learning; CASEL, 2005). Over time, theoretically speaking, the development of these SEL competencies in students results in a shift from being controlled by external factors to behaving in accordance with one's internalized values and assuming responsibility for one's choices.

SEL school-based programs are comprised of two coordinated sets of strategies (CASEL, 2005). The first involves teaching students to process and selectively apply social and emotional skills in a developmentally and contextually appropriate fashion through modeling and practice. Some SEL programs instruct students in applying such skills to specific problems, including interpersonal violence, bullying, school failure, and substance use. The second set of strategies involves the establishment of safe, caring learning environments through improved classroom management and teaching practices. The *Second Step Violence Prevention Curriculum* (Committee for Children, 2004), which is designed to decrease violence through enhanced empathy and social skills and decreases in aggressive behaviors, may be the most commonly used social-emotional learning program. Indeed, the Center for School Counseling Outcome Research and Evaluation (CSCORE) concluded that there is strong empirical support for the *Second Step Violence Prevention Curriculum* (Carey, Dimmitt, Hatch, Lapan, & Whiston, 2008).

The Collaborative for Academic, Social, and Emotional Learning established the acronym of SAFE for representing best practices in implementing SEL programs. S refers to Sequencing, meaning that new and complicated skills are divided into smaller components and sequentially practiced. A stands for Active, which refers to the use of active forms of learning. F refers to Focus, in that sufficient time and practice must be committed in order for students to acquire an SEL behavior. Finally, E stands for Explicit, which means that the learning objectives are very specific.

A meta-analysis provides empirical support for SEL programs (Durlak, Weissberg, Dymnicki, Taylor, & Schellinger, 2011). The results revealed that, in comparison to controls, students participating in SEL programs acquired the intended social and emotional skills and exhibited decreases in emotional distress and the frequency of conduct problems. Moreover, SEL programs resulted in an 11-percentile-point gain in academic achievement. SEL programs were found to be effective across educational levels (elementary, middle, and high school) and in rural, suburban, and urban schools. Programs implemented by school personnel yielded increases in academic achievement, whereas programs implemented by non-school personnel (e.g., university researchers or outside consultants) did not.

Programs that were consistent with the best practice SAFE acronym outperformed programs that did not meet these criteria. Interestingly, programs that included multi-components, meaning programs that included parent training or school-wide initiatives to create new policies in addition to classroom instruction, were not as effective as programs involving classroom instruction alone. The researchers believe that this may have been due to the fact that multi-component programs were less likely to follow the criteria for best practices, and experienced more problems with implementation. The researchers recommended that SEL programs follow best practices as revealed through research. They also noted that while 59% of schools have programming to promote students' social and emotional competence (Foster et al., 2005), many programs do not use evidence-based programs or implement them with poor fidelity (Ringwalt et al., 2009).

Case Study

Josh, a seventh grade student, is enrolled in the Gifted and Talented Program. During a meeting of Josh's team teachers, they express concern for his lack of academic motivation and negative peer relations. The teachers report that, despite his intelligence, Josh is failing several of his classes, as he often fails to complete assignments. Furthermore, they note that Josh seems excluded by both the regular education and gifted students, and report warning several students who appeared to be making fun of him. They refer Josh to you, the school counselor.

Your first impression upon meeting Josh is that he has some of the physical characteristics associated with children who are frequently bullied. He is short and skinny, wears glasses, his hair is disheveled, and his clothing is somewhat outdated. Josh states that he really does not understand why he has been asked to come to your office, as he just wants to be left alone. You explain that the teachers were concerned about his grades and the fact that he often seems lonely. Josh quickly retorts that grades are meaningless as school has not taught him anything, and that he couldn't care less about having friends since all the other students in the school are a "bunch of jerks." Despite Josh's reassurance that everything is okay with him, you remain concerned, sensing that he is very unhappy and negative about many aspects of his life.

In your second meeting, you continue to focus on developing rapport with Josh. Although he claims he does not want to change anything about his life, he seems to enjoy meeting with you, and readily shares with you his interest in science fiction. Your developing sense of Josh is that he is aware of his intelligence, but he is confused and hurt by the rejection by his peers, particularly his fellow gifted students, although he continues to deny any interest in developing friendships. He expresses considerable anger toward his parents, whom he also sees as trying to control him. Josh reports that his father requires him to play basketball in the local recreational league, and insists that Josh try out for the school basketball team each year, which so far he has failed to make. He expresses having no interest in sports. Josh shares that he has tried to explain to his dad that he just wants to be left alone. Josh grudgingly gives his approval for you to meet with his parents, hoping that this might get him out of having to play sports.

Upon meeting Josh's parents, your impression is that they are very concerned about him, taking an active interest in his grades and encouraging him to make friends through requiring him to play sports, which they both reported having been heavily involved in during their childhoods. They express considerable concern, reporting that Josh often avoids them and spends most of his time at home in his room reading science fiction books. His father shared that upon returning from school one day Josh seemed furious, stating that he hated himself and all the kids at school. His parents express feeling helpless and generally seem open to suggestions. You affirm the appropriateness of their expectation of wanting Josh to develop social connections. However, you encourage them to grant Josh more latitude in choosing his social activities, and suggest discussions with him about the types of activities and people with whom he will feel comfortable. His parents decide to continue to require Josh to be socially active but explain to him that he can decide what those activities will be.

You decide to observe Josh in class. You notice that when the teacher asks the students to form into groups to complete a class assignment, Josh sits passively, staring down at his desk, seemingly waiting to be picked. The teacher eventually assigns him to a group with two other students who failed to find a group. During the group interaction, Josh frequently makes sarcastic comments about his classmates' suggestions. One of the group mates responds with a sarcastic remark, and Josh responds by withdrawing from the group, pulling a science fiction book out of his desk.

In your third meeting with Josh, you explore his reactions to your meeting with his parents. Although Josh does not appear pleased that his parents will still require him to be involved in an extracurricular activity, he seems to like the idea that he can select the activity. You ask him what activities he has been considering, and he reports that he is unsure. He agrees to your suggestion that he reviews a list of the school's student clubs and organizations. You indicate that you think that Josh's willingness to consider seeking to become involved in an organization is courageous, as it takes strength to consider taking such a risk. Josh admits to feeling somewhat anxious about joining a group. The remainder of the meeting focuses upon what he has learned about what works and does not work for him in connecting with other students. He is able to identify several of his strengths, including his intelligence and interest in science fiction. You take a risk by sharing that you while you genuinely appreciate Josh's intelligence, you wonder if other students might be annoyed or even hurt by his use of sarcasm. Josh appears to accept this perspective, stating that he notices that sometimes people do seem to get annoyed with him.

Over the course of three additional meetings over the course of a month and a half, Josh eventually joined the drama productions club. By the end of the seventh grade, Josh had appeared to make considerable progress. He seemed to enjoy coming to school and his grades had improved. Although he never seemed to develop friendships among his gifted and talented peers, he no longer seemed upset by their apparent rejection, and thus his need to defend himself through sarcasm dissipated.

Case Study Analysis

Josh shares some of the risk factors common to bully-victims, including negative beliefs about self and others, academic problems, and rejection by peers (Cook et al., 2010), and he can be considered a reactive aggressor rather than a proactive aggressor (e.g., Camodeca & Goossens, 2005). While many children who engage in bullying intentionally seek to harm or embarrass others, Josh appeared to use his sarcastic wit in an attempt to preemptively manage his expectation that he would be rejected.

The school counselor recognized the discrepancy between Josh's verbal statements that he wanted to be left alone, and his actions, which indicated that he enjoyed talking to the school counselor. The school counselor effectively developed rapport with Josh before focusing on his parents' and teachers' expectations that he should learn to interact more effectively with others. The establishment of rapport appeared to increase Josh's willingness to examine adults' expectations of him and made him more receptive to the school counselor's feedback for Josh regarding how his sarcasm was perceived by other students. Another factor that likely contributed to the successful outcome was the fact that Josh was highly intelligent, and merely needed an opportunity to problem-solve about what had become a fairly charged emotional issue between him and his parents.

Although the school counselor only had one in-person consultation with the parents, it most likely made a significant contribution to Josh's successful outcome. When consulting with parents, it is helpful to hypothesize about their strengths and potential areas for improvement. The parents were eager to assist their son and recognized that he needed to develop his social skills. However, the requirement that he attempt to connect with others through sports was developmentally inappropriate, as Josh's parents needed to begin to allow Josh more power, and to help him identify his strengths and interests. They were unfortunately applying to Josh what had worked for them, namely, learning to connect with others through sports.

It is interesting to note that the school counselor did not focus explicitly upon Josh's experiences with bullying, nor did the school counselor focus upon Josh's grades. Provocative victim is a term that is sometimes used to describe bully-victims, one that seemed to fit Josh. Other students probably did not like being the brunt of Josh's sarcasm, and did not see that he was attempting to defend himself psychologically. Rather than acquire information about the nature of the bullying incidents Josh had experienced, the school counselor elected to focus upon helping him to learn to reduce his sarcasm, and helping him develop his social niche. The school counselor intentionally chose not to focus upon Josh's grades because this did not appear to be the most pressing issue to Josh or even his parents.

Summary

Involvement in prevention and peer helping programs offers school counselors an avenue for making a broad impact on the school environment. Whereas stakeholders may fail to identify the subtle improvements generated by individual counseling, involvement in prevention and peer helping programs may be a concrete indicator to students, parents, teachers, and administrators that the school counselor is an integral member of the school staff. As with any activity, school counselors must also weigh the positive impact of involvement in such programs against the time and resources they require. This is particularly true for school counselors who coordinate such programs, as the time involved in effectively implementing such programs can be substantial. Ideally, school counselors should seek to disperse the responsibilities for implementing such programs by adopting a team approach in which there are teachers, parents, and at least one administrator who collaborate in leading the prevention program. A team approach is also probably more likely to infuse the curriculum throughout the school.

References

American School Counselor Association (2010). *Ethical standards for school counselors.* Available online at www. schoolcounselor.org/files/EthicalStandards2010.pdf (accessed December 10, 2014).

American School Counselor Association (2011). *Position statement: Bullying, harassment, and violence prevention programs.* Available online at http://schoolcounselor.org/asca/media/asca/home/position%20statements/PS_Bullying.pdf (accessed December 15, 2014).

American School Counselor Association (2012). *The ASCA national model: A framework for school counseling programs* (3rd ed.). Alexandria, VA: Author.

American School Counselor Association (2015). *Position statement: The school counselor and peer support programs.* Available online at www.schoolcounselor.org/asca/media/asca/PositionStatements/PS_PeerHelping.pdf (accessed September 18, 2015).

Black, D. R., Routson, S., Spight, D. L., Tindall, J. A., & Wegner, C. (2007). NAPP rubric for peer helping programs. *Perspectives in Peer Programs, 20,* 71–92.

Bogner, R. G., & Wagner, M. (2006). Western New York State peer helping/empowerment program survey results. *Perspectives in Peer Programs, 20,* 2–11.

Cameron, J., & Dupuis, A. (1991). Lessons from New Zealand's first school mediation service: Hagley High School 1987–1989. *Australian Dispute Resolution Journal, 2*, 84–92.

Camodeca, M., & Goossens, F. A. (2005). Aggression, social cognitions, anger and sadness in bullies and victims. *Journal of Child Psychology and Psychiatry, 46*, 186–197.

Cantrell, R., Parks-Savage, A., & Rehfuss, J. (2007). Reducing levels of elementary school violence with peer mediation. *Professional School Counseling, 10*, 475–481.

Carey, J. C., Dimmitt, C., Hatch, T. A., Lapan, R. T., & Whiston, S. C. (2008). Report of the National Panel for Evidence-Based School Counseling: Outcome research coding protocol and evaluation of Student Success Skills and Second Step. *Professional School Counseling, 11*, 197–206.

Carruthers, W. L., & Sweeney, B. (1996). Conflict resolution: An examination of the research literature and a model for program evaluation. *The School Counselor, 44*, 5–18.

Centers for Disease Control and Prevention, Injury Prevention and Control: Division of Violence Prevention (2014). *Youth bullying: What does the research say?* Available online at www.cdc.gov/violenceprevention/youthviolence/bullyingresearch/index.html (accessed February 11, 2015).

Centers for Disease Control and Prevention, Youth Risk Behavior Surveillance System (YRBSS) (2013). *2013 National Youth Risk Behavior Survey overview.* Available online at www.cdc.gov/healthyyouth/yrbs/pdf/trends/us_violenceschool_trend_yrbs.pdf (accessed October 11, 2014).

Chen, G., & Weikart, L. A. (2008). Student background, school climate, school disorder, and student achievement: An empirical study of New York City's middle schools. *Journal of School Violence, 7*, 3–20.

Collaborative for Academic, Social, and Emotional Learning (2005). *Safe and sound: An educational leader's guide to evidence-based social and emotional learning programs – Illinois edition.* Chicago: Author.

Committee for Children (2004). *Knowledge assessment for Second Step: A violence prevention curriculum.* Seattle, WA: Author.

Cook, C. R., Williams, K. R., Guerra, N. G., Kim, T. E., & Sadek, S. (2010). Predictors of bullying and victimization in childhood and adolescence: A meta-analytic investigation. *School Psychology Quarterly, 25*, 65–83.

Crick, N. R., & Dodge, K. A. (1996). Social information processing theory mechanisms in reactive and proactive aggression. *Child Development, 67*, 993–1002.

Day-Vines, N., Day-Hairston, B., Carruthers, W., Wall, J., & Lupton-Smith, H. (1996). Conflict resolution: The value of diversity in the recruitment, selection, and training of peer mediators. *School Counselor, 43*, 392–410.

Durlak, J. A., Weissberg, R. P., Dymnicki, A. B., Taylor, R. D., & Schellinger, K. B. (2011). The impact of enhancing students' social and emotional learning: A meta-analysis of school-based universal interventions. *Child Development, 81*, 405–432.

Elias, M. J., Zins, J. E., Weissberg, R. P., Frey, K. S., Greenberg, M. T., Haynes, N. M. Kessler, R., Schwar-Stone, M. E., & Shriver, T. P. (1997). *Promoting social and emotional learning: Guidelines for educators.* Alexandria, VA: Association for Supervision and Curriculum Development.

Foster, S., Rollefson, M., Doksum, T., Noonan, D., Robinson, G., & Teich, J. (2005). *School mental health services in the United States, 2002–2003* [DHHS Pub. No. (SMA) 05-4068]. Rockville, MD: Center for Mental Health Services, Substance Abuse and Mental Health Services Administration.

Hahn, R., Fuqua-Whitley, D., Wethington, H., Lowy, J., Crosby, A., Fullilove, M., Johnson, R., Liberman, A., Moscicki, E., Price, L., Snyder, S., Tuma, F., Cory, S., Stone, G., Mukhopadhaya, K., Chattopadhyay, S., & Dahlberg, L. (2007). *The effectiveness of universal school-based programs for the prevention of violent and aggressive behavior.* Atlanta, GA: Center for Disease Control and Prevention.

Henry, D. B., Tolan, P. H., Gorman-Smith, D., & Schoeny, M. E. (2012). Risk and direct protective factors for youth violence: Results from the Centers for Disease Control and Prevention's multisite violence prevention project. *American Journal of Preventive Medicine, 43*, 67–75.

Johnson, D. W., & Johnson, R. T. (1996). Conflict resolution and peer mediation programs in elementary and secondary schools: A review of the research. *Review of Educational Research, 66*, 459–506.

Johnson, D. W., & Johnson, R. T. (2004). Implementing the teaching students to be peacemakers program. *Theory Into Practice, 43*, 68–79.

Kolbert, J. B., & Field, J. E., (2004, June). The steps of mediation for school counselors. *The Pennsylvania Counselor*, *LI*(5), 14–16.

Lane, K. L., Little, M. A., Casey, A. M., Lambert, W., Wehby, J., Weisenback, J., & Phillips, A. (2009). A comparison of systematic screening tools for emotional and behavioral disorders. *Journal of Emotional and Behavioral Disorders*, *7*, 93–105.

Latham, A. S. (1997). Peer counseling: Proceed with caution. *Educational Leadership*, *55*, 77–78.

McGannon, W., Carey, J., & Dimmitt, C. (2005). *The current status of school counseling outcome research*. Monographs of the Center for School Counseling Outcome Research, *2*. Available online at http://eric.ed.gov/?id=ED512567 (accessed March 23, 2015).

Mitchell, B. S., Stormont, M., & Gage, N. A. (2011). Tier two interventions implemented within the context of a tiered prevention framework. *Behavioral Disorders*, *36*, 241–261.

No Child Left Behind Act of 2001, Pub. L. No. 107–110 (2002).

Olweus, D., & Limber, S. P. (2010). Bullying in school: Evaluation and dissemination of the Olweus Bullying Prevention Program. *American Journal of Orthopsychiatry*, *80*, 124–134.

Park-Higgerson, H., Perumean-Chaney, S. E., Bartolucci, A. A., Grimley, D. M., & Singh, K. P. (2008). The evaluation of school-based violence prevention programs: A meta-analysis. *Journal of School Health*, *78*, 465–479.

Peterson, R. K., & Skiba, R. (2001). Creating school climates that prevent school violence. *The Social Studies*, *92*, 167–175.

Positive Behavior Intervention and Supports: OSEP Technical Assistance Center (n.d.). *SWPBIS for beginners*. Available online at www.pbis.org/school/swpbis-for-beginners (accessed April 11, 2015).

Ringwalt, C., Vincus, A. A., Hanley, S., Ennett, S. T., Bowling, J. M., & Rohrbach, L. A. (2009). The prevalence of evidence-based drug use prevention curricula in US middle schools in 2005. *Prevention Science*, *10*, 33–40.

Sellman, E. (2011). Peer mediation services for conflict resolution in schools: What transformations in activity characterize successful implementation? *British Educational Research Journal*, *37*, 45–60.

Skiba, R., & Peterson, R. (2000). *Creating a positive climate: Peer mediation. Safe & Responsive Schools*. Available online at www.schoolcounselor.org/asca/media/asca/Resource%20Center/Mentoring-Peer%20Mediation/Sample%20Documents/PeerMediation.pdf (accessed October 8, 2014).

Smith, S. W., & Daunic, A. P. (2002). Using conflict resolution and peer mediation to support positive behavior. In G. Algozzine & P. Kay (Eds.), *Preventing problem behaviors: A handbook of successful of successful prevention strategies* (pp. 142–161). Thousand Oaks, CA: Corwin Press.

Snyder, H. N., & Sickmund, M. (1999). *Juvenile and offender victims: 1999 national report*. Washington, DC: Office of Juvenile Justice and Delinquency Prevention.

Sugai, G., Horner, R., & Algozzine, B. (2011). Reducing the effectiveness of bullying behavior in schools. Available online at www.pbis.org/common/cms/files/pbisresources/PBIS_Bullying_Behavior_Apr19_2011.pdf (accessed March 3, 2016).

Ttofi, M. M., & Farrington, D. P. (2011). Effectiveness of school-based programs to reduce bullying: A systematic and meta-analytic review. *Journal of Experimental Criminology*, *7*, 27–56.

US Department of Education (2014). *Indicators of school crime and safety: 2013*. Available online at http://nces.ed.gov/pubs2014/2014042.pdf (accessed April 21, 2015).

Young, A., Hardy, V., Hamilton, C., Biernessen, K., Sun, L., & Niebergall, S. (2009). Empowering students: Using data to transform a bullying prevention and intervention program. *Professional School Counseling*, *12*, 413–420.

Chapter Twelve
Helping Students with Exceptionalities

Box 12.1

2016 CACREP School Counseling Specialty Area Standards

2.d School counselor roles in school leadership and multidisciplinary teams

3.d Interventions to promote academic development

3.e Use of developmentally appropriate career counseling interventions and assessments

3.g Strategies to facilitate school and postsecondary transitions

---

The ASCA National Model® (2012) themes of advocacy and social justice indicate that school counselors should seek to promote the academic, social/emotional, and career development of all students. Historically, school counselors' involvement with students with disabilities has been idiosyncratic, meaning that it has depended upon the formal or informal role description of the school counselor in a particular school or district. However, as the school counseling profession has sought to play a more active role in educational reform, school counselors have been encouraged by the ASCA and the Education Trust to seek to identify and address achievement gaps of all typically disadvantaged groups, including students with disabilities.

Activities provided to children with exceptionalities by school counselors often center around: (a) delivering counseling support as described in Chapter 6; (b) encouraging increased family involvement in the child's educational process, such as understanding the nature of the child's exceptionality and the supports and adaptations required for improved school functioning; and (c) consulting and collaborating with other school staff to comprehensively promote the child's success, often through 504 plans or Individualized Education Plans (IEPs), and addressing the unique career development needs of students with disabilities. It is important to note that ASCA also cautions school counselors to refrain from engaging in any inappropriate *supervisory* responsibilities for children receiving special education services, including oversight regarding the writing or implementation of the IEP, or serving as the formal district representative (i.e., local educational agent; LEA) responsible for fiduciary considerations on behalf of the district. Additionally, although school counselors are considered to be important members of the child study team, they do not singularly make decisions about the child's placement or grade retention (ASCA, 2013a).

In order to identify the best approach for helping students with special needs, it is best to review a few definitions and the responsibilities required by schools. In this way, school counselors can feel more surefooted in the decisions they make and approaches used to engage families. Since 1973, all children – including those with disabilities – have been guaranteed the right to a free and appropriate public education (FAPE; National Center for Learning Disabilities, 2014). Appropriate means an *Individualized Education Plan* (IEP).

Students who do not meet IDEA's eligibility requirements may not receive special education services, although they may qualify to receive accommodations within the general education setting if they meet the conditions set forth by Section 504 of the Vocational Rehabilitation Act of 1973, which requires that students have a "physical or mental impairment which substantially limits one or more of such person's major life activities and has a record of impairment." Major life activities include such things as walking, seeing, hearing, and learning. Conditions for which students typically receive a 504 plan include a temporary (e.g., broken leg) or permanent (e.g., asthma, diabetes, epilepsy) medical condition, emotional disorders (e.g., depression, anxiety, obsessive-compulsive disorder), etc. In summary, for students who do not meet the eligibility requirements for an IEP, schools and parents have the option of considering a 504 plan.

IDEA has gone through several reauthorizations, with each review adding to the list of services required for students with disabilities. For example, IDEA now requires a LEA, also known as a school, to ensure due process to settle disputes, to provide educational services to students in the least restrictive environment (LRE) in their home district, and most recently the definition has been modified to mean the student is included in general education classes to the greatest extent possible (National Center for Learning Disabilities, 2014). Students with an IEP have a highly defined set of parameters for service provision, including how they are evaluated (comprehensive evaluation), when they are evaluated (every three years at a minimum), who must be consulted, timelines for decisions, access to services that meet their individual needs, LRE, written notification for changes in their placements, timelines for reviewing the IEP progress, annual reviews about the appropriateness of IEP goals, and access to an impartial hearing when there are disputes (DREDF, n.d.) in order to ensure their education program is *individualized*. There are strong sanctions for failing to adhere to special education legal requirements (e.g., district reimbursement for attorney fees; district-funded compensatory education; the Department of Education can refer noncompliant states to the Department of Justice; the Office of Special Education Programs (OSEP) can withhold funds in whole or in part from states, based on the degree of noncompliance found, among other options; Wright & Wright, n.d.).

Special Education Overview

There are two models for school districts to use in determining a student's eligibility for special education services. For a referral for a learning problem, schools may use the traditional process, which is referred to as the discrepancy model, which requires the student to exhibit a significant difference between his or her achievement and intelligence, as measured by individualized, standardized instruments that measure academic achievement and intellectual functioning, and ideally are normed on the same sample of students (e.g., the WISC-IV and the WIAT-III).

Box 12.2

Acceptance for RtI Models May Be Growing

A national sample of practicing school psychologists and members of the National Association of School Psychologists were surveyed to assess levels of acceptability for the ability/achievement discrepancy model and the Response to Intervention (RtI) model as part of the identification process for students with specific **learning disabilities**. Significantly higher levels of acceptability were found for the RtI model. Even more encouraging, as levels of exposure to the RtI model increased, acceptability ratings for the RtI model increased and ratings for the discrepancy model decreased. Variations in acceptability ratings for the RtI model were also found to occur in relation to school psychologists' school setting. Specifically, school psychologists employed at middle and high schools demonstrated lower levels of acceptability for the RtI model compared with those employed at elementary and multiple settings (O'Donnell, 2011).

Additionally, a fairly recent authorization of IDEA provides schools with the option of using the RtI model. The RtI model involves a tiered intervention system in which focused, empirically supported interventions are provided to students who are exhibiting below than expected academic progress. Students may be deemed to be eligible for special education services if they fail to respond to these tiered interventions. The RtI model will be discussed in greater depth later in this chapter.

Box 12.3

Did you know?

One of the reasons why the federal government permitted an alternative process for identifying students' eligibility for special education services is because of the assertion that minority students are overidentified as disabled and disproportionately represented in special education (e.g., Sullivan & Bal, 2013). However, a recent study found that minority children were less likely than similar White, English-speaking children to be identified as disabled and thus receive special education services (Morgan et al., 2015).

Both models for identifying eligibility for special education require that a student is failing to demonstrate adequate academic progress. It is important to note that some students may have a medical or mental health diagnosis (e.g., ADHD) but not receive special education services because there is no educational need. That is, they are learning *and* developing at a rate that is commensurate with their age-mates. To elucidate, the disorder does not significantly interfere with the child's academic or social-emotional development. Although school child study teams often look to failing grades as an indicator of school problems, teams need to be aware that failing grades are not a specific requirement for special education services; grades are given for many reasons (e.g., participation, effort, improvements, etc.) in addition to basic knowledge. Inadequate social-emotional progress is also a problematic educational outcome (Assistance to States for the Education of Children With Disabilities and Preschool Grants for Children With Disabilities, 2006c) and can be a qualifier for special education even if grades are good.

If a student demonstrates minor needs related to a diagnosed disability, a 504 plan may be used instead of an IEP.

Box 12.4

What is a 504 Plan?

"Section 504 is a federal law designed to protect the rights of individuals with disabilities in programs and activities that receive Federal financial assistance from the US Department of Education (ED)…the Section 504 regulations require a school district to provide a 'free appropriate public education' (FAPE) to each qualified student with a disability who is in the school district's jurisdiction, regardless of the nature or severity of the disability. Under Section 504, FAPE consists of the provision of regular or special education and related aids and services designed to meet the student's individual educational needs as adequately as the needs of nondisabled students are met" (US Department of Education, n.d.-a).

What is a 504 Plan?

For example, a fifth grade student diagnosed with ADHD is earning mostly "B's" and a few "C's" in his classes; his friendships are well developed. Teachers describe him as "hyper" and complain his homework is often "destroyed" (e.g., folded, crushed, torn, or crumbled) before it is turned in. Upon inspection, his locker is disorganized and jammed with old papers, folders, and projects. In this case, a school child study team may use a 504 plan to help improve the student's organization skills (e.g., clean the locker, teach him how to use shelves or drawers so that materials can be reliably located, teach him how to use an organizer so he can plan for short- and long-term assignments, show him how to manage a backpack to increase its usefulness) in order to help improve the probability of getting homework to and from school in better condition.

Box 12.5

"Dear Colleague" Letter for 504 Eligibility

In 2012, the US Department of Education's (ED) Office for Civil Rights (OCR) issued guidance regarding the effects of the Americans with Disabilities Act Amendments Act of 2008 on public elementary and secondary programs. In the form of a "Dear Colleague" letter, school districts were advised to use an expanded definition of and services for students with disabilities. The recommendation of the letter is that students who traditionally may not have been identified under Section 504 and Title II under ADA should be reevaluated and tested under a broadened definition (Wright & Wright, 2012).

Given the student's satisfactory grades and adequate social-emotional development, it would be appropriate to argue that while there is a diagnosed disorder (i.e., ADHD), there is no educational need that could not be addressed by a less intrusive placement or intervention system. Likely, a 504 plan would be sufficient. Indeed, as long as the student continues to develop on this trajectory, this is appropriate. The use of a 504 plan becomes inappropriate when the student's disorder interferes with his education. Once his educational outcomes (e.g., social-emotional functioning, academic achievement) are negatively impacted, a special education eligibility evaluation must then be initiated. Moreover, when the school is aware that the student has a diagnosis and is aware that he is not succeeding, the school is required to seek services to help him benefit from his educational environment; this requirement is called Child Find.

Child Find. Child Find is an IDEA mandate to find and identify all students with a disability from birth to 21 years of age. This includes all children in the district catchment area; those who attend private or parochial schools; those who are homeless, migrants, immigrants; are wards of the State – everyone. States manage to fulfill this requirement in a variety of ways. Often, infants and toddlers are identified through pediatricians and are referred either to the district's early intervention services or to the relevant agency (e.g., cystic fibrosis foundation), which coordinates with the district services.

Box 12.6

Child Find (Section 300.111)

(a) General.
   (1) The State must have in effect policies and procedures to ensure that
      (i) All children with disabilities residing in the State, including children with disabilities who are homeless children or are wards of the State, and children with disabilities attending private schools, regardless of the severity of their disability, and who are in need of special education and related services, are identified, located, and evaluated; and
      (ii) A practical method is developed and implemented to determine which children are currently receiving needed special education and related services.
(b) Use of term developmental delay. The following provisions apply with respect to implementing the child find requirements of this section:
   (1) A State that adopts a definition of developmental delay under Sec. 300.8(b) determines whether the term applies to children aged three through nine, or to a subset of that age range (e.g., ages three through five).
   (2) A State may not require an LEA to adopt and use the term developmental delay for any children within its jurisdiction.
   (3) If an LEA uses the term developmental delay for children described in Sec. 300.8(b), the LEA must conform to both the State's definition of that term and to the age range that has been adopted by the State.
   (4) If a State does not adopt the term developmental delay, an LEA may not independently use that term as a basis for establishing a child's eligibility under this part.
(c) Other children in child find. Child find also must include
   (1) Children who are suspected of being a child with a disability under Sec. 300.8 and in need of special education, even though they are advancing from grade to grade; and
   (2) Highly mobile children, including migrant children.
(d) Construction. Nothing in the Act requires that children be classified by their disability so long as each child who has a disability that is listed in Sec. 300.8 and who, by reason of that disability, needs special education and related services is regarded as a child with a disability under Part B of the Act (Authority: 20 U.S.C. 1401(3)); 1412(a)(3); US Department of Education, n.d.-b).

For other children who are not yet school age, many districts set up screening procedures several times a year advertising widely to all community members to bring their children in to school or community facilities to ask questions about health concerns, determine if their development is within normal ranges and, by law, to identify the presence of a disability. Rotating through each area of development, the child's health, vision, hearing, motor abilities (e.g., gross motor skills such as walking, running, jumping, and fine motor skills including holding a crayon, closing /opening buttons, using zippers), communication abilities (e.g., listening and comprehension as well as nonverbal and verbal expression), cognitive development (memory, learning, attention), academic (pre-math, pre-reading, pre-writing) skills, social skills, and emotional control are reviewed and results are compared to criterion-referenced age expectations. When delays are present, early intervention services are provided to children aged three and younger, usually free of charge or on a sliding scale. When disabilities are present, special education services are required and provided free of charge by the district or agency designated by the district. Note that states have the choice to recognize and support the remediation of childhood delays – problems that are not yet a considered a disability – for children between the ages of three and nine, or any age grouping therein (e.g., three to five years, etc.).

The Child Find requirement to identify students with disabilities extends throughout the child's educational experience (i.e., until he or she graduates). Furthermore, the requirement extends to all children residing in the district even if they attend a different school (e.g., private, parochial, etc.). Once children are attending school, the teachers, parents, administrators, and counselors monitor child development and progress and should work together to find students with disabilities. When a student at a private school requires a special education evaluation or services, the public and private schools coordinate in order to meet the child's needs. Some public schools share their professional staff with the private school. Other schools may hire independent or statewide services to be implemented at the private school. However it happens, the home district (e.g., catchment area where the student lives) ensures that each child has access to the same services as those that would be provided in their building.

Problems may occur when school personnel fail to understand how to implement the Child Find process, by confusing the requirement to find students with disabilities to mean that every child should be considered for special education services even if the school child study team does not believe that the student needs specialized instruction. That is, overzealous school child study teams try to show they considered the possibility of a disability for each child, but are then unprepared when they must justify their declination to provide a service should a disability later be identified. In this case, the school child study team is now arguing that there is no need for specialized instruction even though the child was initially referred for consideration for special education services. This may become problematic because, although most children who need special education services: (a) have a disability, and (b) are either failing classes or exhibiting disruptive behavior that are interfering with learning, neither is an absolute requirement for eligibility. For example, a student with an anxiety disorder may be earning passing grades in her classes, behaving appropriately in her classes, but yet be demonstrating impaired social and friendship development. The child study team who referred her (just in case) is notified that she has a disability and for the child study team to now conclude that the referral was not based on an actual educational concern appears unreasonable. Moreover, how and why a student would be referred for special education consideration without an educational need calls into question of the judgment of the child study team itself.

School counselors can help school child study teams by reminding them that children who are referred for special education consideration should, by definition, be showing problems, and that such a problem cannot be remediated via general education practices or a 504 plan. Stated simply, there is no reason (need) to refer a child for special education eligibility consideration if he or she is not having difficulty or if the difficulty can be resolved with less intensive and intrusive adjustments. School counselors can help children and families by guiding them through the school's established evaluation processes (discussed in detail below). Also, families need to understand some of the limitations of the law; for example, some disabilities (e.g., nonverbal learning disabilities) are not yet recognized. Indeed, prior to 1991, ADHD was not recognized as a disabling condition for which children were eligible to receive special education support (Rabiner, 2006). Yet, families of children with ADHD needed guidance regarding navigating the system in order to receive help.

In summary, it is appropriate for school personnel and parents to request an evaluation for special education for children who appear to be having difficulty, either academically, emotionally, behaviorally, or socially; however, step one of that process is identifying the need (National Dissemination Center for Children with Disabilities, 2010). Indeed, the child's need for specialized instruction should drive the reason for the request. If the school identifies such a need, it should be communicated to parents in seeking their permission to evaluate their child for eligibility for special education services.

Special Education Eligibility

The process for determining if a student is eligible for special education services includes a comprehensive psychoeducational evaluation that is completed by the school psychologist. Independent psychological evaluations paid for and provided by parents to the school may be accepted, in part or in whole, if deemed appropriate by the child study team, including the school psychologist. Because psychoeducational evaluations are required to cover all areas of behavioral and educational concern – and outside evaluations may not reference how a child behaves across various educational settings – additional information likely needs to be added and considered. Parents may also seek an independent education evaluation (IEE) if they are in disagreement with the school's findings in the comprehensive evaluation; parents may ask the school to pay for the IEE.

The most traditional mechanism to determine if a student has a disability is through the comprehensive psychoeducational evaluation mentioned above. Such an evaluation includes input from all relevant stakeholders (e.g., child, parents, teachers, counselors), an observation of the student in a variety of environments (e.g., large and small group instruction, independent seat work, unstructured free time between classes or lunch, with adults and peers, etc.), and a review of the child's cognitive ability, academic achievement, and social-emotional status and skills.

However, the referral question (need) drives the manner in which the evaluation is conducted. For example, if the referral question is to determine the presence of ADHD, the cognitive processes and behaviors associated with ADHD will specifically be evaluated. The purpose of the evaluation is not only to determine if ADHD symptoms are present, but also to determine if there is another cause of the behaviors, instead of an ADHD diagnosis. For example, the symptoms of irritability and distractibility may be associated with ADHD, but may also be indicative of depression. Perhaps what is the most important information for school counselors to know is that many symptoms occur across disorders. While it is true that attention problems are a core symptom of ADHD, children with other disorders will show attention difficulties as well. In addition to depression, as noted above, a child experiencing adjustment difficulties, a grief reaction, a learning disability, an intellectual disability, or trauma and violence can all have attention problems. Sorting out the etiology of the problem is an essential goal of the examination. Once identified, evidence-based interventions aimed at the target problem can then be recommended.

Although the special education evaluation process is well known, there are some controversies regarding best practices. Determining the presence of a learning disability has long been a source of controversy. This hot button issue has several layers. First, determining the presence of a learning disability is a common referral question requiring many hours of services in schools. About 13% of all children between the ages of three and twenty-one will be identified with a disability, 5% (almost a third) of which are learning disabled. In comparison, children with speech and language disorders comprise about 2.5% and all other disability categories represent about 1% each of the disability population (US Department of Education, 2013). Second, some learning problems are the result of poor instruction and thus are not the result of a disability. Finally, the solutions offered through the special education eligibility process are often only available after children have been left untreated for years and are far behind in skills. In fact, the learning disability controversy has resulted in the development of a Response to Intervention (RtI) model for identifying learning problems/disabilities to avoid the delay of intervention to children who are badly in need of educational assistance

Response to Intervention (RtI). RtI is a three-tiered model (Fuchs & Fuchs, 2006) often depicted in the shape of a triangle. At its base, Tier 1 represents interventions that are meant for use with all students in a regular education setting. These techniques are proactive and empirically supported, and designed to prevent problems for students. Despite such interventions, it is anticipated that approximately 15% of children will require more intensive support and are served in Tier 2 after failing to respond to interventions in Tier 1. About 5% of students will require even more intensive instruction in Tier 3 (small tip of the triangle) after failing to respond at Tier 2. The movement to more intensive intervention is both to select interventions that are tailored to the specific child, and to ensure the evidence for the usefulness of the intervention for that child. Given that fewer children require Tier 2 interventions, and fewer yet require Tier 3 interventions, making sure that there is evidence for a specific intervention and matching the intervention to the child's needs becomes complicated. Indeed, some districts argue that Tier 3 is essentially individualized instruction, akin to what is provided in special education programming.

Advocates for RtI assert that the tiered system solves the problems listed above (e.g., learning disabilities are relatively common, some learning problems are the result of poor instruction, such problems need to be addressed before children are failing). Specifically, RtI is designed to prevent learning problems, since all instructional techniques have an established evidence base in a tiered intervention system, and then allows for a quick progression to more intensive services given an ongoing need, regardless of disability status. However, using the RtI system to diagnose a learning disability is not without criticism, although these concerns will be reviewed in a later section.

Box 12.7

Using RtI to Determine Learning Disabilities in IDEA (2004) Regulations

With regard to identifying children with SLD, the regulations: (1) allow a local educational agency (LEA) to consider a child's response to scientific, research-based intervention as part of the SLD determination process; (2) allow States to use other alternative research-based procedures for determining whether a child has an SLD; (3) provide that States may not require the use of a severe discrepancy between intellectual ability and achievement to determine whether a child has an SLD; and (4) require a public agency to use the State criteria in determining whether a child has an SLD and discuss the role that response to scientific research-based interventions plays in a comprehensive evaluation process (US Department of Education, 2007).

Specific learning disability. The federal law defines a specific learning disability as:

...a disorder in one or more of the basic psychological processes involved in understanding or in using language, spoken or written, that may manifest itself in an imperfect ability to listen, think, speak, read, write, spell, or to do mathematical calculations, including conditions such as perceptual disabilities, brain injury, minimal brain dysfunction, dyslexia and developmental aphasia.

...the term does not include learning problems that are primarily the result of visual, hearing, or motor disabilities, of mental retardation, of emotional disturbance, or of environmental, cultural, or economic disadvantage.

(Assistance to States for the Education of Children With Disabilities and Preschool Grants for Children With Disabilities, 2006c).

The problem with the definition is that it is unclear regarding the meaning of "an imperfect ability." Some disorders are redundantly listed (e.g., reading and dyslexia; deaf, deaf-blindness and hearing impairment; blindness and visual impairments) while others are missing (i.e., nonverbal learning disability). Regardless, it is clear that the definition assumes underlying psychological (neurological) processes resulting in a learning disability, which is consistent with the findings in the literature (WLD, n.d.).

Historically, a significant difference between the child's cognitive abilities and academic performance was required (IQ-achievement discrepancy) to identify a learning disability. However the IQ-achievement discrepancy requirement was removed in the 2004 IDEA revision, which ushered in the use of RtI and other assessment approaches (e.g., measuring the underlying neurological processes associated with cognitive and academic skills but without concern for the IQ-achievement discrepancy) to identify a learning disability. Yet, the implementation of these revisions is not uniformly adopted by states and what is allowed in one state (e.g., relying on RtI data to determine a learning disability) may not be permissible in another. Furthermore, RtI data alone does not negate the requirement for a comprehensive evaluation (Assistance to States for the Education of Children With Disabilities and Preschool Grants for Children With Disabilities, 2006c).

It is important to note that some districts have not yet been able to shown that their Tier 1 curriculum is appropriate for an increasingly diverse student population, delivered with fidelity, and has an appropriate evidence base for a specific child. As described by Kovaleski (2012), it is inappropriate to make a decision about a child's failure to respond, "R," if we cannot assure the usefulness of the intervention, "I." Relatedly, how the school child study team goes about selecting the interventions for a particular child without information about the underlying neurological difficulties is unclear. Tier 2 interventions may be selected from a list of what is most likely to work for children within a specific content area (e.g., reading), but there is a lack of clarity regarding the selection of Tier 2 interventions if the student does not respond to the Tier 1 interventions. That is, without the requisite information about the child's neurocognitive strengths and weaknesses, it is difficult to know which intervention should work better than the one already tried. Furthermore, how the use of RtI to identify a learning disability impacts the number of children served in special education is not yet known (Zirkel, 2010).

The role of the school counselor is to help the school child study team to identify and gather relevant data regarding the child's strengths and why the child is not learning (Geltner & Leibforth, 2008; Ockerman, Mason, & Hollenbeck, 2012). This may include information about the classroom instruction, previous supports that have been tried, and where and how progress is made. Also, school counselors are an important point of contact for the child to express his or her impressions of the classroom, the teacher, instructional materials, etc. Moreover, school counselors' connection to the everyday building activities is an invaluable resource for school child study teams.

Special Education Teams

After the evaluation is complete, the school child study team meets to determine if the child is a student with a disability, if there is an educational need, and thus, if the child is eligible for special education

Table 12.1 IDEA Special Education Categories

Autism	Multiple disabilities
Deaf-blindness	Orthopedic impairment
Deafness	Other health impairment
Developmental delay*	Specific learning disability
Emotional disturbance	Speech or language impairment
Hearing impairment	Traumatic brain injury
Intellectual disability	Visual impairment, including blindness

Note: * required for children from birth–three years and is allowed, but not required, up to the age of nine.

services. Parents, a general education teacher, a special education teacher, a school psychologist (someone qualified to interpret test results), and someone authorized to represent the school regarding curriculum and financial decisions are all required to participate on the school child study team; the child, when appropriate, school counselors, and other community members may join the child study team as needed. Next, the child study team meets to discuss the child's needs and write the IEP goals. An important point here is that the child's needs drive the IEP. That is, regardless of disability area, the IEP should be written to ensure that all of the child's needs are addressed. Children with ADHD may need reading help or children with autism may need counseling support, for example. How and when (but at least annually) feedback on IEP goals is provided should also be established.

IDEA Categories of Eligibility

At present, IDEA recognizes 14 areas of eligibility (see Table 12.1). Prior to reviewing these in detail, it is important to address some issues that may represent potential points of confusion for school child study teams. Special education categories do not always match well with psychological, psychiatric, or developmental disability disorders as described by the Diagnostic and Statistical Manual of Mental Disorders (DSM). Indeed, IDEA categories are designed to be broad and general. Furthermore, because the school child study team determines eligibility decisions, a formal diagnosis is not required.

Although this is meant to allow schools flexibility, it can interfere with selecting evidence-based interventions. As discussed previously, many symptoms are associated with numerous disorders; lack of clarity does not help child study teams sort through which interventions are most likely to be effective. Consequently, it is important that school counselors encourage child study teams to be specific in describing the nature of the child's difficulty and insist on clarity in purpose when providing supports.

Developmental considerations. Children may be identified as eligible for special education at any age between birth and 21 years. However, there are some general timelines to observe. Severe deficits (e.g., classic autism, intellectual disabilities) and significant health issues are typically noticed very early in the child's development. As discussed previously, pediatricians often notice problems in infants and toddlers. Learning disabilities often begin to be noticed in preschool or elementary school age children when academic requirements increase. In fact, behavior difficulties in an otherwise unremarkable preschooler – that is, the child has met developmental milestones and is without a history of abuse or neglect – are more likely an indication of a learning problem than serious emotional disturbance. Social-emotional disabilities tend to show up in adolescents.

There are many reasons why a learning problem could appear later than expected. Perhaps, the support given in the general education classroom was enough to mute the impact of a disability, for example. Unfortunately, it is possible that the diagnosis may have been missed or the school child study team was slow to act. Adults working with young children tend to want to wait and see if the children grow out of their difficulties. This tendency can leave minor problems unattended until they have become major deficits. School counselors can support teachers and parents in obtaining needed services, which may or may not include special education level intensity, as soon as possible. It is well documented that early intervention has the best chance of producing the best outcomes. Children with minimal differences in their skills in comparison to typical age-mates are easier to assist than those with significant differences.

It is also true that children who show significant problems at a younger age tend to have the most difficult time in achieving the performance of their typical peers. Simply put, they do not have a bank of skills to fall back on. A good point of comparison is when a person experiences depression. If that person's depressive disorder evidences itself when he or she is 38, his or her coping skills are well developed, as he or she has enjoyed good social support over many years and as such has more to fall back on when stressed. If the person is eight, however, he or she has only had a short time to develop immature coping skills and the development of subsequent skills are likely to be affected by this event, even if symptoms are controlled relatively quickly. In sum, how quickly adults respond to the child's needs is of utmost importance. School counselors can help assure nervous parents and teachers that they are correct in asking for school support.

Direct services with children. School counselors can support children by helping them to understand their disability in a manner that is developmentally appropriate. Children need to know about their symptoms and how to manage them. Most importantly, children need to know that they are not the disorder. A primary reason for using children-first language is to ensure that adults maintain the perspective that the child has a disability as opposed to viewing the child as disabled. Respecting the child is adults' primary concern. By keeping the disorder or symptoms separate from the child, that allows the child to join with the teacher, parent, and counselor to combat the symptoms. The message therefore is, "We are all working together, as a child study team, to manage the…autism," for example. Relatedly, helping the child to build assertiveness skills so that he or she is comfortable in self-advocacy will not only help the child but it also helps parents and teachers hear – from the child himself or herself – what is needed. Continued communication is essential for many reasons but most central here is the issue that the child's needs will change as he or she ages.

For example, children with autism have deficits in social interactions. A child who may show limited interest in socializing as an elementary student may become interested in friendships or even dating as an adolescent. While the disorder may interfere with the expression of their social contact, their wants and desires can develop alongside the onset of puberty. Adults can teach the child communication skills which will likely increase the likelihood that the child can express their changing desires. A change in dating and intimacy interests for a child with autism may alert the child study team to add social skill instruction that includes the differences between friends and people you date (e.g., how to initiate these different relationships, how to pursue a dating interest, actions appropriate between people who date as compared to those between friends, etc.).

Indirect services with children. School counselors provide indirect services to children by helping the adults in their lives, with the idea that supported adults are better prepared to effectively help children. When adults are troubled, they often do not have the attention, motivation, or energy level to understand the needs of, or to assist, the child. Furthermore, each may be angry at having to deal with the disability altogether. Parents can be devastated when they realize their child has a disability. Many feel a sense of loss as they reconcile the realities of the child they have with the child they planned to have. It is not uncommon to find parents in all stages of grief; some are in denial, angry, bargaining, or experiencing feelings of depression, while others accept the disability.

The school counselor is an essential individual to bridge the gap between school personnel and family members in creating a platform to allow for a combined effort on behalf of the child (Baumberger & Harper, 2007; Milsom, 2007). Alongside the parents, the school child study team will have a long-term role in supporting the child. Over the years, school counselors are often the most consistent school child study team member who works with a child; teachers change by grade, while school counselors are assigned to a whole building of grades. By forecasting the school counselor's long-standing support for the parents, school counselors can help parents move through their grieving more effectively and comfortably.

Teachers can show similar patterns of frustration with children who have disabilities. General education teachers are prepared to work with children who are developing typically. They may not be as well prepared to deal with a child with a disability, although some states are increasing the special education requirements for regular education teacher certification. Given that a child with a disability who has an IEP requires individualization to instruction, teachers often have to modify their teaching practices significantly. There may be numerous students with IEPs in the general education classroom, magnifying the demand on teachers' time and energy. Furthermore, because some teachers may not have training in accommodating students with special needs in the classroom, this lack of knowledge may lead to feelings of inadequacy or humiliation. When teachers are unable to manage the classroom as they planned, feelings of resentment and anger may be outwardly expressed to the class or directly to the child.

School counselors can help distressed teachers in many ways. First, providing an empathic ear when teachers need to vent is often helpful. Second, coordinating resources, such as collaborating with special educators, the reading specialist, or the school psychologist in order to assist the general education teacher in his or her own skill development not only will help with the teacher's immediate frustrations but also will be good for the education of future children with disabilities in their classroom. School counselors can also contribute to the professional development planning in their building; noticing patterns in teacher and parent needs can determine what type of professional development programming should be delivered. At times, school counselors may communicate with principals about the teachers' needs; good principals will find additional ways to support stressed teachers. For example, rotating highly desirable activities (e.g., teaching honors students) or giving a special education teacher a year in general education to refresh his or her energy are all suggestions that counselors can use with administrators to support the whole teaching staff.

IDEA definitions. All special education categories carry the qualifier that the problem conditions interfere with children's ability to *benefit from their educational environment* (Assistance to States for the Education of Children With Disabilities and Preschool Grants for Children With Disabilities, 2006b). Recall the previous discussion about need; youth who require special education services need these individualized education programs to learn. Also, recall that failing grades are not a requirement for eligibility (Assistance to States for the Education of Children With Disabilities and Preschool Grants for Children With Disabilities, 2006b) and that poor social-emotional development may comprise the majority of the child's difficulty that is adversely affecting their ability to benefit from their educational environment. Each category is listed below.

Autism. Autism is a developmental disability (Assistance to States for the Education of Children With Disabilities and Preschool Grants for Children With Disabilities, 2006b). In contrast to psychiatric disorders, in which symptoms can diminish, autism is considered a lifelong disorder. In some high functioning individuals, when adequate treatments are provided, symptoms can diminish or be well managed. Autism occurs on a spectrum (i.e., Autism Spectrum Disorders; ASD), meaning that students will vary in the number and severity of their symptoms. Symptoms include poor (verbal and nonverbal) communication skills and social interactions, often evident by the age of three. Although the DSM-V requires restrictive/repetitive behaviors for a diagnosis of autism, IDEA only considers these symptoms as sometimes associated.

Because there is such variability in how individuals with ASD behave, this disorder is especially difficult for parents and teachers to accommodate and treat. For youth with severe impairments, their deficits are obvious and while requiring intensive interventions, most adults trained in evidence-based treatment strategies can readily see behavioral patterns that require interventions. However, for individuals whose symptoms are less severe, adults often find working with these youth to be very frustrating. In some ways, the demands of treatment increase with the child's degree of functioning, because it is less clear where and when a youth with high functioning autism spectrum disorder (HFA) will fail to understand how to act. Further, it is hard to predict when children with HFA will fail to use a skill set that they already hold; teachers and parents alike will comment, "I know he knows better." Implied in the comment is that they do not understand why the child failed to act appropriately given his knowledge.

Also, because stress can worsen symptoms, a muted deficit in a high functioning individual may not be evident until there is an extreme behavioral response. Consider the early adolescent who ran away from police when they approached to ask him a question about a local robbery. The teenager was not originally suspected of wrongdoing until his response of running away gave the police the impression that he was hiding something. Indeed, it is likely that their loud and hurried approach contributed to his actions; apparently lights were flashing as they pulled over and they used a speaker to call his attention. However, his parents and the youth himself indicated that he knew there was no reason to run away from the police as they are people "here to keep the community safe."

Deaf-blindness. This category is meant to acknowledge children who simultaneously have hearing and visual impairments and require interventions that are beyond those provided to only the deaf or only the blind – both separate special education eligibility categories. A hearing impairment is also listed as a disabling condition. This is an example where there is some redundancy in the law but it is meant to expand care.

Deaf. This is a severe hearing impairment that interferes in processing spoken language. It covers hearing loss that interferes with education; amplification devices are often necessary for the child to benefit from classroom instruction, but are not a requirement for qualification.

Developmental delay. The term developmental delay, as described by IDEA, is best understood as below average development but not yet out-of-range to a degree that a disability is present. As discussed previously, each state can determine what is meant by a delay in child development that would result in services being provided. The Individuals with Disabilities Education Act (part C) ensures early intervention services for children from birth to age three, while IDEA (part B) allows for services for children aged three through nine. Recall that children with disabilities are served through special education. This educational label should not be confused with formal diagnostic terms used to describe developmental disabilities (e.g., autism, intellectual disability).

Emotional disturbance. An emotional disturbance (ED) is "a condition exhibiting one or more of the following characteristics over a long period of time and to a marked degree that adversely affects a child's educational performance":

(a) An inability to learn that cannot be explained by intellectual, sensory, or health factors.
(b) An inability to build or maintain satisfactory interpersonal relationships with peers and teachers.
(c) Inappropriate types of behavior or feelings under normal circumstances.
(d) A general pervasive mood of unhappiness or depression.
(e) A tendency to develop physical symptoms or fears associated with personal or school problems.

The term includes schizophrenia. The term does not apply to children who are socially maladjusted, unless it is determined that they have an emotional disturbance.

(IDEA Amendments of 1997; 1999, § 300.7(c)(4)(ii))

This disability category can be highly controversial. It includes children with internalizing disorders such as anxiety, depression, and somatic disorders (where emotional distress is experienced as physical pain) as well as externalizing disorders such as conduct disorder, oppositional defiant disorder, bipolar disorder, in addition to schizophrenia. However, the criteria are not well defined, they do not match well with DSM descriptions of psychological disorders and, most significantly, require a distinction for individuals who are socially maladjusted. Social maladjustment is not defined.

Hearing impairment. Hearing impairment is similar to deafness, which is listed above, but is meant to apply to children with transient conditions. That is, permanent hearing loss is not required.

Intellectual disability (ID). An intellectual disability, formerly termed mental retardation, is an individual of significantly low general intellectual functioning *and* adaptive behavior skills which, IDEA notes, occurs "in the developmental period" associated with school attendance. Although not required, schools often use the qualifications set by the American Association on Intellectual and Developmental Disabilities (AAIDD), which recognizes the complexity associated with individuals with ID. For example, AAIDD recognizes that individuals with ID may have some skills (e.g., up to a score of 75) that are above the standard score of 70 that is strictly used by most states. This may represent an appreciation that tailored interventions can increase an individual's skills, scores can change over time, and that there is some error in any score. The error in a score is often described as how confident we are that the score is an accurate reflection in the person's functioning (e.g., we are 90% confident that the score is between 67–73). Using the AAIDD definition is useful because it is the standard most often used by state agencies providing adult care. Essentially, using the same criteria allows for an easier transition from child to adult services.

Multiple disabilities. Like deaf-blindness, this category is meant to acknowledge children who have several disabilities simultaneously. This category reminds school child study teams that addressing only one problem or providing services in only one setting cannot meet the child's needs. It does exclude deaf-blindness, as this condition has its own category.

Orthopedic impairment. This category is somewhat broad. It includes impairments that are due to genetic conditions, disease, injury, or other concerns.

Other health impairment (OHI). Often referred to by its initials OHI, this category includes impairments in "strength, vitality, or alertness," including issues of heightened alertness and under arousal. It includes impairments from ADHD in addition to acute and chronic health problems (e.g., asthma, diabetes, epilepsy, a heart condition, hemophilia, lead poisoning, leukemia, nephritis, rheumatic fever, sickle cell anemia, and Tourette syndrome). Although both ADHD and ADD are listed in the description, ADD is not a current term used in the DSM. Rather, there are three types of ADHD as recognized by the DSM-V, ADHD with Predominantly Hyperactive-Impulsive Presentation, ADHD with Predominantly Inattentive Presentation, and ADHD Combined Presentation.

Specific learning disability. The criteria for learning disabilities were reviewed previously. Recall that the essential components of an SLD are that underlying psychological processes result in the imperfect ability to listen, think, speak, read, write, spell, or to do mathematical calculations. In practice, this means that students can qualify for a learning disability in the following eight areas:

- oral expression (explaining thoughts through oral communication)
- listening comprehension (understanding what is heard)
- written expression (communication in writing)

- basic reading skills (the link between letters and their sounds/phonemes)
- reading fluency skills (reading words quickly and easily)
- reading comprehension (understanding what is read)
- mathematical calculation (the link between math symbols and the action required)
- mathematical problem-solving (the process of working through a problem to find a solution).

A learning disability *cannot* be the result of cultural factors (e.g., the student's background is different than that of the school or larger society; he or she has limited experience in the culture, poor acculturation), environmental factors (e.g., the student has changed schools often, he or she was exposed to traumatic events, he or she is homeless), economic disadvantage (e.g., exposed to poor nutrition, abused, neglected), or limited English proficiency.

For students whose primary language is not English, a learning disability is not an appropriate diagnosis if their English language acquisition skills are not adequate. In short, a person cannot be considered disabled just because they are unable to speak English. School psychologists are required to assess a student's Basic Interpersonal Communication Skills (BICS), which typically takes about two years to develop, and a student's Cognitive Academic Language Proficiency (CALP), which typically takes between five and seven years to acquire when considering if an English language learner may qualify for a learning disability. A CALP is required for a student to function effectively in an academic classroom. Obviously, children who are learning English as a second language will often have poor performance in their academic courses until their CALP has developed adequately.

The school child study team must ensure that student failure to learn was not due to lack of appropriate instruction in reading or math. Furthermore, child study teams must show that prior to the referral, the child received appropriate instruction in the general education settings that was delivered by personnel qualified to teach the subject and that there is documentation that the teacher assessed the student's performance several times over a reasonable period of time. Finally, those results were to be shared with parents before a special education evaluation was initiated.

Speech and language. This category covers voice disorders (e.g., an inability to produce speech sounds correctly or fluently), which includes stuttering and impaired articulation as well as language impairment (e.g., delayed language acquisition). Language skill acquisition includes similar skills to those listed in the specific learning disabilities section (i.e., understanding and expressing ideas orally, understanding the sounds associated with letters with enough speed that word comprehension is possible). Language skills that are included in this category overlap with the language skills needed for reading. Children who show early speech and language problems who are not treated successfully are also likely to go on to developing reading difficulties at school age.

Traumatic brain injury (TBI). This category refers to individuals injured by an external force (e.g., car accident) to the head. TBI has become an increasing concern for parents and school personnel as school-sponsored sports teams, intramural sports, and extracurricular athletic programs have shown an increase in sports-related concussions and accidents (Halstead & Walter, 2010).

Visual impairment and blindness. Similar to the hearing impairment category listed above, visual impairment is meant to capture children with transient conditions and students who have impairment even with visual correction (e.g., eyeglasses, materials that are magnified, large print). Permanent vision loss is not required.

Transition Services

Advising students on the transition from high school to the world of work or postsecondary education is a core activity for school counselors. Although all youth have some similar needs, transition planning for special education students (Assistance to States for the Education of Children With Disabilities and Preschool Grants for Children With Disabilities, 2006a) requires the child study team to address a set of specific skills "in preparing for adulthood." The plan must be in place by the time the youth turns 16 and the child must participate in its development. The goals in the plan must be measurable, where specific strategies are coordinated.

Transition services (Assistance to States for the Education of Children With Disabilities and Preschool Grants for Children With Disabilities, 2006a) should articulate what the child needs to prepare for life after high school. That is, what are the child's interests and skills in living independently, participating in the community, employment options, career plans, and postsecondary education? What academic and functional skills are needed to facilitate transition? Will the child continue to need services in adulthood? What are the child's strengths? Given the child's strengths, interests, and needs, the IEP should include a statement of the goals and reflect a plan for how instruction, community experiences, and related services (e.g., counseling) can come together to develop the child's employment and daily living skills.

The school counselor can continue to support parental involvement not only in IEP discussions about career options but also by supporting the changing family dynamics as this important milestone approaches. Like all post-high school experiences, there is a time of adjustment for parents and their children. Parents often face a loss of identity, purpose, and their right to advocate for their coming-of-age child.

Although not formally part of a transition plan, there is a requirement for students with IEPs to have an *Age of Majority* notification. Schools are required to notify the student about the educational rights he or she has, if any, when maturing into adulthood. Furthermore, the parents of students with IEPs also need to be notified of the transfer of educational rights from them to the child. The notification must occur at least one year before the *Age of Majority* notification. The transfer of parent rights to the child may vary across states, and information regarding this transfer may be accessed here: http://minors.uslegal.com/age-of-majority. In the case in which the child does not have the ability to provide informed consent (e.g., not competent to act on his or her own behalf), the parents would retain their rights regarding their child.

Case Study

John, a 12-year-old boy, has been referred to the child study team by his teachers three months into his sixth grade year. John is receiving mostly "D's" in his academic subjects, and the teachers report that he frequently does not submit homework assignments and that he often appears "lost" in class. In collecting data regarding John's progress and health history, the child study team reviews documentation that has been provided by John's physician, indicating that John was previously diagnosed with ADHD – Predominantly Inattentive Type. John's student file indicates that in fifth grade he was provided a 504 plan as a result of his ADHD diagnosis. The accommodations listed in the 504 plan included sitting near the front of the classroom, additional time for testing, receiving tests in portions to reduce John's sense of being overwhelmed, and having the teacher check his agenda planner to ensure that he was accurately recording the assignments.

A child study team meeting is scheduled, at which John's parents, his two child study team teachers, a special education teacher, the assistant principal, the school counselor, and the school psychologist attends. At this meeting, John's mother forcefully demands that her son receive an IEP because he is not succeeding in his academic classes. The school psychologist informs John's parents of the special education process, explaining that a plan of accommodations within a general education setting first must be created and John's response to the accommodations must be evaluated before it can determined whether a full-scale evaluation should be conducted to determine John's eligibility for special education services. The child study team then decides that a period of intervention in John's classes will be implemented, including some of the successful strategies used previously, and self-monitoring techniques to increase John's attention to tasks and improve his work completion, after which the child study team will determine whether the interventions have been successful.

After a six-week intervention period, the child study team determines that John has not made a sufficient rate of progress. The supports provided have not resulted in improved functioning (e.g., academic performance, feelings of being overwhelmed) in the classroom. Also, the child study team suspects that his ADHD diagnosis is significantly interfering with his ability to benefit from the instruction provided. Consequently, a multidisciplinary evaluation is conducted. At the subsequent feedback session, the school psychologist explains that John continues to meet the criteria for a diagnosis of Attention-Deficit/Hyperactivity Disorder – Predominantly Inattentive Type and that his scores on a measurement of emotional functioning indicate that he meets the criteria for an Anxiety Disorder. Based upon this assessment data, the child study team determines that John qualifies for special education services under the criteria outlined in the Individuals with Disabilities Education Act (IDEA); specifically, he qualifies under the educational category of OHI and ED. Although John's mother agrees that he is not progressing academically, she indicates she has reservations about the conclusions of the child study team. The child study team informs her that she is free to disagree with the conclusions of the child study team; she may express her disagreement in writing, and attach this to the report. An additional meeting is scheduled to develop John's IEP, in which the child study team will discuss with John's parents the form, duration, and location of the specially designed instruction that will be used to address his educational needs.

At the IEP meeting, the child study team suggests that John receive push-in special education services, so that he can receive accommodations in real-time in the general education classroom, in addition to twice weekly counseling sessions conducted by the school counselor. In response to this proposal, John's mother forcefully disagrees, explaining that she knows her son has a learning disability. She demands that the school do more, in particular, that they send John to a special school for students with ADHD. John's father attempts to express a different opinion, but John's mother ignores him. John's mother becomes angry, and storms out of the meeting before its conclusion. Her husband sits looking dejected, and eventually also leaves the meeting.

Stimulus Questions

1. What should be the next course of action for the school counselor?
2. How could the school counselor work to connect with John's parents to reconcile their wishes regarding John's education in light of the proposal made by the child study team?
3. What supplemental support could the school counselor provide to John's teachers to help him adjust to special education supports delivered in the general education classroom?

Gifted and Talented Students

In addition to helping children with psychological disorders who are placed in special education, school child study teams also concern themselves with children who show other exceptionalities, such those identified as gifted and talented (GT). Some states require that schools identify and provide differentiated educational programs for GT students, while others do not. Schools manage gifted education in a variety of ways. Because gifted education does not mandate inclusion or the least restrictive environment (LRE) in the way that special education does, many schools use pull-out (exclusion) classes to deliver gifted content. Some districts allow for talent development in specialized schools (e.g., performing arts, engineering, science). Some schools use online courses. Advanced Placement classes (AP) are common in high school, as is allowing students to take college coursework. However, the most successful GT school programs use differentiated instruction to enrich the learning of intellectually advanced students alongside their peers.

Box 12.8

ASCA's Position on Gifted and Talented Programs

The professional school counselor delivers a comprehensive school counseling program as an integral component of the school's efforts to meet the academic and developmental needs of all students. Gifted and talented students have unique and diverse needs that are addressed by professional school counselors within the scope of the comprehensive school counseling program and in collaboration with other educators and stakeholders (ASCA, 2013b).

Used with permission by ASCA.

Current research shows that giftedness is best thought of as a confluence of events. Yes, children are bright; in some states, "bright" is explicitly defined, such as having an IQ of 130 or above (i.e., performing at or better than 98% of the population), along with teacher and parent recommendations of support. Yet giftedness is also about the child's attitude, passion, commitment, and motivation to succeed (Pfeiffer, 2014). In fact, for a child whose skill level exceeds the standard curriculum, who shows an intense interest in learning a particular topic, and is able to persist in their work effort, enrichment may be appropriate in either a pull-out or inclusion model.

The issue that school counselors need to be sensitive to is the myth that giftedness is a stable trait. In fact, cognitive skills fluctuate as children age, as do their interests and opportunities. When these match well, much success is possible. When they do not match, then the experience is not positive. Enrichment in a subject that is not of interest to a child is simply extra work and is not likely to be a positive experience. Furthermore, it is important for children who are gifted to understand that effort, attitude, and persistence matter – gifted education is not about sliding by because you are already smart. Moreover, for youth who were nearly eligible but did not require enrichment, they should be retested, as their skills can improve and when matched with their interest, such students can flourish in enrichment programming. School counselors should attend to the interests of gifted and very bright students so that they can aid them in finding opportunities to excel. Opportunities matched with interests provide a sense of accomplishment and support positive social-emotional development (Elijah, 2011).

Greene (2006) provides interventions for school counselors to address the unique career needs of GT students. GT students are more likely to experience multipotentiality, which refers to the ability for a high level of competency for a variety of tasks. This apparent strength can be problematic for GT students in that it can result in frustration with having to let go of some interests. Multipotentiality is associated with frequent changing of a major focus of study, delayed decision-making, and premature choices (Stewart, 1999). Often, GT students are directed toward prestigious occupations, such as becoming a doctor, lawyer, or engineer. Greene (2006) recommends that GT students should be encouraged to explore their various interests, including their values, life goals, and leisure activities. Also, GT students and their parents should be made aware that a career decision made at the end of high school is merely one of many potential choices.

GT students are also more likely than their non-gifted peers to exhibit early career emergence, showing unusually strong talents and intense interest as early as elementary school (Greene, 2006). Too much encouragement from parents and teachers may diminish the child's interest, but requiring diversification may reduce the child's passion. Greene recommends that school counselors encourage the parents and teachers of GT students to seek to achieve a balance between encouraging and challenging the child's pursuit of his or her interest while also encouraging the child to engage in novel experiences.

GT students have a greater tendency toward perfectionism and social responsibility than their non-GT peers (Greene, 2006). The overly perfectionistic GT student may manage his or her anxiety with making the "wrong" decision by avoiding a decision or acquiescing to an adult. Because GT students often have a heightened sense of sensitivity and commitment to social justice, Greene (2006) recommends that school counselors explore with GT students the importance of selecting a career that is compatible with their values and interests, versus focusing strictly on abilities given that GT students have abilities which they are not necessarily interested in pursuing.

Summary

School counselors today enjoy a supportive role in working with children and families facing significant educational challenges. In particular, school counselors are in a unique position to maintain a stable relationship with families that feel vulnerable because of a child's difficulty in his or her educational progress. Whether faced with a struggling student, a student with a disability, or a student with an exceptionality, the communication provided by school counselors can help parents, teachers, and administrators solve immediate and short-term educational problems, access general education supports (e.g., school-wide anti-bullying programs), participate in the development of 504 plans (e.g., adjustments, modifications, and/or enrichments to the curriculum), or navigate the special education eligibility process.

References

American School Counselor Association (2012). *The ASCA national model: A framework for for school counseling programs* (3rd ed.). Alexandria, VA: Author.

American School Counselor Association (2013a). *The school counselor and students with disabilities*. Available online at www.schoolcounselor.org/asca/media/asca/PositionStatements/PositionStatPositi.pdf (accessed January 21, 2015).

American School Counselor Association (2013b). *The school counselor and gifted and talented student programs*. Available online at https://www.schoolcounselor.org/asca/media/asca/home/position%20statements/PS_Gifted.pdf (accessed Februry 10, 2015).

Assistance to States for the Education of Children With Disabilities and Preschool Grants for Children With Disabilities, 34 C.F.R. § 300.43 (2006a).

Assistance to States for the Education of Children With Disabilities and Preschool Grants for Children With Disabilities, 34 C.F.R. § 300.8(c)(1)(i)-(ii) (2006b).

Assistance to States for the Education of Children With Disabilities and Preschool Grants for Children With Disabilities, 71 Fed. Reg. 156, 46648 (codified at 34 C.F.R. pts. 300.304, 300.304(b), and 300.305) (2006c).

Baumberger, J. P., & Harper, R. E. (2007). *Assisting students with disabilities: A handbook for school counselors* (2nd ed.). Thousand Oaks, CA: Corwin Press.

Disability Rights Education and Defense Fund (n.d.). *A comparison of ADA, IDEA, and Section 504*. Available online at http://dredf.org/advocacy/comparison.html (accessed November 11, 2014).

Elijah, K. (2011). Meeting the guidance and counseling needs of gifted students in school settings. *Journal of School Counseling, 9*, 1–19. Available online at http://eric.ed.gov/?id=EJ933180 (accessed October 13, 2014).

Fuchs, D., & Fuchs, L. S. (2006). Introduction to response to intervention: What, why, and how valid is it? *Reading Research Quarterly, 41*, 93–99.

Geltner, J. A., & Leibforth, T. N. (2008). Advocacy in the IEP process: Strengths-based school counseling in action. *Professional School Counseling, 12*, 162–165.

Greene, M. J. (2006). Helping build lives: Career and life development of gifted and talented Students. *Professional School Counselor, 10*, 34–42.

Halstead, M. E., & Walter, K. D. (2010). Sport-related concussion in children and adolescents. *Pediatrics, 126*, 597–615.

Individuals with Disabilities Education Act Amendments of 1997 [IDEA]. (1999).

Kovaleski, J. (2012). *RTI and SLD identification in Pennsylvania*. Available online at http://rtinetwork.org/rti-blog/entry/1/195 (accessed November 16, 2014).

LD OnLine (n.d.). *What is a Learning Disability?* Available online at www.ldonline.org/ldbasics/whatisld (accessed October 22, 2014).

Milsom, A. (2007). Interventions to assist students with disabilities through school transitions. *Professional School Counseling, 10*, 273–278.

Morgan, P. L., Farkas, G., Hillmeier, M. H., Mattison, R., Maczuga, S., Li, H., & Cook, M. (2015). Minorities are disproportionately underrepresented in special education: Longitudinal evidence across five disability conditions. *Educational Researcher, 44*, 278–292.

National Center for Learning Disabilities (2014). *What is FAPE, and what can it mean to my child?* Available online at www.ncld.org/parents-child-disabilities/ld-rights/what-is-fape-what-can-it-mean-my-child (accessed March 27, 2015).

National Dissemination Center for Children with Disabilities (2010). *10 basic steps in special education*. Available online at http://nichcy.org/schoolage/steps (accessed December 2, 2014).

Ockerman, M. S., Mason, E. C, & Hollenbeck, A. F. (2012). Integrating RTI with school counseling programs: Being a proactive professional school counselor. *Journal of School Counseling, 10*, 1–37. Available online at http://eric.ed.gov/?id=EJ978870 (accessed December 20, 2014).

O'Donnell, P. S. (2011). Identifying students with specific learning disabilities: School psychologists' acceptability of the discrepancy model versus response to intervention. *Journal of Disability Policy Studies, 22*, 83–94.

Rabiner, D. (2006). *Educational rights for children with ADHD/ADD*. Available online at www.helpforadd.com/educational-rights (accessed October 21, 2014).

Stewart, J. B. (1999). Career counseling for the academically gifted student. *Canadian Journal of Counseling, 33*, 3–12.

Sullivan, A. L., & Bal, A. (2013). Disproportionately in special education: Effects of individual and school variables on disability risk. *Exceptional Children, 79*, 475–494.

US Department of Education (n.d.-a). *Protecting students with disabilities*. Available online at www2.ed.gov/about/offices/list/ocr/504faq.html (accessed May 26, 2015).

US Department of Education (n.d.-b). Sec. 300.111 Child find. In *Building the legacy: IDEA 2004*. Available online at http://idea.ed.gov/explore/view/p/%2Croot%2Cregs%2C300%2CB%2C300%252E111%2Cc%2C (accessed October 4, 2014).

US Department of Education (2007). *Questions and answers on response to intervention (RTI) and early intervening services*. Available online at http://idea.ed.gov/explore/view/p/,root,dynamic,QaCorner,8, (accessed December 11, 2014).

US Department of Education (2013). Elementary and secondary education. *Digest of Education Statistics 2012 (2)*. Available online at http://nces.ed.gov/pubs2014/2014015.pdf (accessed November 15, 2014).

Wright, P. W. & Wright, P. D. (n.d). *Wrightslaw: Back to school on civil rights, part I*. Available online at www.wright-slaw.com/law/reports/IDEA_Compliance_1.htm (accessed February 2, 2015).

Wright, P. W., & Wright, P. D. (2012). *Wrightslaw: Discrimination – Section 504 and ADA*. Available online at www.wrightslaw.com/info/sec504.index.htm (accessed October 27, 2014).

Zirkel, P. A. (2010). The legal meaning of specific learning disability for special education eligibility. *Teaching Exceptional Children, 42*, 62–67.

Chapter Thirteen
Crisis Intervention, Response, and Recovery

Box 13.1

2016 CACREP School Counseling Specialty Area Standards

2.d School counselor roles in school leadership and multidisciplinary teams

2.e School counselor roles and responsibilities in relation to the school emergency management plans, and crises, disasters, and trauma

2.g Characteristics, risk factors, and warning signs of students at risk for mental health and behavioral disorders

2.k Community resources and referral resources

News reports highlighting school violence have understandably focused our collective attention on the manner in which schools are prepared to help children and their families when unexpected events occur. The very unlikely event of a school shooting as well as the more common acts of school violence, such as childhood bullying, have resulted in the need for school-wide crisis training. Specifically, today's school teams need to be prepared to prevent, intervene, and recover from crisis situations. Common problems in crisis preparedness are a lack of basic knowledge about how people react and the appropriate timing for the implementation of intervention strategies. While many students and staff feel confident in the fact that their school has a crisis plan, often, they do not do not know the expected roles for students and staff and when the plan should be implemented, because such plans are not regularly practiced (Heath, Sheen, Annandale, & Lyman, 2005). This chapter provides an overview of the best practices for crisis prevention, intervention, and response, and discusses the school counselor's role in preventing and managing crises.

What Counts as a Crisis?

A crisis often refers to a sudden and unexpected set of events, which is associated with emotional, social, or cognitive instability. In schools, there is a sense of disruption of students' or staffs' feelings of psychological well-being and/or the learning environment (Brock et al., 2009). A crisis can result from experiencing acts of war and terrorism, disasters (natural or human-caused), threatened or actual violent injury or death, among other causes.

Adults and children can experience a variety of symptoms after a crisis event. It is typical for 80–85% of individuals exposed to a crisis incident to show a noticeable symptom within 24 hours; about half of these individuals can continue to be affected for three or more weeks (California Department of Corrections and Rehabilitation, n.d.). Symptom intensity tends to be associated with the severity of the incident, but not always. Symptoms that may be observed in children and adults include:

- anxiety, fear, and worry about safety of self and others
- guilt
- mistrust, withdrawal from others or activities
- irritability, anger
- decreased attention and/or concentration
- increase in impulsivity, risk-taking behavior, hyperactivity
- over- or under-reaction to noises, physical contact, sudden movements
- heightened difficulty with authority, redirection, or criticism
- re-experiencing the trauma (e.g., nightmares or disturbing memories)
- hyperarousal (e.g., sleep disturbance, tendency to be easily startled)
- avoidance behaviors (e.g., resisting going to places that remind them of the event)
- emotional numbing (e.g., seeming to have no feeling about the event).

There are four variables that contribute to the experience of traumatization in a crisis: the event predictability, intensity, duration, and consequences (Brock et al., 2009). Although individuals vary in their sensitivities, as a general rule, human-caused, violent events tend to be more traumatizing than natural disasters. It is not uncommon for students to experience drops in academic performance, increases in behavioral difficulties, increases in absenteeism and tardiness, as well as a worsening of previous problems.

There is no right or wrong way for an individual to cope with a crisis event. Most people, including those showing the symptoms identified above, recover without further difficulty. However, there are some students and staff who will require extra support. It is important for the school team to monitor how people are functioning. At times, schools can be so focused on students that they are slow to notice staff who also require support; it is important to assess and monitor all student and staff responses.

School counselors can assist in crisis preparedness by educating parents, students, and staff about typical responses and coping (Crepeau-Hobson, Sievering, Armstrong, & Stonis, 2012). Pamphlets and brochures are an excellent way for students to take home this information. Ensuring educational information is available in the languages spoken by the district's population is essential for good home-school communications.

School Counselor's Role in Crisis Prevention, Intervention, and Response

ASCA's position statement (2013) on safe schools and crisis response states that one way school counselors demonstrate leadership is through involvement in safe school initiatives and critical response preparation and intervention. The position statement lists specific crisis prevention and response practices for school counselors, which are listed in Table 13.1.

Table 13.1 ASCA's Crisis Prevention and Response Preparedness Practices

- individual and group counseling
- advocacy for student safety
- interventions for students at risk of dropping out or harming self or others
- peer mediation training, conflict resolution programs and anti-bullying programs
- support of student initiated programs such as Students Against Violence Everywhere
- family, faculty and staff education programs
- facilitation of open communication between students and caring adults
- defusing critical incidents and providing related stress debriefing
- district and school response team planning and practices
- partnering with community resources

This excerpt from ASCA's position statement is reprinted here with kind permission.
American School Counselor Association (2013). *The professional school counselor and crisis/critical incident response in the schools.* Available online at www.schoolcounselor.org/asca/media/asca/PositionStatements/PS_SafeSchools.pdf (accessed May 18, 2015).

ASCA's position statement references Fein's (2003) seminal work regarding the impact of school shootings upon school leaders, and Fein, Carlisle, and Isaacson's (2008) identification of the implications for school counselors. Fein et al. (2008) identified several implications for school counselors in responding to any serious crisis. Fein's (2003) study of school leaders at four schools which experienced a school shooting revealed that school counselors often assumed a leadership position in the aftermath of a school shooting, even though they did not necessarily have a formal role in the school's crisis response plan. Fein urged school counselors to seek formal roles on the school's crisis response team given that their training and skill set prepares them for leadership in response to a crisis. He recommended that school leaders and counselors be certified in critical incident stress debriefing (CISD) methods in order to serve others and understand how to engage in self-care. CISD will be described in the next section.

Fein (2003) found that in addition to the stress of secondary trauma, school counselors reported stress in dealing with the additional responsibilities that interfered with their other duties, and the role conflict associated with providing a leadership role in responding to the crisis. He recommended that schools establish co-leaders in order to disperse the responsibilities. Fein encouraged school counselors and administrators to understand that role ambiguity may occur, as leaders of the crisis response team may outrank an administrator during the implementation of a school's response to a crisis. Fein (2003) found that formal school leaders were reluctant to formally pursue help from others, but school counselors reported that they often provided informal help to school administrators, allowing an administrator to ventilate feelings. Finally, Fein et al. (2008) encouraged school counselors to take care of themselves by limiting their critical response shift to 3–4 hours and obtain debriefing from a trained personnel member.

Critical Incident Stress Debriefing (CISD)

CISD is a group-based, seven-stage, crisis intervention process for persons who are exposed to trauma, and persons who assist those exposed to trauma, who are often referred to as victims of "secondary trauma" (Mitchell, 1983). The group process gradually engages persons exposed to trauma in exploration of their reactions and feelings to the traumatic event, which are processed within a group experience. In the fact-gathering stage, victims are encouraged to report the facts of what they encountered. The debriefer does not encourage victims to express their feelings, but acknowledges any feelings expressed. In the thought stage, the debriefer asks victims to recall the thoughts they had during the traumatic incident. In the reaction stage, victims are encouraged to share their reactions to the incident, as the leader may ask such a question as "What was the worst part about seeing Jennifer attacked?" In the symptom stage, the leaders ask the group to share any physical or cognitive symptoms they have experienced since the incident, and the leader seeks to normalize the symptoms, asking group members to raise their hand if they have experienced the symptoms of other group members. In the teaching stage, the leader educates the group about the symptoms of post-traumatic stress disorder (PTSD), identifying common immediate (e.g., anxiety, sleep disturbances) and delayed reactions (e.g., limited range of emotions, frequent dreams of being attacked) to experiencing a traumatic event. The leader will also have the group members discuss how they have coped with the event and how their support network has assisted them.

While Fein et al. (2008) recommend that school counselors receive formal training in CISD, it should be noted that there are questions about the effectiveness of the approach. Based upon a review of the research literature, Wei, Szumilas, and Kutcher (2010) concluded that there is limited research on the use of CISD in schools, and the available research even suggests that the approach may be ineffective or even harmful.

What is a Good Crisis Plan?

The US Department of Education (2013) recommends that schools develop a school Emergency Operations Plan (EOP) addressing the areas of concern before, during, and after an incident. Prevention, Mitigation, Protection, Response, and Recovery contexts are described in the Guide for Developing High-Quality School Emergency Operations Plans (US Department of Education, 2013) and are summarized below.

Prevention

Prevention describes the actions taken by a school to avoid an incident occurring. Prevention activities in the school can address targeted or known risks associated with crime or violence such as bullying or suicide prevention programs. Programs aimed at increasing school connectedness are associated with violence prevention efforts (Tillery, Varjas, Roach, Kuperminc, & Meyers, 2013), including responsible reporting of safety concerns (Catalano, Oesterle, Fleming, & Hawkins, 2004).

Mitigation

Mitigation means the capacity to eliminate or reduce the loss of life and property damage by lessening the impact of the emergency. In the school setting, this includes how the buildings are managed (e.g., the setup of monitored entry points, visitor screenings) and maintained (e.g., anchoring large bookshelves to walls, property fencing designating boundaries; Sorensen, Hayes, & Atlas, 2013; US Department of Education, 2008).

Protection

Protection means the ability to protect students, staff, property, and visitors from hazards or potential threats. School safeguards such as video monitoring, metal detectors, and surveillance around school entrance and exit areas are associated with school protection (Reeves et al., 2012).

Response

Response refers to the capability to stabilize an emergency situation once it has begun or it is clear that it cannot be prevented. Response means establishing a safe and secure environment and facilitating recovery. When responding to a crisis, school teams enact their (previously written) emergency management plans in order to ensure the physical and psychological safety of the students and staff.

Recovery

This involves the actions implemented to restore the learning environment. It is important to note that as the school system returns to its typical functioning, the whole school crisis team should be properly debriefed. The implementation team's care needs to be an intentional part of the recovery process (Brock, 2011).

How to Build a Good Crisis Plan

A good crisis plan is developed through dialogues within the school, as well as with the community at large. Various school personnel need to be included in planning meetings, as well as relevant community partners. Diverse cultural and linguistic groups in the community also need to be present.

School participants for the school safety and school crisis teams should include administrators, teachers, facility staff, mental health professionals (e.g., school counselors, psychologists, and social workers), parents, and students; all provide different and important perspectives. Community members should include first responders and community agencies involved in emergency management (e.g., shelters, Red Cross, etc.), community mental health services, spiritual leaders, and immigrant community contacts that can help address the needs of cultural and linguistic groups represented in the building.

The school safety team focuses on identifying potential hazards (e.g., prevention needs relevant to the school's population) as well as known strengths and weaknesses specific to the building that would impact the school's ability to protect or mitigate the impact of an emergency. The school crisis team, which may include some or all of the members of the safety team, focuses on the implementation procedures for mitigating and responding to a crisis. The school crisis team also plans the implementation of the recovery strategies.

The US Department of Education (2013) identifies several assessment strategies used to determine the risk and vulnerability that should be considered by the school safety team. The considerations are discussed in the following section.

Site Assessment

This assessment focuses on identifying the risks and vulnerability of the building(s) and the school grounds. It is designed to provide information about potential hazards and areas that are vulnerable as well as identify which areas provide a safe, accessible shelter where students, staff, emergency responders, and volunteers can gather.

Culture and Climate Assessment

This assessment focuses both on the students' and staffs' perceptions of physical safety and psychological well-being in the building. Its purpose is to identify problematic behaviors or practices that would interfere with a healthy school culture (e.g., where students and staff are free to report concerns). For example, a school where bullying is rampant and unaddressed by the school staff would not promote good communications between students or between students and staff. Bullying is also thought to diminish feelings of connectedness between students and their school (Skues, Cunningham, & Pokharel, 2005). Results from the culture and climate assessment could indicate a need for a bullying prevention program in order to increase students' sense of psychological safety. Results could suggest a need to improve the school's awareness of the different cultural and linguistic populations represented in the district, the coping strategies preferred by different groups, and the resources these groups can bring to support the school's efforts (Heath et al., 2005). Reeves et al. (2011) provide an example of a physical and psychological safety vulnerability assessment.

School Threat Assessment

A threat assessment is used to identify if communications or behaviors exhibited by a student, staff member, or other individual may pose a threat. The purpose of the assessment is to prevent the incident and refer the individual(s) for support and services, if appropriate.

Box 13.2

Did you know?

An investigation by the US Secret Service and US Department of Education revealed that of the 41 school shootings that occurred between 1974–2000, 71% of the school shooters were victims of bullying (Vossekuil, Fein, Reddy, Borum, & Modzeleski, 2004).

The threat assessment team should include school mental health personnel (e.g., school counselors, psychologists, or social workers) with appropriate training in the methods of assessment, school personnel familiar with the individual and the context, as well as relevant community agency personnel (e.g., law enforcement, mental health personnel). Given the need to consider the mental status of the individual at the time of the threat, this team is necessarily different than the school safety team and crisis response teams; however, membership from the crisis response team may overlap. Cornell and Sheras (2006) have developed an evidence-based threat assessment guideline (National Registry of Evidence-Based Programs and Practices [NREPP], 2013) that has been shown to be used effectively by school teams (Strong & Cornell, 2008). It is important to note, however, that some threats may require ongoing assessment and intervention from the school team.

Capacity Assessment

This assessment identifies the available resources for responding to both evacuation and in-place crisis responses, and includes material resources (e.g., equipment and supplies) and staff assets (e.g., who is trained in CPR, who can assist individuals with disabilities, who can assist with various cultural groups including English language learners and their families, etc.).

The US Department of Homeland Security (2013) has published a document titled *K-12 School Security Checklist* that helps schools assess many of the areas listed above and includes psychological safety (www.illinois.gov/ready/SiteCollectionDocuments/K-12SchoolSecurityPracticesChecklist.pdf). The National

Association of School Psychologists (NASP) provide resources and the rationale for the processes and practices needed to ensure school safety (www.nasponline.org/resources/handouts/Framework_for_Safe_and_Successful_School_Environments.pdf).

How to Prevent a Crisis

School counselors play an important role in delivering the support services that can prevent or mitigate a crisis. This is because the school counselor is often aware of which students and families are in distress and can help school teams direct support services toward those in need. Also, school counselors are aware of the cultural and linguistic diversity in the building and can help districts to incorporate diversity needs into the programs provided. As such, most school counselors are likely to find themselves on the crisis and threat assessment teams charged with addressing the psychological safety of students and staff.

Psychological safety initiatives focus on a person's emotional and behavioral well-being (Brock et al., 2009; Reeves et al., 2011; Reeves et al., 2012). Programs tend to be multi-tiered, where universal supports are provided to all students, targeted interventions are provided for those who are at risk, and intensive interventions are aimed at those who are experiencing extreme distress. Common multi-tiered programs include:

- academic support through Response to Intervention (RtI; see Chapter 12 for a full description);
- positive behavior support (Positive Behavior Interventions and Supports, n.d.) which uses the RtI model for behavioral improvement;
- a social-emotional learning curriculum that addresses safety, school climate, and anti-bullying more directly (Safe and Civil Schools, n.d.);
- programs aimed at improving home-school partnerships.

Durlak, Dymnicki, Taylor, and Schellinger (2011) conducted a meta-analysis that revealed that schools using evidence-based programs with a high level of fidelity at the universal level of intervention demonstrated a positive impact upon student behavior. The researchers concluded that high expectations for academic success, engaging teaching practices, caring student-teacher relationships, and a safe and orderly classroom environment were essential for effectiveness at the universal level of intervention.

School counselors have several roles within the tiered framework of crisis intervention. At the universal level of intervention, school counselors can lead home-school partnership activities, support teachers in implementing programs with fidelity, or provide direct instruction on the problem-solving portions of these programs. For the targeted and intensive intervention levels, the school counselor ensures good communication between team members. Effective communication is necessary because as targeted and intensive interventions are paired and added onto the universal support, those new team members will require a bridge to what has already been done, where the child continues to show challenges, and access to how the counselor has approached the parent or guardian. The school's vulnerability assessments and academic and behavioral data should drive the selection of targeted interventions.

Responding to a Crisis as it Happens

Responding to a crisis is a complex matter that requires everyone in the building to know their role and to implement it in coordination. The school counselor is likely to serve as a conduit between the school crisis team, which is managing the system, and the teachers, who are in more immediate contact with students. The perspective of the school crisis team and the teachers are presented below.

In the Classroom

Well-informed teachers, prepared for clear communications, who are able to remain calm during uncertainty, are key assets in managing a crisis. All school staff require in-service instruction and practice regarding crisis responding. Individual teacher responses need to be understood in the context of the system response.

The first priority in crisis communications is to reassure all children that they are safe. Children require an honest explanation about what is happening. In low trust school environments, that honesty may need to be explicitly stated, "I will tell you all that I know, as soon as I know it." In linguistically diverse environments, that communication needs to be delivered in a manner that is understood by the children in the class. Explanations need to be developmentally appropriate to best meet the needs of students (National Association of School Psychologists, 2007).

- Elementary children require a brief statement with concrete reassurance about their safety. Teachers should point out locked doors, how the school has practiced fire drills, and how adults are always making sure children are safe (e.g., in the cafeteria, on the playground, on the bus).
- Older elementary and some middle school children will often wonder how the teacher can know if they are really safe. This group needs help sorting reality from fantasy. Teachers can provide reassurances, such as the school has a safety plan, and the police and fire department respond within three minutes when we practice for an emergency situation.
- Middle and high school students often wonder if society is really safe, if a school can really protect anyone. This group should be encouraged to give their suggestions for school safety improvements and prompted to use the strategies in place for responsible reporting of safety concerns. They often need to talk about the differences between gossiping, tattling, and responsible reporting. What are appropriate (e.g., talking with friends and family) and inappropriate (e.g., use of violence, drugs, alcohol) ways to solve problems? Who else in the community is dedicated to helping others: doctors, policeman, faith leaders, etc.? What is the possibility vs. the probability of a violent act at school? Adolescents can be informed that schools are one of the safest places for children, and they are safer now than they have been in 20 years (Robers, Kemp, & Truman, 2013).

All children should be encouraged but not forced to talk. Listening to children's thoughts and feelings will help the school crisis team know who may require additional support. Teachers need to be explicitly told that the school counselor wants to know whom they are concerned about and why; teachers need to know not to wait a couple of weeks to let the counselor, or other members of the school crisis team, know how the children are responding. Some example statements for teachers in such discussions include:

- Reassuring statements: We are in a safe place. We have followed the plan; everyone (police, fire department, your parents) knows where to come and find us when it's time. We are here together; we can help each other while we wait.
- Explanations: The principal has told us there was a fire. The principal has called for help. Help is on the way/already here.

- Listen: Your thoughts are important. Tell me more about how you are thinking/feeling. I can see how you might think of it that way.
- Talk about it: Lots of people have more thoughts or feelings as time goes by; we can talk about that if it comes up for you.

While open communication is encouraged, returning to routines is also important. If students are to remain in their classroom, returning to classroom-like activities may facilitate a sense of normalcy. This does not necessarily mean that the scheduled test should resume as planned during a lockdown, but rather that educational activities can help pass the time and reinforce that the students are safe, the plan is being carried out, and school routines can resume. At times, however, students will be evacuated to another location, and teachers may be pressed to be creative. One French teacher employed a French version of Simon Says during an hour outside to help pass the time and keep track of wandering teenagers (Heath, Sheen, Annandale, & Lyman, 2005). To the extent that students and staff know what to do, more rapid recovery is more likely.

Box 13.3

Tips for parents and school personnel can be found here:
www.nasponline.org/resources/crisis_safety/terror_general.aspx

---

Box 13.4

Tips for helping students with disabilities can be found here:
www.nasponline.org/resources/crisis_safety/specpop_general.aspx

---

At the Building Level

The National Education Association (NEA, n.d.) provides a comprehensive overview, along with checklists, of the types of considerations that need to be addressed when the crisis is happening in the publication, *School crisis guide: Help and healing in a time of crisis*. As stated, school teams should have roles delegated (who is doing what and when) along with redundant checks to make sure that all of the responses are covered during the crisis event. No detail is too small. An excellent resource, the NEA lists nine priorities to complete in the first hour (please see Table 13.2).

In addition to the initial response, the NEA provides a detailed list of the steps/functions that need to be addressed in the first day of the crisis. Included are implementing the established operating procedures as well as communication plans and use of volunteer support (please see Tables 13.3 and 13.4). The NEA also provides guidance on how to manage Day Two and the First Week of a crisis. School counselors may wish to review the *School crisis guide: Help and healing in a time of crisis* at the beginning of each school year in order to refresh their knowledge and to participate in discussions about their role on any of the school teams (e.g., school safety, school crisis, threat assessment) as the academic year begins.

Table 13.2 Being Responsive During a Crisis: Day One – First Hour

---

Assess the crisis
- What must be done immediately to protect lives? Should the school go on lockdown, evacuate or close off areas of the building or grounds?
- Are people injured?
- Is medical attention needed?

Call for assistance
- Contact police and fire/rescue agencies.
- Contact leadership and crisis team at district central office.

Mobilize the site
- Initiate site-based emergency plan.
- Activate incident command team and protocols. Call for school buses, if needed.
- Determine if actions (e.g., lockdown) must be taken at neighboring schools.

Manage media relations
- Establish a media briefing area.
- Work with law enforcement to set a designated area and perimeter for media.
- Identify the spokesperson (site-based or district official).
- Develop an initial media release. (See Appendix E.)
- Provide school and district fact sheets. (See Appendix F.)
- Hold a press briefing in conjunction with law enforcement.
- Control rumors by getting facts out as soon as information is verified.
- Take into account that personal communication tools, such as cell phones and text messaging, allow students to contact media and others directly.

Establish network to account for missing and injured
- Determine who is safe and who is not accounted for.
- Establish a liaison with local hospitals, if necessary.

Contact mental health support
- Request counselors and other trained professionals from neighboring schools.
- Contract district crisis response team.
- Contact local mental health agencies or centers.
- Contact state and national agencies who can provide immediate support to students and staff.

The NEA's model is reprinted here with kind permission.
National Education Association: Health Information Network (n.d.). *School crisis guide: Help and healing in a time of crisis*. Washington, DC: Author. Available online at http://neahealthyfutures.org/wp-content/uploads/2015/05/schoolcrisisguide.pdf

Crisis Recovery

The response after the crisis is as important as the response during the event. School counselors will find that they are needed to provide support to students and staff as well to help ensure the delivery of the response plan. Accordingly, the NEA provides a back to school checklist that school counselors may find helpful to review (please see Table 13.5).

Crisis Preparedness is Essential

No school can prevent every crisis; some events are simply unstoppable. However, it is clear that schools are required to be prepared for a crisis; the No Child Left Behind (NCLB) legislation requires schools to develop safety and crisis plans (2002). Child safety remains a high priority as noted in the 2013 White House Now is the Time initiative, which provides strategies and funding recommendations regarding making schools safer as well as how to increase access to mental health services.

Table 13.3 Being Responsive During a Crisis: Day One – First 12 Hours

Plan for communications command center to be operational in the next day or two.
- Determine best location based on crisis site. Consult with school principal, facilities manager, security and law enforcement.
- Develop a list of supplies that will be needed at the command post. (See Appendix G.)
- Assign a volunteer coordinator who will solicit communications experts and volunteers from local, state and national sources, if needed. (See Appendix H.)
- Establish communications channels for internal and external audiences.
- Initiate phone tree and email to staff, students and parents. Carefully craft a script with what is known and not known to share with students and families.
- Create a recorded message on the district voice messaging system and update regularly as new information becomes available. Include a phone number where people with questions can reach a "real" person.
- Update the district and school Web sites with information about the crisis. Cross-reference hotline numbers and provide links to other resources, such as mental health support.
- Set up an information hotline staffed by central office personnel or trained volunteers from the teacher's association, retired administrators, etc. Provide a script and answers to frequently asked questions. Have operators log calls and keep track of new questions that arise.
- Develop fact sheet template to be used throughout the crisis. Send fact sheet electronically to internal and external audiences daily at a set time, such as 10 a.m. (See Appendix I.)
- Send group email. Send an email to staff at the affected site and all other central and school sites in the district with the latest information about what happened and what is being done. Provide information on how to get updates through the Web site and hotline.
- Deal with rumors. Make sure all central and school-based staffs have accurate information that they can share in the community to squelch rumors. Recognize how technology – such as cell phones and text messaging – can accelerate the spreading of rumors.
- Provide scripts for office personnel on answering questions or giving directions to staging area or other locations.

Prioritize stakeholders. Take care of internal audiences first, such as:
- Staff at the affected site, other schools, central office, substitutes and retired staff.
- Students and parents at the affected site.
- Students and parents at neighboring schools.
- Families district wide.
- Key community leaders such as school board members, other elected officials and clergy.
- Media. Provide service to local media first, then national and international.

Continue meeting priority needs. These issues include facilities and people management.
- Reunite families. Have a list of all students and check them off when they are picked up by parents or legal guardian.
- Contact local hospitals. Establish a liaison between the school district and the hospitals to get ongoing reports of victims' conditions.
- Secure building and grounds. Work with law enforcement to secure perimeter of school.
- Get top district officials to the scene. The superintendent and/or top administrators, along with key communications department staff, should tour the scene as soon as possible. Decide whether the superintendent will make a media statement.

Manage media relations. The media will want ongoing information. Be available, open and honest.
- Designate a spokesperson who can serve throughout the crisis. If the school district has a communications office, it's ideal for the director to serve as spokesperson. Determine carefully whether the principal, superintendent or school board members will make public statements and who is most appropriate.
- Consider:
  - Is the official emotionally ready and able to give a statement?
  - Does the community/media expect a high-level official to take an active, visible communications role?
  - What are the legal considerations and long-term implications?
  - Which official is appropriate: Who has the most information and represents the district best in the public arena?
- Prepare officials for their roles:
  - Provide talking points in writing.
  - Prepare a list of frequently asked questions and answers.
  - Practice, including asking difficult questions.
  - Determine a specific length of time for the interview or media conference. Begin and end on time.

Continued

Table 13.3 (*cont.*)

- Put the communications director in charge to introduce the spokesperson, manage the question-and-answer period and decide when the interview should end.
- Meet with media spokespersons from law enforcement and the fire/rescue agencies to determine how you will coordinate release of information.
- Develop a call log and track media calls, news agency and reporter names, and questions asked.
- Set up a regular schedule of press briefings. During the first few hours, as the incident is unfolding, hourly press briefings may be required, even if there is nothing new to report. That frequency can decrease as the situation stabilizes. NEA provides advice on how to deal with the media at: http://neahealthyfutures.org/wp-content/uploads/2015/05/schoolcrisisguide.pdf
- Discuss how the identity of victims will be released. Names should not be released until they are verified. Law enforcement, fire and rescue, hospitals and families should be involved in this decision.
- Provide information about evacuation. The media is very helpful in getting information out quickly, so families know where their children are and how to be reunited.
- Express sympathy and acknowledge pain and grief suffered by victims, their families and the community. Connect on a human level. Grant permission to feel the range of feelings associated with a crisis.
- Thank individuals and agencies. Acknowledge the good work of school staff, first responders and community agencies.

<u>Take care of staff.</u> Set up a staff meeting as soon as practical to talk with staff and express support and caring. Practice active listening, allowing staff to safely vent and be heard.

<u>Make decision about classes the next day at affected schools as well as other schools in the district.</u> Release information about the following day as soon as possible.

The NEA's model is reprinted here with kind permission.
National Education Association: Health Information Network (n.d.). *School crisis guide: Help and healing in a time of crisis.* Washington, DC: Author. Available online at http://neahealthyfutures.org/wp-content/uploads/2015/05/schoolcrisisguide.pdf

Table 13.4 Being Responsive During a Crisis: Day One – Evening

<u>Meet with first responders and school/district crisis team.</u>

- Discuss what worked and what didn't. Talk about the next steps and how the agencies will work together over the next few days. Determine where and when the agency representatives will next meet. Establish a process to coordinate media response.
- Hold meeting with school incident command team, school/district crisis team and communications team to address the following issues:
  - What worked well: Did we follow our emergency plan? Did it work as expected? How did we communicate? Did we do everything we could to ensure safety?
  - What must we improve: What parts of the plan didn't work? Were responses prompt and appropriate?
  - What lies ahead: What can we expect tomorrow? How will we communicate to key stakeholders?

<u>Plan for the next day for issues that affect students and school staff.</u>

- Will school be open?
- Where will students and staff gather?
- What actions must we take immediately regarding mental health, safety and security, internal communications and media?
- Whom do we need to contact in our community, such as elected officials, former board members, hospitals, first responders, opinion leaders, district leadership, principals, staff, parents, attorneys, etc.?
- What help do we need, such as volunteers for hotline, phone banks, media relations, family liaisons, etc.?

The NEA's model is reprinted here with kind permission.
National Education Association: Health Information Network (n.d.). *School crisis guide: Help and healing in a time of crisis.* Washington, DC: Author. Available online at http://neahealthyfutures.org/wp-content/uploads/2015/05/schoolcrisisguide.pdf

Table 13.5 Being Responsive During a Crisis: Back to School – When Students and Staff Return

---

<u>Support students and families to help them feel safe; promote healing and a sense of normalcy.</u>
- Develop a re-entry plan, such as tours of the building, where students and their parents can return to school for a short time and feel comfortable.
- Help people feel safe. Make sure parents and students know about the presence of new adults in the building, such as police, mental health counselors, and volunteer door and hall monitors. Encourage parents to be in the school as volunteer support, door monitors, etc.
- Decide on the first-day schedule. Do you want to have a half or full day of classes? Some schools begin with having students meet and talk with the teacher whose class they were in when the tragedy struck. Schools also should have mental health professionals available.
- Provide meaningful opportunities to mark the occasion. Consider whether you want to start the day with a moment of silence. Students might write letters to those injured or thank-you notes to the first responders.
- Offer the option of homeschooling to those who can't return to school.
- Develop routines that make students feel secure, such as rules about leaving the building, student movement in hallways and staircases, and reporting suspicious incidents.

<u>Provide support for staff so they feel capable of being caregivers and educators.</u>
- Actively listen to staff concerns and issues. Reflect concerns back to staff, providing support and answering questions.
- Have a meeting with all staff, administrators and mental health professionals before school starts to discuss curriculum and talking points. NEA's examples are found here: http://neahealthyfutures.org/wp-content/uploads/2015/05/schoolcrisisguide.pdf
- NASP provides examples in English, Spanish, Korean, Vietnamese, French, Amharic, Chinese, Portuguese, Somali, Arabic and Kurdish here: www.nasponline.org/resources/crisis_safety/
- Ensure office staff know the latest developments and have a script for answering phone calls.
- Set up a "safe room" where staff can go for a break or to seek guidance from a mental health professional.
- Have substitute teachers available to take over classes if teachers need a break.
- Make mental health support available in the classroom and throughout the building.

<u>Provide classroom activities for teachers to use with students.</u>
- The NEA provides examples here: http://crisisguide.neahin.org/crisisguide/tools/p4_4.html
- Schoolsecurity.org provides examples here: www.schoolsecurity.org/resources/Practical%20Suggestions%20for%20Crisis%20Debriefing%20for%20Schools.pdf

<u>Take care of the community</u> by inviting first responders to visit the school and serve them a "thank-you" lunch on a day students are not present.

<u>Consider operational issues that make staff and students feel more comfortable.</u> For example, think about changing the sounds of the fire and emergency alarms. Also consider changing the "look" of affected parts of the building; don't use rooms where violence, injuries or death occurred; and visually block off damaged areas.

<u>Manage media coverage of the first day back.</u>
- Establish policies regarding media presence on school grounds and in the building.
- Establish a perimeter for photographers and satellite trucks.
- Set guidelines on still and video cameras in the building.
- Consider holding a meeting or conference call with the media prior to the first day back to set the tone and parameters for the day.
- Remember the goal is to establish a normal routine, heal and foster a sense of safety.
- Host a media tour when students are NOT in school, so reporters have footage to use later. The NEA has examples at http://crisisguide.neahin.org/crisisguide/tools/p2_3.html.

The NEA's model is reprinted here with kind permission.
National Education Association: Health Informa\tion Network (n.d.). *School crisis guide: Help and healing in a time of crisis*. Washington, DC: Author. Available online at http://neahealthyfutures.org/wp-content/uploads/2015/05/schoolcrisisguide.pdf

Counseling Victims of Trauma

Many students who are exposed to trauma, either as the result of a crisis occurring in a school or community, or through other forms of trauma (e.g., victims of sexual, physical, or emotional abuse, witnessing domestic violence, etc.) can benefit from more intensive, ongoing support. A meta-analysis of evidence-based counseling approaches for treating youth who have been exposed to traumatic events found that interventions generally produce positive but modest reductions in post-traumatic stress, depressive symptoms, anxiety symptoms, and externalizing behavioral problems (Silverman et al., 2008). The study also revealed that cognitive-behavioral theory (CBT) interventions were more effective than non-CBT approaches. The authors concluded that there are common elements of effective counseling interventions for youth who have been exposed to trauma. These common elements include educating youth about common reactions to trauma, providing them with skills to manage anxiety and other emotions, learning to label and process thoughts and emotions associated with trauma, discussing and organizing one's memory of the traumatic event, and problem-solving regarding safety and relationships.

The approaches indicated for children who have experienced trauma are grounded in Beck's cognitive theory (Beck & Emery, 1985). Beck found that trauma significantly modifies a person's worldview, and leads children to view themselves as less capable, fearful of the environment, and to believe that they will not be successful in life and that their life will be shortened. Students who have experienced trauma are likely to display a number of specific cognitive distortions. Traumatized children may display dichotomous thinking, believing that situations are completely safe or unsafe. They may magnify negative information or minimize positive information. Such children may overgeneralize, believing that one negative event, such as a fight in the hallway, means that the school is completely unsafe. Or, they may personalize, thinking that uncontrollable events are their fault. The three primary goals in the cognitive therapy approach to counseling traumatized children are to provide strategies for controlling intrusive thoughts, teaching skills to manage the physical symptoms (e.g., tense muscles), and to increase children's confidence that they function effectively in environments that provoke anxiety. Brown (1996) describes how elementary school counselors can identify and counsel children who have been traumatized.

Most of the studies examined in the previously mentioned meta-analysis conducted by Silverman et al. (2008) involved non-school-based interventions. However, the *Group Cognitive-Behavioral Intervention for Trauma in Schools* (CBITS) has also received empirical support (Jaycox et al., 2009). CBITS seeks to reduce symptoms of post-traumatic stress, anxiety, and depression, and in ten weekly group (5–8 students) sessions, each covering one class period. Students learn about the symptoms of common reactions to trauma, are gradually encouraged to explore their thoughts and feelings regarding the trauma through writing and/or drawing, receive cognitive (e.g., thought stopping), and coping skills training (e.g., relaxation), and social skills training.

Support for Students Exposed to Trauma (SSET) is an adapted form of CBITS which is designed to be delivered by paraprofessionals and teachers within classroom and small group settings. The SSET has been shown to decrease students' levels of PTSD and trauma-related anxiety (Jaycox et al., 2009). The SSET manual can be downloaded for free at the following link: www.rand.org/pubs/technical_reports/2009/RAND_TR675.pdf. CBITS, which is available through Sopris West Publishers, and the SSET include detailed lessons and worksheets that can be easily implemented in schools. Both SSET and CBITS have been found to be effective with students of diverse economic, religious, and ethnic/cultural backgrounds, and non-English speaking students.

Suicide Postvention and Prevention

The crisis response and recovery activities detailed earlier are applicable to various types of crises, but it is important to note that the response and recovery activities that are implemented should be adapted to the specific form of crisis. Suicide by a student may require modification of the crisis response and recovery, and efforts to decrease the likelihood of subsequent suicide attempts by students have been termed suicide postvention. The goals of school-based suicide postvention efforts are to (1) provide emotional support to survivors, (2) decrease the likelihood of additional imitation or cluster suicides, and (3) assist the school in returning to normal routines (Fineran, 2012). In the following section, we provide a synopsis of Fineran's (2012) review of the literature regarding aspects of crisis response and recovery efforts that are specific to crisis response and recovery regarding a student suicide.

Box 13.5

Common Misbeliefs of School Professionals Regarding Suicide (Granello & Granello, 2007)

1. Talking about suicide increases the likelihood students will attempt suicide.
2. Schools may be sued if they have a suicide prevention program.
3. Suicide prevention programs lead to what is referred to as "copycat suicides."

After a Student Completes Suicide

A meeting before school with all personnel may be organized to inform the staff of the incident, provide basic facts while remaining sensitive to the family's privacy, and announce any changes to the school's schedule (Fineran, 2012). School personnel should address the death directly and honestly with students as ignoring may undervalue students' distress. Students should be informed of the death in simultaneous small group settings rather than making a school-wide announcement. Parents should be notified in a written letter or individual phone calls. A school counselor should contact the parents/guardians of the deceased child to determine their preferences for disclosure, obtain information on funeral arrangements, inform them of the school's postvention response, identify siblings and friends who may be in need of more intense assistance, and offer support, including references for mental health agencies and survivor support groups. School counselors should develop a plan to include school counselors from other buildings and external mental health professionals in order to sufficiently staff crisis centers (Fineran, 2012). School counselors may need to intentionally pursue students who may be particularly affected by the suicide, given that many students are reluctant to ask for assistance.

School counselors should conduct small, postvention groups for students who may be potentially at risk following a student's suicide. School counselors may find that following the initial shock and denial regarding the student's suicide, students may experience a wide variety of responses, including significant guilt, anger, and cognitive distortions (Fineran, 2012). School counselors can emphasize that there is no particular right way to feel following a suicide. Survivors should be encouraged to identify and express feelings, and learn to distinguish between less effective and effective coping mechanisms, including how students can obtain assistance from their support network. The leader should encourage students not to focus on the specific student suicide, and should discuss suicide in general. Also, students should be encouraged to focus on their memories of the life of the deceased student, as opposed to dwelling on the circumstances surrounding his or her death.

School counselors may also consider conducting school counseling classroom lessons, particularly if a large segment of the student population appears to be affected by a student's suicide. Research suggests that a suicide curriculum should consist of at least three classes of 40–45 minutes or a semester-long class, as these formats have been shown to decrease suicidal ideation, depression, and hopelessness (Kalafat & Elias, 1994). In contrast, having one lesson on suicide prevention has been found to be ineffective (e.g., Kalafat, 2003). The curriculum should focus on protective factors, including social competence, problem-solving, coping strategies, social support, and decision-making, as this type of curriculum has been found to decrease suicidal thoughts and plans (e.g., Evans, Smith, Hill, Albers, & Neufeld, 1996). In addition, Capuzzi (2009) recommends that students be provided with a realistic understanding of suicide, including the impact upon family and friends, the ability to recognize symptoms in themselves and friends, knowledge of school and community resources, and learn about the myths about suicide. The stress model, which implies that suicide is a normal response to stress, should be avoided as it has been found to be potentially harmful as it appears to "normalize" suicide (e.g., Hayden & Lauer, 2000). Also, media portrayals should be avoided as they appear to glamorize suicide (Kalafat, 2003).

Special Considerations in Suicide Postvention

Memorials. There is disagreement among experts regarding how to honor the deceased student (Fineran, 2012). In general, it is recommended that schools avoid memorial services or shrines within the school as this may encourage students' suicidal ideation. More appropriate memorial activities include a small tribute such as a yearbook photo, suicide prevention fundraiser, a moment of silence, or creating a memorial scholarship fund.

Media. Only the deceased student's school activities and facts about the suicide should be reported, and speculation about the student's motivation for committing suicide should be avoided (Fineran, 2012). All statements to the media should be approved by the family of the student. To avoid imitation suicides, the method or location of the suicide should not be revealed. The media should be encouraged to emphasize the impact of suicide and provide the contact information of local mental health agencies for those in need.

Ongoing care. Generally it is recommended that schools return to the routine schedule as soon as possible, while recognizing that students may take months to years to recover. Attention should be paid to students' emotional status, particularly students who were close to the deceased, have mental health issues, have attempted suicide, or those who are identified by parents and staff. Staff and parents can be encouraged to watch for students who appear disoriented, confused, impatient, sad, inattentive, or disruptive. School counselors can monitor attendance patterns and changes in social and academic behavior. It is recommended that students' reactions be closely monitored for six months following a suicide, and less intense monitoring should be conducted for one to two years thereafter. Monitoring may include checking in with particularly at-risk students, soliciting the perspectives of staff and parents, and conducting school-wide depression and suicide screenings.

Suicide Prevention and Lesbian, Gay, Bisexual, Transgender, and Questioning (LGBTQ) Students

A review of the literature found that LGBTQ youth are between two and seven times more likely than straight youth to attempt suicide (Haas et al., 2011). Although there are no studies regarding the effectiveness of suicide prevention programs that are specifically designed for LGBTQ youth, LGBTQ students in schools with a Gay-Straight Alliance (GSA) have fewer suicide attempts than schools without GSAs, and GSAs have also been found to be associated with less truancy, substance use, and sex with casual partners (Poteat, Sinclair, DiGiovanni, Koenig, & Russell, 2013). GSAs are based on a youth empowerment model in which youth assume leadership roles, with adult support, to engage in collaborative efforts to increase school safety and address inequality in schools. They also offer youth peer support to deal with homophobic victimization and parental rejection and provide opportunities to socialize. ASCA's (2014) position statement regarding LGBTQ youth encourages school counselors to advocate for the creation of safe spaces for LGBTQ students such as GSAs. The Gay, Lesbian & Straight Education Network (GLSEN) provides a free guide for establishing a GSA on their website.

Suicide Intervention

School counselors frequently conduct informal assessments of a student's potential for suicide, to determine the level of intent and the possible need for referral for a formal mental health evaluation and services (Dass-Brailsford, 2007). In situations in which the school counselor believes that a student poses a significant risk for suicide, the school counselor should contact the school's mental health liaison and request that he or she come to the school to conduct a formal mental health evaluation. Most school districts have an arrangement with a local community mental health agency to conduct such evaluations. According to Dass-Brailsford, suicidal intent can be assessed by examining suicidal thoughts and the ability to control them and determining if the student has a plan, the presence of which increases the suicide potential, and assessing the lethality of the plan. Other high or severe risk indicators include the following behaviors: a long period of having suicidal thoughts or depressive symptoms, isolation from peers and family, contact with other suicidal persons, high emotional sensitivity, self-injury, drug use, aggressive behaviors, bipolar disorder, psychosis, and sudden behavioral changes (Hays, Craigen, Knight, Healey, & Sikes, 2009). See Box 13.6 for recommended questions for assessing a student's suicidal intent.

Box 13.6

Questions to Assess a Student's Suicidal Intent (Capuzzi, 2009)

1. What are the things in your life that are bothering you?
2. Are you thinking about attempting suicide?
3. How long have you been thinking of suicide?
4. Do you have a plan to commit suicide?
5. Do you know someone who has committed suicide?
6. Have you attempted suicide in the past?
7. Do you use alcohol or other drugs?
8. Have you lost people close to you in the past year, or before this past year that you never talked about?

Interventions for students with suicidal ideation is both short- and long-term. Short-term interventions involve the counselors' response in the course of assessing for suicide, and are listed in Box 13.7:

Box 13.7

Short-term Interventions When Assessing Suicidal Intent (Dollarhide & Saginak, 2012)

1. Remain with the student.
2. Ask direct questions to assess the risk.
3. Encourage the student to identify his or her feelings.
4. Focus on the present, vs. the past or future.

---

5. Express genuine concern for the student.
6. Encourage the student to identify alternatives to suicide without minimizing the student's concerns.
7. Use active listening skills and accept the student's perspectives unconditionally.
8. Implement your school's crisis plan and notify the crisis team in the building.
9. Contact and inform the student's parents/guardians.
10. Refer the student to a mental health agency.

The most effective approach for suicidal students involves wraparound care which includes family support, community resources, and school monitoring for support and safety (e.g., Capuzzi, 2009). School counselors support suicidal students who are currently in treatment or who have recently returned to school from treatment by periodically checking in with the student to reinforce the student's use of coping mechanisms to deal with the stressors related to the student's suicidal intent, and the potential negative attention from peers if the student's suicidal ideation became known (e.g., Capuzzi, 2009).

Summary

Being prepared is essential for adequately serving students, and in reducing the district's legal risk. If there is a failure to make a good faith effort to create safe schools, especially if the risk was obvious and foreseeable (Taylor, 2001), the school district may be vulnerable to a lawsuit for negligence (US Department of Education, 2007). As such, the call to action regarding crisis preparedness continues. School counselors have the training and skill set to significantly contribute to crisis efforts, and should seek to assume a formal role and leadership position in preventing and responding to crises.

References

American School Counselor Association (2013). *The professional school counselor and crisis/critical incident response in the schools*. Available online at www.schoolcounselor.org/asca/media/asca/PositionStatements/PS_SafeSchools.pdf (accessed May 18, 2015).

American School Counselor Association (2014). *Position statement: The school counselor and LGBTQ youth*. Available online at www.schoolcounselor.org/asca/media/asca/PositionStatements/PS_LGBTQ.pdf (accessed September 17, 2015).

Beck, A. T., & Emery, G. (1985). *Anxiety disorders and phobias: A cognitive perspective*. New York: Basic Books.

Brock, S. E. (2011). *Crisis intervention and recovery: The roles of school-based mental health professionals* (2nd ed.). Bethesda, MD: National Association of School Psychologists.

Brock, S. E., Nickerson, A. B., Reeves, M. A., Jimerson, S. R., Lieberman, R. A, & Feinberg, T. A. (2009). *School crisis prevention & intervention: The PREPaRE model*. Bethesda, MD: National Association of School Psychologists.

Brown, D. (1996). Counseling the victims of violence who develop posttraumatic stress disorder. *Elementary School Guidance and Counseling, 30*, 218–227.

California Department of Corrections and Rehabilitation (n.d.). *Normal post incident stress symptoms and how to cope with them*. Available online at www.cdcr.ca.gov/victim_services/docs/normal_post_incident_stress_symptoms.pdf (accessed February 19, 2015).

Capuzzi, D. (2009). *Suicide prevention in the schools: Guidelines for middle and high school settings* (2nd ed.). Alexandria, VA: American Counseling Association.

Catalano, R. F., Oesterle, S., Fleming, C. B., & Hawkins, J. D. (2004). The importance of bonding to school for healthy development: Findings from the Social Development Research Group. *Journal of School Health, 74*, 252–261.

Cornell, D., & Sheras, P. (2006). *Guidelines for responding to student threats of violence*. Longmont, CO: Sopris West.

Crepeau-Hobson, F., Sievering, K. S., Armstrong, C., & Stonis, J. (2012). A coordinated mental health crisis response: Lessons learned from three Colorado school shootings. *Journal of School Violence, 11*, 207–225.

Dass-Brailsford, P. (2007). *A practical approach to trauma: Empowering interventions.* Thousand Oaks, CA: Sage.

Dollarhide, C. T., & Saginak, K. A. (2012). *Comprehensive school counseling programs: K-12 delivery systems in action* (2nd ed.). Toronto: Pearson.

Durlak, J. A., Weissberg, R. P., Dymnicki, A. B., Taylor, R. D., & Schellinger, K. B. (2011). The impact of enhancing students' social and emotional learning: A meta-analysis of school-based interventions. *Child Development, 82*, 405–432. doi:10.1111/j.1467-8624.2010.01564.x

Evans, W., Smith, M., Hill, G., Albers, E., & Neufeld, J. (1996). Rural adolescent views of risk and protective factors associated with suicide. *Crisis Intervention, 3*, 1–12.

Fein, A. (2003). *There and back again: School shootings as experienced by school leaders.* Lanham, MD: Scarecrow Education.

Fein, A. H., Carlisle, C. S., & Isaacson, N. S. (2008). School shootings and counselor leadership: Four lessons from the field. *Professional School Counseling, 11*, 246–252.

Fineran, K. R. (2012). Suicide postvention in schools: The role of the school counselor. *Journal of Professional Counseling: Practice, Theory, and Research, 39*, 14–28.

Granello, D. H., & Granello, P. F. (2007). *Suicide: An essential guide for helping professionals and educators.* Boston, MA: Pearson.

Haas, A. P., Eliason, M., Mays, V. M., Mathy, R. M., Cochran, S. D., D'Augelli, A. R., Silverman, M. M., Fisher, P. W., Hughes, T., Rosario, M., Russell, S. T., Malley, E., Reed, J., Litts, D. A., Haller, E., Sell, R. L., Remafedi, G., Bradford., J., Beautrais, A. L., Brown, G. K., Diamond, G. M., Friedman, M. S., Garofalo, R., Turner, M. S., Hollibaugh, A., & Clayton, P. J. (2011). Suicide and suicide risk in lesbian, gay, bisexual, and transgender populations: Review and recommendations. *Journal of Homosexuality, 58*(1), 10–51.

Hayden, D. C., & Lauer, P. (2000). Prevalence of suicide programs in schools and roadblocks to implementation. *Suicide and Life-Threatening Behavior, 30*, 239–251.

Hays, D. G., Craigen, L. M., Knight, J., Healey, A., & Sikes, A. (2009). Duty to warn and protect against self-destructive behaviors and interpersonal violence. *Journal of School Counseling, 7*, 1–30.

Heath, M. A., Sheen, D., Annandale, N., & Lyman, B. (2005). In M. A. Heath & D. Sheen (Eds.), *School-based crisis intervention: Preparing all personnel to assist* (pp. 23–43). New York: Guilford Press.

Jaycox, L. H., Langley, A. K., Dean, K. L., Stein, B. D., Wong, M., Sharma, P., & Kataoka, S. H. (2009). *Making it easier for school staff to help traumatized students* (RAND Publication No. RB-9443-1-NIMH). Santa Monica, CA: RAND.

Kalafat, J. (2003). School approaches to youth suicide prevention. *American Behavioral Scientist, 46*, 1211–1223.

Kalafat, J., & Elias, M. (1994). An evaluation of school-based suicide awareness intervention. *Suicide and Life Threatening Behavior, 24*, 224–233.

Mitchell, J. T. (1983). When disaster strikes…The critical incident stress debriefing process. *Journal of Emergency Medical Services, 8*, 36–39.

National Association of School Psychologists (2007). Talking to children about violence: Information for parents and educators. *Crisis and School Safety.* Available online at http://apps.nasponline.org/resources-and-publications/podcasts/podcast.aspx?id=102 (accessed January 11, 2015).

National Education Association: Health Information Network (n.d.). *School crisis guide: Help and healing in a time of crisis.* Washington, DC: Author. Available online at http://neahealthyfutures.org/wp-content/uploads/2015/05/schoolcrisisguide.pdf (accessed September 21, 2015).

National Registry of Evidence-Based Programs and Practices (2013). *Virginia student threat assessment guidelines.* Available online at http://regionalk12smhi.org/resourceItem.cfm?topic=BULLY&type=BSTPRAC&id=243 (accessed March 3, 2016).

No Child Left Behind Act of 2001, Pub. L. No. 107–110, § 115, Stat 4114. (2002).

Positive Behavioral Interventions & Supports (n.d.). *Is school-wide positive behavior support an evidence-based practice?* Available online at www.pbis.org/research (accessed May 5, 2015).

Potetat, V. P., Sinclair, K. O., DiGiovanni, C. D., Koenig, B. W., & Russell, S. T. (2013). Gay–straight alliances are associated with student health: A multischool comparison of LGBTQ and heterosexual youth. *Journal of Research on Adolescence, 23*, 319–330.

Reeves, M., Conolly-Wilson, C., Pesce, R., Lazzaro, B., & Brock, S. (2012). Preparing for the comprehensive school crisis response. In S. Brock & S. Jimerson (Eds.), *Best practices in school crisis prevention and intervention* (2nd ed.). Bethesda, MD: National Association of School Psychologists.

Reeves, M. A., Nickerson, A. B., Connolly-Wilson, C. N., Susan, M. K., Lazzaro, B. R., Jimerson, S. R., & Pesce, R. C. (2011). *PREPaRE workshop 1: Crisis prevention and preparedness: Comprehensive school safety planning* (2nd ed.). Bethesda, MD: National Association of School Psychologists.

Robers, S., Kemp, J., & Truman, J. (2013). *Indicators of school crime and safety: 2012* (NCES 2013–036/NCJ 241446). Washington, DC: National Center for Education Statistics, US Department of Education, and Bureau of Justice Statistics, Office of Justice Programs, US Department of Justice.

Safe and Civil Schools (n.d). *Welcome to safe and civil schools.* Available online at www.safeandcivilschools.com (accessed January 28, 2015).

Silverman, W. K., Ortiz, C. D., Viswesvaran, C., Burns, B. J., Kolko, D. J., Putnam, F. W., & Amaya-Jackson, L. (2008). Evidence-based psychosocial treatments for children and adolescents exposed to traumatic events. *Journal of Clinical Child & Adolescent Psychology, 37*(1), 156–183.

Skues, J. L., Cunningham, E. G., & Pokharel, T. (2005). The influence of bullying behaviours on sense of school connectedness, motivation and self-esteem. *Australian Journal of Guidance and Counselling, 15*, 17–26.

Sorensen, S., Hayes, J. G., & Atlas, R. (2013). Understanding CPTED and situational crimeprevention. In R. Atlas (Ed.), *21st century security and CPTED: Designing for critical infrastructure protection and crime prevention* (pp. 53–78). Fort Lauderdale, FL: CRC Press.

Strong, K., & Cornell, D. (2008). Student threat assessment in Memphis City Schools: A descriptive report. *Behavioral Disorders, 34*, 42–54.

Taylor, K. R. (September, 2001). Student suicide: Could you be held liable? *Principal Leadership.* Available online at www.nassp.org/portals/0/content/48901.pdf (accessed October 15, 2014).

Tillery, A. D., Varjas, K., Roach, A. T., Kuperminc, G. P., & Meyers, J. (2013). The importance of adult connections in adolescents' sense of school belonging: Implications for schools and practitioners. *Journal of School Violence, 12*, 134–155.

The White House (2013). *Now is the time: The President's plan to protect our children and our communities by reducing gun violence.* Available online at www.whitehouse.gov/sites/default/files/docs/wh_now_is_the_time_full.pdf (accessed December 23, 2014).

US Department of Education (2013). *Guide for developing high-quality school emergency operations plans.* Washington, DC: Author.

US Department of Education, Office of Safe and Drug-Free Schools (2007). *Practical information on crisis planning: A guide for schools and communities.* Washington, DC: Author.

US Department of Education, Office of Safe and Drug-Free Schools (2008). *A guide to vulnerability assessments: Key principles for safe schools.* Washington, DC: Author. Available online at https://rems.ed.gov/docs/VA_Report_2008.pdf (accessed February 3, 2015).

US Department of Homeland Security (2013). *K-12 school security checklist.* Washington, DC: Author.

Vossekuil, B., Fein, R. A., Reddy, M., Borum, R., & Modzeleski, W. (2004). *The final report and findings of the Safe School Initiative: Implications for the prevention of school attacks in the United States.* Washington, DC: US Department of Education.

Wei, Y., Szumilas, M., & Kutcher, S. (2010). Effectiveness on mental health of psychological debriefing for crisis intervention in schools. *Educational Psychological Review, 22*, 339–347.

Chapter Fourteen
Legal and Ethical Concerns in School Counseling

Box 14.1

2016 CACREP School Counseling Specialty Area Standards

2.b   School counselor roles in consultation with families, P-12 and postsecondary school personnel, and community agencies

2.g   Characteristics, risk factors, and warning signs of students at risk for mental and behavioral disorders

2.n   Legal and ethical considerations specific to school counseling

---

What do I do if my principal wants me to disclose what I hear during a counseling session? If a parent asks do I have to tell him or her what his or her child said to me? What records do I keep and how do I maintain them in a confidential manner? When do I call a parent about a child who is cutting him- or herself?

Unfortunately, there are seldom clear answers to the questions in the preceding paragraph, as the correct response will often depend upon the specifics of the situation. Furthermore, the ambiguity in discerning the right answer may be heightened because of the presence of competing principles. For example, the first question regarding the principal's request for disclosure of information provided by a student in a counseling session may involve the maintenance of the school's safety versus the student's right to privacy. Moreover, the difficulties encountered in ethical decision-making are often referred to as "ethical dilemmas."

In order to answer the questions presented in the first paragraph, school counselors must be familiar with a variety of sources pertaining to the practice of school counseling. The primary sources that influence the ethical practice of school counseling include ethical standards, federal and state laws and regulations, case law, and school district policies.

In this chapter, we will focus upon what we consider to be the foundational aspects of the *Ethical Standards for School Counselors* (ASCA, 2010), and discuss laws and regulations associated with these Standards. In order to obtain a more detailed understanding of all of ASCA's *Ethical Standards*, we highly recommend that school counseling students download this document, which can be obtained for free on ASCA's website.

Negligence and Malpractice

Professionals as a whole seek to practice ethically and in a manner consistent with the law as it benefits consumers and promotes the profession as a whole. Furthermore, school counselors want to practice in an ethical manner because they can be found civilly liable if they fail to exercise "due care" in meeting their professional responsibilities (Stone, 2013). While school counselors are rarely sued, and in most states employees are protected from personal liability as long as they are not acting in a willful or wanton manner (Euben, 2003), it is important that school counselors understand how to decrease the likelihood of being sued.

School counselors can be found to be negligent if they "owed a duty," or in other words, failed to act, and their failure results in an injury or damage. An example of negligence would be a school counselor who did not report suspicions of child abuse (Linde, 2007). Most courts have ruled that school counselors did not owe a duty to provide accurate academic advice, prevent suicide, or inform parents when their child is considering abortion (Stone, 2013).

School counselors are more likely to be accused of malpractice than negligence. Malpractice is defined as "professional misconduct or any unreasonable lack of skill in the performance of professional duties" (Lovett, as cited in Hopkins & Anderson, 1990, p. 48). A finding of malpractice requires that a student experienced harm as a result of the school counselor's lack of skill or appropriate behavior (Linde, 2007). An example of malpractice would be if a school counselor conducted eye movement desensitization and reprocessing (EMDR) with a student who suffered sexual abuse, when the school counselor had not received the necessary training to use EMDR.

The standard of practice is used in any court proceeding to determine if the school counselor's conduct was within accepted practice (Stone, 2013). Often, the testimony of a witness who is considered to be an expert within the profession is used to determine whether or not the professional met the acceptable standard of care. Other sources used by the courts to determine the appropriate standard of care include the counselor's involvement and adherence to the requirements of credentialing bodies, the ethical standards of the respective professional organizations, involvement in continuing education, and school board policies. School counselors are most likely to experience legal troubles for failing to follow or violating school board policies (Linde, 2007). This highlights the importance for school counselors to know the communities they serve. For example, a school counselor who worked in a district in which there was a large percentage of Latino or Asian American families should understand that encouraging students to follow their career aspirations regardless of their family expectations might conflict with the more communal worldview of the students and their families.

The first thing a school counselor should do if confronted with a legal action is contact a lawyer and then inform his or her supervisor (Linde, 2007). The school counselor should not attempt to resolve the conflict with the student, the student's parents, or the family's lawyer without the advice of a lawyer. Also, the school counselor should not discuss the case with anyone other than his or her lawyer or supervisor.

Laws, Regulations, and District Policies

As mentioned previously, in addition to ethical standards, school counselors must also understand laws, regulations, and school district policies when engaging in ethical decision-making. As we review some of the more important *Ethical Standards for School Counselors* (ASCA, 2010), we will refer to these other sources that influence the practice of school counseling when pertinent. First, we will provide an overview of these legal sources.

The common law tradition of the United States involves the continual emergence of new legislation. Laws that are enacted by state and national legislatures are referred to as statutory law.

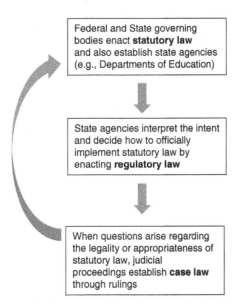

Figure 14.1 Types of laws affecting school counselors.

Government agencies, such as state departments of education, are established by state and national legislatures to develop what is referred to as regulatory law in order to implement the intent of legal statutes. Case law represents rulings from judicial proceedings that interpret either the legality or intent of statutory laws.

Local school board policies and regulations tend to have more influence than laws upon the day-to-day practice of school counselors. For example, school districts may adopt policies regarding the role of school counselors, such as if parents should be notified if their child is receiving individual or group counseling, etc. In contrast to larger school districts, which are more likely to have an identified director specifically for the school counseling program and official policies and procedures governing school counselors, it is not uncommon for smaller districts to lack policies specific to school counselors. Also, in smaller school districts, while administrators may assert that the ethical policies and procedures governing teachers are the same for school counselors, this is not necessarily the case. Most school counselors adhere to the ethical codes of professional counseling organizations, and not professional organizations associated with teaching.

School districts also cannot implement policies and procedures that are inconsistent with state laws and regulations (Schmidt, 2014). For example, if a state statute designates communications between a student and his or her school counselor to be of a privileged nature (an issue we will discuss later in this chapter), then school districts cannot deny privileged communication status. It is not uncommon for districts and/or administrators to want school counselors to engage in practices that may conflict with state laws or ethical standards. School officials may not be aware of regulations specific to school counseling, and thus school counselors must be knowledgeable about the laws, regulations, and ethics that govern the profession, and seek to resolve potential conflicts, which usually involves first speaking with an administrator or the supervisor of the school counseling program.

Ethical Standards for School Counselors (ASCA, 2010)

Most school counselors abide by ASCA's *Ethical Standards for School Counselors* (2010). The *Ethical Standards for School Counselors*, like most ethical standards, are aspirational in nature, identifying what generally is considered ideal or best practice. They do not always indicate the clear choices that school counselors should make to avoid conflict and legal involvement and address the needs for the involved parties. The *Ethical Standards* acknowledge that its members must also be "knowledgeable of laws, regulations and policies relating to students" (A.1.d).

School counselors operate in a broad contextual field and have obligations to various stakeholders. Possibly in recognition of the different populations served by school counselors, the *Ethical Standards for School Counselors* (ASCA, 2010) are divided according to the school counselor's responsibilities to students, parents/guardians, other professionals, the school and community, the school counseling profession, and maintenance of the standards. While the *Ethical Standards* acknowledge that school counselors have responsibilities to various stakeholders, the standards recognize that school counselors "have a primary obligation to students..." (A.1.a). A primary way in which school counselors fulfill this obligation to students is through seeking to implement and maintain a school counseling program which promotes "the educational, academic, career, personal, and social needs and encourage the maximum development of every student" (A.1.b). We believe that the most foundational aspects of the *Ethical Standards* are mostly contained in the section on Responsibilities, including the sections regarding Confidentiality (A.2) and Danger to Self or Others (A.7). However, we will also examine the section regarding the Responsibilities to Parents/Guardians (B), and Maintenance of Standards (G).

Confidentiality

The importance of confidentiality to the school counseling profession is highlighted by the fact that it is cited as one of the five basic tenets enumerated in the Preamble of the *Ethical Standards* (ASCA, 2010), and within the Responsibilities to Students there is an entire section devoted to it.

Box 14.5

Confidentiality – each person's right to privacy within a counseling relationship.

Confidentiality can be considered the most vital aspect of a school counselor's relationship with students, and yet it is also the most difficult ethical issue to negotiate. Confidentiality refers to each person's right to privacy within a counseling relationship. It is based upon the ethical principle that the counseling relationship fosters autonomy by providing a secure environment in which students can explore their thoughts, feelings, actions, and goals to develop the insight essential for improving one's decision-making capabilities. The notion is that if students believed that information that they share within a counseling relationship might be communicated to teachers, administrators, or their parents, they would not engage in free exploration. In other words, without the assurance of confidentiality, many students may not come to the school counselor, or self-disclose difficult issues (Ford, Milstein, Halpern-Felsher, & Irwin, 1997).

Although all educators like to believe that every child comes to school ready to learn, unfortunately, there are many issues that interfere with children's realization of their academic potential. Assisting a child in managing personal issues in a confidential setting can enable children to actualize their academic potential. One of the most important roles of a school counselor, who can be considered the professional most qualified to help students with socio-emotional issues, is to help children manage personal obstacles that interfere with their learning. Ledyard (1998, p. 172) states, "If confidentiality is not established through an educated source such as the school counselor, students may unwittingly confide in unreliable or ill-informed sources for help with their problems." The school counselor's training in promoting social/emotional development is an area of expertise that sets these professionals apart from other education professionals.

When initiating a relationship with a student, school counselors are expected to obtain informed consent, meaning that they communicate to the student the purposes, goals, techniques, and procedures of counseling, and the potential limitations of confidentiality (A.2), which are explained in greater depth later in this chapter.

Box 14.6

Informed Consent – an individual must be deemed competent (e.g., able to make decisions regarding his or her own well-being) and be made aware of the purposes, goals, techniques, and procedures of counseling, as well as the potential limits to confidentiality, before counselors can ethically begin a therapeutic relationship.

The *Ethical Standards* require that the student has the developmental capacity to understand the limits of confidentiality (A.2.a), but it does not provide the criteria for determining a student's capacity for providing informed consent. A further complication is that some courts have ruled that that minors lack the capacity to understand and enter into confidential relationships (Schmidt, 2014).

The legal status of minors is highly ambiguous (Stone, 2013). For example, there is considerable variation between state regulations in regards to when students can drive, marry, engage in sexual relations, enter contracts, and consent to medical services. Eighteen is commonly considered the legal age of majority unless otherwise specified in state statutes. Minors generally are not able to make decisions on their own behalf. Rather, the Supreme Court has ruled that parents have a legal right to make critical decisions about their children (Isaacs & Stone, 1999), and as a consequence, parents are considered to have a legal right to information shared by their children in counseling sessions. Some courts have also ruled that minors cannot legally enter into counseling without parental consent because it is considered a contractual relationship (Remley & Herlihy, 2013).

State statutes often can provide school counselors with some guidance in making a determination of minor status and a child's capacity for informed consent. In some states, there are statutes identifying the age at which children can consent to mental health services without parental permission. For example, in Pennsylvania, at the age of 14, an individual has the right to enter or decline mental health services. Therefore, it can implied from this statute that in Pennsylvania, students who are at least 14 years old and do not have any cognitive limitations that might impair their reasoning, may give informed consent.

Privileged Communication

Whereas confidentiality is an ethical principle, privileged communication is a legal term, meaning that communication revealed to a professional is protected from having to be revealed in a court of law. State laws vary considerably in regards to privileged communication. In some states, privilege is granted to clients in counseling relationships (Remley & Herlihy, 2013), while in other states, there are specific statutes that provide privilege to communications between a student and a school counselor. The right of privilege may be waived, meaning that if granted permission by the student, the school counselor is required to share this information in a court proceeding. States vary in regards to whether the right of privilege belongs to the student or the parent. Stone (2013) found that almost half of school counselors were not aware if their state granted privilege. Not knowing this important legality can be considered ethical negligence.

Box 14.7

Privileged Communication – a legal (not ethical) term indicating which types of conversations and interactions are not required to be revealed in a court of law.

Courts typically have ruled that communications beyond two people are not privileged (Schmidt, 2013). Thus, the *Ethical Standards* indicate that school counselors explain to students that "confidentiality in group counseling cannot be guaranteed" (A.6.c).

Limitations to Confidentiality

Parents' rights and confidentiality. One of the most important limitations to confidentiality is the recognition enunciated in the *Ethical Standards* of "parents'/guardians' legal and inherent rights to be the guiding voice in their children's lives, especially in value-laden issues" (A.2.d). Also, court rulings usually are more likely to recognize parents' legal right to information related to their child's counseling (Herlihy &

Corey, 2006). Herein lies the essential dilemma. The profession regards confidentiality as the cornerstone of counseling, and yet this principle is not always recognized by courts.

School counselors must favor parents' rights over the student's rights when students may be a threat to self or others. Most notably, the *Ethical Standards* state that school counselors must "inform parents/guardians and/or appropriate authorities when a student poses a danger to self or others" (A.7.a). School counselors are required to breach confidentiality to "prevent serious and foreseeable harm to the student" (A.2.c). The *Ethical Standards* provide some guidelines for school counselors in negotiating the delicate balance between students' and parents' rights. The *Ethical Standards* indicate that the age of the child and consideration of the "circumstances requiring the breach" are essential factors when considering violating confidentiality and sharing information with parents (A.2.e). The discussion regarding the "circumstances requiring the breach" go on to mention the phrase "value-laden issues," which can be inferred to include such issues as abortion, sexual activity, contraceptive services, etc., and situations in which a child may be at risk of harm to self and others.

The fact that the *Ethical Standards* require school counselors to "Report risk assessments to parents" (A.7.b) obviously implies that school counselors are expected to assess the child's potential for harming self or others. The *Ethical Standards* and laws do not provide operational definitions for the terms "foreseeable" and "harm." School counselors are expected to receive training and be familiar with the current literature regarding some of the self-destructive behaviors (e.g., depression, suicide, self-injury, eating disorders) and forms of interpersonal violence (e.g., bullying and dating violence) in which some youth engage. Hays et al. (2009) provide comprehensive risk assessment guidelines for these common behaviors of concern, and this document can be available to download for free in the archives of the *Journal of School Counseling*.

Danger to self or others. The terms used within the *Ethical Standards* of "serious and foreseeable harm" are not clearly defined within the *Ethical Standards* or by law. Foreseeable, as defined by the American Heritage dictionary (1985), means "to see or know beforehand." Use of the term "foreseeable" means that the behavior in question is in regards to a future and not a past action.

Box 14.8

Foreseeable – implies that school counselors are required to break confidentiality only if there are reasons to suggest that the student will be a danger to self or others in the future.

In other words, school counselors are generally not required to inform parents and/or authorities of actions that have occurred in the past only in as much as they may be indicators of the potential for future harm. For example, as surprising as this may sound, in the absence of state statutes or district policies, a school counselor may not have to break confidentiality in situations in which a student has committed a violent act, stolen property, or used illicit substances unless that data suggests that the student represents a threat to self or others in the future.

The term "serious" is also not easily defined. While a school counselor may be concerned about an adolescent's future use of alcohol or drugs, the adolescent's use must rise to the level of "serious harm" in order to justify a breach of confidentiality. Most likely, a high school student who reports that he or she plans to imbibe alcohol or smoke marijuana during a weekend party does not rise to the level of "serious." However, an adolescent who reports that he or she plans to use cocaine or heroin could constitute a situation involving "serious harm" given the potential for single-use lethality with these drugs. Although a future act may be illegal, such as in the case of underage drinking, using cigarettes, shoplifting, prostitution, etc., if it does not necessarily entail serious harm to self or others, school counselors are not required by law to report a crime that has already been committed (Fischer & Sorenson, 1996).

However, the school counselor must still consider the degree to which the parents should be involved in a situation in which a child is engaging in an illegal act (Stone, 2013). Stone provides the example of a 16-year-old girl who informs her school counselor that she has shoplifted on a consistent basis. The school counselor can help the girl understand the potential ramifications of her behavior, and may consider referring the girl to a community agency so that she can develop insight regarding her behavior. While the school counselor may decide to involve the girl's parents in the counseling process, the school counselor does not necessarily need to reveal that the girl admitted to shoplifting. The best course of action is for the school counselor to encourage the girl to voluntarily involve her parents in the counseling process, and the school counselor can offer to meet with the girl and her parents to explore the issue together.

Remley and Herlihy (2013) assert that the most effective way for school counselors to justify their ethical decision-making is to act in accordance with the way a reasonable counselor would act in a similar situation. Thus, it can be helpful to know how professional school counselors reason about violating confidentiality when confronted with risk-taking behaviors among students. A national survey found that professional school counselors report being more likely to breach confidentiality when behaviors are more intense (e.g., ranging from a small to large amount of alcohol use) and of greater frequency/duration (e.g., ranging from once several months ago to monthly for several months; Moyer & Sullivan, 2008). There is considerable agreement among school counselors, however, that it is ethical to violate confidentiality when students are engaging in suicidal behaviors, even at the lowest levels of frequency/duration and intensity. School counselors were also likely to favor breaching confidentiality for behaviors involving self-mutilation, substance use, and antisocial acts, but the level of agreement for these acts did not reach the level of consistency demonstrated by school counselors when asked about reporting students' suicidal behaviors. For sexual behaviors and alcohol use, school counselors generally only recommended breaching confidentiality for higher levels of frequency and intensity, and were very unlikely to favor breaking confidentiality for any level of smoking.

Many school counselors tend to side in favor of parents' rights when assessing a child's risk potential, and this tendency would most likely be supported by many school administrators and courts. However, school counselors must remember that the *Ethical Standards* emphasize a student's right to privacy and confidentiality. School counselors are urged to remember that they have a special role in helping students. The role of the school counselor is somewhat different from that of teachers and administrators, who are expected to uphold and maintain school rules and student codes of conduct. The specialized training of school counselors provides them with the skills to help students address socio-emotional issues that contribute to their engagement in self-destructive behaviors and interpersonal violence. In other words, school counselors can help some students learn to meet their needs in more effective, socially acceptable ways. If students believe that the school counselor would breach confidentiality for any sensitive topic, students are likely to cease sharing information that could be vital to the counseling process. The importance of maintaining confidentiality is further supported by the fact that the *Ethical Standards* require that confidentiality is only breached "after deliberation and consultation with other counseling professionals" (A.7.a).

Suicide. While suicidal ideation would certainly seem to meet the definition of "serious," it is not uncommon for adolescents to contemplate suicide, which raises the issue of whether a student admitting to suicide ideation constitutes "foreseeability." School counselors can assess the degree of risk for suicide by asking about the frequency of the student's suicidal thoughts, whether he or she has a plan for completing the act, determining the potential lethality of the plan, and whether the student has attempted suicide in the past, etc.

The courts have yielded contradictory rulings regarding the school counselor's responsibility in breaching confidentiality in regards to a student's suicidal threats (Stone, 2013). In the case of *Eisel v. Montgomery County Board of Education* (1991), the Maryland Court of Appeals ruled that school counselors had a duty to notify the parents of a 13-year-old student named Nicole Eisel who informed peers that she intended to kill herself. Several of Nicole's friends informed their school counselor about Nicole's suicidal threats, and their school counselor informed Nicole's school counselor. The two school counselors questioned Nicole but she denied making any such threats. The school counselors did not inform Nicole's parents or the administrators about the suicidal statements. Soon after, Nicole and a friend committed suicide.

The Maryland Court of Appeals cited the loco parentis doctrine which states that educators legally serve in the role of parents. Furthermore, the Court ruled that school counselors have a special duty to engage in reasonable care to protect a student from harm, defining reasonable care to include attempting to prevent a suicide when informed of a student's suicidal intent. Thus, in Maryland, school counselors must warn both a parent and administrator of suicidal threats made by a student to a school counselor. This includes even indirect threats, such as rumors that a student has threatened suicide, regardless of the perceived seriousness of the threat. Since the Eisel ruling, courts in some states have ruled that school counselors are liable for failing to notify parents of a student whom has written or talked to others about killing themselves, whereas other state courts have yielded opposite rulings (Stone, 2013).

Sexual activity and abortion. As mentioned earlier, ASCA's *Ethical Standards* (2010) indicate that school counselors must recognize that parents have a right to provide guidance to their children, "especially in value-laden issues" (A.2.d). Few topics can be more value-laden than those regarding sexuality. School boards have the right to adopt policies restricting school counselors' discussion of specified topics with students, and some school boards have forbidden school counselors from discussing sexual activity and abortion (Stone, 2013). In considering whether to breach confidentiality, school counselors must be familiar with their state's laws regarding whether minors may seek contraceptive services and obtain an abortion or prenatal care without parental consent.

Box 14.9

Contraceptive Service: Twenty-six states allow minors (12 and older) to obtain contraceptive services without parental consent, while 20 states permit only certain categories of minors.

Sexually Transmitted Infection (STI) Service: All states permit minors to consent to STI services.

Abortion: The majority of states require parental involvement in a minor having an abortion.

Prenatal Care: Thirty-two states permit all minors to consent to prenatal care (Guttmacher Institute, 2015).

There is considerable variation between states in regards to the lawful age of consent for sexual activity (Stone, 2013). In some states, is it illegal for two persons under the age of 18 to engage in sexual relations. The age of consent is as young as 14 in some states, and as old as 17 in other states. A related issue is statutory rape, which is defined as an adult who engages in a sexual relationship with a minor. States, again, have different laws regarding the age difference to qualify as statutory rape. To determine if a situation may be defined as statutory rape, school counselors can consult with the district's legal counsel or contact the Child Protective Services or police department.

Sexually transmitted diseases. One topic upon which the ASCA *Ethical Standards* (2010) is extremely explicit is in regards to situations in which a student is engaging in sexual activity and has a disease that is communicable and fatal (A.2.f). In such situations, the school counselor may breach confidentiality by informing a third party if the student who has the disease does not notify his or her partner and cease engaging in behaviors that put a third party at risk.

Child abuse. Obviously, while parents have a right to information in situations in which there is the potential for "foreseeable and serious harm" to their child, a school counselor should not inform parents when he or she suspects that a parent or a caregiver has committed child abuse or neglect (42 USCS 5101). The term child abuse refers to a range of behaviors that includes physical, emotional/psychological, and sexual abuse, neglect, and inadequate supervision. Federal law designates all educators as mandated reporters, which requires that they must report suspected abuse or neglect, usually within 24 to 72 hours of first "having reason to suspect." Reporters are free from liability for reporting suspected child abuse/neglect, even if a subsequent investigation determines that there is no evidence of abuse/neglect, as long as the report was made without malice, meaning that the school counselor was not personally motivated to harm the alleged perpetrator. Most states have serious penalties for failing to report suspected child abuse/neglect. Mandated reporters are only responsible for reporting suspected abuse to Child Protective Services, who are responsible for investigating reported cases.

Duty to warn. Although the term "duty to warn" is not explicitly stated, the *Ethical Standards* (ASCA, 2010) imply that school counselors have a "duty to warn," which means that they must consider breaching a student's confidentiality by warning the intended target if the student poses a danger to others. The basis for the duty to warn standard stems from the *Tarasoff v. Board of Regents of California* case (1976; Stone, 2013). In this case, the client, a graduate student, informed his psychologist that he intended to kill a girl, whose last name was Tarasoff, and who had rejected his advances. The psychologist informed the police, who arrested but then released the client who, soon after, murdered Tarasoff. The California Supreme Court ruled that the psychologist had a duty not only to protect but to also warn the intended victim and her parents, as the relationship between a psychologist and parents is special and outweighed the psychologist's obligation to protect the client's privacy.

Since the Tarasoff ruling, some state courts have extended the duty to warn standard while others have limited this obligation (Stone, 2013). Generally, a duty to warn is required in situations where potential victims can be identified. Courts have generally ruled that foreseeability is an essential condition for a duty to warn. If a school counselor was informed that a child was a potential danger and failed to take action, the school counselor could be considered negligent.

Duty to protect. Some courts have ruled that school counselors, within the school setting, also have a duty to protect. The case of *Gammon v. Edwardsville Community Unit School District* (1980) illustrates an example in which a school counselor was ruled to have failed to meet his or her duty to protect a child (Stone, 2013). An eighth grade student informed her school counselor that other students told the girl that another girl made physical threats toward her. The school counselor, who had worked closely with the girl who allegedly had been making threats, conducted an unsuccessful mediation with the two girls. Subsequently, the school counselor met individually with the student making the threats, warning her that she would be suspended if she engaged in physical aggression. The school counselor also met privately with the apprehensive student and encouraged her to avoid the girl making the threats. The school counselor did not inform an administrator or notify the recess supervisors who were supervising the girls later that day. During recess, the aggressor punched the victim, which resulted in a skull fracture that required surgery. The Court ruled that the school counselor violated in loco parentis by failing to attempt to protect the child, and that the school counselor had sufficient proof of the potential for harm. However, other courts in cases involving similar circumstances, such as in the case of *Sugg v. Albuquerque Pub. Sch. Dis.* (1999), have not ruled that the school counselor has a duty to protect.

Bullying. While school counselors may decide to breach confidentiality in situations in which there is the potential for a student to direct physical violence toward another student, the issue of whether to violate confidentiality in regards to bullying incidents is often more ambiguous. In addition to acts of overt physical aggression, bullying also encompasses more indirect forms of aggression, including verbal aggression, relational/social aggression, and cyberbullying. It is not clear whether school counselors have a duty to protect in cases of bullying. In some states, such as New Hampshire, school counselors are required by statute to break confidentiality in situations involving bullying (New Hampshire Regulatory Statutes, 2004). However, the courts have generally ruled that school personnel and schools are not liable for failing to intervene in cases of bullying (Stone, 2013). It can be argued that some forms of verbal and relational/social aggression and cyberbullying represent forms of free speech, which is protected within the US Constitution. However, the US Supreme Court has ruled that certain types of speech, including fighting words, obscenities, defamation, and true threats are not protected forms of speech.

Recommendations for dealing with student violence and bullying. Ideally, school counselors should use collaboration, advocacy, and leadership in order to increase school safety, and thus decrease the need to consider breaching confidentiality for situations involving violence and bullying between students.

Box 14.10

Reasons to **ALWAYS** break confidentiality:

- student is a danger to self (e.g., suicidal thoughts and actions)
- student is a danger to others → danger must be "foreseeable" and "serious"
- student reports experiencing abuse
- student has been diagnosed with a communicable disease and is exposing a partner to the disease
- whenever federal or state law, or district policy mandates reporting.
  (Confidentiality regulations vary by state)

Reasons to (strongly) **CONSIDER** breaking confidentiality:

- drug or alcohol use (especially at elevated rates of intensity and frequency)
- sexual activity
- pregnancy/abortion
- self-harm
- bullying.

Comprehensive strategies for improving the school climate and decreasing school violence are explored in Chapter 11: Prevention/Auxiliary Programming. However, school counselors in any school are likely to encounter situations in which they must consider breaching confidentiality to protect other students. Stone (2013) recommends that school counselors report all bullying incidents to an administrator and collaborate with the administrator in determining whether further investigation and involvement of school personnel is warranted. For example, a student who has demonstrated a pattern of aggression may indicate a need for further involvement. Stone (2013) also asserts that courts will most likely apply the principle of *in loco parentis* and rule that school counselors have a duty to protect students.

Probably the most effective way that school counselors can manage the ambiguity regarding confidentiality is to be proactive in educating students and parents about the importance of confidentiality and its limitations. The *Ethical Standards* (ASCA, 2010) indicate that school counselors should explain the importance and limits of confidentiality through school counseling lessons, the student handbook, brochure, and school website, in addition to informing students orally (A.2.b). School counselors must "endeavor to establish, as appropriate, a collaborative relationship with parents/guardians to facilitate students' maximum development" (B.1.a). School counselors can establish such collaborative relationships with parents by proactively informing parents about confidentiality, the *Ethical Standards* (ASCA, 2010), informed consent, and the nature of a school counseling program. Many parental concerns can be allayed through presentations about the school counseling curriculum and professional responsibilities. Reassuring parents that the school counselor will definitely contact them at any time they feel their child might be in danger to themselves or others may go a long way to assuage concerns.

When working with individual parents, empathic and non-judgmental communication can bridge a gap between school personnel, the student, and the parents. Sometimes allowing parents to vent while validating their concerns may be all that is necessary to quell a conflict. Who better to offer the emotional support needed and be able to provide a forum in which exasperated parents can share their frustrations than the professional school counselor, who has honed those mediation skills (Kaplan, 1995)?

McCurdy and Murray (2003) suggest using effective professional judgment for deciding on "appropriate" inclusion of parents. Most certainly, it is not the school counselor's job to become "the informant" for the parents. In order to avoid this role, it may be helpful to simply ask the parents what they wish to know. Likewise, asking the child what he or she wants to share has value and may eliminate the problem. When a parent's request for disclosure of his or her child's counseling sessions arises, it may offer a teaching opportunity. This may open the door to a discussion between the parent and school counselor about the value of the support being offered to the child, while also modeling effective communication. Another effective strategy may be to offer the school counselor's office as a venue for a discussion between parent and child. School counselors can also suggest that the parent directly asks the child about the content of the counseling sessions because, in many cases, the child wants to share his or her feelings with their parents, but lacks the necessary skills. In many ways, confidentiality is not about keeping someone's secrets as much as it is about helping someone learn how to effectively share them (Williams, 2009).

A parent's request to learn about the content of a counseling session can also be handled by reinforcing to the parent the importance of his or her child's developmental growth that is necessary for independent thinking (Mitchell, Disque, & Robertson, 2002). The school counselor's intention is to help the child practice talking about his or her feelings so they can effectively share information with his or her parents. This knowledge may help minimize parental skepticism, especially when they understand that the counseling office is a safe place to practice the child's communication skills. Additionally, educating parents about the value of a trusting relationship in the school setting is as important as helping them understand how a breach of confidentiality may harm the child and inhibit his or her willingness to share information honestly. This simple information sharing may mitigate the parent's request to breach confidentiality.

Courts have generally ruled that parents have a right to know the information shared by their child within counseling sessions, but that does not mean that parents have a right to all of the information shared by the child. School counselors still have a responsibility to serve and protect the students with whom they work, and, therefore, school counselors need to be mindful of the information shared with the parent that is above and beyond what the parent is asking for, or what the counselor is required to share by law. For example, children may have expressed negative feelings toward a parent, and sharing such information will only increase the tension between the student and his or her parent. When breaking the student's confidentiality in sharing information with the parent, the school counselor should first seek to only share that information that may be helpful to the parent. The school counselor may provide suggestions that could improve the parent's relationship with their child. For example, rather than divulge that a student has stated that he or she hates his or her mother, the school counselor can share ideas about how the parent can hear and understand his or her child's anger.

Confidentiality and School Administration

The ASCA (2010) *Ethical Standards* require school counselors to inform school officials of activities that "may be potentially disruptive or damaging to the school's mission, personnel, and property while honoring the confidentiality between the student and the school counselor" (D.1.b). Unlike the obligation to inform parents of potential risk-taking behavior, school counselors in the vast majority of states are not legally required to breach confidentiality and inform administrators of students' risk-taking behaviors (Glosoff & Pate, 2002). Neither laws nor the *Ethical Standards* provide an operational definition of what may be considered potentially disruptive or damaging behavior. A national survey revealed that school counselors thought it was more ethical to reveal private information shared by students to administrators when the behaviors were directly observed versus behaviors that were reported by students, and when the behaviors occurred on school grounds during school hours (Moyer, Sullivan, & Growcock, 2012).

Family Education Rights and Privacy Act of 1974 (FERPA)

In regards to maintaining the confidentiality of student records, the *ASCA's Ethical Standards for School Counselors* (2010) require that school counselors adhere to school policies and state and federal laws, including the laws within the Family Educational Rights and Privacy Act of 1974 (FERPA).

Box 14.11

Family Educational Rights and Privacy Act of 1974 (FERPA) – federal legislation that describes how all written information, including educational records, should be handled and maintained within schools. It also states that parents must have access to their child's educational records.

FERPA is federal legislation that regulates educational records and outlines how all written information concerning a student must be handled and distributed in order to protect the student and her or his family (Stone, 2013). Ideally, school counselors are not responsible for managing educational records, but they should have a deep understanding of FERPA guidelines in order to advocate for students' and parents' rights. FERPA grants parents of minor students the right to access their child's official school records, which includes cumulative folders, test data, academic reports, attendance and discipline records, health information, family background, etc. Parents' rights to review, seek to amend, and disclose education records are transferred to the student once he or she reaches 18 years of age. However, once a student turns 18, parents may still have access to their child's education record if the child is still financially dependent. FERPA grants non-custodial parents all the same rights as custodial parents to their child's education record as long as there is not a court order explicitly prohibiting the non-custodial parent's access (Alexander & Alexander, 2009). Step-parents have the same rights as custodial parents if he or she resides in the same residence as the child.

Parents and eligible students have the right to challenge the accuracy of information. If a school refuses to amend an education record, parents or the eligible student may request a hearing. If the school continues to refuse to amend the educational records, parents or the eligible student may add a statement of disagreement which the school is required to disclose when sharing records with other institutions/persons.

Under FERPA guidelines, schools must have written permission from parents or the eligible student before releasing information from a student's educational record. Universities, military and employment recruiters, and class ring and yearbook companies frequently request directory information. FERPA does permit districts to disseminate "directory information," which includes students' contact information, without the consent of parents of eligible students. If a district elects to make student directory information available, parents have the right of opting their child out of the information dissemination. Schools may use a variety of ways to inform parents of their rights under FERPA, including the student handbook, special letters, emails, etc. If a district decides to make directory information available, they cannot discriminate between groups of requestors. In other words, they cannot provide directory information to one university, but deny it to another.

Exceptions within FERPA. FERPA indicates that educators who have a "legitimate educational interest" may have access to a student's educational records without parental permission. Legitimate educational interest means that a teacher or other school professional may review an educational record for the purposes of performing tasks within the professionals' job descriptions. The information gathered through a record review may be related to a student's educational progress, discipline referrals, or may provide information regarding a service related to the student or to the student's family, such as counseling. School counselors have a legitimate educational interest in performing tasks associated with the position, but may not access a student's record out of curiosity. School districts must establish procedures to ensure that school officials, including outside service providers, only access educational records for which they have legitimate educational interests. FERPA allows school officials to disclose information from a student's educational record in an emergency in order to protect the health or safety of students or other individuals. In such situations, school officials may release information and records to appropriate parties, which may include law enforcement, public health officials, and medical personnel.

School Counselors' Notes

Although time does not allow for school counselors to engage in extensive note-taking, it is considered best practice for a school counselor to document his or her time on task. These notes may merely include first names or initials of the student and a brief comment regarding the topic of discussion. The comments may be as generic as:

Student: AF
Topic: Family issues.

This documentation can be used as data regarding time on task without breaking confidentiality. On the other hand, it is imperative to maintain the safety and confidentiality of school counseling records that may require more documentation. Ethically, it is important to keep school counseling records, but it is also important to keep these records separate from the student's cumulative file, which is considered an educational record (A.8.b). FERPA designates that "sole possession records" are not considered educational records, thus they are not subject to the disclosure accorded by FERPA. The criteria for a school counselor's notes to be considered sole possession notes are:

1. They serve as memory aids.
2. They are not accessible or shared verbally or in written form with others.
3. They are created solely for the person possessing them.
4. They include only observation and professional opinions.
   Sole possession notes are best kept in a personal and secured manner. The notes should be put in a locked place when not in use.

(Stone, 2013)

Box 14.12

Sole Possession Notes – a school counselor's case documentation that consists of brief memory aids intended only for the school counselor and are not added to a student's educational file and, therefore, are not covered under FERPA.

If the school counselor's notes are kept on a school-owned computer, they are considered the possession of the school. School counselors must also establish and follow a consistent policy for the purging of their notes. For example, the school counselor may destroy their notes for all students who have graduated from the school, or are no longer assigned to the school counselor. School counselors cannot destroy their notes on a discriminate basis. For example, it is unethical to destroy one's notes for a specific child for fear that the notes would reveal sensitive information about the child or call into question the school counselor's ethical decisions.

When the occasion occurs that more extensive documentation is necessary for the difficult cases such as suicidal threats, self-mutilation, child abuse, etc., case notes must be handled in a thorough and professional manner. Included in these notes are only objective observations and procedures. It is not appropriate to include personal commentary, judgments, or thoughts in these extensive notes. It is wise practice to include in the notes lists of school professionals with whom the school counselor consulted, what decision was made, and why a decision occurred when documenting a difficult situation. Always consider that a court may subpoena the school counselor to make his or her notes available. In the time of continuous new technology, confidential record-keeping can be more tenuous and vulnerable.

Subpoenas

A survey of school counselors revealed that one third of the respondents reported that they had been asked to testify in court (Stone, 2013). The vast majority of the school counselor testimony requests concerned custody issues and child abuse. School counselors frequently receive subpoenas, and commonly these subpoenas are either a request for documentation or to testify in court. Upon receiving a subpoena, a school counselor should contract the school district's lawyer to review his or her options. Lawyers for defendants or plaintiffs frequently submit such subpoenas, but the school counselor does not necessarily need to comply with the subpoena. In contrast, a subpoena from a judge typically requires compliance.

Case Study

Madison is a highly motivated, 13-year-old, seventh grade student who receives mostly "A's." Her teachers regard her as the model student, frequently providing assistance to teachers and performing beyond their expectations. The teachers report that Madison is a particularly skilled writer, and that she enjoys sharing her "emotionally deep" poetry with them. However, Madison's teachers report that she frequently appears "down" in that she rarely smiles or appears happy, and they have referred Madison to you, the school counselor.

In your first meeting with Madison, you explain that her teachers were concerned that she often seemed "down." She readily shares that she often feels rejected by other students, stating "I just don't get people. I try to be friendly, but they act like I don't exist. What is wrong with me?" In exploring Madison's sadness on a 10-point scale, she reports feeling at about a "3." In response to your question, "Have you ever thought about hurting yourself?", Madison, after some hesitation, says no, but her nonverbal reactions indicate to you that she may have had such thoughts as she appears uncomfortable but she isn't necessarily angry or upset with you asking such questions. You explain to her that it is not uncommon for people to think about hurting themselves. You state that you understand that she might feel uncomfortable telling you, but that you would like to help her if she is having such thoughts. She states that she doesn't want to talk about it. You ask her again, but she denies attempting to hurt herself and she changes the subject, complaining that no one likes her. While Madison's thinking in general appears irrational, she readily generates and comprehends abstract thought. She agrees to meet with you again in several days.

Madison initiates the second meeting by stating that she recently intentionally scalded herself in the shower and in previous weeks she had made scratches on her arm with a needle which drew blood. When asked if her parents know that she has hurt herself, Madison does not want them to know, believing that her mother would probably say something like, "That is a really stupid thing to do." In the past two weeks, she also reports several incidents where she thought her heart was racing, felt dizzy, and thought, "I'm going to die." When she mentioned one of these episodes to her mother, her mother's response was, "Don't worry about it, it will go away."

You remind Madison that you are obligated to notify those that can help her if she is a threat to hurt herself. You explain that you're concerned about her and want to help. In order to do that, her parents need to know about the problems she is having, because you believe that they know her the best, and are the ones who are most likely to be able to help her. You inform her that you will be contacting her parents later that day, asking them to meet about some problems that Madison has been having. She declines to be present as she fears that they will be angry at her for sharing her problems with someone outside of the family. You tell Madison that you will tell her parents specifically about her self-injury and possible panic attacks.

When you reach Madison's mother, Mrs. Smith, she seems confused but reluctantly agrees to bring along her husband for a meeting later that day. Mr. and Mrs. Smith readily admit that they are aware of Madison engaging in several incidents of self-injurious behavior during the past year, and that Madison's pediatrician encouraged them to seek counseling for her. However, Mr. and Mrs. Smith seem to be strongly united in seeing Madison as "dramatic," and believe that she will "grow out of it." You share with the Smiths what the research literature indicates about some of the potential dangers of self-injury, but this seems to only further harden their position that there is no need for concern. You switch tactics, asking them to identify what would indicate to them that Madison is having a problem, and while they do not identify any specific behaviors, their responses seem to be a bit more thoughtful, suggesting that they are thinking differently about the problem. When asked what they would like Madison to develop at this point in her life, they indicate that they would like her to have more friends. They ask for your help in assisting Madison with making friends, and you agree to include Madison in a social skills group. You also explain how that you cannot, however, focus exclusively upon Madison's self-injurious behaviors. You conclude the session by reiterating your concern that Madison is at risk of harming herself, and you provide the parents with the contact information for three mental health agencies in the area which provide counseling services to children and their families.

Over the next several months you assist Madison in developing friendships. She attends a six-week social skills group, and you meet with her every other week for individual counseling. Madison demonstrates progress in making friends. She develops awareness that she tends to over-pursue very popular girls who are not interested in becoming friends with her. She begins to seek out girls and boys who have similar interests, and are receptive to being friends with her. Madison also learns skills to manage her anxiety when connecting with peers.

Madison reports that her parents never pursued the referrals you provided them. During your individual counseling sessions, Madison reports being angry and confused with her parents, particularly her mother, whom she describes as suffocating. Through individual counseling, eventually she comes to realize that her mother and father have difficulty hearing about Madison's emotions. She realizes that it is acceptable for her to have strong feelings, including toward her parents, but she concludes that she must be thoughtful about how she manages her emotions in a constructive way, which she does through her poetry, and she must be careful about how she shares her thoughts and feelings with her parents. You occasionally check in with her about her attempts at self-injury, but she appears to be truthful in reporting that she has not acted upon any urges to hurt herself.

Analysis of Case Study

Madison's presenting problems indicate that she and her family are in need of services that would be more appropriately provided within an agency vs. a school setting, and the school counselor correctly provided the parents with appropriate referrals (A.5.a). The school counselor effectively handled breaching confidentiality by informing Madison of the limits of confidentiality, conducting an informal risk assessment, and offering her options for how to inform her parents. The fact that Madison's parents are not interested in pursuing a referral, which unfortunately is a fairly common response among parents, presents a dilemma for the school counselor. The role of the school counselor dictates that they seek to assist all students, and thus are not able to provide long-term counseling. However, the school counselor also had an ethical obligation to assist Madison, and the school counselor appeared to achieve an effective compromise in respecting the parents' right to make decisions for Madison, while also attempting to assist Madison in at least a more limited fashion.

Summary

Because of the complexity of ethical decision-making when working in a school setting with minors, professional school counselors should utilize a specific ethical decision-making model. Stone's Solutions to Ethical Problems (STEPS) for ethical decision-making have actually been incorporated within the ASCA (2010) *Ethical Standards* (G.3). Consultation with other seasoned professionals is an important and necessary ethical expectation and an important system of support. Reaching out to other professionals for the benefit of your career and the benefit of the children you serve is an ethical mandate. Involvement within the state school counseling professional association can be extremely beneficial, as often professional school counselors who participate in state professional associations are the most knowledgeable about the regulations within the state. Finally, documenting all steps taken in the ethical decision-making process is essential.

References

Alexander, K., & Alexander, M. D. (2009). *The law of schools, students, teachers in a nutshell* (4th ed.). Eagsan, MN: West Publishing.

American School Counselor Association (2010). *Ethical standards for school counselors.* Available online at www.schoolcounselor.org/files/EthicalStandards2010.pdf (accessed December 10, 2014).

Euben, D. R. (2003). Educational malpractice: Faculty beware? *Academe, 89,* 102–107.

Family Education Rights and Privacy Act, 20 U.S.C. $1232g (1974).

Fischer, L., & Sorenson, P. (1996). *School law for counselors, psychologists, and social workers.* White Plains, NY: Longman.

Ford, C. A., Milstein, S. G., Halpern-Felsher, B. L., & Irwin, C. E., Jr. (1997). Influence of physician confidentiality assurances on adolescents' willingness to discuss information and seek future health care: A randomized controlled trial. *Journal of the American Medical Association, 278,* 1029–1034.

Glosoff, H. L., & Pate, R. H., Jr. (2002). Privacy and confidentiality in school counseling. *Professional School Counseling, 6*(1), 20–27.

Guttmacher Institute (2015, January). *State policies in brief: An overview of minors' consent law.* Available online at www.guttmacher.org/statecenter/spibs/spib_OMCL.pdf (accessed February 19, 2015).

Hays, D. G., Craigen, L. M., Knight, J., Healey, A., & Sikes, A. (2009). Duty to warn and protect against self-destructive behaviors and interpersonal violence. *Journal of School Counseling, 7,* 1–30.

Herlihy, B., & Corey, G. (2006). Confidentiality. In B. Herlihy & G. Corey (Eds.), *American Counseling Association ethical standards casebook* (6th ed.; pp. 205–217). Alexandra, VA: American Counselor Association.

Hopkins, B. R., & Anderson, B. S. (1990). *The counselor and the law* (3rd ed.). Alexandria, VA: American Counseling Association.

Houghton Mifflin. (1985). *The American heritage dictionary* (2nd college edition). Boston, MA: Houghton Mifflin.

Isaacs, M. L., & Stone, C. (1999). School counselors and confidentiality: Factors affecting professional choices. *Professional School Counseling, 2,* 258–266.

Kaplan, L. S. (1995). Principals versus counselors: Resolving tensions from different practice models. *School Counselor, 42,* 261–267.

Ledyard, P. (1998). Counseling minors: Ethical and legal issues. *Counseling and Values, 42,* 171–177.

Linde, L. E. (2007). Ethical, legal, and professional issues in school counseling. In B. T. Erford (Ed.), *Transforming the school counseling profession* (pp. 51–73). Upper Saddle River, NJ: Merrill Prentice Hall.

McCurdy, K. G., & Murray, K. C. (2003). Confidentiality issues when minor children disclose family secrets in family counseling. *The Family Journal: Counseling and Therapy for Couples and Families, 11,* 393–398.

Mitchell, C. W., Disque, J. G., & Robertson, P. (2002). When parents want to know: Responding to parental demands for confidential information. *Professional School Counselor, 6,* 156–161.

Moyer, M., & Sullivan, J. (2008). Student risk-taking behaviors: When do school counselors break confidentiality? *Professional School Counseling, 11,* 236–245.

Moyer, M. S., Sullivan, J. R., & Growcock, D. (2012). When is it ethical to inform administrators about student risk-taking behaviors? Perceptions of school counselors. *Professional School Counseling, 15,* 98–109.

New Hampshire Regulatory Statutes (2004). H.R.S.A. 193-F:3(II).

Remley, T. P., Jr., & Herlihy, B. (Eds.). (2013). *Ethical, legal, and professional issues in counseling* (4th ed.). Upper Saddle River, NJ: Merrill Prentice Hall.

Schmidt, J. J. (2013). *Counseling in schools: Comprehensive programs of responsive services for all students* (6th ed.). Toronto: Pearson.

Stone, C. (2013). *School counseling principles: Ethics and law.* Alexandria, VA: American School Counselor Association.

Williams, R. L. (2009, July). *Confidentiality dilemma: Ethical issues in school counseling.* Paper presented at the annual meeting of American School Counselor Association Conference, Dallas, TX.

APPENDIX A

Group Counseling Parent Consent Letter: English Language Version

August 15th, 2014

Dear Parent/Guardian,

Your daughter has shown interest or has been nominated by her teachers to join "Smart-Girl". "Smart-Girl" is an enrichment program designed to teach young girls skills they will need for success during their adolescent years. Girls will discuss issues such as critical thinking, mood management, refusal skills, body image, leadership and bullying, among others. Girls also participate in activities such as role playing, journal writing, art projects, and many other fun activities.

The "Smart-Girl" group will meet every Thursday from 3:15 pm to 4:30 pm, from September 11, 2014 until November 20, 2014. The groups will be led by Erika Serrano (ELL teacher), Brenda Fritzler (teacher in Green pod), and Kris Goen (resource teacher). Matthew McClain, Baker Central School Counselor, will serve as program manager.

Due to the overwhelming interest and nature of the program, participants must be able to attend most sessions. Former sessions proved to be quite successful with many of the girls finding it valuable and applicable to their lives. It is our hope that this group will empower our young girls with the knowledge, skills, and confidence to face the challenges of the upcoming years. We hope you will allow your student to participate in this wonderful and exciting group! Please return this permission slip, and attached form (portions of the attached form are optional, and information is used by the Smart Girl program office – no personal information is published) to school no later than **Friday, September 5th, 2014**. Your daughter will be notified if she is attending this session by Wednesday, September 10th, 2014. Our first "Smart-Girl" session will start on Thursday, September 11th, 2014.

If you have any questions regarding "Smart-Girl", you can visit the website www.smart-girl.org or please feel free to contact Matthew McClain.

Sincerely,

Erika Serrano, Brenda Fritzler and Kris Goen

Matthew McClain 867–8422 Ext. 44218

****

_____ **Yes**, I would like my daughter to be a part of the Smart-Girl group at Baker on Thursdays from 3:15 pm to 4:30 pm. I will make sure I have made arrangements for her to walk home or for someone to pick her up at 4:30 pm (if transportation is a concern, please contact Mr. McClain)

_____ **No**, I would not like my daughter to be a part of the Smart-Girl group at Baker.

_____   _____

Print Daughter's Name   Print Parent's Name

_____   _____

Daughter's Signature   Parent's Signature

APPENDIX B
Group Counseling Parent Consent Letter: Spanish Language Version

15 de Agosto de 2014

Estimado Padre/Guardián,

Su hija ha mostrado interés o ha sido nombrado por sus maestros para unir *"Smart-Girl"*. "Smart-Girl" es un programa de enriquecimiento de diseñó para enseñar chicas jóvenes habilidades que necesitarán para el éxito durante sus años adolescentes. Las chicas discutirán asuntos como pensamiento crítico, gestión de humor, habilidades de negativa, imagen de cuerpo, el liderazgo e intimidar, entre otros. Las chicas también toman parte en actividades como el juego de roles, como escritura de diario, como proyectos de arte, y como muchas otras actividades divertidas.

El grupo de las "Smart-Girl" se encontrará todos los jueves de 3:15 P.M. a 4:30 P.M., del 11 de Septiembre de 2014 hasta el 20 de Noviembre de 2014. "Smart-Girl" no encontrarán sobre interrupción de primavera. Las sesiones serán dirigidas por Erika Serrano (Maestra del ELL), Brenda Friztler (Maestra del equipo Verde), y Kris Goen (Maestra del recursos). Matthew McClain, Consejero de Escuela de Baker Central, servirá como Director de Programa.

Debido al interés y la naturaleza abrumadores del programa, los participantes necesitan asistir la mayoría de las sesiones. Las sesiones anteriores resultaron bastante exitosas con muchas de las chicas que encuentran valioso y aplicable a sus vidas. Es nuestra esperanza que este grupo autorizará a nuestras jóvenes chicas con el conocimiento, las habilidades, y la confianza a encarar los desafíos de los años próximos. ¡Esperamos que permita a su estudiante tomar parte en este grupo maravilloso y emocionante! Regrese por favor este permiso y forma conectada (porciones de la forma conectada son opcionales, y la información es utilizada por la oficina del programa de "Smart-Girl" – ninguna información personal es publicada) al escuela no mas tarde que el **Viernes, el 5 de Septiembre de 2014**. Su hija será notificada si asiste esta sesión para el Miércoles, 10 de Septiembre de 2014. Nuestra primera sesión de "Smart-Girl" comenzará el Jueves, 11 de Septiembre de 2014.

Si tiene cualquier pregunta con respecto a "Smart-Girl", puede visitar el sitio web www.smart-girl.org o sentirse por favor libre contactar a Matthew McClain.

Sinceramente,

Erika Serrano, Brenda Fritzler and Kris Goen

Matthew McClain 867–8422 Ext. 44218

****

_____ **Si,** Quiero que mi hija sea una parte del grupo de "Smart-Girl" en Baker los Jueves de las 3:15 a 4:30 de la tarde. Me aseguraré de que he hecho arreglos para ella que ande a casa o que alguien la recoja a las 4:30 de la tarde (si transporte es una preocupación, contacte por favor a Sr. McClain).

_____ **No,** yo no quiero que mi hija sea una parte del grupo de las "Smart-Girl", en Baker.

_____   _____

Imprima el Nombre de Hija   Imprima el Nombre de Padre

_____   _____

Firma de Hija   Firma de Padre

APPENDIX C
The ASCA National Model® (2012) Group Counseling Student SMART Goals Worksheet

Specific
What is the specific issue you hope to address in this group?

Student A: I hope to be able to talk to my mom without fighting. I hope to learn a better way to get my point across to her without getting angry.

Measurable
How will we measure your growth?

Student A: I would like to not fight with her every day, but understand that this will be hard, so I will try not fight with her for 5 days out of the week.

Attainable
What outcome would be realistic to expect, given the timeline for the group?

Student A: I think this goal is realistic, because we used to never fight, so I think this is possible.

Results-Oriented
What is the result you hope to achieve? (the change you will see).

Student A: My mom and I will communicate without yelling or slamming doors. I will not get grounded for yelling at my mom.

Time Bound
When will your goal be accomplished?

Student A: I will try to accomplish my goal within the next 8 weeks, the time of my group meetings.

Student:_____Semester/Year:_____

School Counselor(s):_____

Based on the information above, write a single goal statement sentence

Example: By the end of the semester, the number of times I am absent will decrease by 50%

_____

_____

_____

Modified from *the ASCA National Model®*. Templates available online at www.schoolcounselor.org/school-counselors-members/asca-national-model/asca-national-model-templates.

APPENDIX D
Middle School Career and College Readiness Standards (MS-CCRS)

Standards	Competencies	Indicators
Standard #1: **Self-Awareness** An understanding of how one's unique interests, talents, and aspirations play a role in decision-making and interpersonal relationships. Individual thoughts and feelings that get students excited about life and learning, and the ability to articulate passions and dreams; including recognizing challenges and potential barriers to attaining goals, and how healthy lifestyles contribute to personal and professional success.	**Competency 1:** Students will demonstrate knowledge, understanding, and personal awareness of her/his individual talents, interests, hopes, dreams, and passions.	**Indicator-1** Each student will participate in self-discovery exercises/assessments in order to begin the process of uncovering potentially hidden talents, interests, and aspirations. **Indicator-2** Each student will begin to identify the unique characteristics and attributes that set her/him apart from other people and allow them to express themselves as individuals. **Indicator-3** Each student will begin to articulate, through written essay or other creative work, how her/his unique attributes may contribute to or possibly hinder their academic and/or career success.
	Competency 2: Students will demonstrate personal understanding of how their mindsets and behaviors impact their personal learning styles, self-management, and social skills.	**Indicator-1** Each student will begin to develop appropriate critical thinking skills to make informed, ethical, and socially responsible decisions regarding their personal wants, needs, and aspirations in relation to her/his academic and/or postsecondary goals. **Indicator-2** Each student will begin to develop effective collaboration and cooperation skills by engaging in extracurricular activities with others who share the same interests, passions, or personal goals for success. **Indicator-3** Each student will learn the importance of self-determination and self-discipline and how to apply it to learning in order to enhance her/his aptitude and self-confidence when faced with difficult tasks.

Continued

Standards	Competencies	Indicators
		Indicator-4 Each student will begin to develop her/his ability to work independently toward achieving an academic or personal goal.
		Indicator-5 Each student will understand the importance of balancing academic, personal, and community activities in order to achieve a holistic sense of wellness.
	Competency 3: Students will demonstrate personal awareness and social maturity through the development of positive relationships with peers, teachers, and other adults.	**Indicator-1** Each student will learn how to develop a personal/professional network of adult mentors that she/he may access for guidance and support when developing career or postsecondary goals.
		Indicator-2 Each student will participate in specific assessments that identify unique, individual, leadership qualities. Those leadership qualities may be developed and enhanced through practice and self-reflection.
		Indicator-3 Each student will learn to identify the types of individuals (peers or adults) upon whom she/he may rely for support in order to effectively transition through challenging situations at home, school, or within her/his community.
		Indicator-4 Each student will begin to develop and practice self-advocacy skills and be able to assert herself/himself through the use of appropriate oral and written communication.
Standard #2: **Career Awareness** Knowing the difference between jobs, occupations, and careers. Being aware of a wide range of local regional, national, and global career pathways and opportunities while giving consideration to economic, cultural influences, and the impact of stereotypes on career choice.	**Competency 1:** Students will demonstrate knowledge and awareness about career pathways in local, regional, national, and global arenas as evidenced by the relevant indicators.	**Indicator-1** Students will determine their career pathway, and identify at least three jobs within that pathway that they would consider upon obtaining the necessary training or education.
		Indicator-2 Students will select a career pathway of interest to them, and take courses within that pathway.
	Competency 2: Students will be able to explain the influences of culture and stereotypes on their own career options, as evidenced by the relevant indicators.	**Indicator-1** Students will identify a stereotype that causes barriers to a career pathway that they are interested in, and be able to state three ways to overcome those obstacles or challenges to their success.
		Indicator-2 Students can explain how their own family and/or community culture may impact their career goals.
	Competency 3: Students will be able to understand the economic influences and impact on career pathways.	**Indicator-1** Students will be able to identify how the average salary of a particular career choice influences lifestyles.
		Indicator-2 Students can identify and utilize two resources that can inform them about career pathways.
Standard #3: **Postsecondary Aspirations** Career exploration centered on students' passions, interests, dreams, visions of their future self, and perceived options.	**Competency 1:** Students will have the opportunity to explore occupations based on dreams, passions, and individual interests.	**Indicator-1:** Students will be able to articulate future visions of themselves within the workforce.
		Indicator-2 Students will be able to identify life interests and how they relate to their postsecondary vision of themselves.

Continued

Standards	Competencies	Indicators
	Competency 2: Students will be knowledgeable about members in their community who represent a variety of career pathways.	**Indicator-1** Students will be able to identify several professionals in their community, and "real world" information regarding careers that exist within their community. **Indicator-2** Students will be able to identify professionals whose careers are not represented within their local community, but exist in other places.
	Competency 3: Students will, through guidance and support from their school counselor, parents/caregivers, family members, and community, explore how their dreams and interests translate into career fulfillment.	**Indicator-1** Students will be able to create a post-secondary goal, based on their future vision of themselves within the workforce. **Indicator-2** Students will be able to identify how their values and academic aspirations support future life needs, wants, and goals.
Standard #4: **Postsecondary Options** The awareness of a variety of postsecondary and career opportunities and advancements available using tools such as career clusters, personality assessments, and learning style inventories to highlight individual strengths and capabilities.	**Competency 1:** Students will develop awareness of self by assessing motivations, abilities, limitations, interests and skills.	**Indicator-1** Students will demonstrate an understanding of "self" based on information given using career and college-ready assessments. **Indicator-2** Students will be able to identify personal strengths and weaknesses. **Indicator-3** Students will use critical thinking to assess possible career pathways that best fit their skills, abilities, and interests. **Indicator-4** Students will demonstrate the ability to communicate an academic action plan for future goals and achievements, based on acquired self-knowledge.
	Competency 2: Students will become knowledgeable about a variety of post-secondary opportunities, including two-year and four-year degree programs, apprenticeships, military service, career and technical colleges, and service-learning programs such as Job Corps.	**Indicator-1** Students will know the difference between types of colleges, as well as technical and apprenticeship programs. **Indicator-2** Students will make cognitive connections between self-knowledge and post-secondary opportunities. **Indicator-3** Students will demonstrate the ability to navigate and use tools such as CollegeInColorado.org, among other online resources as determined by the school or district. **Indicator-4** Students will evaluate the costs, benefits, and challenges (to include personal, social, environmental, and/or family implications) of post-secondary opportunities.
	Competency 3: Students will gain exposure to basic academic and life skills necessary to reach their optimal postsecondary potential.	**Indicator-1** Students will identify advanced placement opportunities, extra-curricular clubs, organizations and college preparation programs available to them. **Indicator-2** Students will demonstrate knowledge of basic vocabulary and information associated with application and interviewing processes. **Indicator-3** Students will understand the application and interviewing process: to include how to dress for success, how to identify strengths and abilities, and how to communicate verbally and on written assessments.

Continued

Standards	Competencies	Indicators
Standard #5: **Environmental Expectations** An ecological system in which school, family, community, culture, and world view influence the students' career development and post-secondary plans.	**Competency 1** Students will understand how their academic environmental resources influence their career choice.	**Indicator-1** Students will have access to programs and activities which focus on issues of equitable distribution of resources. **Indicator-2** Students will categorize available academic resources in their region that minimize academic environmental limitations. **Indicator-3** Students will identify academic environmental strengths and limitations.
	Competency 2 Students will increase their awareness of risky behaviors and how they can adversely influence postsecondary and career options.	**Indicator-1** Students will identify negative environmental associations, which can have an impact on post-secondary options and career choices. **Indicator-2** Students will identify positive environmental resources (community after-school programs and clubs) which have a beneficial impact on post-secondary and career choices.
	Competency 3 Students will understand how values and beliefs within multiple environments (school, home, and community) influence future career and other postsecondary options.	**Indicator-1** Students will identify their cultural and environmental norms, values, and beliefs as they relate to career choice. **Indicator-2** Students will be able to identify family structural and financial limitations influencing postsecondary and career options. **Indicator-3** Student will be able to identify limitations to their career choice based on their geographical region. **Indicator-4** Students will understand environmental factors that influence their physical, emotional, and mental health in relation to career choice.
Standard #6: **Academic Planning** The skills and knowledge necessary to map out and pass the academic courses required to achieve postsecondary goals.	**Competency 1:** Students will acquire the academic discipline necessary for 8th Grade course completion (*academic discipline* includes organization, planning, and effort).	**Indicator-1** Students will demonstrate the ability to complete coursework in a timely manner using some type of organizational system (e.g., electronic calendar). **Indicator-2** Students will use appropriate conflict resolution skills on an individual basis, resulting in reduction of disciplinary outcomes. **Indicator-3** Students will demonstrate self-advocacy through use of appropriate communication skills when engaging teachers, parents, and fellow students as issues arise over coursework.
	Competency 2: Students will gain knowledge on how the Common Core State Standards apply to future career clusters and other postsecondary options.	**Indicator-1** Students will be able to explain the importance of communication skills, teamwork, and problem-solving skills in the workplace. **Indicator-2** Students will demonstrate reasoning skills such as critical thinking, using logic, and forming arguments in a socially acceptable manner. **Indicator-3** Students will apply personal responsibility and accountability skills to promote a reduction in their tardiness and absentee rates.

Continued

Standards	Competencies	Indicators
	Competency 3: Students will understand which courses are necessary to complete graduation requirements in high school to promote individual career readiness.	**Indicator-1** Students will apply information from personal interests, values, and abilities assessments to select a career cluster. **Indicator-2** Students will select high school coursework that is compatible with individual career cluster interests.
Standard #7: **Employability Skills** To define, develop, and hone skills that increase the likelihood of becoming and remaining successfully employed and civically responsible citizens.	**Competency 1:** Students are able to locate, access, and utilize various systems in order to gain employability information (what skills are needed for particular jobs/careers?).	**Indicator-1** Students will identify relevant employability systems, including interpersonal, technological, and community. **Indicator-2** Students will evaluate employability resources for their applicability and reliability within their community and the world of work.
	Competency 2: Students will identify and develop personal and professional employability traits.	**Indicator-1** Students will summarize their personal and professional strengths. **Indicator-2** Students will generate realistic goals to enhance their personal and professional traits in relation to a given career pathway.
	Competency 3: Students will identify and develop essential employability skills.	**Indicator-1** Students will become aware of academic competencies related to basic employability skills (i.e. math, writing). **Indicator-2** Students will generate goals and an action plan for improving their basic employability skills (i.e. math, writing). **Indicator-3** Students will develop awareness of the impact academics have on future career choices.
Standard #8: **Financial Literacy** The ability to recognize financial aid vocabulary and know what options are available to pay for post-secondary options.	**Competency 1:** Students will complete 8th grade with the preparation essential to meeting the needs for their postsecondary options.	**Indicator-1** Students will be able to identify the various forms of financial aid, including grants, scholarships, and loans. **Indicator-2** Students will be able to locate and organize financial aid information. **Indicator-3** Students will become familiar with financial aid vocabulary.
	Competency 2: Students will complete 8th grade with the skills to find and apply for federal financial aid to assist them in attending postsecondary options.	**Indicator-1** Students will know what the FASFA is and be able to locate the information necessary to assist them in completing the application process. **Indicator-2** Students will know the purpose of determining the *cost of attendance* (COA) for a particular post-secondary institution, and how it is determined. **Indicator-3** Students will know what *expected family contribution* (EFC) means and how it is calculated.

Continued

Standards	Competencies	Indicators
	Competency 3: Students will complete 8th grade with knowledge of all financial options available to them through their state to pursue postsecondary options.	**Indicator-1** Students will know the online or pencil and paper planning tools used by the school or district, and how to use these for postsecondary exploration and planning (i.e., Naviance®, Career Cruising®).
		Indicator-2 Students will complete at least one application for state funding (i.e., scholarship, grant).
		Indicator-3 Students will determine what payment options are best suited to support their postsecondary plans.

Adapted from Williams, R., & Morgan, L. W. (2014). *Middle school career and college readiness standards for professional school counselors in Colorado*. Denver, CO: Colorado Department of Education. Reprinted with permission.

APPENDIX E
NEA Template for Initial Media Release: School Crisis

For immediate release

Contact: NAME

PHONE NUMBER

DATE OF RELEASE:

Headline: NAME OF SCHOOL, INCIDENT

Describe situation: At approximately TIME, DATE, TYPE OF INCIDENT occurred at SCHOOL NAME, LOCATION.

Describe action being taken: Our school and district crisis response teams as well as emergency responders (LIST AGENCY NAMES) are on scene.

Our major concern is for the safety of our students and staff.

List information for parents/staff:

Parents can meet their students at LOCATION ADDRESS.

Insert quote from principal/central administrator:

For more information:

Hotline number

District voice mail number

District Web site address

National Education Association Health Information Network. (n.d.). *Media relations in a crisis: Immediate issues.* Available online at: http://crisisguide.neahin.org/crisisguide/tools/index.html

APPENDIX F
NEA Sample School Fact Sheet: School Crisis

- About the school district
  - Name
  - Location
  - Number of schools
  - Cost per pupil
  - District mission
  - School calendar
  - Board of Education members, superintendent
- About the school
  - Name
  - Location
  - Articulation area
  - Grades
  - School enrollment
  - School colors
  - School mascot
  - Motto/mission
  - Principal
  - Number of teachers
  - Facility: When built, remodeled
  - School programs
  - Extracurricular activities
  - Graduates
  - History
  - Test scores

National Education Association Health Information Network. (n.d.). *School fact sheet template.* Available online at: http://crisisguide.neahin.org/crisisguide/tools/index.html

NEA Sample Communications Command Post Supplies

First Day of Crisis

Office supplies. Chairs, desks, bulletin boards, flip charts, stamps or a postage meter, poster-making machine, computers, printers, fax machines, telephones, cell phones and chargers, digital cameras, TV, radios, copy machine, file folders, paper, message pads, school and district letterhead, pens, pencils.

Communications supplies. Media request forms, script for volunteers, fact sheets, frequently asked questions, press releases.

Key lists. Staff and student telephone directories, media directory, map of school and area.

Food and beverages. Volunteers might solicit donations from local restaurants.

Emergency supplies. Flashlights, police radio, two-way radios.

National Education Association Health Information Network. (n.d.). *Sample communications command post supplies*. Available online at http://crisisguide.neahin.org/crisisguide/tools/index.html

APPENDIX H
NEA Sample Volunteer Information

Answering the phone in crisis communications center and phone banks

- Volunteers should be equipped with a script on how to answer phone, daily fact sheets and press releases, and frequently asked questions. Volunteers should read and become familiar with all materials before answering calls.
- Volunteers should identify themselves as such and stick to the scripted information.
- The greeting for answering the phone is: "[INSERT NAME], Crisis Communications Center, may I help you?"
- If the volunteer is asked his name, respond, "I am a volunteer helping the district fulfill media requests and am not an official spokesperson. If you wish to attribute a statement, I will be glad to take your contact information and be sure that a district spokesperson returns your call."
- If the call is from the public, parents or staff, the volunteer may answer questions that are factual in nature. Take messages and record questions that need additional research.

Responding to the media

- If the call is from a member of the media, record questions and requests on the media request form. The goal is to provide the media with fast, accurate information to meet their deadlines.

Media Request for <u>Information</u>
Reporter_____
Media outlet_____
Phone_____
Cell phone_____
Deadline_____
Specific question_____
Message taken by_____

Date and time of request_____
Media request for <u>Interview</u>
Request interview with_____
Media outlet and reporter name_____

   ___TV
   ___Newspaper
   ___Magazine
   ___Radio
   ___Other

Phone_____
Cell phone_____
Date interview to be held_____
Location and logistics of interview:
___In person
___By phone

Topic_____
Anticipated length of interview_____
Other interviewees_____
Message taken by_____
Date and time of request_____

- After completing the form, file them in the designated folders – local, regional, major national and others. Even though the phones will continue to ring, it's important to file the forms as quickly as possible.
- The volunteer may answer questions about factual information, such as how many students are enrolled. If other data is requested, the volunteer should fill out a media request for information or media request for interview form and file it in the appropriate location for communications staff response.
- The priority for responding to the media is local first, regional second, major national third, and international and tabloids last.

Assisting the communications center coordinator with the following duties
<u>Morning</u>:

- Finalize master schedule of events for the day and make available to all phone bank volunteers.
- Finalize the daily fact sheet, and fax and email to appropriate lists. Post on Web site.
- Make sure each phone station has updated materials and supplies.
- Monitor the content of morning newspapers, wire stories and broadcast media.

<u>Afternoon</u>:

- Attend interagency communications director briefings and take notes.
- Prepare and distribute updated schedules and fact sheets, and post on Web site.
- Prepare and copy updated fact sheets for press briefings.
- Attend all press briefings, take notes and tape comments.

- Research questions from phone bank and update FAQs.

<u>Evening:</u>

- Complete master schedule for next day.
- Remove outdated information from volunteer folders and replace with new.
- Back up computer files.
- Participate in end-of-day meeting to ensure media requests have been fulfilled and to discuss issues that arose.
- Assemble "to do" list for following day and assign volunteers.

Other duties for volunteers

- Check incoming faxes and emails.
- Monitor Web sites and blogs.
- Monitor the contents of newspapers, radio and television reports.
- Organize and research phone bank and crisis center questions.
- Inventory and obtain supplies, such as paper, pens and pencils.
- Make sure each phone station has adequate supplies throughout the day.
- Supply copy and fax machines with paper.
- Catalog letters, cards and gifts.
- Write thank-you notes to donors.
- Keep running lists of items that need attention.

National Education Association Health Information Network. (n.d.). *Sample volunteer information.* Available online at: http://crisisguide.neahin.org/crisisguide/tools/index.html

APPENDIX I
NEA Daily Fact Sheet Example

School District:

School Name:

Date:

Contact:

Contact Phone/Cell Phone:

Latest information:

Press briefing schedule:

Donations:

Condolences:

Funeral arrangements:

Mental health support:

Parent information line:

Web site:

National Education Association Health Information Network. (n.d.). *Daily fact sheet template*. Available online at: http://crisisguide.neahin.org/crisisguide/tools/index.html

Index

Carlisle, C. S. 255–256
Carrizales, D. 83
Carrol, A. G. 36
Carruthers, W. L. 222, 224
Carta, J. J. 181–182
Carter, D. 82
case law 273–276
case notes 287
Casey, A. M. 220
Catalano, R. F. 256
Chambers, T. V. 46
change agents 1, 24, 31, 45, 51, 56, 197, 214
Center for School Counseling Outcome Research and
  Evaluation (CSCORE) 33, 68, 96, 226
certification 3, 4, 89
Chapman, C. 180
check-in/check-out (CICO) 36–37, 83, 220
Chen, G. 215
Chen-Hayes, S. F. 51–53
Chickie-Wolfe, L. A. 174–177
child abuse 265, 274, 282, 287
Child Find 235–237
Child Protective Services 121, 281–282
child study team 36, 153, 233, 237, 240–241
Chizhik, A. W. 56
choice theory 116, 134
Cholewa, V. 56
Choy, S. 180
Chung, R. C. 125, 134
circle format 147
civil liability 274
Clark, M. A. 55, 171, 174, 179–180, 184
Clayton, P. J. 268
closing-the-gap action plans 29–30, 183–184
Cockman, C. R. 88–89, 93–95, 179
Cocco, K. 209
Cochran, S. D. 268
cognitive-behavioral theory 109, 120–123, 218, 266
Colbert, R. D. 38
Cole, R. 155
collaboration 31, 45, 54, 57, 152–160, 173
collaborative consultation 160
Collaborative for Academic, Social, and Emotional Learning
  (CASEL) 226
collaborative teams 59
college admission 51, 153, 158, 197
college admission essay 207
college and career readiness 35, 59, 152, 158, 180, 192, 194,
  197–198, 207, 209
college application 25, 59, 206, 207
College Board 16, 46, 58, 195–196, 206–208
College Navigator 208
Commission on the Reorganization of Secondary Education
  (CRSE) 20
Common Application 207
Common Core State Standards 24, 30, 33, 34, 90, 104, 180,
  196, 300
common factors model 108

community asset mapping 159–160
community partnership programs 182
comprehensive school counseling 11, 25–26, 28, 32, 69, 132,
  152, 154, 172, 198, 249
Condron, D. J. 47
confidentiality 127–128, 143, 277–290
conflict resolution 178, 216, 220, 222–223
Connolly-Wilson, C. N. 256, 258–259
Constantine, M. G. 49
consultation 26, 36, 52–53, 55, 152, 160–169
contraceptive services 279, 281
Conyne, R. K. 136
Cook, C. R. 217, 228
Cook, J. B. 73, 177
Cook, M. 234
Cooley, L. 137, 139–140, 145–146
cooperative learning 91
Coping Cat Program 121
Corey, G. 125, 130, 135, 279
Corey, M. S. 125, 135
Cornell, D. 258
Cornely, L. 183
Council for the Accreditation of Counseling and Related
  Educational Programs (CACREP) iv, 1, 20–21, 24, 45, 66,
  88, 107, 125, 152, 171, 192, 214, 232, 253, 273
Cox, D. D. 182
Coyne, A. 181
Craigen, L. M. 269, 279
Crepeau-Hobson, F. 254
Crick, N. R. 217–218
crisis intervention 254–255, 259
crisis prevention 253–255, 259
critical incident stress debriefing (CISD) 255–256
Crone, D. A. 83
Crosby, A. 216
crosswalking 90, 96
Crothers, L. M. 54, 79
Crowell, J. L. 136
Cruz, R. de la 18
cultural awareness 93, 104, 127, 129, 158
cultural biography 52
culturally responsive teaching 54
culture and climate assessment 257–258
Cunningham, E. G. 258
curriculum development 88, 92, 94
curriculum mapping 179, 189
Curtis, M. J. 166

Dahir, C. A. 10, 19, 74–75, 97, 194, 198
Dailey, D. 70
daily behavior report card (DBRC) 83, 220
Dahlberg, L. 216
Daluga-Guenther, N. 25, 39–40
Damico, J. 132
D'Andrea, M. 114
D'Augelli, A. R. 268
Daniels, H. 155
Darling-Hammond, L. 180

homogeneous group 134
Hopkins, B. R. 274
horizontal articulation 88, 93
Horner, R. H. 36, 83–84, 219–220, 226
Hourse, R. J. 173
House, R. M. 180, 183
Hughes, A. 31, 69, 172
Hughes, K. L. 195
Hughey, K. 90
humanism 10
Hurt, K. 54–57

identity development 183, 205
Imbeau, M. B. 94
immigrant student 46
impact evaluation 69
indirect service 30, 52–53, 242
Individualized Education Plan (IEP) 153, 158, 209, 233–234, 241, 243–244, 247
individual planning 68, 179, 187, 204, 210
Individuals with Disabilities Education Act (IDEA) 35, 208–210, 233–234, 236, 239–241, 243–245, 248
informed consent 127–128, 181, 277–278
inquiry learning 56
in-service 153, 174
intellectual disability 209, 238, 241, 245
institutional theory 13, 15
Instructional Support Team (IST) 153
integrators 10
internalizing behavior 82–84, 217, 220
International Baccalaureate (IB) 71, 74
International Model for School Counseling Programs 27
interval observation 84
Iowa Test of Basic Skills (ITBS) (test) 71, 74
Irwin, C. E. Jr. 277
Irwin, L. K. 84
Isaacs, M. L. 278
Isaacson, N. S. 255–256
Ivey, A. E. 111
Ivey, M. B. 111

Jacobi, M. 157
Jansorn, N. R. 155
Jasper, M. 137
Jaycox, L. H. 266
Jimerson, S. R. 254, 256, 258–259
job shadowing 9, 52, 209
Johnson, A. H. 17
Johnson, C. 10
Johnson, D. 134
Johnson, D. W. 221
Johnson, J. 25, 193
Johnson, R. T. 221
Johnson, S. 10
Jondahl, S. E. 102–103
Jones, M. T. 158, 195, 197
Jordan, W. J. 158

journaling 91, 95, 292
Juhnke, G. A. 161

Kaffenberger, C. J. 36, 72, 125, 177
Kahn, B. B. 161
Kalafat, J. 267–268
Kalberg, J. R. 81, 83
Kamphaus, R. W. 37
Kataoka, S. H. 266
Kaplan, D. M. 16
Kaplan, L. S. 128, 284
Karp, M. M. 195
Keller, T. 89
Kelley, S. D. 108
Kelly, F. D. 180–181
Kemp, J. 260
Kendall, P. C. 120–121
Kern, C. W. 157
Khoury-Kassabri, M. 38
Kim, T. E. 217, 228
Kindaichi, M. M. 49
Kish, L. 79
Kneale, M. M. 59–60
Knight, J. 269, 279
Knokey 209–210
Koenig, W. 268
Kohlberg's theory of moral development 93
Kolb, D. 57
Kolbert, J. B. 54, 79, 224
Kolko, D. J. 266
Kolodinsky, P. 199
Kovalik, S. J. 100
Koth, C. W. 133
Kovaleski, J. 240
Kozlowski, K. 129
Kratochwill, T. R. 37, 102, 160, 166–168
Kuperminc, G. P. 256
Kutcher, S. 256

Ladson-Billings, G. 46
Laird, J. 180
Lambert, M. J. 108
Lambert, W. 220
Lamberto, R. 27
Lambie, G. W. 59
Lane, K. L. 81, 83, 220
Langevin, J. 194
Langley, A. K. 266
Lantz, A. 95, 100, 103, 129–130, 137, 146
Lapan, T. L. 33, 62, 68, 90, 172, 226
Latham, A. S. 221
Latino American students 29, 32, 46–47, 53, 55–57, 60–62, 158–159, 177, 180–181
Latino families 157, 275
Lauer, P. 268
Lazzaro, B. R. 256, 258–259
leadership 29, 31, 33–34, 45, 49, 51, 58–59
leadership group 129, 134, 159

Montopoli, G. 199
Moore-Thomas, C. 158, 197
Morgan, L. W. 194, 302
Morgan, P. L. 234
motivational interviewing (MI) 109, 184, 187–188
Moyer, M. S. 280, 285
Mullis, F. 165
Murphy, J. J. 118–119
Murray, K. C. 284
Myers, G. E. 12, 19
Myrick, R. D. 10, 16
multicultural 2–8, 50, 52, 55, 63, 129, 159
multicultural competency 55
multiple-gate screening 37, 81, 83, 220
Mutillo, A. J. 173

Nakasato, J. 36
National Association of Guidance Supervision and Counselor
    Trainers 20
National Association of Peer Programs 225
National Association of School Psychologists (NASP) 234,
    260, 264
National Board of Certified Counselors (NBCC) 20–21
National Career Clusters Framework 200–201
National Center for Transforming School Counseling 31
National Certified Counselor (NCC) 20–21
National Certified School Counselor (NCSC) 20–21
National Defense Education Act (NDEA) 5, 18,
    21
National Dropout Prevention Network 181
National Education Association (NEA) 20, 261–262,
    264–265, 309
National Office of School Counselor Advocacy (NOSCA)
    196, 198
National Panel for School Counseling Evidence-Based
    Practice 68
National Vocational Guidance Association (NVGA)
    10–11, 18, 20
Native American 32
Naviance 205–207, 302
needs assessment 53, 60, 71, 92–93, 96, 153
negligence 270, 274, 278
Nesson, L. 54
Net Price Calculator 208
Neufeld, J. 268
Newman, L. 209–210
Newmyer, M. D. 136
Nickerson, A. B. 254, 256, 258–259
Niebergall, S. 219
Nikels, H. J. 133
Niles, S. G. 179, 199
No Child Left Behind (NCLB) Act 15, 19, 21, 24–25, 31–33,
    45, 66, 71, 75, 90, 154–155, 168, 194, 215, 261
Noonan, D. 227
Norcross, J. C. 184, 186–187, 189
Noorulamin, S. 95, 100, 103, 129–130, 137,
    146
Norwood, E. 108

North, R. D. 9
note-taking 58, 91, 286
Now is the Time initiative 262

Occupational Information and Guidance Service (OIGS) 20
Ockerman, M. S. 35, 240
O'Donnell, P. S. 234
Oescher, J. 31
Oesterle, S. 256
office discipline referral (ODR) 37, 81–82, 220
Olsen, K. D. 100
Olweus, D. 41, 216, 219–220
Olweus Bullying Prevention Program (OBPP) 41, 219–220
opportunistic experiment 68
organizational theory 13
Orozco, G. L. 182
O'Shea, A. J. 79
Ortiz, C. D. 266
other health impairment (OHI) 245, 248
Ott, A. N. 25, 193
outcome data 28, 40, 57, 61, 72–74, 77–78, 101

Paisley, P. 126
parental consent 129, 142, 278, 281
parental permission 128–129, 286, 292, 294
parent involvement 72, 75, 155, 181–182
Parents and Friends of Lesbians and Gays (PFLAG) 54
parents' rights 278–280, 284–285
parent-teacher association (PTA) 59, 77
parent-teacher conference 155–156, 165
Park-Higgerson, H. 216
Parks-Savage, A. 222
Parsons, F. 2, 9–10
Partnership for 21st Century Skills (P21) 200
Pate, R. H. Jr. 285
Paulsen, C. A. 70
PeaceBuilders program 216
Peace Pal Program 222
Pederson, W. 199
peer helping/support 214, 221, 225, 229
peer mediation 52, 214, 218, 221–224, 255
peer mentoring 36, 181, 218, 221
peer tutoring 181–182, 189, 221, 225
Peluso, P. 62, 177
Penaloza, R. V. 48
Pender, D. A. 136
perception data 72–73, 74, 78, 101, 225
performance-based assessment 73, 80
Perkins, G. 31
person-centered theory 109, 112, 119, 121–122, 184
Perumean-Chaney, S. E. 216
Perusse, R. 31, 38, 69, 90, 93–95, 102–103, 125, 133, 139, 172
Pesce, R. C. 256, 258–259
Peterson, J. S. 89
Peterson, R. K. 221–222
Petroski, G. F. 172
Phillips, A. 220
Piaget's theory of cognitive development 93, 114

Sullivan, K. 18
summarizing 35, 91, 114, 161, 166
Sun, L. 219
Super's theory of career development 93
Support for Students Exposed to Trauma (SSET) 266
Susan, M. K. 256, 258–259
Swan, S. 187
Sweeney, B. 222
Systematic Screening for Behavioral Disorders (SSBD) 37, 83, 220
systems advocacy 52–53
systems consultation 164–165
systems-ecological theory 24, 38–41
systems level 173
Szumilas, M. 256

Tai, W. L. 68, 89, 150
Tarasoff v. Board of Regents of California 282
Tatum, B. 52
Tarvydas, V. M 16
Taylor, K. R. 270
Taylor, L. 119
Taylor, R. D. 226, 259
Teachers Involve Parents in Schoolwork (TIPS) 183
Teaching Students to be Peacemakers Program (TSP) 222
Teich, J. 227
Terenzini, P. T. 158
Terriquez, V. 158–159
Terry, J. 187
test-taking skills 174–175
Tevis, T. L. 196
Thomas, R. V. 136
Thompson, R. A. 9–10, 14, 20
threat assessment 258–259, 261
Thurston, C. J. 182
Tillery, A. D. 256
Time Elapsed Analysis & Reporting System (TEARS) 76
time management 82, 132, 157, 176, 181
Tindall, J. A. 225
Tobin, R. 180
Todd, A. W. 36, 84
Tolan, P. H. 216
Tominey, S. L. 115
Tomlinson, C. A. 93–94
Tope, D. 47
tracking 48, 70, 171
trait/factor theory 9–10, 13
trauma 129, 238, 246, 254–256, 265–266
traumatic brain injury (TBI) 241, 246
Tran, O. K. 83
Transforming School Counseling Initiative 24, 31, 38, 40–41, 67, 172–173
transition services/planning 209, 246–247
transtheoretical model (TTM) of change 184–186, 188
Traxler, A. E. 9
Truman, J. 260
Trusty, J. 172, 179, 181–183
Ttofi, M. M. 41, 218
Turk, D. C. 168

Urban, T. 173
Urbano, A. 50, 56

Valiga, M. J. 10
value laden issues 278–279, 281
Van Atta, R. 18
Vandiver, F. M. 155
Van Someren, K. R. 168
Van Velsor, P. 182
Van Voorhis, F. L. 155, 183
Varjas, K. 256
Veach, L. J. 125
Vision into Action 10, 19
universal screen 35, 37, 81, 83
Villares, E. 62
Vincus, A. A. 227
violence prevention 154, 216, 226, 256
vision statement 28
Visweswaran, C. 266
visual imagery 123
vocationalists 9
Vocational Education Act 5, 18
Vocational Education Amendments 18
vocopher 11
Vossekuil, B. 258

Wadenya, R. O. 157
Wadsworth, J. 209
Wagner, M. 221
Wagner, R. 209–210
Walberg, H. J. 177
Waldo, E. 194
Walker, H. M. 83
Wall, J. 224
Walter, K. D. 246
Wampold, B. E. 108
Wang, M. C. 177
Ward, C. A. 32
Watanbe, S. 180
Weaver, R. 9
Webb, L. 62, 68, 77–78, 96, 174, 177
Weber, C. 34
Wegner, C. 225
Wehby, J. 220
Wei, Y. 256
Weikart, L. A. 215
Weintraub, A. L. 165
Weisenback, J. 220
Weishaar, M. E. 122–123
Weissberg, R. P. 226, 259
Wells, D. S. 54
Wesman, A. G. 205
West-Olatunji, C. 56
Westwood, C. A. 165
Wethington, H. 216
What I Like to Do Inventory 209
What Works Clearinghouse 96
White, J. 165

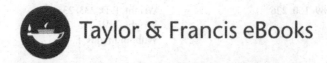